Correctional Counseling & Rehabilitation

5th Edition

Patricia Van Voorhis / University of Cincinnati

Michael Braswell / East Tennessee State University

David Lester / Stockton State College

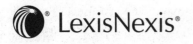 LexisNexis®

 **anderson publishing**
A member of the LexisNexis Group

Correctional Counseling and Rehabilitation, Fifth Edition

Copyright © 1987, 1992, 1997, 2000, 2004
Matthew Bender & Company, Inc., a member of the LexisNexis Group

Phone 877-374-2919
Web Site www.lexisnexis.com/anderson/criminaljustice

LexisNexis and the Knowledge Burst logo are trademarks of Reed Elsevier Properties, Inc.
Anderson Publishing is a registered trademark of Anderson Publishing, a member of the LexisNexis Group

Van Voorhis, Patricia.
    Correctional counseling and rehabilitation / Patricia Van Voorhis, Michael
C. Braswell, David Lester.— 5th ed.
        p. cm.
    Rev. ed. of: Correctional counseling & rehabilitation. 4th ed. ©2000.
    Includes bibliographical references and index.
    ISBN 1-59345-967-X (softbound)
    1. Correctional pyschology. 2. Prisoners--Counseling of. 3.
    Psychotherapy. I. Braswell, Michael. II. Lester, David, 1942- III. Van
    Voorhis, Patricia. Correctional counseling & rehabilitation. IV. Title.
    HV9276.V35 2004
    365'.66--dc22   2004023427

Cover design by Tin Box Studio, Inc.

EDITOR Elisabeth Roszmann Ebben
ACQUISITIONS EDITOR Michael C. Braswell

Contents

Preface

I am pleased to introduce the fifth edition of *Correctional Counseling and Rehabilitation*. In putting the finishing touches on this book, I could not help but reflect on the extraordinary changes that have occurred in corrections since the first edition was released in 1987. I would like to share some of these musings as I pack this manuscript up for its final trip to the publisher.

The history of this text now spans almost 20 years, and it is nothing short of an understatement to say that this edition is being released to an academic and political climate much more embracing of the rehabilitative ideal than was the case when the first edition was released. Our first edition was released to an audience that was not sympathetic to the notion of changing offender behavior. The field of corrections was then reeling from Martinson's (1974) research and ultimate admonition that "nothing works." Strong efforts to show that his research was flawed (Palmer, 1975), were not being heard in policy circles. The Reagan administration was scoring political points with the dictate, "lock them up and throw away the key." Funding priorities supported a "punitive state" rather than a "therapeutic state" (Cullen & Gendreau, 2000), by promoting determinate sentencing and punishment or "penal harm" (Clear, 1994) over rehabilitation.

At that time, I had only recently completed my doctoral studies. Graduate school training and two mentors in particular—psychologists Marguerite Warren and Hans Toch—had introduced me and my fellow students at the University at Albany to the notion of "planned change." Psychologically based correctional treatment fit well within the curriculum of "planned change" and my graduate school colleagues and I were treated to the rich history of correctional rehabilitation. Rita Warren summed up the shift in policy succinctly when one day she said in frustration, "We have learned too much to just throw these programs away." But as noted above, more than 70 years of rehabilitative programming (some good and some bad) did give way to budget cuts and punitive ideals embodied by such new options as boot camps, "three strikes," Scared Straight, and other politically motivated, but untested, correctional "innovations." Suffice it to say, the first edition of this book sold to a very small number of academic holdouts—the few criminal justice departments that continued to teach correctional rehabilitation.

By the late 1980s, another group of psychologists held similar reactions to the early Martinson research and resulting policy shifts, noting that the findings just didn't sound "quite right." They began a series of meta-analyses of the existing evaluation research. Canadian psychologists Paul Gendreau, Don Andrews, Jim Bonta, Robert Hoge, and others commenced archiving and empirically summarizing hundreds of controlled studies of correctional treatment. Similar efforts were later undertaken at the University of Maryland (Sherman et al., 1997) and with the Campbell Collaboration Crime and Justice Group. The conclusions from this body of research were clear: specific correctional treatment programs work. Although the early editions of *Correctional Counseling and Rehabilitation* predated the earliest meta-analysis, subsequent editions, including the present one, repeat throughout that behavioral, social learning, cognitive-behavioral, and family therapy can reduce recidivism by as much as 30 percent in comparison to the programs where inappropriate correctional interventions are administered or those where no programming is offered.

Over time, policy makers have come to embrace the notion of "evidence-based practice" (MacKenzie, 2000). Embarrassed by the realization that some of the most politically favored panaceas, such as boot camps, intermediate sanctions, and Scared Straight, often increased the likelihood of future offending, policy makers were encouraged to choose programs that had been studied and found to work. Indeed, if the goal is to change the behavior of offenders, there is now no need to follow a hunch. Moreover, correctional programming is the only option for changing offender behavior. Correctional scholars and policy makers have and will continue to debate the merits of incapacitation, deterrence, and retribution—alternative correctional goals—but research shows that such policies do little to change offender behavior. They may have their own goals, which some will consider worthy in their own right, such as punishment and making it nearly impossible for an individual to commit a new crime (albeit only for the period of correctional supervision), but long-term behavioral change is not the benefit of such correctional policies. The research is clear, and the evidence has continued to mount, especially over the past five years.

Necessity has also prompted renewed interest in rehabilitation. In late 1970s, correctional populations, which had remained fairly steady since the 1930s, began to grow at an extraordinary rate. Dramatic increases were seen in both institutions and community corrections. For the most part the population boom was not the result of increases in violent, street, or white-collar crimes. Rather, correctional populations expanded to accommodate the "War on Drugs." Cuts in spending for community mental health also sent mentally ill individuals to prisons in unprecedented numbers (Austin et al., 2000). Simply put, corrections now has to deal with more troubled offenders than in the past. The need for programs solidly grounded in mental health is urgent and has prompted not only increased commitment to correctional treatment, but new policies and organizational structures designed with rehabilitation in mind, e.g., reentry, prison transition, drug courts, and mental health courts.

In contrast to the earlier years of our careers, my colleagues and I have observed dramatic changes in the ways that universities and correctional agencies work together. We know and communicate frequently with commissioners and directors of these agencies and work regularly with their administrators as well as their clients. Our work has a much more direct influence on correctional programming, assessment, and research endeavors. In another sense, though, I am pleased to say that the field changes what we do in our home universities, and influences how and what is taught in university classes. Our work with correctional agencies also underscores the fact that we do not know everything. Gaps exist in our knowledge about what works for female offenders (Bloom et al., 2003) and how best to address the needs of minorities. The field brings us up a bit short on the issue of new types of offenders—such as terrorists and those addicted to crystal methamphetamine.

These are not necessarily liberal transitions, and certainly these are not times in which correctional rehabilitation enjoys ample funding. Indeed, the public still favors punishment, though not in the absence of correctional rehabilitation (Cullen et al., 2000). Treatment budgets are again being cut in the face of declining state revenues. Such cuts are not taking place willingly, and my compliments to those states and programs that have found ways to keep programming alive. Many rehabilitation programs are, after all, cost-effective (Aos et al., 1999).

When recent trends are considered, this edition is being released to a favorable audience, and when I consider where we have been over the past 20 years, this seems miraculous. But while the audience may have shifted over time, this text continues to do what it always promised to do: (a) present the central modalities of correctional treatment, (b) offer a view to the foundations of correctional intervention (e.g., psychoanalytical strategies and early group practices, and (c) offer a more detailed attention to strategies that have been found to reduce offender recidivism (e.g., sound assessments, and behavioral, social learning, cognitive-behavioral, and family therapies). My co-authors and I have intended this book to serve as a primer, of sorts, showing readers what is available, and offering a strong picture of what each theoretically grounded treatment modality should look like.

We hope that the book will contribute a clear picture of what should be going on "inside" correctional programs. A thorough understanding of the clinical dimensions of the most effective modalities is essential to effective correctional programming. Indeed, a cognitive-behavioral program must be a cognitive-behavioral program if is going to prove effective in reducing recidivism. Programs that exist on paper but not in practice, or those that "drift away" from the core components of a modality don't work because they don't happen. We encourage readers to understand that it is not the organizational framework of a program (e.g., halfway house, intensive supervision, drug court, day reporting center) that changes offender behavior; it is the modality within (behavioral, social learning, cognitive-behavioral, or family therapy) that does so. Absent program modalities that are firmly grounded in psychological theory, the administrative shell of a program will do little to change behavior.

I would like to thank my co-authors, Mickey Braswell and David Lester, for their ongoing assistance with this text. Additionally, Biz Ebben, the editor for this and previous editions, contributed phenomenal attention to detail, skilled attention to the language, and many late-night e-mails. She also policed some deadlines, albeit patiently. That was a good thing—otherwise we might still be writing. Thanks also to Jordanna Ross for her assistance with some of the research for the book. I now see that my golf buddy, Jeanne Busemeyer, is a talented indexer as well as a "scratch golfer." Many thanks.

Colleagues have greatly influenced our thinking on this and previous editions. Special thanks to Donald Andrews, Barbara Bloom, Joanne Belknap, Jim Bonta, Frank Cullen, Stephanie Covington, Paul Gendreau, Barry Glick, Ed Latessa, Doris MacKenzie, Ned Megargee, Barbara Owens, Ted Palmer, Marilyn Van Dieten, and most recently, Paula Smith.

Finally, some readers of previous editions of this text and students of corrections classes at the University of Cincinnati (taught by Ed Latessa, Frank Cullen, Larry Travis, John Wooldredge, and myself) have developed their own commitments to the field of corrections. At early stages of their careers they have offered much to the field through their research, training, and consultations. I have come to admire their willingness to reach out to the field as well as their skill in doing so. I especially would like to recognize Brandon Applegate, Shannon Barton, Kelly Brown, Dena Hanley, Steve Haas, Betsy Matthews, Melissa Moon, Colleen Kadleck, Lisa Spruance, Chris Lowenkamp, Debra Shaffer, Kim Sperber, Martha Henderson, Dana Hubbard, Shelley Listwan, Jennifer Pealer, Lori Brusman Lovins, Brian Lovins, Alex Holsinger, Kristi Holsinger, Tony Flores, Jill Potts, Emily Salisbury, Jody Sundt, Charlene Taylor, and Georgia Spiropoulis.

Patricia Van Voorhis

Notes

Aos, S., P. Phipps, R. Barnoski & R. Lieb. (1999). *The Comparative Costs and Benefits of Programs to Reduce Crime: A Review of National Research Findings with Implications for Washington State*. Olympia, WA: Washington State Institute for Public Policy (available at www.wa.gov/wsipp).

Clear, T. (1994). *Harm in American Penology: Offenders, Victims, and Their Communities*. Albany, NY: State University of New York Press.

Cullen, F.T., B.S., Fisher & B.K. Applegate. (2000). "Public Opinion About Punishment and Corrections." In M. Tonry (ed.), *Crime and Justice: A Review of Research*, Vol. 27. Chicago: University of Chicago Press.

MacKenzie, D. (2000). "Evidence-based Corrections: Identifying What Works." *Crime and Delinquency*, 46, 457-471.

Palmer, T. (1975). "Martinson Revisited." *Journal of Research in Crime and Delinquency*, 12, 133-152.

Part One

A Professional Framework for Correctional Counseling

The object of Part One of this text is to encourage the reader to develop a personal sense of what correctional counseling is about. Prior to presenting specific strategies and theories of counseling in later chapters, we wish to devote some time to what the career is like. Such an awareness includes a general understanding of essential counseling skills and responsibilities. It is also important to examine more specifically the professional context of correctional counseling; that is, how it relates both formally and informally to the rest of the correctional process. Part One also discusses a number of challenges unique to correctional counselors in comparison with counselors working with non-offenders.

In Chapter 1, the key professional and human dimensions of the counseling relationship are presented. Kimberly Dodson, Michael Braswell, and Michael Bush discuss the importance of timing, effective risking, and the characteristics of a therapeutic relationship. Readers are introduced to the essentials of effective communication and the importance of developing sensitivity to gender and ethnic differences. The authors show how varied the counseling function is across different correctional settings (community versus institutional), as well as across different contexts such as probation, parole, education, recreation, institutional counseling, psychotherapy, and spiritual counseling.

In Chapter 2, William Elliott and Jeffrey Schrink help readers to better understand the world of corrections through the eyes of the correctional counselor. Particular attention is paid to such job stressors as prison overcrowding, excessive paperwork, involuntary clients, large caseloads, inmate conning behaviors, and staff burnout. They introduce readers to valuable strategies for coping with challenging environments and offenders who are resistant to treatment. Their discussion of ethics and standards of practice for counselors is crucial to anyone in the role of therapist or counselor.

Part One encourages the reader to become personally involved in the correctional counseling process, to understand that there is an inevitable blending of personal beliefs, professional feelings, and practice. To the extent that the goal of this section is realized, the remainder of the book will become more interesting and meaningful. Correctional counseling is more than learning about counseling techniques. It is also vitally involved with learning through experience; clarifying and developing one's own feelings and beliefs concerning helping others, particularly offenders.

Chapter 1

The Function of Correctional Counseling and Treatment

Kimberly Dodson, Michael Braswell, and Michael Bush

Correctional counseling and treatment involve a variety of mental health and related helping professionals working with people who have been identified as delinquent or criminal. Their services span numerous correctional settings, including correctional institutions, community-based residential settings, probation and parole, human service programs that contract with correctional agencies, and most recently, specialized mental health and drug courts.

Correctional counseling requires a combination of skill, knowledge, and experience—all of which shape the counselor's professional attitude and style. Each offender presents the counselor with a unique counseling situation and challenge that, in many instances, offers little promise of an adequate resolution. For example, imagine yourself the counselor in the following case:

> John has been in prison for two years. He is a likeable inmate who works in the prison library. Usually quiet, John has a remarkable talent for repairing damaged books. He has saved the prison library hundreds of dollars by his handiwork.
>
> As his counselor, you try to see him at least once a month to find out how he is getting along. He always indicates that he is doing all right and that he is optimistic regarding his parole hearing, which is only nine months away. John has some reason to feel good about his chances for making parole. He is a first-time offender who got into a drunken brawl at a tavern and seriously injured another man. As a result of the altercation, he was sentenced to six years in the state penitentiary. Although John had experienced

severe drinking problems for a number of years, fighting had never been a part of the problem. Since being in prison, he has completed intensive substance abuse therapy, joined Alcoholics Anonymous and has even successfully completed several college-level courses in library science. Needless to say, counseling John is a pleasant experience for the most part because of his own motivation.

However, in the last several weeks John's behavior and attitude have changed. His wife, who has been visiting him faithfully every Sunday, has not shown up for the last two visitation days. Cell block rumor is that she is seeing another man and is planning to file for divorce. To make matters worse, the man she is involved with is an alcoholic himself. John has quit coming to work and stays to himself in the cell block. He has also been losing weight and looks haggard and distraught.

As his counselor you want to help, but John, who has always been quiet, has now become even more withdrawn. You are not sure how to approach him. You have considered talking to his wife or his parents. If John's depression continues to worsen, his behavior may become unpredictable. He might become aggressive and get into a fight with someone in the cell block or he might turn his anger inward and attempt suicide. You have to approach him, but how? You have to do something in an attempt to help him, but what? (Braswell, Fletcher & Miller, 1990).

As a correctional counselor, you are aware that the odds are substantially against a marriage surviving the extended imprisonment of one of the spouses. Yet John is your client and he is distraught. Will his unhappiness explode in a cell block confrontation, endangering the safety of prison staff or other inmates? Or will it, perhaps, result in an internal explosion in the form of emotional illness or self-inflicted injury? Although your therapeutic options and resources are limited, you will have to do the best you can. Will your counseling efforts be successful in resolving John's crisis? If they are not, will you and John be able to live with the consequences?

The following chapters will attempt to:

1. introduce you to some of the professional and human dimensions of the correctional counseling process;

2. help you better understand characteristics of the offender-client and the correctional counselor;

3. examine a variety of correctional counseling and psychotherapy approaches; and

4. consider selected special issues and problems in counseling offenders.

Goals of Offender Counseling and Treatment

This book focuses on "correctional" counseling and treatment. While it seems that current politics favor the term "correctional," the idea of "correctional" counseling may not be compatible with what most counselors consider the legitimate interest and purposes of helping offenders. For instance, is the primary goal of counselors who work in prison one of correcting offenders for successful readjustment to the outside world, or is their primary role concerned with offenders' adjustment to the institutional world of the prison? Or should correctional counselors be concerned with both possibilities, including the offender becoming more responsible and peaceful whether he or she eventually gets out of prison or spends the rest of his or her life incarcerated? Similarly, does the basic goal of probation and parole counselors revolve around therapeutically correcting offenders under their supervision or are they more concerned with the enforcement of the conditions of probation and parole? More fundamentally, one might ask whether there is any substantial evidence that counselors could "correct" offenders if they wanted to? In fact, correctional counselors often relate frustration over their inability to conduct interventions geared to helping offenders reform and change the course of their lives. For example, prison case mangers and counselors tell of devoting most of their time to facilitating inmates' adjustment to the institution rather than to their more long-term adjustment to a normal/prosocial life on the outside (see Elliot and Schrink's discussion in Chapter 2). Similarly, probation and parole counselors maintain that their time is overburdened by enforcement of the conditions of probation and parole, leaving little time for assisting offenders' reintegration and community adjustment.

The goals of offender counseling and treatment are frustrated by the convergence of three recent trends:

1. Political and scholarly debate concerning the effectiveness of offender therapy (e.g., Andrews & Bonta, 2003; Cullen & Gendreau, 2000; Gaes et al., 1999; Lipsey, 1992; Martinson, 1974; Van Voorhis, Cullen & Applegate, 1995).

2. A litigiously based drive for hyper-vigilant, if not excessive, agency accountability (Hepburn, 1989).

3. Declining fiscal and personnel resources resulting from prison overcrowding and severe cuts to local, state, and federal correctional treatment budgets.

What seems to be a more appropriate focus is to view correctional counselors as helping professionals who attempt to apply their skills and expertise in correctional and related settings. In doing so, they try to focus on the strategies that are likely to reduce future offending. The primary goal of these counselors appears to be one of intervening therapeutically with various clients, the majority of whom happen to be offenders. To name a few, these interventions may address prison adjustment, prisoner re-entry, risk of future offending, substance abuse, education and employment, and mental health concerns.

The Counseling Process

Correctional counseling and psychotherapy are comprised of a process that involves three essential abilities:

1. a sense of timing

2. effective risking

3. high-quality therapeutic relationships

In order for one to develop a sense of **timing**, the counselor needs to pay careful attention to whatever the client is communicating. Communication is the lifeblood of relationships. It is the way we get to know each other. Communication includes what we say and do not say; what we hear and do not hear. It includes the way we look, dress, and feel. In this regard, Virginia Satir's work continues to have meaning for us today. In defining communication, Satir (1972) states, "Communication covers the whole range of ways people pass information back and forth; it includes the information they give and receive, and the ways that the information is needed. Communication covers how people make meaning of the information" (p. 20).

There are six basic elements of communication that everyone contributes to the communication process (exceptions to this would include such disabilities as blindness or deafness):

1. The body is an element of communication that moves and has form and shape. How a person moves, as well as his or her physical appearance, can provide the correctional counselor with significant information. An unclean physical appearance, for example, might be indicative of depression. The body language of crossed arms may be indirectly signaling to keep our distance.

2. Values are another element of communication. They are usually reflected in a person's behavioral habits and verbal communication, especially concerning what people "ought and ought not to do."

3. Another important element of communication are the expectations a person brings to an experience. These expectations are, for the most part, based upon past experiences and are inclined to influence the way a person perceives his or her own and others' communication. Sometimes negative expecta-

tions (e.g., all offenders are bad and untrustworthy) can contribute to a person experiencing poor communication and human relations skills and eventually might encourage a destructive self-fulfilling prophecy.

4. The sense organs (i.e., eyes, ears, nose, mouth, and skin) enable a person to see, hear, smell, taste, and be touched.

5. Words and a person's voice combine to provide that individual with the ability to talk, which is essential to all verbal communication.

6. Finally, the brain stores the knowledge a person has acquired from past experiences. All of these elements work together in each person's communication process (Satir, 1972).

Good communication does not occur automatically. Communication can be constructive or destructive. To be an effective and helpful communicator, one must be skilled at listening, interpreting, and expressing oneself. As much as possible, when interacting with others, the counselor needs to listen in a nonjudgmental manner. Because the client is typically an offender, it is easy to come to view such a relationship in terms of "us versus them." The offender, however, has already been judged and found guilty. As counselors, we need to be clear and open-minded in an effort to establish a basis for trust with the person we are working with if we are to have any hope in establishing a basis for meaningful communication.

Many counselors, particularly those who work with offenders, may find it difficult to pay adequate attention to their clients' communication. Perhaps this difficulty is, to a large extent, the result of the counselor's professional and personal attitude, an attitude that is a reflection of the counselor's dual responsibility (i.e., security and treatment) and, as mentioned previously, the retributive feelings of society in general. Indeed, we live in a social system that is often punishment-oriented. In addition, the counselor who works in a correctional setting is typically concerned first with security/custody needs of the agency and community, and second with the treatment and rehabilitation needs of the offender.

A part of the basis for meaningful communication also includes being sensitive to, and able to interact with, an ethnically and culturally diverse offender population. As counselors, we often are inclined to filter everyone and everything through our dominant culture—middle-class values. However, we are a pluralistic society that includes black, white, Asian, Native, and Hispanic and Latino Americans. Each of these groups, to some extent, has its own values and ways of communicating. Yonas and Garland (1994) suggest four ways to sensitize helping professionals to ethnic variations:

1. sensitize practitioners to ethnic variations in approaches to problem solving;

2. provide greater understanding of the general perspectives, common problems, and specific needs of the people from specific ethnic backgrounds;

3. clarify the likely sources and probable nature of conflicts between service providers and clients from specific ethnic groups; and

4. suggest ways in which the organizational structure and operating procedures of the criminal justice system complement or come into conflict with the values, orientations, and lifestyles of people from specific ethnic backgrounds.

Gender responsivity has become another concern for correctional counselors. This concern emerges from increasing accusations that prevailing correctional treatment focuses primarily on male offenders and ignores women offenders (Chesney Lind, 2000). Or at best, the current intervention and assessment models were developed for males and applied to females with no thought to relevance or effectiveness (Morash, Bynum & Koons, 1998). In recent research focusing on gender-responsive approaches to counseling women offenders, Bloom, Owen & Covington (2003) put forward several guiding principles for gender-responsive policies and programs. Those most relevant to correctional treatment and counseling are as follows:

1. Acknowledge that gender makes a difference.

2. Create environments based on safety, respect, and dignity.

3. Develop interventions that are relational in their approach, focusing on healthy connections to children, family, significant others, and the community.

4. Address substance abuse, trauma, and mental health issues in an *integrated* and culturally relevant manner.

For the counselor to develop a sense of timing, he or she must be able to respect "where clients are" in terms of their value systems, life experiences, and needs, yet not necessarily respect "what the clients have done" in terms of their behavior. Respecting and understanding where the client is helps the counselor to have a more accurate perception of the general condition of the offender and aids in the implementation of a meaningful treatment strategy. "Listening" is essentially a clinical art that enables the counselor to build a base relationship with his or her client that can increase the potential for positive change to occur. Developing the ability to fully listen to a client requires both patience and perseverance. Giving advice to a client before adequately understanding what he or she is trying to communicate is like a physician attempting to provide medical treatment before an adequate assessment has been rendered concerning the nature of the patient's illness. Perhaps, in the final analysis, counselors would do well to remember the old adage: "It is not so much 'what' you say as it is 'when' and 'how' you say it."

Effective risking is a skill or an ability that the counselor attempts to impart to his or her client. The offense that brings the client to the counselor could be viewed as the primary "symptom" of other, deeper conflicts. An important goal of the counseling relationship is to help the offender develop more acceptable ways of relating to his or her environment.

Risking in a general sense is not new to many offenders. Every time they have tried to commit crimes they have risked arrest and possible imprisonment. Risking in a therapeutic sense—a serious effort to substantially change one's attitude and behavior—is a commitment neither an offender nor a non-offender would take lightly. Such a risk, if unsuccessful, could prove to be devastating to a person's emotional stability and, perhaps, physical survival. For instance, during the era of self-discovery and encounter groups in the 1970s, there were a number of casualties. Individuals experiencing the close intimacy and support of an extended small group occasionally chose to make radical changes in their lives. These changes involved careers, marriages, and other major areas of life. The result of taking such risks in some cases was emotional illness and even suicide. In other words, problems that have taken a lifetime to evolve rarely can be changed quickly or with a single decision. Offenders in prison face the additional problem of feeling as though they cannot appear to conform too closely to establishment values. They must keep up the proper image in the cell block or face, in some cases, potentially violent consequences. The key to taking risks is to learn to take risks effectively. Some offenders often act impulsively without thinking through their actions in terms of what the consequences may be. The counselor should attempt to help the client assess the costs of his or her actions. In other words: if I choose to take a risk, what will it cost me? The costs may be measured in time (e.g., a possible prison sentence), money, more positive or negative relationships, or even life or death.

When evaluating the potential costs of a particular risk, the counselor can help the offender make a more relevant and effective choice by examining three fundamental existential questions: Who I am? Where am I going? Why? These questions provide a counseling focus that is both "here and now" and responsibility-based. "Who am I?" can provide a catalyst for helping the client to put into better perspective the successes and failures of his or her past, as well as the as-yet unrealized hopes and fears of the future in the context of the present—the "here and now." Where am I going?" suggests two questions: "Where do I currently see myself?" and "Where do I see myself in the future?" These questions have particular application in helping offenders with risk-taking regarding vocational and career decisions. "Why" enables the counselor to help his or her client experience a greater sense of responsibility and accountability for the choices he or she makes and the risks he or she takes. In fully exploring the "why" of a person's choice, the counselor can help the individual clarify his or her priorities and make a more informed decision in terms of personal meaning and responsibility to others.

High-quality **therapeutic relationships** have a lot to do with whether an offender changes (Andrews, 1980). Notice, for example, how often people try to do the right thing because they want the respect of parents and friends more than they want just a good grade in college or a job promotion. Good relationships often motivate people to action. In the context of therapeutic relationships, clients also transfer both positive and negative feelings to the counselor as a part of the dynamics of the relationship process. How the counselor responds to these feelings will have a substantial impact on any potential attitude change on the part of the offender. The therapeutic relationship is also important during times when the offender's life just does not seem fair. The support of the therapeutic relationship sustains offenders during times when, despite their best efforts, life is discouraging. As Van Wormer (1999) observes, "Sometimes one encounter or one supportive relationship—whether it be a teacher, social worker, or priest—can offer a turning point in a life of crime" (p. 51).

Therapeutic intention is a key quality the counselor attempts to impart to his or her client through modeling and other aspects of the therapeutic relationship. Therapeutic intention refers to the counselor's or the client's attempts to put their good intentions into action. Indeed, to persevere—to continue trying—may be more important to long-term correctional rehabilitation and stability than more immediate treatment outcomes. This is because life offers no rewards or guarantees for people doing the right thing.

Types of Correctional Counseling

Within the correctional setting, counselors are generally divided into two categories: (1) community-based and (2) institutional.

Community-based counselors include probation and parole service professionals, halfway house counselors, case managers for drug courts or mental health courts, and probation or parole officers with specialized caseloads (e.g., for mental health clients or sex offenders). Counselors working in pretrial or supervised release settings could also be included in this group. Other, yet very important, professional resources include mental health centers, public schools, employment agencies, volunteers, private helping centers (e.g., alcohol and drug counseling), and pastoral counselors and other faith-based agencies and organizations.

Probation is perhaps most utilized as an alternative to sentencing juveniles and adult offenders to correctional institutions. Essentially, probation consists of mandating an offender to a community-based treatment or other correctional program rather than incarcerating him or her. Probation officers are responsible for managing and supervising offenders who have been placed on community-based orders (e.g., community service, home detention, etc.) by the courts.

Parole officers supervise and monitor offenders who have been released on parole from prison. Unlike probation officers, who usually work with offenders before incarceration, parole officers work with offenders after they have been incarcerated for a period of time. The work of some parole officers actually begins prior to release as they prepare offenders for their return home.

The treatment and counseling functions of probation and parole have increased in recent years. For example, these officers are often required to conduct intake risk/needs assessments (see Chapter 7) or screen for mental health or substance abuse problems. In addition, many probation and parole officers now facilitate cognitive behavioral treatment groups on topics such as anger management, cognitive skills, or life skills (see Chapters 8 and 9). Finally, both probation and parole officers are responsible for monitoring and assessing probationer and parolee compliance with court-ordered conditions of release. If offenders fail to comply with conditions of release, both probation and parole officers may initiate **revocation** proceedings (i.e., a process that responds to violations of the conditions of probation or parole) against such offenders.

It is important to note that the roles of both probation and parole officers are, to some extent, conflictual in nature. These professionals are faced with reconciling the competing roles of public safety and the rehabilitation and reintegration of the offender (Purkiss et al., 2003). In other words, probation and parole officers are charged with ensuring public safety, while at the same time being asked to help their clients. One problem with this dual role centers on the issue of counselor/client confidentiality. If the offender is aware that his or her probation/parole officer must investigate and enforce the conditions of probation/parole, building a truly confidential relationship is likely to be significantly reduced. The confidentiality dilemma of "treatment versus security" is a conflict that all correctional counselors share to some extent.

Institutional counselors and treatment professionals often include: intake assessment staff, institutional parole officers, psychologists, psychiatrists, social workers, counselors, case managers, chaplains, educators, vocational instructors, and recreation specialists. These professionals will work with the inmate to varying degrees, depending on his or her individual needs. However, the majority of inmates are usually assigned to a counselor (sometimes referred to as a prison case manager or an institutional parole officer) with whom they have considerable interaction during their incarceration. Like their community counterparts, institutional counselors are responsible for supervising and monitoring offenders. However, these individuals also perform a number of other important duties, which include:

1. monitoring and assessing inmate adjustment problems;

2. assessing risk and needs, or administering institutional custody assessments;

3. developing and recommending interventions considered most beneficial for the rehabilitation of inmates;

4. advising and counseling inmates regarding their problems and monitoring and evaluating their progress; and

5. communicating with inmates' families and contacts in the community to maintain established bonds outside the institution.

In addition, counselors prepare reports for parole boards and make recommendations concerning an inmate's release. More importantly, they play a crucial role in the inmate's transition from the institutional setting to community life. For example, counselors provide discharge planning so that, upon release, parolees can be referred to community-based programs that fit their individual needs. Ideally, institutional and community-based counselors coordinate their efforts to make an inmate's transition from the correctional institution to the community easier.

Another institutional counselor who often plays an important role in the inmate's life is the prison chaplain. Chaplains perform a number of duties, including conducting religious services and funeral services, counseling troubled inmates, conveying news of family tragedies to prisoners, and helping to link parolees to community religious or faith-based resources. However, the chaplain's primary focus is often on helping inmates survive the stresses of prison life.

In correctional institutions, there are four basic categories of treatment programming:

1. Education

2. Recreation

3. Counseling/Casework

4. Psychotherapy

The **educational specialist** working in a prison or the correctional educator in general is confronted with a less-than-ideal population of potential students. As a group, offenders represent a profound record of failure. Moreover, both juvenile delinquent (Hodges, Guiliotti & Porpotage, 1994) and adult offenders (Kirsch et al., 1993) evidence lower literacy levels than their counterparts in the general population. The failure of many of these offenders within the mainstream educational system is primarily the result of unidentified or unaddressed learning disabilities (Parkinson, Dulfano & Nink, 2003; Corley, 1996).

Unfortunately, traditional educational approaches do not work with most offenders, and matching inmates with the appropriate instructional or educational programs often presents a considerable challenge for correctional educators. However, being able to meet these educational challenges may translate into a significant payoff for society. Research consistently demonstrates that inmates who participate in educational programs have lower recidivism rates (see, e.g., Parkinson, Dulfano & Nink, 2003; Phipps et al., 1999; Ryan, 1995; Steurer & Smith, 2003; Wilson, Gallagher & MacKenzie, 2000) and better community adjustment (McCollum, 1994).

Even so, many national organizations, such as the American Correctional Association (ACA) and the Correctional Education Association (CEA), have noted a number of deficiencies in the educational opportunities available in prison, and they continue to push for changes within correctional education. The United Nations Economic and Social Council (UNESC), for example, endorses correctional education standards, which include:

1. All prisoners should have access to education;

2. Prisoners should have access to literacy programs, basic education, vocational training, creative, religious and cultural activities, recreational education and activities, social education, higher education, and library facilities;

3. Prison administrators and managers should facilitate and support education as much as possible;

4. Disincentives to prisoners who participate in approved formal educational programs should be avoided;

5. Wherever possible, prisoners should be allowed to participate in education outside prison;

6. Where education has to take place within the prison, the outside community should be involved as fully as possible;

7. Vocational education should aim at the greater development of the individual and be sensitive to trends in the labor market;

8. Creative and cultural activities should be given a significant role because they have a special potential for enabling prisoners to develop and express themselves;

9. Educational opportunities should aim at developing the whole person, bearing in mind the prisoner's social, economic and cultural background (National Institute of Correctional Education, 2004).

The latter of these standards recognizes the importance of allowing an inmate to reach his or her full potential and develop as a "whole" person by providing as many educational opportunities as possible. However, providing educational opportunities is not enough. Because many inmates may feel that society views them as failures, not worthy of further investment, their success may hinge on the relationships they build with correctional educators or other treatment professionals. As with client-counselor relationships, the interpersonal skills the educator brings to his or her relationship with an offender will often determine success or failure (Dennison, 1969; Van Wormer, 1999).

Recreational programs offer distinct advantages over other treatment programs. For instance, one does not have to be able to read and write in order to participate in and learn from recreational programs. Even physically disabled offenders can engage in a variety of recreational activities (e.g., arts and crafts, music, table games). A major problem regarding correctional recreation has been one of perception. Too often, the correctional recreation specialist has been no more that an athletic "coach," coordinating a few recreational activities such as softball, basketball, and weightlifting, which are meaningful to only a small percentage of the inmate population.

The "treatment versus security" dilemma is nowhere more evident than in the area of correctional recreation. If a correctional institution does not utilize a varied and comprehensive recreation program, inmates are left with a substantial amount of idle time and very few appropriate outlets for venting any frustrations or tensions they might be experiencing. Such a situation can, of course, result in an increase in physical and emotional conflicts among prisoners, ranging from sexual assaults to personal depression. Indeed, if a correctional institution operates a varied and comprehensive recreational program, new problems as well as benefits will probably occur. More recreational programs and activities result in a more complex scheduling process. Inmate meals, work assignments, education programs, and other aspects of institutional life need to operate smoothly in conjunction with recreational activities. Another concern is for the security of recreational events. Inadequate and ineffective supervision could result in a security and treatment nightmare.

A number of innovations have occurred in recreation and related programming that have implications for corrections. Outward Bound and therapeutic wilderness programs have been used with juvenile offenders eligible for incarceration (Castellano & Soderstrom, 1992). The programs provide a rugged outdoor experience, usually of one or two weeks in duration, in which youths engage in:

1. physical conditioning (e.g., running and hiking);

2. technical training (e.g., lifesaving, solo survival);

3. safety training; and

4. team training (e.g., rescue and firefighting).

An important aspect of the program is teaching the youth that they are capable of doing more than they think they can do and that they can learn to trust others.

Exercise as therapy has gained increasing attention with the general public as well as with mental health and correctional treatment programs. Strenuous physical exercise has demonstrated positive psychological benefits for adolescents and for drug- and alcohol-addicted individuals (Buffone, 1980).

Counseling and case management functions (the subject of the remainder of this book) provide a cohesiveness that enables institutional and other programmatic activities to run as smoothly as possible. Traditionally, counselors work with both individual clients and conduct group counseling sessions relating to different kinds of problems (e.g., drug abuse, sexual offending, anger management, and suicide prevention). Formally, and more importantly, informally, counselors function as "crisis-intervenors." From the newly arrived first-time offender who is anxious and depressed, to the inmate who has just been turned down for parole, the counselor must intervene in a diverse and varied array of interpersonal situations. Counselors try to help offenders adjust to and function in the institution with a minimum amount of interpersonal frustration and deterioration. Effective treatment or rehabilitation does occur, but in the context of many challenges. For example, treatment is often secondary to general crisis intervention and maintenance functions. In addition, some offenders genuinely want to change; others do not. Some offenders come to a point in their lives where they want to chart a more positive and meaningful course; other offenders are comfortable with their criminal careers and engage in counseling as a means of improving their situation in prison and their chances of getting out as soon as possible.

The use of correctional counseling as opposed to **psychotherapy** has been an issue of continuing debate. Arguments have been raised regarding the differentiation of the two along lines of theory behind the technique (e.g., psychoanalysis as psychotherapy); degree of emotional disturbance and psychopathology (i.e., more serious disturbances require psychotherapy); clinical work setting (e.g., medical or educational); and level of professional education and training (e.g., the M.D. psychiatrist is a psychotherapist; the Ph.D. or Psy.D. psychologist is a psychotherapist; and the M.A. counseling psychologist is a counselor). Generally speaking, psychotherapists have doctorate degrees (M.D., Ph.D., Psy.D., D.S.W.). In a fundamental sense, however, it is often difficult to determine where counseling stops and psychotherapy begins, especially in correctional settings where most treatment practitioners are counselors with M.A. (Master of Arts) degrees or social workers with M.S.W (Master's in Social Work) degrees. It is often difficult to distinguish between the two on the basis of clientele, structure, theory, process, and methodology (Braswell & Seay, 1984; Ivey & Simek-Downing, 1980).

This is not to suggest that there is little difference between the M.D. psychiatrist who can prescribe medication and who has completed a psychiatric residency and a M.A. level counselor. There are obvious and significant differences between the two. It is rather an attempt to point out that, in reality, most institutional and agency clinical treatment professionals who provide counseling or psychotherapy services that are available to offenders are trained at a master's level of expertise. Finally, any attempt to define correctional counseling and psychotherapy would include several elements:

1. A clear clinical/professional identity in which some counselors or therapists happen to work primarily with human beings who happen to be offenders;

2. The ability to effectively incorporate and communicate the helping skills of timing, risking, and therapeutic relationship; and

3. The capacity for maintaining the perspective of "therapeutic intention"—that one's helping attitude and efforts in a sustained, preserving manner may be more important than measured outcomes such as recidivism rates.

Effectiveness of Offender Counseling and Treatment

There has been considerable debate among practitioners and researchers regarding the effectiveness of offender counseling and treatment. However, whether offender counseling is effective may depend to a large extent on what meaning one gives the word "effective." For some people, effective counseling and treatment is whatever keeps the prison routine running smoothly, with little regard for preparing the offender to return and readjust to the outside community. For others, effective treatment programs are equated with whatever programs are cheapest to implement and maintain in terms of financial costs. Finally, for many policy makers, members of the general public, and correctional practitioners, reductions in recidivism represent the benchmark measure of effectiveness. Regardless of one's perspective, the role, function, and degree of success attributed to offender treatment programs have represented areas of heightened controversy, with support ranging from heavy emphasis on rehabilitation and community reintegration to very little reliance, if any, on correctional counseling and treatment programs (Cullen & Gendreau, 2000; Cullen & Wright, 1996; Cullen, Wright & Applegate, 1995; DiIulio, 1991; Gaes et al., 1999; Palmer, 1992; Whitehead & Lab, 1989).

A number of approaches have been used to try to measure the effectiveness of offender treatment. The most respected approaches include long-term, post-treatment, follow-up measures, experimental designs (using comparison groups), and personality or attitudinal change as measured by psychological tests. In examining these approaches, it is apparent that the most accepted evaluation techniques are driven by quantitative methodology. However, in recent years, some researchers have advocated for renewed attention to qualitative studies (Creswell, 1994; Glesne, 1999; Maxwell, 1996). Researchers who endorse qualitative methodology argue that the complexity of human behavior cannot be quantified, and that it is qualitative inquiry that allows us to gain a more thorough understanding of the dynamics of human behavior.

One of the most respected evaluation methodologies utilizes the statistical technique of **meta-analysis**. Meta-analysis affords an opportunity to summarize results across many studies, thereby combining many research samples into one large sample and creating a summary statistic (effect size) that gauges the effectiveness of all or specific types of program modalities. Meta analyses correct for many of the methodological problems of individual studies, including low base rates and small sample sizes (Lipsey & Wilson, 2001). As will be seen in later chapters of this book, a series of meta-analyses offers strong recommendations regarding the effectiveness of behavioral, social learning, and cognitive behavioral interventions for offenders (e.g., Andrews et al., 1990; Lipsey, 1992; Sherman et al., 1997).

Undoubtedly, both practitioners and researchers will continue to debate the merits of program evaluation techniques. It is also likely that they will continue to question the effectiveness of correctional counseling and treatment programs. However, there seems to be a general consensus among many practitioners and researchers regarding the elements that comprise an effective counseling or treatment program. These elements include:

1. a cooperative treatment community where health care, education, vocational, recreational, mental health and substance abuse professionals work together in a comprehensive, integrated approach in intervening with offenders and promoting prosocial, productive behavior;

2. administrative and institutional support in providing adequate resources and opportunities to develop and implement meaningful treatment and related programs;

3. a variety of practical life skills and treatment experiences that reinforce personal accountability and relevance both within the institution and in the community;

4. a method for matching characteristics of the offender, therapist, and program—referred to as the *principle of responsivity*;

5. program evaluation in order to (a) identify and understand which programs work and which do not, (b) monitor the strengths and weaknesses of effective programs, and (c) identify opportunities for improvement;

6. a willingness to change and move away from the status quo in order to explore more creative treatment alternatives;

7. relapse prevention strategies to assist the offender in the community upon completion of the formal phase of a treatment program in a correctional facility; and

8. well-trained treatment staff who have attained appropriate educational credentials (Adapted from Dodson & Braswell, 2003).

Conclusions

Correctional counselors are involved in both community-based and institution-based programs for offenders. The nature of their jobs involves both security and treatment issues and indicates that probation and parole officers be considered a part of this group as well.

Pre-release, post-release, and family readjustment counseling all fall within the domain of the correctional counselor. He or she uses a variety of interpersonal skills and psychological treatments in working with offender-clients and their families.

Ambiguity and contradictions abound in many correctional counseling environments, in which counselors may often have to provide educational, recreational, and related services in addition to their counseling and case management responsibilities. Treatment and security concerns may also place the correctional counselor in the middle of conflicts between offenders and security and administrative personnel.

The continuing debate regarding treatment effectiveness creates varied perspectives concerning the professional role of the correctional counselor. Are correctional counselors rehabilitation professionals, maintenance and adjustment counselors, security personnel, educators, or recreation coordinators?

The scope and purpose of offender counseling covers a dynamic range of professional expertise and responsibility that continues to evolve and challenge the creative energies of the counselor who chooses to work in a correctional environment.

Key Concepts and Terms

community-based counselors	psychotherapy
counseling and case management	recreational programs
educational specialists	therapeutic intention
effective risking	therapeutic relationship
institutional counselors	timing
meta-analysis	

Discussion Questions

1. What are some of the issues involved in differentiating between offender and correctional counseling?

2. What are the three essential abilities an offender counselor or therapist needs to possess?

3. What is meant by gender-responsivity and how might it be demonstrated?

4. What are the six basic elements of communication and how do they relate to the "abilities" in question two?

5. What are four ways in which correctional counselors become more sensitive to the ethnic and cultural diversity of offenders?

6. Discuss the crucial role that both education and recreation specialists play as part of the correctional counseling team.

7. Is correctional treatment effective?

Chapter 2

Understanding the Special Challenges Faced by the Correctional Counselor in the Prison Setting

William N. Elliott and Jeffrey L. Schrink

The following vignettes were extracted from a 23-year-old criminology graduate's first 90 days on the job as a correctional counselor in a state-operated juvenile correctional facility.

> The counselor took a group of juvenile offenders to a nearby county juvenile detention center to conduct peer counseling with the youth at the county facility. At one point during the discussion, the counselor walked up behind one of the county detainees, a rather frail-looking 10-year-old boy, and placed his hand on the youth's shoulder. The boy screamed in terror and ran into the corner of the group room and assumed the fetal position.

> After only six weeks on the job, the counselor approached the assistant superintendent of the institution and passionately requested that an offender be considered for an early release from custody. The following week, the assistant superintendent informed the counselor that the youth, while watching a movie with other offenders at a local theater, had stolen a pack of cigarettes from a woman's purse. This theft jeopardized the opportunity for other offenders to visit the theater.

> The counselor, following his orientation training, was directed by the superintendent to surreptitiously record an interview with two juvenile offenders. The superintendent believed that the offenders had engaged in sexual contact with an adult prisoner who was regarded as a "trusty."

> Two months after the counselor assumed his position, a colleague transferred to another division of the Department of Correction. The neophyte counselor was thus left with two caseloads totaling 100 offenders and all of the attendant responsibilities: admission summaries, progress reports, telephone calls, supportive counseling, crisis intervention, classification team meetings, etc.

The neophyte counselor featured in these vignettes was the first author who, with a recently awarded graduate degree in hand and assistance from the second author, had secured a counseling position with a state correctional facility for male delinquents. Each situation not only served as a painful, albeit necessary, learning experience, but serves as a vivid illustration of the special challenges that face the correctional counselor. In the first illustration, the counselor discovered that basic **counseling principles** and **techniques** were woefully inadequate in offender treatment (in this case a youth who had been the victim of sexual abuse by his father).

In the second vignette the counselor learned too late that he had fallen prey to *ingratiation* (Elliott & Verdeyen, 2002), a subtle form of **resistance to treatment.** (The offender had told the counselor that he wished that the latter had been his father. This endeared the youth to the counselor so much that the former was not held as accountable for program achievement as other offenders.) In the third instance, the counselor was confronted by the first of many **ethical dilemmas** (client confidentiality) inherent in correctional counseling. In the final scenario, the counselor was besieged by a huge caseload with excessive paperwork, two of the many **contextual demands** confronting the correctional counselor.

Preliminary Considerations

Before examining the four special challenges cited above, it is important to define correctional counseling for the purposes of this chapter. Correctional counseling is understood by the authors as an intensive, purposeful, interactive process between a counselor, who is professionally prepared to deal with the special problems posed by a correctional environment, and a client, who has been found guilty of committing a crime or active delinquency and placed in a correctional facility. Although academic and experiential qualifications for correctional counselors may vary across jurisdictional boundaries, most corrections departments require at least an undergraduate degree in criminology/criminal justice or a social or behavioral science. Additionally, higher job classifications have been developed to attract individuals with relevant experience or graduate degrees in counseling and related fields. The caliber of individuals who work as correctional counselors runs the gamut from highly dedicated professionals who take their work seriously to those who just put in the hours to get their paychecks.

Principles and Techniques

Beginning correctional counselors are often admonished to forget everything they have learned about traditional counseling techniques. Traditional counseling strategies are dismissed as either irrelevant or susceptible to manipulation by offenders. The authors disagree with the notion that standard counseling methods are inherently useless or ineffective. Rather, conventional counseling principles and techniques must be applied in a unique manner to offender populations. For example, it is universally agreed that a warm, **collaborative relationship** between the counselor and client is required if counseling interventions are to be successful. This is no less true in correctional counseling. However, the correctional counselor must build a relationship through which he or she can confront the offender with the irresponsible decisions and behavior that culminated in incarceration. Indeed, Glasser (1965) argues that the correctional counselor's basic job is to be involved with the offender and then to persuade him or her to face reality.

The importance of establishing a meaningful relationship with the offender cannot be overstated. Myers and Jackson (2002) assert that, without personal involvement on the part of the counselor, there will no significant connection with the offender and, therefore, counseling will not hold the offender's attention. In discussing the appropriateness of this relationship, however, it is important to introduce the notion of **interpersonal boundaries.** A boundary is the invisible line that separates individuals according to their needs, feelings, emotional health, privacy concerns, and other human issues. Counselors examine interpersonal boundaries according to their appropriateness. For example, it would be inappropriate for a stranger to ask us about the intimate details of our lives. However, such discussions are typically not inappropriate with a spouse. Similarly, it is appropriate for parents to exercise authority over their children, but not appropriate for them to exercise such authority over other adults. Counselors also cautiously maintain appropriate boundaries with clients. It is appropriate to develop a therapeutic relationship with clients but inappropriate to develop a sexually intimate relationship with a client.

Unfortunately, many correctional counselors are reluctant to build personal involvement with offenders because they fear becoming overly emotionally involved with them. Indeed, managing interpersonal boundaries with offenders is important for several reasons, not the least of which is preventing manipulation and exploitation (Elliott & Verdeyen, 2002). However, a trusting and open working relationship is not synonymous with emotional over-involvement and poor boundary management. To the contrary, a collaborative relationship between the counselor and offender is seen as a necessary precursor to successful counseling (Harris, 1995). The counseling relationship, or therapeutic alliance, has been systematically shown to be related to positive outcomes in treatment (Drapeau, Korner & Brunet, 2004).

In traditional counseling a lot of time is spent both inquiring into and listening to offenders' complaints about the actions of other people, the world they live in, and so forth; the list is endless. The authors contend that it is less productive to probe at length for the problems of offenders. Counselors who sacrifice valuable time and energy exploring the offender's past for antecedents of current problems may be ignoring a more likely cause of the offender's behavior. That is, it is typically a **"here and now"** style of thinking that supports and maintains the offender's antisocial behavior (Walters, 1990). Moreover, complaining is usually an effort to avoid talking about the issues that really need to be discussed. The authors suggest that such historical investigations are not only fruitless, but at times counterproductive. Moreover, such inquiries provide the offender with yet one more excuse or justification for his or her criminality.

The authors strongly endorse **group counseling** as the preferred modality for providing offender treatment. Groups provide the offender with a wealth of new information gathered from interactions with other individuals who can relate to the offender's current situation and issues. In addition, groups create an external feedback mechanism (offenders challenging each other) with the prospect of internalization somewhere down the line (Walters, 2001). Working in groups is also important because peer group pressure and influence are inherently therapeutic (Vorrath & Brentro, 1985). Moreover, group members will typically refuse to accept excuses from, and are not bashful about offering hard-hitting feedback to, their peers (Myers & Jackson, 2002). Correctional counselors who lack requisite training and experience are encouraged to conduct psychoeducational groups that are highly structured and largely didactic in nature (Elliott & Walters, 1991, 1997). Typically, such groups are time-limited and offer a specific curriculum, including a workbook for participants (Caputo, 2004).

Whenever possible, counselors are advised to seek **collateral information** regarding the offenders they are treating. Indeed, counselors should find out as much as they can about an offender's behavior in his or her housing unit, classroom, work area, or elsewhere. Such investigations can be most enlightening because many offenders are masters of deceit and can present themselves in a favorable light in the presence of the counselor (Samenow, 1984). Therefore, it is crucial that the counselor rely on something other than the offender's self-report. Reading the offender's central file, observing his or her behavior in different contexts and talking with other staff who know the offender are ways in which the counselor can form a reliable and comprehensive impression of the offender (Elliott & Verdeyen, 2002). Housing unit officers are especially valuable sources of information, because they spend more time with the offender than any other staff.

Whether counseling offenders in groups or individually, the counselor must adopt and adhere to some kind of conceptual framework for his or her treatment efforts. Unfortunately, there is no "magic bullet" for effectively treating offenders. However, focal **cognitive-behavioral interventions** directed at specific criminal thinking styles have some efficacy at reducing criminal risk and recidivism (McMackin, Tansi & LaFratta, 2004) (see Chapter 9, Cognitive Therapies). Many cognitive-behavioral techniques can be used with offenders, including Rational-Emotive Therapy (Ellis, 1962); Rational Behavior Therapy (Maultsby, 1975); and Rational Cognitive Therapy (Smith & Lombardo, 2001). However, the authors are unequivocal and enthusiastic advocates of the cognitive-behavioral strategies developed by Yochelson and Samenow (1976, 1977) and extended by Walters (1990). These approaches, referred to as "The Criminal Personality" and "The Criminal Lifestyle," respectively, emphasize the identification and amelioration of recurrent and pervasive criminal thinking patterns.

Yochelson and Samenow (1976) described 52 specific **thinking errors** uncovered in their intensive case studies of inmates housed at St. Elizabeth's Hospital in Washington, D.C. Walters (1990) modified and consolidated these thinking errors into a set of eight interactive criminal thinking patterns, which serve as the centerpiece of his comprehensive theory of criminal behavior. Yochelson and Samenow's model enjoys widespread popularity among counselors in several state institutions, whereas Walters' theory figures prominently in the Federal Bureau of Prisons' Psychology Treatment Programs. Regardless of the model selected for use, it is clear that challenging the cognitive distortions or "thinking errors" employed by offenders to justify their offending is an integral part of treatment (Houston, 1998). Indeed, Samenow (1984) maintains that any treatment approach is inherently futile unless it influences the offender to change his or her thinking.

Elliott and Verdeyen (2002) have adapted the Walters (1990) model in a manner that renders it "user friendly" to correctional counselors who seek to challenge criminal thinking exhibited by offenders in groups. In Figure 2.1, Walters' eight primary criminal thinking patterns are listed in the left-hand column while the corresponding cognitive distortions described by Elliott and Verdeyen appear in the right-hand column. As noted above, the authors of this chapter encourage the correctional counselor to focus his or her efforts on incipient criminal thinking regardless of the treatment context. However, the counselor is warned that doing so will require a maximum degree of patience and commitment. After all, in some cases, the protective shield of justifications, rationalizations, and excuses used by offenders has been developed over the course of a lifetime of violating the laws of society (Walters, 2001).

Resistance to Treatment

Some counseling texts suggest that the counseling relationship can only occur with the mutual consent of both the client and counselor. This is perhaps the ideal relationship, but it is not often found in many contexts, especially corrections. Many offenders are, after all, confined in institutions against their will; participation in correctional counseling is, by definition, arguably involuntary. However, even if some offenders do voluntarily involve themselves in counseling programs, the counselor may still be confronted by fierce resistance. Criminal behavior is highly reinforcing (Walters, 2001) and ego syntonic, that is, consistent with the offender's view of right or wrong (Harris, 1995). Therefore, the offender sees no reason to change and presents little motivation to do so during treatment. Moreover, the very nature of the prison environment promotes an "us versus them" atmosphere in which inmates may view counselors as "cops" and counseling sessions as "snitch sessions" (Morgan, 2003).

Figure 2.1
Eight Primary Criminal Thinking Patterns

Walters (1990)	Elliott and Verdeyen (2002)
Mollification	The Blaming Game
Cutoff	I Feel Nothing
Entitlement	I Should Get What I Want
Power Orientation	I'm in Charge
Sentimentality	Look at Me Being Good
Superoptimism	I Can Get by with Anything
Cognitive Indolence	That's Too Much Work
Discontinuity	I Talk One Way and Act Another

Resistance to treatment can assume many forms: Harris (1995) identifies some of the more common ones: withholding information, missing appointments, discrediting or dismissing the counseling process, failing to do homework assignments, and declining to cooperate with the counselor in overt or covert ways. Of course, many offenders are outwardly compliant, which can also be a form of resistance (Stanchfield, 2001). It may not be obvious for quite some time that such offenders are merely going through the motions and saying the right words while failing to internalize any of the information presented during counseling sessions. Elliott and Verdeyen (2002) describe 12 specific types of resistance that correctional counselors can expect to confront. These "dirty dozen" **power and control tactics** employed by offenders in counseling are presented in Figure 2.2.

Figure 2.2
**The Dirty Dozen: Power and Control Tactics Exhibited by Inmates
in Counseling (Elliott & Verdeyen, 2002)**

TACTIC	EXAMPLE
Testing	Offender completes the first few and last few pages of a workbook just to see if the counselor actually reads the workbook.
Diversion	Offender asks the counselor for help with an in-class assignment while another offender sets the clock ahead by 15 minutes.
Extortion	Offender threatens to file a complaint against the counselor unless she (counselor) immediately enrolls the offender in a psychoeducational group.
Sphere of Influence	Offender obtains documentation from an influential citizen to support the claim that he requires residential substance abuse treatment solely to receive a one-year sentence reduction.
Disreputation	Offender circulates a petition calling for the reassignment of a counselor labeled as "racist."
Rumor Clinic	Offender spreads a rumor that the counselor is an alcoholic and is thus unfit to conduct substance abuse groups.
Solidarity	Several offenders refuse to attend group counseling sessions because of the expulsion of a group member.
Negotiation	Offender offers to clean the counselor's office in exchange for retaking a drug education examination that he (offender) had failed.
Revenge	Offender damages the TV/VCR in a group room after she is expelled from a group because of poor attendance and disruptive behavior.
Ingratiation	Offender tells counselor that she (counselor) is responsible for motivating the offender to turn his life around.
Splitting	Offender tells female counselor that a male colleague said that women had no business working with male inmates.
Boundary Intrusion	Offender compliments counselor on her perfume and asks if her husband or boyfriend likes it.

Many correctional counselors understandably become impatient with and frustrated by these encounters with resistance. They either dismiss the offender as unmotivated for counseling or respond irritably and try to coerce the offender into adopting a receptive attitude and cooperative behavior (Harris, 1995). The latter approach inevitably sets the stage for a power struggle between the counselor and offender that signals the death knell for successful counseling. Such **power struggles** and the confrontation they entail are counterproductive for several reasons. First, research has consistently shown that confrontation arouses defenses, activates resistance, and deteriorates into a means of attack and an attempt to tear someone down (Elliott, 2002). Second, offenders will always emerge victorious from power struggles because the mere act of engaging the counselor in such a conflict reinforces an offender's inflated sense of self-importance (Elliott & Verdeyen, 2002). Finally, power struggles often reveal the counselor's vulnerabilities or "hot buttons" and, therefore, must be actively avoided to prevent the undermining of the counselor's credibility.

It is thus imperative that correctional counselors become adept at managing resistance and using *indirect* methods for engaging offenders in the counseling process. Elliott (2002) has identified three such strategies that simultaneously challenge incipient criminal thinking and prevent futile and protracted struggles for control. Elliott refers to these strategies as the "**3Rs**" of managing offender resistance to counseling: **redirection, reframing**, and **reversal of responsibility**. The "3Rs,"derived from the first author's experience in a Positive Peer Culture (Vorrath & Brentro, 1985) program for juvenile offenders, are illustrated in Figure 2.3.

Figure 2.3
The "3Rs" of Managing Offender Resistance to Counseling (Elliott, 2002)

STRATEGY	TECHNIQUES
Redirection: Return focus of attention to task/issue at hand.	1. Ignore resistance. 2. Employ undefocusing (Stanchfield, 2001). 3. Focus on offender's contribution to problem/conflict. 4. Focus on current/relevant issues. 5. Solicit other group members' reactions to offender's resistance.
Reframing: Encourage offender to adopt a different perspective re: the source of his/her resistance.	1. Address semantics 2. Place a positive spin on the resistance. 3. Place a negative spin on the resistance. 4. Relabel resistance in terms of its underlying criminal thinking pattern(s).
Reversal of Responsibility: Reflect offender's resistance back to him/her in a manner that assigns personal responsibility and demands accountability.	1. Paraphrase resistance with attention to its underlying (criminal) meaning. 2. Ask challenging, open-ended questions. 3. Encourage offender to make a value judgment re: his/her resistance. 4. Deliver responses as tentative observations.

Whether or not the counselor chooses to adopt the "3Rs," he or she is encouraged to remember that one of the most important elements in managing resistance is to avoid extended debates with offenders. Counselors should point out the self-defeating nature of offenders' behavior and clarify the short-term and long-term consequences of continuing to engage in such behavior. However, the counselor cannot force the offender to make the decision to adopt a prosocial lifestyle. All he or she can really do is supply the offender with information and feedback. The choice to continue a pattern of criminal behavior or create a prosocial way of life is the exclusive province of the offender (Walters, 2001).

Ethical Dilemmas

A summary of the Ethical Standards of the American Counseling Association is offered in Figure 2.4 and may be viewed in greater detail by consulting their Web page, www.counseling.org.

Competent and well-intentioned correctional counselors sometimes struggle both with each other and with themselves over what appear to be conflicting ethical demands that arise when abstract ethical standards collide with the practical realities of counseling within the correctional environment. Some argue that such dilemmas naturally arise because of a basic and unavoidable conflict between two opposing philosophies: **treatment** and **security**. Because the primary mission of correctional institutions is custody and security, counselors are often required to assume roles and responsibilities in addition to and perhaps inconsistent with that of counselor or helper. The so called treatment/custody dichotomy is but one of several ethical dilemmas to be examined in this section.

The Treatment versus Security Dichotomy. The premise that treatment and security interests are mutually in conflict is debatable and seems to be based on a narrow definition of "security." The purpose of maintaining effective security and control within a correctional facility is more than preventing escape. Another primary goal is to protect inmates from each other and themselves, thus promoting the safety and general welfare of all concerned (Dignam, 2003). This is hardly inconsistent with a treatment philosophy. Indeed, the authors of this chapter would argue that treatment can only occur within an environment characterized by safety, security, and structure.

Definition of the Client. Monahan (1980) asked the question, "Who is the client?" in highlighting the conflicting loyalties inherent in correctional treatment. The nature of correctional counseling, given the many and varied tasks counselors are asked to perform, suggests that there are several client candidates at various times. The crux of the ethical issue is typically couched in terms of the counselor's perceived divided loyalties between the competing interests of the offender and those of the institution. Monahan himself partially resolves the dilemma by observing that the question "Who is the client?" is not a multiple-choice item; the objectives and interests of each party can overlap. Monahan's (1980:5) qualified conclusion is that the offender and the institution are *both* clients of the counselor "in different roles and with varying priorities."

Dual or Multiple Relationships. One of the most common ethical dilemmas voiced by correctional treatment professionals concerns the problem of dual or multiple relationships. Specifically, when required to relieve a correctional officer in a housing unit or participate in a search for contraband in an institution, many counselors push the ethical "panic button." Dignam (2003:50), however, argues that a counselor may indeed feel uncomfortable when performing tasks that are unrelated to treatment, ". . . but performing a task that is merely different from a clinician's typical regimen is not tantamount to behaving unethically, at least not in the context of dual or multiple relationships." Unless it can be convincingly demonstrated that offenders' welfare would be somehow jeopardized or that they could be exploited in the process, the performance of security-related tasks does not pose significant ethical problems.

Boundaries of Competence and Maintaining Expertise. Given the complex and diverse nature of offender populations, it is ethically imperative that counselors be sufficiently knowledgeable and competent to treat offenders. Counselors can begin or continue to meet this ethical obligation by supplementing their training and experience in areas pertinent to working with offenders. Independent study options include reading on topics such as criminal personality (Yochelson & Samenow, 1976, 1977), lifestyle criminality (Walters, 1990), substance abuse treatment (Wanberg & Milkman, 1998; Walters, 1998), psychopathy (Hare, 1993), managing deception and manipulation (Elliott & Verdeyen, 2002), and **suicide prevention** (White, 1999). It is equally important for counselors to realize that they cannot be all things to all people. The full range of offender needs and problems can be found in prisons, and counselors need to be careful that they function within the boundaries of their expertise (Dignam, 2003).

Confidentiality. It is axiomatic that confidentiality is essential to the counseling relationship, because it provides the client with the comfort of knowing that what is said during sessions will not be repeated outside the counseling context. However, when counseling takes place within a jail or prison, confidentiality often conflicts with institutional security. For example, if an offender discloses his or her intent to escape during a counseling session, the counselor must decide whether to breach a confidentiality. Obviously, in such a situation, the counselor will be under intense pressure to divulge the information to a third party, most likely administrative or custodial personnel. Agency policy may even dictate that the counselor be required to disclose information that might constitute a threat to institutional safety or security. Moreover, there is a statutory requirement known as the "duty to warn," which requires that confidentiality be superseded by the need to protect an identifiable third party from harm (Walsh, 2003). At the same time, ethical standards governing the counseling profession maintain that counselors report to proper authorities when clients indicate an intention to harm themselves or others. This standard pertains regardless of whether the client is an offender.

Given the reality that there are relatively severe limits on an offender's privacy and confidentiality, it can be argued that the more important ethical issue for counselors is to ensure that all recipients of services are fully aware of such limits. Obviously, informing offenders of limits and restrictions on privacy and confidentiality should occur prior to engaging in the counseling process (Dignam, 2003). At a minimum, counselors need to clarify for themselves and with the offender what communication will be kept strictly confidential and what protections they do and do not have in the counseling relationship (Harris, 1995).

Figure 2.4
Summary of American Counseling Association's Ethical Standards of Practice (ACA, 1995)

---

1. **Nondiscrimination.** Counselors respect diversity and must not discriminate against clients because of age, color, culture, disability, ethnic group, gender, race, religion, sexual orientation, marital status, or socioeconomic status.

2. **Disclosure to Clients.** Counselors must adequately inform clients, preferably in writing, regarding the counseling process and counseling relationship at or before the time it begins and throughout the relationship.

3. **Dual Relationships.** Counselors must make every effort to avoid dual relationships with clients that could impair their professional judgment or increase the risk of harm to clients. A dual relationship exists when a counselor maintains relationships with the client that are in addition to the counseling relationship (e.g., counselor and employer; counselor and best friend, etc.). When a dual relationship cannot be avoided, counselors must take appropriate steps to ensure that judgment is not impaired and that no exploitation occurs.

4. **Sexual Intimacies with Clients.** Counselors must not engage in any type of sexual intimacies with current clients and must not engage in sexual intimacies with former clients within a minimum of two years after terminating the counseling relationship.

5. **Protecting Clients During Group Work.** Counselors must take steps to protect clients from physical or psychological trauma resulting from interactions during group work.

6. **Termination.** Counselors must assist in making appropriate arrangements for the continuation of treatment of clients, when necessary, following termination of counseling relationships.

7. **Inability to Assist Clients.** Counselors must avoid entering or immediately terminate a counseling relationship if it is determined that they are unable to be of professional assistance to a client. The counselor may assist in making an appropriate referral for the client.

Figure 2.4, *continued*

8. **Confidentiality Requirement.** Counselors must keep information related to counseling services confidential unless disclosure is in the best interest of clients, is required for the welfare of others, or is required by law. When disclosure is required, only information that is essential is revealed and the client is informed of such disclosure.

9. **Confidentiality Requirements for Subordinates.** Counselors must take measures to ensure that the privacy and confidentiality of clients are maintained by subordinates.

10. **Confidentiality in Group Work.** Counselors must clearly communicate to group members that confidentiality cannot be guaranteed in group work.

11. **Confidentiality of Records.** Counselors must maintain appropriate confidentiality in creating, storing, accessing, transferring, and disposing of counseling records.

12. **Permission to Record or Observe.** Counselors must obtain prior consent from clients in order to record electronically or observe sessions.

13. **Disclosure or Transfer of Records.** Counselors must obtain client consent to disclose or transfer records to third parties, unless legal exceptions exist.

14. **Data Disguise Required.** Counselors must disguise the identity of the client when using data for training, research, or publication.

15. **Boundaries of Competence.** Counselors must practice only within the boundaries of their competence.

16. **Continuing Education.** Counselors must engage in continuing education to maintain their professional competence.

17. **Impairment of Professionals.** Counselors must refrain from offering professional services when their personal problems or conflicts may cause harm to a client or others.

18. **Credentials Claimed.** Counselors must claim or imply only professional credentials possessed and must correct any known misrepresentations of their credentials by others.

19. **Sexual Harassment.** Counselors must not engage in sexual harassment.

20. **Use of Assessments.** Counselors must: (a) perform only testing and assessment services for which they are competent; (b) not allow the use of psychological assessment techniques by unqualified persons under their supervision; (c) use assessment instruments in the manner for which they were intended; (d) provide explanations to clients prior to assessment about the nature and purposes of assessment and the specific uses of the results; (e) ensure that accurate and appropriate interpretations accompany any release of testing and assessment information; and (f) avoid use of data or test results that are invalid, obsolete, or outdated for the current purpose.

21. **Precautions to Avoid Injury in Research.** In conducting or overseeing research, counselors must: (a) avoid causing physical, social, or psychological harm or injury to subjects in research; (b) keep confidential information obtained about research participants; (c) report all variables and conditions known to the investigator that may have affected research data or outcomes; and (d) not distort or misrepresent research data, nor fabricate or intentionally bias research results.

Contextual Demands

There are a host of issues and demands arising from the correctional environment itself. These confront the counselor on a routine basis and make his or her job that much more difficult and stressful. The counselor's ability to effectively negotiate these demands will, to a large degree, determine his or her susceptibility to the burnout that so often afflicts helping professionals. Several of the most prominent of these contextual demands are examined in this section.

Working in a Bureaucracy. A prison is the epitome of a bureaucracy. It is an organization dominated by rules and paperwork, often ignoring individuals in favor of procedures and precedents (Pollock, 1998). Moreover, correctional institutions adhere to a paramilitary style of management with a vertical chain of command (Elliott & Verdeyen, 2002). Obviously, some people feel more comfortable working within, and adapt more readily to, such a structure than others. Correctional treatment professionals may especially have a difficult time coping with the regimentation and rigidity so endemic to prison operation. Counselors who attempt to "buck the system" run into the proverbial brick wall and end up frustrated, disillusioned, and of little or no value to offenders. Counselors who, on the other hand, devote their time and energy to carving out a niche for themselves within the bureaucracy will become valuable members of the correctional "team."

Handling Excessive Paperwork. The written record is the single most important item in the criminal justice system. No matter how insignificant or important the event, everything that is done for, by, or to an offender either originates or culminates in some type of correctional report or record (Schrink, 1976). The exact nature and function of the reports and records and the kind of person responsible for developing and maintaining them vary somewhat depending on the stage of the criminal justice system involved. At the correctional level, it is the counselor who is most responsible for collecting information and writing reports. Several different types of records and reports must be periodically developed for each offender. Because there are so many inmates on a typical caseload, the resulting paperwork can often be enormous. Time spent on paperwork reduces the opportunities for the counselor to interact with the client. Unfortunately, some ineffective counselors have learned to hide behind this paperwork. One positive development that may help the correctional counselor better manage paperwork is the increasing availability of relatively inexpensive personal computers and software.

Managing Large Caseloads. Counselors are often expected to maintain a caseload that may exceed 100 inmates. The sheer size of the caseload is further exacerbated by the fact that there is usually a fairly rapid turnover of the inmates on the caseload. If the average stay of an inmate in an institution is two years and a counselor has a caseload of 125 inmates, the counselor may never really get to know any of the inmates before they are discharged.

Not only is the caseload large, but it is also diverse. The counselor must accept any and all inmates assigned, and few opportunities exist for developing a specialized caseload. Often the inmates have little in common beyond the fact that they have been convicted of a crime and sentenced to some type of correctional facility or program. It is not unusual for a counselor in an institution housing adult felons to have inmates on his or her caseload who have been convicted of murder, robbery, rape, child molestation, drunk driving, public intoxication, and any number of other offenses.

Under such pressure, it may be tempting for the correctional counselor to focus on the inmates with whom he or she enjoys interacting rather than with those inmates who need help the most. Offenders should be seen because they need to be seen, not because they want to structure their free time around the counselor. Similarly, they should not be seen just because the counselor likes to interact with them and is able to rationalize that he or she cannot help everyone on his or her caseload anyway.

Responding to Racial and Ethnic Skewing. Today more than 60 percent of prisoners are black or Hispanic, and there is no indication that this racial and ethnic skew is going to abate anytime in the near future. This racial and ethnic skewing can complicate the efforts of correctional counselors, because they, like most people, have a tendency to resort to ethnocentrism when dealing with others who are different from them. **Ethnocentrism** involves judging other people on the basis of one's own beliefs rather than those of others. Closely related to ethnocentrism is the all-too-common human tendency to **stereotype** others; that is, to judge people on assumed group characteristics rather than to see them and react to them as individuals. Obviously, ethnocentrism and stereotyping are prescriptions for failure in a correctional setting.

The correctional counselor can avoid many of the problems relating to ethnocentrism and stereotyping if he or she assumes a more racially and ethnically sensitive approach. Such an approach is often referred to as "cross-cultural" or **multicultural counseling** (Dillard, 1987). Specifically, correctional counselors need to try to broaden and deepen their knowledge and understanding of racially and ethnically diverse groups so that they can appreciate where these individuals "are coming from" and then begin to see them as individuals rather than as some larger group.

Working With Special Needs Offenders. Novice correctional counselors are often surprised to find that their caseloads consist of offenders with severe mental illnesses, developmental disabilities, and substance abuse problems. Increasingly, such "special needs offenders" are found in prison populations and present unique treatment needs and challenges to counselors. Counselors working with female offenders will be confronted by additional demands in that such offenders often present a variety of family and social problems, including their relationships with their children and histories of physical or sexual abuse.

One of the fastest growing subpopulations since the 1960s has been offenders with mental illness. In 1998, it was estimated that nearly 300,000 mentally ill inmates were housed in prisons and jails, constituting 15 percent of the prison population (Schwartz, 2003). Correctional institutions have often had a difficult time responding to the needs of this group. In 1991, it was estimated that only 50 percent of those with severe mental illness and 25 percent of those with moderate mental illness in U.S. prisons received an appropriate level of care (Schwartz, 2003).

Another significant group of inmates who are particularly vulnerable to abuses within prisons are those with developmental disabilities. Inmates with mental retardation or other cognitive impairments may be tempting targets for physical or sexual abuse. In addition, the first author has observed that such individuals are often enlisted by other inmates to assist in the commission of crimes within the institution. They may also confess to infractions they are not guilty of.

Of the 1.3 million prisoners confined in U.S. correctional facilities, 21 percent of state prisoners, 50 percent of federal inmates, and 26 percent of jail detainees are incarcerated for drug-related offenses (Peters & Matthews, 2003). Moreover, there have been many links drawn between substance abuse and criminal behavior (Walters, 1998). Substance abusers report significantly greater criminal activity and have more extensive criminal records than do non-users, while those with greater histories of criminal activity are more likely to report prior substance abuse (Peters & Matthews, 2003). In recognition of the scope of substance abuse problems among jail and prison inmates, correctional counselors should regard substance abuse treatment as an essential element of counseling services offered to the inmate population. Walters (1998) offers comprehensive and specific guidelines for the construction and implementation of effective substance abuse treatment services (see also Chapter 12, Treating Substance Abuse in Offender Populations).

One of the most widely accepted findings in the criminological research is that men are arrested at a higher rate than women (Holtfreter, Reisig & Morash, 2004). Although the gender gap remains large, it has narrowed over the past three decades (Pollock, 1998). Female offenders are much more likely to seek counseling services, although they may be no more motivated for sincere change than their male counterparts (Elliott & Verdeyen, 2002). Moreover, female offenders actively seek counseling to address issues of prior sexual/physical abuse and separation from their children (Hislop, 2001). Accordingly, the correctional counselor who works in a women's prison will be expected to provide a variety of counseling services to a significant portion of the population.

Providing Crisis Intervention Services. Counseling incarcerated offenders with deeply ingrained criminal tendencies is a daunting task, and true cognitive and behavioral change may not be possible in many cases (Harris, 1995). Indeed, the character pathology of the typical offender is seen by some as nonamenable to change (McMackin, Tansi & LaFratta, 2004). Therefore, working with such offenders, especially in institutions, often boils down to helping inmates manage incipient crises.

Correctional institutions are unquestionably stressful environments and offenders must deal with a host of issues resulting from incarceration. These include, but are certainly not limited to, separation from family members, imposition of structure in one's life, loss of previous coping strategies (e.g., alcohol and drug use), and fear of the prison environment itself (e.g., physical or sexual violence) (Morgan, 2003). Some offenders thrive under the environmental structure and the "inmate code" (i.e., unwritten rules of conduct) (Elliott & Verdeyen, 2002). Many simply adapt and blend into the environment, while others experience significant adjustment difficulties and internal distress. Accordingly, crisis intervention and brief supportive counseling services are necessary to assist this latter group in adjusting to their newfound lives as inmates.

Adjustment difficulties, of course, are not limited to newly incarcerated inmates; rather, chronic anxiety and stress are inevitable byproducts of incarceration (Morgan, 2003). Offenders with both short- and long-term sentences will encounter various stressors and life issues they must handle. For example, it is not uncommon for family members or significant others to discontinue communication with offenders, thus depriving the latter of a valuable source of social support (Lynch & Sabol, 2001). Even offenders nearing their release experience apprehension and anxiety, a process referred to as "getting short." Issues such as becoming reacquainted with family members, finding a job, and avoiding criminal behavior become primary areas of concern.

The correctional counselor will, at some point in his or her career, be called upon to provide crisis support services to suicidal inmates. Suicide is the leading cause of death in lock-ups and jails, and the second leading cause of death in prisons (Morgan, 2003). It is thus necessary for counselors to be thoroughly familiar with the demographic, historical, situational, and psychological risk factors for suicide (White, 1999). In addition, the counselor will need to be prepared to provide support services to the special needs offenders referred to in an earlier subsection. Finally, the correctional counselor will undoubtedly be required to offer supportive services to offenders who are physically or sexually abused by predatory inmates.

Surviving the Brutality of the Prison Environment. It is obvious that prisons are brutal environments. Correctional workers witness overt displays of violence by inmates, receive verbal abuse and threats from offenders, and observe or, if necessary, participate in the application of physical force to manage a disruptive prisoner. Such exposure to violence and aggression may be a bitter pill for many counselors to swallow; after all, many enter the correctional field to "help" offenders and "find the good" in them. However, virtually everyone who has made correctional work his or her career has experienced a "normalization" process (Welo, 2001) that can diminish the shock, disgust, fear, and anger experienced after witnessing violence and other antisocial behavior.

Unfortunately, correctional counselors are subjected to even more encounters with the violence and the destructiveness perpetrated by offenders. Counselors are expected to familiarize themselves with the presentence investigation reports and other documents concerning the offenders assigned to their caseload. Such reports are replete with the "horror stories of [the offenders'] crimes, the victims' impact statements, the anguish of their family members, and [their] . . . degree of criminality" (Welo, 2001:166). Repeated exposure to accounts of the pain and misery caused by offenders can lead to cynicism, disillusionment and, ultimately, burnout (Elliott & Verdeyen, 2002).

Final Considerations

This chapter has been devoted to an exploration of the numerous and diverse challenges faced by the correctional counselor. It is hoped that the reader now has a keen appreciation for the complexities inherent in developing counseling strategies that are effective with a hostile and resistant population, resolving the various ethical dilemmas endemic to counseling in a correctional institution, and negotiating the unique contextual demands of counseling in a prison environment. However, this discussion would be incomplete without attending to the issue of **burnout prevention**.

In a concerted effort to assist the correctional counselor in not succumbing to burnout and its deleterious physical and emotional consequences, Elliott and Verdeyen (2002) have offered 10 strategies for burnout prevention and career satisfaction. These strategies, dubbed "The Ten Commandments for Prison Staff," are listed in Figure 2.5. Finally, the authors of this chapter recommend that the correctional counselor do his or her best to maintain and exercise a healthy sense of humor. Even so-called "gallows humor" can be an effective way of distancing oneself from shocking, disgusting, or dangerous situations and preventing unwarranted emotional and behavioral responses to such situations (Kauffman, 1988). Likewise, one of the most successful ways to cope with offender deception and manipulation is to reflect on the lessons to be learned from such victimization, laugh at oneself, and move on (Elliott & Verdeyen, 2002).

Figure 2.5
Ten Commandments for Prison Staff (Elliott & Verdeyen, 2002)

1. Go home safe and sound at the end of the day.

2. Establish realistic expectations (for self, offenders, and other staff).

3. Set firm and consistent limits.

4. Avoid power struggles.

5. Manage interpersonal boundaries.

6. Don't take things personally.

7. Strive for an attitude of healthy skepticism.

8. Don't fight the bureaucracy.

9. Ask for help (from supervisors and colleagues).

10. Don't take your work home with you.

Key Concepts and Terms

brutality of prisons
burnout prevention
cognitive-behavioral interventions
collaborative relationship
collateral information
contextual demands
counseling principles
counseling techniques
criminal lifestyle
criminal personality
crisis intervention
dual/multiple relationships
ethical dilemmas
ethnocentrism
group counseling

"here and now"
interpersonal boundaries
positive peer culture
power and control tactics
power struggles
redirection
reframing
resistance to treatment
reversal of responsibility
special needs offenders
stereotyping
suicide prevention
thinking errors
treatment versus security dichotomy

Discussion Questions

1. Discuss the importance of identifying and challenging criminal thinking when counseling offenders.

2. Explain why group counseling is the preferred modality in offender treatment.

3. Describe the strategies recommended by the authors for managing offender resistance to counseling.

4. What are some of the ethical dilemmas facing the correctional counselor? How can they be successfully resolved?

5. Discuss some of the contextual demands encountered by the correctional counselor that make his or her job more stressful.

Part Two

Historical Foundations of Correctional Counseling and Treatment

---

Many of the therapeutic strategies discussed in the next three chapters are not practiced in corrections today—at least not in their purest form. Contemporary counseling emerged from the historical approaches discussed in Chapters 3 through 5, however. Professionals should be familiar with them. For example, while we certainly do not practice psychoanalysis as professional counselors, it would be unusual to be in professional circles and not hear discussion of defense mechanisms, ego controls, transference, projection, and other concepts credited to psychoanalytic and psychodynamic traditions. Similarly, more contemporary learning theories (social learning and cognitive behavioral models of counseling) incorporate a strong understanding of stimuli, reinforcement, and punishment. Simply put, it is not possible to be in the helping professions and not have an understanding of its traditions. The goal of the next three chapters is to do just that.

The psychoanalytic tradition discussed in Chapter 3 is of important historical note and contributes to the roots of many counseling approaches. While the psychoanalytic and psychodynamic models may be of limited practical value to corrections, they still provide an important foundation for subsequent developments in therapy and counseling. In addition, some of the components of psychodynamic thought (e.g., therapeutic alliance, defense mechanisms, and the notion of ego controls) are important considerations for counselors regardless of clinical orientation. Moreover, many of the clinical dimensions appeared in later traditions as modified but familiar constructs.

Chapter 4 presents the radical behavioral approaches of classical and operant conditioning. While classical conditioning is not widely used in corrections, except occasionally for special populations (e.g., sex offenders), operant conditioning, in the form of token economies, is pervasive, especially in correctional settings for juveniles.

Finally, Chapter 5 makes it clear that almost any correctional modality can be delivered in either group or individual settings. In corrections, group counseling programs are far more than simple cost-saving ventures. In Chapter 5, Lester and Van Voorhis list several functions of group programs. These often cannot be achieved as efficiently by individual, one-on-one therapies. They include: (a) peer support; (b) role modeling opportunities; (c) opportunities to help others; (d) opportunities to practice new skills; (e) increased opportunities for learning; and (f) dealing with the stigma of having problems such as a criminal record or an addiction. For some clients, group counseling sessions may actually be a more potent form of planned change than individual counseling. From a discussion of the core concepts of group process, Chapter 5 offers an overview of some of the early efforts at group therapy in corrections: Transactional Analysis, milieu therapy (in the form of the therapeutic community), Guided Group Interaction, Reality Therapy, and Person-Centered Therapy. As will be seen, research found several of these to be unsuccessful, while others evolved over time to become more successful—learning, that is, from the mistakes of the past.

Chapter 3

Psychoanalytic Therapy

David Lester and Patricia Van Voorhis

Psychoanalytic therapy[1] is based on a theory of the human mind that focuses on unconscious as well as conscious thoughts and desires. Some of these unconscious ideas are those that we had as children and that became unconscious because we were punished for having such ideas. Others were not our ideas originally, but rather ideas that our parents and other people imposed upon us.

Psychoanalytic therapy seeks to minimize the effect of these unconscious ideas on our behavior by making us aware of them; in other words, by giving us insight into the psychological forces operating in our minds. This insight enables us to evaluate these ideas consciously and therefore rationally. We can then make more appropriate choices when confronted with problem situations.

Psychoanalysis was developed by Sigmund Freud at the end of the nineteenth century and the beginning of the twentieth century. It is a theory of both normal and abnormal behavior and their development. In addition, it is a method of therapy.

Psychoanalytic theory is very complex. Freud himself changed his opinions and modified his theory continually throughout his lifetime, and subsequent psychoanalysts have also modified the theory. Consequently, we must remember that there is no single theory of psychoanalysis. There are instead many variations, each centered around a common set of assumptions.

Psychoanalysis was the first major technique of psychotherapy. It stimulated interest in this method of treatment and provided the basis for all subsequent methods of therapy. Many systems of psychotherapy are modifications of Freud's original technique. Even the systems that seem most different from psychoanalysis are usually reactions against one or more of Freud's ideas. Thus, psychoanalysis is both the seminal theory of human behavior and the seminal system of psychotherapy.

Before we describe the technique of psychoanalysis, it is necessary first to give a brief sketch of some of the assumptions made by psychoanalytic theory.

Psychoanalytic/Psychodynamic[2] Theory

The basic assumption made by Freud was that all behavior is motivated. The crucial word here is "all." All behavior is motivated, including our choice of career, our choice of a spouse, our choice of clothes today, and even such trivial behaviors as tugging your earlobe or stroking your nose as you read this page. This assumption is often called the **principle of psychic determinism**. Freud argued that each behavior was not determined simply by one wish or motive, but probably by many. Furthermore, some of these wishes are unconscious, so that we remain unaware of them and the fact that they are determining our behavior.

Freud talked about three major subsets of wishes that are developmental in nature. (He also referred to these as three components of the personality). **Id** wishes are those that we possessed very early in life. They are simple, somewhat primitive and unorganized, and often aggressive. When a small child says to his parent, "I'm going to smash you with a cement truck," this is a good example of an id wish. Id wishes rarely get satisfied directly, and many of them become unconscious as we grow up.

Superego wishes are wishes that we take over and adopt from other people, chiefly our parents. There are two kinds: the prohibitions that are commonly called our conscience ("Don't lie to your mother!" and "Clean your plate or you won't get any dessert") and the wishes that characterize what we would like to be, commonly called our **ego ideal** ("I want to be a lawyer when I grow up, just like my daddy").

Ego wishes are complex, organized, realistic, and mature wishes, best exemplified by the kinds of wishes we show most of the time. The ego's function is to balance the desires of the id, the demands of the superego, and the requirements of one's immediate environment.

The terms *id*, *superego*, and *ego* are best thought of as adjectives, and not as little structures inside your skull. Let us say that you become angry with your father because of something he does or says to you. An id wish might be that you would like to hit him and really hurt him. A superego wish might be that it is wrong to hit your parents, and Daddy, upon whom you modeled yourself, never hits people. An ego wish might be that you love your father. Despite difficulties you have in relating to him, you feel a good deal of affection for him. But you also feel some anger. Eventually you write him a letter telling him how mad he made you. This behavior is motivated by, and a compromise of, all of these wishes (and probably many more that derive from your particular situation). Thus, the ego functions primarily as a psychological "thermostat" that attempts to regulate id and superego wishes and express them in socially acceptable and productive behavior.

As we mature, we gain control over these wishes. We form derivative desires that emerge from the desires we had as children. The desire to suck at mother's breast leads to desires to suck at a bottle, a pacifier and thumb, candy, cigarettes and pipes, the end of your pencil as you read this book, to touch your lips with your finger as you sit in class, to kiss and touch the person you love with your lips, and so on. The early desire to drink your mother's milk has now developed into a liking for several hundred kinds of food.

The derivative desires give you control, because, if you have to give up one object of your desire, for example, Lobster Newburg, you have many other objects to take its place. A baby has few alternatives. Often a baby will not drink strange fluids. Furthermore, as you grow up, you can feed yourself and prepare your own foods; the baby has to rely on his or her mother.

A crucial concept for Freud was **anxiety**, and he argued that anxiety is created in two ways. First, you become anxious whenever any wish of yours (conscious or unconscious) is deprived. Second, you become anxious whenever an unconscious wish is likely to become conscious to you. This poses the basic dilemma of humankind. Let us say you have an unconscious desire to attack your father. If you deprive that desire, you will become anxious. However, if you do anything that may make you aware of it, you will also become anxious. The solution may be to satisfy it partially without realizing that you are really doing, so you turn the anger inward upon yourself and feel only depression, but no anger. Or you meet someone who is like your father in some respects, and get into a fight with him, without realizing the similarity—for example, your employer or a guy in a bar. Or you decide that your father hates you (rather than you hating him), and you avoid him. On a related note, one of Freud's predecessors, Breuer, recognized that traumatic and unresolved events can also leave us with deep anxieties and unresolved issues that may motivate later irrational feelings and behaviors (Redl & Toch, 1979).

All psychiatric symptoms and all abnormal behavior (as well as much of normal behavior) are ways out of dilemmas—ways to satisfy unconscious desires without becoming conscious of them. A five-year-old boy may have been consciously attracted to his mother, but he realized that he could never marry her. So he decided to marry a girl like his mother when he grew up. When he became an adult, he had forgotten his desires at the age of five, so that when he married a woman like his mother, he did not realize the unconscious motives behind his choice.

The **defense mechanisms** further describe these alternatives. For instance, in **displacement**, you might express anger toward your employer rather than your father, in **reaction formation** you unconsciously feel anger toward your father but assert that you like him, and in **projection** you decide that he hates you. Defense mechanisms occur when the ego cannot manage the wishes of the id or the superego. Some defense mechanisms can be fairly benign and normal adaptations to stress. However, when overly defense individuals lose their ability to manage their defenses, consistent dysfunctional behavior, even violence, can be the result. Figure 3.1 defines and gives examples of a number of defense mechanisms.

Figure 3.1
Selected Psychoanalytic Defense Mechanisms

Repression:
An active attempt to push desires and thoughts out of one's consciousness or to keep material from reaching consciousness. Example: You forget that you owned a pet that was run over by a car when you were a child.

Displacement:
A change in the primary object of a feeling or desire to a secondary one that is less threatening. Example: You are angry at your boss but you yell at your husband or wife instead.

Sublimation:
Here the displacement is more long-term and the object chosen is socially acceptable. Example: You want to hit and hurt your father, but you become a professional boxer or football player.

Denial:
The truth of certain facts or experiences is denied, rather than forgotten as in repression. Example: Your daughter dies, but you act as if she is still alive, keeping a bed made up for her.

Reaction Formation:
A desire is changed or transformed into the opposite feeling or desire. Example: You hate or deeply resent your father, but you tell everyone how much you love him and act toward him in a loving manner.

Projection:
You have an unconscious desire or thought, but you attribute it to someone else instead of acknowledging it in yourself. Example: You no longer love someone, but instead accuse him or her of no longer loving you.

Rationalization:
The process of finding an acceptable reason for doing something unacceptable. Example: You punish your child harshly, but say "I'm doing this for your own good."

Regression:
You replace your desires or thoughts with those from an earlier stage of your development. Example: You are under stress and get angry at someone who works for you so you throw a temper tantrum.

Whether the psychoanalyst addresses the behavior of a criminal or a non-criminal, he or she always asks, "What is the real reason this person is doing that?" The psychoanalyst wonders about the conscious reasons, but more importantly, attempts to uncover the unconscious reasons for the behavior.

It is important to recognize that psychoanalysis has undergone many transformations since Freud first set forth his ideas during the late 1800s. In fact, psychoanalytic therapy has since evolved into **psychodynamic therapy**. One recent branch of psychodynamic thought, **ego psychology**, de-emphasizes Freud's focus on a deterministic id. Ego psychologists focus instead on the development of the ego. Much of the writing in this area examines how the ego's functioning improves or expands with development. Mature egos, in other words, deal with reality in flexible and adaptive ways (Hartmann, 1951). We also credit these psychologists with forming the notion of the ego defense mechanisms discussed above.

Another group of theorists, writing since the 1950s, developed theories of **object relations**. *Object* in these theories refers to people; so object relations refers to the set of cognitive and emotional processes that affect our ability to function in intimate relationships. Object relations also moves away from Freud's focus on deterministic drives by assuming that humans are highly motivated by their need to be in relationship with others (Cashdan, 1988). From the standpoint of object relations theory, humans internalize aspects of maternal as well as other early relationships. The vestiges of these relationships often affect present-day relationships. They may also govern feelings toward ourselves (e.g., self-esteem) and others (e.g., hostility). Many of these theories also assert that the mother-child relationship is the most important relationship in terms of its effect on future relationships. However, recurrent focus on the mother has had its critics. In fact, later feminist therapists (see Caplan & Hall-McCorquodale, 1985) and advocates (Steinem, 1994) referred to such the psychoanalytic and psychodynamic models as "mother blaming" approaches. As will be seen in later chapters on family therapy and substance abuse therapies, object relations theory underlies many of the present-day psychoanalytic approaches to psychotherapy.

Psychoanalytic Therapy

The goal of psychoanalysis can be stated in many ways, but a simple way is to say that the goal is to make conscious what is unconscious to you. If you can become conscious of your unconscious desires, then you will not necessarily satisfy them directly, but at least you will be able to make more appropriate choices in the future. If you realize that you have been proposing to and marrying people who are parental substitutes, the next time you are in love you can at last ask yourself, "Now that I know that my love for this person is based in part upon the fact that he or she resembles my parent, do I really want to propose to and marry him or her?" Psychoanalysis does not attempt to direct your choice, but rather attempts to make it an informed choice.

Doing this is difficult. To **become conscious of unconscious desires** will make you anxious, even to the point of panic. At the same time, the new awareness may relate to some very distressing information, such as when a client is moved to emotionally respond to his or her early child abuse. The process must be done slowly and carefully, with the guidance of a psycho-analyst. The process is not one in which the connection of the present to the past is enough to allow the client to move on. Rather the past is "rehearsed, sorted out, coped with, and (ultimately) set aside" (Redl & Toch, 1979).

Psychoanalysis, in its classic form, often involved three to five meetings a week for three to seven years or more. At a minimum rate of $200 an hour, psychoanalysis continues to be mostly accessible to the wealthy.

What are the techniques of psychoanalysis? One involves relaxing by lying on a couch (or sitting in a chair) and engaging in a process of free associa-tion. In **free association** a person says out loud whatever comes to mind, with-out censoring. If this seems easy, be assured that it is not. Few of us, if any, can permit ourselves to know what we are thinking. How often do we distract ourselves from our thoughts, forbid ourselves to feel what we are experiencing, or distract ourselves by taking a drink or a sleeping pill or busying ourselves with some activity? Free association becomes even more difficult with another person present, our psychoanalyst. Some psychoanalysts say that it is only after many years of psychoanalysis, that one can truly free associate.

There are additional "**windows to the unconscious**." Dreams are also believed to be manifestations of our subconscious thoughts. And in the psychoanalytical tradition, stumbles in our speech or "Freudian slips" are believed to emanate from unconscious desires. For example, our friends would smile if we inadvertently stated that we were "getting rid of a math exam" rather than getting ready for it.

Your psychoanalyst also listens to what you say and assesses how you behave toward him or her. The psychoanalyst behaves very neutrally toward you, so that when you attribute thoughts and desires to him or her, the analyst wonders why you do so. This is called **transference**. You treat the analyst not as he or she really is, but as if the analyst were some other important person from your life. Some psychoanalysts say that the end of psychoanalysis is when this transference is finally understood and resolved by the client.

Finally, the psychoanalyst **interprets** your behavior to you and slowly tries to help you realize the unconscious motives behind your behavior. The analyst rarely comes right out and tells you what he or she thinks the motive really is, but prefers to wait until you discover it yourself. The analyst may listen to you tell about an argument you had with your spouse, and merely ask, "I wonder if that reminds you of any arguments you've had with other people?" hoping that you will see the parallels. Psychoanalysts say that the best interpretations are those that the client makes himself or herself. This is why the technique is a slow one.

Because most of your unconscious desires derive from wishes you had as a child, and because most of your superego wishes derive from wishes you took over from your parents, psychoanalysts place a great deal of importance on your childhood. Much of psychoanalysis is spent discussing these early years and your parents and siblings. It is therefore often described as a historical approach to therapy.

The most recent approaches to psychoanalytic therapy are more flexible than the classic representations of its use. Your therapy today would rely on more than free association, dream therapy, and transference. You might also notice that it is more present-oriented. Without discarding the importance of the past and windows to the unconscious, psychotherapists working in a psychodynamic tradition today may place greater emphasis on the present; the **therapeutic alliance** between client and therapist is as important as transference. Therapists can be directive on occasion, offering concrete suggestions rather than waiting for the client to "work through" various aspects of the therapy. Finally, most current applications of psychoanalysis do not last for years or involve multiple sessions per week.

Therapy incorporating object relations involves a process in which the client and therapist develop a therapeutic alliance, which in time involves the client directing **projective identifications** onto the therapist or to others. Projective identification is a defense mechanism in which a client sees an unacceptable aspect of himself or herself in another person. One might see, for example, a client asking why the therapist is angry with him or her. Not being angry, the therapist recognized the client's comment as a projection. The projection is then interpreted for the client, e.g., the anger is the client's. The client is then afforded the opportunity to acknowledge and accept his or her repressed anger, and to perhaps acquire a better understanding of the source of the anger. The intention may not be to make anger go away, but rather to accept and understand its source and to deal with it in an appropriate manner.

Psychoanalytic Approaches to Crime

In dealing with a criminal, the psychoanalyst asks him- or herself, "What are the conscious and unconscious desires in this person that are motivating his or her criminal behavior?" Or alternatively, "What typical prosocial desires that we find in most people are not available to this person, so that he or she fails to inhibit his or her antisocial behavior?" The answer for each criminal is quite unique to that particular person. In other words, if we were to try to state a general rule here, such as "Burglars are usually motivated by . . ." then we would probably be incorrect in applying this to each and every burglar. Even so, case studies, such as the one that follows, are useful tools for illustrating the process of a therapeutic approach. We present the following case of an exhibitionist and describe what the psychoanalyst discovered.

The Case of an Angry Exhibitionist

To illustrate what a psychoanalyst might discover about a client, here is a summary of a case reported by McCawley (1965). The client was a theological student who was having marital problems with his first wife when he first began to expose himself to young girls and boys. His wife was critical of his ambitions, belittled him, and often interrupted their sexual intercourse, refusing to resume it. He was also about to be given increased responsibility at the seminary. After exposing himself, he was arrested and placed on probation. Soon he had to leave the seminary, and his wife divorced him.

His second wife was sympathetic to him and sexually compatible with him. His father offered him money to start a small business, but began to complain about the way he ran the business. As this stress grew in magnitude, the client again began exposing himself. When he exposed himself to a female child, he was arrested.

Therapy with this client uncovered the fact that the client's father was a compulsive businessman who was often away from home as the client grew up. The father belittled the client and was generally hostile toward him. The mother was hostile to all of her children, frequently reproaching them for their ingratitude.

Thus, the client was emotionally deprived of affection from his parents, and McCawley guessed that he failed to model himself on them (or, in psychoanalytic terms, to identify with them). He had few friends as a child due to his geographical isolation, but at school he developed one close relationship with another boy. The boys would expose their genitals to each other quite frequently. This relationship was the most satisfying one that the client had in his formative years, and McCawley felt that, when under stress, the client regressed to this stage in his development.

At the time of the first episode, the client was overwhelmed by feelings of inferiority and sexual inadequacy. At the time of the second episode, he was feeling inadequate about his business acumen. On each occasion he was angry, with his first wife and then his father. But it took time for him to admit his anger in the counseling sessions. He eventually realized that the first arrest had removed him both from an intolerable marriage situation and from the increased responsibility at the seminary. The second episode rescued him from business pressures.

The anger he felt toward his first wife and then his father was increased by the intense unconscious anger that he had felt toward both his father and his mother during his childhood as a result of their rejection of him and their hostility toward him. The relationship with his first wife recapitulated the relationship with his mother and was, therefore, especially stressful for him. The business venture with his father recapitulated the earlier relationship with his father. The regression to a behavior pattern (exposing himself) he had once shown in childhood was symbolic of his desire to be a child again and avoid adult responsibilities.

For a client to discover these connections between his adult behaviors and the events of his childhood takes a great deal of time. To become aware of feelings and desires that have long been repressed requires time. And the bare bones of the problems faced by this client only scratch the surface of his complex internal conflicts and problems. However, as the client sees the connections between his childhood experiences and his adult behavior, and as he becomes aware of his hitherto unconscious wishes and feelings, he can begin to make more appropriate choices for his behavior. For example, he can find socially acceptable ways of expressing his anger toward his father or toward his second wife if he so chooses. Or he can choose to avoid situations in which this anger might be aroused. The increased self-awareness and self-insight that would result from psychoanalysis would enable him to conduct his life in a more rational and satisfying manner.

Aggressive Delinquents

Redl and Wineman (1951) have described a treatment program they devised for a group of delinquent children. The children showed typical delinquent behaviors: assault, theft, lying, truancy, and so on. But in addition, there was an aggressiveness and uncontrolled aspect to their behavior that made them virtually unmanageable. Redl and Wineman tried to treat them in summer camps and in part-time contacts, but they eventually set up a home for five of them that existed for about 18 months before funds were depleted. How did Redl and Wineman describe these children?

Ego Deficits

Redl and Wineman considered the possibility that the impulses of these children might be abnormally strong, that is, that their id wishes might be greater in number and of greater intensity than normal children. But they rejected this possibility and suggested instead that the problem lay in the control that their ego wishes had over their id wishes.

Redl and Wineman pointed out that the ego keeps us in touch with reality. The ego fulfills the following functions for the normal person:[1] It perceives and judges the external environment. It also monitors what is going on in our bodies and maintains some awareness of our id wishes and our superego wishes. The ego not only knows what the demands of reality are, but has the power to change our behavior in line with those demands. It both tells us that we have to go to the dentist and gets us there.

The ego also has a selective function. It chooses among alternatives and selects the best course of action for us. Finally, the ego synthesizes or balances all of the wishes within us, all of the parts of our personalities, to achieve some degree of integration.

Redl and Wineman suggested that the ego of the delinquent cannot perform adequately, and they spelled out some of its failures.

Ego Failures

1. The delinquent ego cannot tolerate the emotions that accompany frustration. It insists upon a total gratification of the wishes. It cannot, in other words, control the wishes of the id.

2. The delinquent ego cannot deal with the emotions of insecurity, anxiety, and fear. When confronted with these emotions, the delinquent tends to abandon the activity in panic and deny the emotion, or he attacks ferociously and destroys indiscriminately whatever is within reach.

3. The delinquent ego fails to give clear-cut danger signals if the youth is tempted and is not able to resist temptation. Exciting things in the environment tempt the youth, and he gives in. In addition, he is susceptible to contagion from others. If another boy jumps onto the dining table, then he may join in, too. The threshold for this group intoxication is extremely low. Related to this was the difficulty the boys had in using toys and gadgets for their intended purpose rather than using them as missiles or simply destroying them.

4. The delinquent ego has difficulty taking care of possessions that are valued and that the boy wants to keep.

5. The delinquent ego has difficulty dealing with a new situation. The boys would claim that the situation was not new, that they had visited this or that town before. Alternatively, they would aggressively handle a new object with panicky haste. A third alternative was to ridicule what was strange.

6. The delinquent ego is easily flooded by memories of the past. If a counselor struggled with a boy in trying to control him, the boy would respond as if his brutal father were trying to kill him.

7. The delinquent ego cannot cope with the emotion of guilt. In the face of such guilt, the delinquent tends to respond with panic, denial, and destructiveness.

8. The delinquent ego has difficulty remembering its own contribution to the consequences that befell the boy. It simply forgets the actions that precipitated the catastrophes in life.

9. The delinquent ego finds it difficult to be content with some reward. It unreasonably demands more. It has difficulty remembering previous satisfactions and so doubts whether it will enjoy an activity such as playing baseball.

10. The delinquent ego is not realistic about rules or routines. If the boy is told "tomorrow," he acts as if he has been told "never."

11. In some respects the delinquent ego is interpersonally blind. The boy will act in a way that he should realize will make the other boys beat him up, but he fails to predict this accurately. He fails to learn from experience or from what happens to other people.

12. Failure is reacted to with feelings of complete failure or hostility to the adult. Success is reacted to with conceit and reckless behavior. The delinquent boy has difficulty coping with competition.

Ego Strengths

On the other hand, the delinquent ego has many strengths and can cope well in many situations. If impulse gratification is involved, the delinquent ego can function superbly.

1. The delinquent ego keeps guilt feelings under control. The boys repress the motivation behind antisocial behavior, leaving themselves free to brag about the incident. They use such rationalizations as, "He did it first," "Everybody else does such things," "We were all in on it," "But somebody else did that same thing to me before," "He had it coming to him," "I had to do it or I would have lost face," "I didn't use the proceeds anyway," and so on.

2. The delinquent ego is good at seeking out support for antisocial behavior—ferreting out like-minded boys, provoking behaviors in others that will give them the excuse to act antisocially, exploiting gang excitement, searching out activities and locales that favor delinquent behavior, and so on.

3. The delinquent ego resists change. If confronted with distressing facts, the boy will clam up. Or he will show an improvement in behavior that simply gets his supervisors off his back. The group will ostracize those who reform. The delinquent boy will avoid persons who threaten the delinquent lifestyle, those who are kind to the delinquent, for example. He will run away from a good foster home.

4. More than simply resisting change, the delinquent ego fights change actively. The delinquent ego can diagnose a counselor's weak spots or can pick out another boy who will be useful in the delinquent exploits. The delinquent ego can argue well and divert conversations away from problem areas. It can

provoke behavior from others that justifies its response. It can form friendships with counselors and adults without letting itself be influenced.

In summary, then, the ego of the delinquent has difficulty coping with many of life's events and with many normal emotions. On the other hand, the delinquent ego has great resourcefulness in aiding and abetting delinquent behavior.

The Delinquent Superego

Redl and Wineman also felt that the delinquent superego was faulty. They saw the function of the normal superego as possessing certain values and standards and as giving warning signals when issues concerning values and conscience were involved. Delinquents have superegos. Redl and Wineman said they had not yet met anyone who had no superego. But the delinquent superego has characteristic features that contribute to the delinquent lifestyle.

1. The delinquent superego has peculiar values. Often, the delinquent superego has identified with a delinquent code of behavior. As Eysenck (1970) has suggested, the delinquent has internalized standards and values, but they are those of a delinquent subculture rather than of the larger society. However, there may often be islands of standards and values from the larger society.

2. The delinquent superego also is poor at signaling danger. If it operates at all, it produces a post-action guilt rather than a pre-action (or anticipatory) guilt.

The Sources

How did these peculiarities of the delinquent ego and superego develop? The superego developed in the way that it did because there were no adequate role models for the delinquent as he grew up. His parents behaved inconsistently, or brutally, so the child never came to love them and respect them enough to use them for models. But even should the boy identify with his parents or model himself on them, his parents' behavior was often so disturbed and antisocial that he learned inappropriate behavior.

Learning is not the only source of superego development. Early parental nurturing, bonding, and attachments are critical to the development of internalized prosocial values. Thus, the child of parents who fail to provide love, warmth, and comfort often has trouble internalizing a generalized concern for the well-being of others. In this respect, we might be particularly concerned for children of abusive, neglectful, or addicted parents (Bowlby, 1969).

A normal child also needs to be helped to develop a strong ego. He has to be taught how to deal with frustration and with his emotions of anxiety and fear and guilt. Left to his own resources, he will not develop these skills. And if he is abused and neglected and hated, then he will have even more difficulty learning such skills. This, in fact, is a general principle in psychoanalytic theory—namely that all disturbed behavior is a result of severe frustration (or trauma) that takes place during the child's early years, from birth to the ages of six or seven.

Here are a couple of vignettes that Redl and Wineman have given to illustrate the behavior of their boys. First, two examples of ego deficits:

> The kids burst out of the station wagon in their usual exuberant mood and barged madly up the steps into the house. Luckily, this time the door was open so the usual pounding, kicking of door, etc., wasn't necessary. I was in my office tied up in a phone call and the door was closed. Mike yelled for me, shouting something about his jackknife, which I was keeping in the drawer for him. I put my hand over the receiver and said "O.K., come on in." But the lock had slipped on the door and he could not open it. Before I even had a chance to excuse myself from my phone conversation and say "Just a minute, I'll be back," he was pounding on the door, kicking it, called me a "sonofabitch" repetitively. I opened the door and gave him his knife. Even this failed to quiet his furor and, when I commented on the obvious fact that I hadn't even meant to make him wait, that the lock had slipped, all I got was a snarling, contemptuous "Shit." (Entry: 4/7/47, David Wineman) (Redl & Wineman, 1951:92).

> We have finally worked out a haircut schedule. It was Joe's turn to go with me today to get his hair cut. This produced quite a reaction in Larry, who burst into my quarters today after learning from Joe that he was going with me to the barber. He demanded that he be taken today and that's all there was to it. I reminded him that we had all sat down and worked out the schedule and that he agreed to come after Joe because his shopping trip came before Joe's. He was blind to this reasoning, however, completely swept away by his involvement in this particular need of the moment. "Yeah," he whined and screamed at the same time, "Now I'll never git one. I'll never have one, never, never." Again I remonstrated, "But, Larry, you know you'll go tomorrow, we worked it out that way, and I've always done what we planned to do, you know that." "No," he screamed, "I'll never git mine." (Entry: 2/7/47, Emily Kener) (Redl & Wineman, 1951:143).

And here are two examples of the delinquent ego showing its strength:

> On one occasion the whole Pioneer group had been involved in a very dangerous and destructive episode of throwing bricks from the top of the garage. We decided to "rub-in" the total unaccept-

ability of such behavior. Andy, especially, was fascinating in his real indignation at even being approached on the subject. Tearfully he shouted at the Director who was doing the interviewing, "Yeah, everybody was doing it and you talk to me. Why is it my fault?" When it was pointed out to him that we were not saying it was all his fault but that he was responsible for his individual share of the matter, he was still unable to admit the point: "But we were all in on it. Why talk to me?" (Redl & Wineman, 1951:176).

We found our Pioneers time and again magically drawn to activities which, though innocent looking at the start, would invariably end up by exposing them to more excitement and temptational challenge than they could take. They would invariably drift into alleys where irate neighbors might be expected to chase them away, so that destructive window breaking then would be considered an understandable "act of revenge."

They would discover, of all the many basements of the various University buildings, the one which contained a Coke machine which seemed to be all too ready to respond to buttons instead of nickels—it happened to be in the Law School of all places, too. Or they would carefully seek out stores whose keeper could be expected to be of a less watchful type, or browse around the rooms of counselors at camp whose tendency not to be not too vigilant with cigarettes or cash lying around was known to them. In the cases we have in mind, they did not enter those premises with a decision to steal. All their ego did was to drive them toward "situational lure," knowing it could leave the rest to predictable "chance" (Redl & Wineman, 1951:188-189).

Implications for Treatment

Redl and Wineman felt that treatment for the children with whom they worked had to take place in a setting that was treatment-oriented all the time. They set up a house in which about five boys lived together with a trained staff. The treatment described by Redl and Wineman ended not because the boys were considered able to function in society, but because funding ended. Thus, the treatment might have taken several years if it had been allowed to continue. Redl and Wineman described three components of the program.

1. A Hygienic Environment: The staff must be fully trained so as to protect the boys from the kinds of traumatic handling they had experienced in their earlier lives. The staff should give the boys love and tokens regardless of the boys' behavior. To withhold rewards and love if the boys misbehave would be like withholding medicine from patients who fail to get well. The house should be similar to the boys' previous homes in decor

and furnishings so that they will feel at ease. In a similar vein, Redl and Toch (1979) remind us that harsh punishment of the delinquent child from an abusive home may only serve to confirm his or her view of the world as an arbitrary and abusive place. We should, instead, disconfirm the hostility, disinterest, and cruelty that characterizes the delinquent's life and ultimately disarm the fodder for his or her future motivation.

2. Focus on Ego Support: The major therapeutic emphasis initially is on building up the boys' egos. To strengthen their consciences without giving them ways of handling the guilt would be premature. The major technique for giving the boys alternative strategies for behavior is through recreation. Suitably chosen recreational activities allow the child to discharge impulses, but within a structured setting. Play must be made gratifying for these boys.

3. Exploitation of Live Events: Because the staff is always around the boys, any events that happen in day-to-day living can be exploited before the event becomes forgotten. Also, the staff can try to teach alternative behaviors when the behaviors are relevant, instead of sometime later during a scheduled therapeutic interview.

Psychoanalysis for Criminals

Schoenfeld (1971) has argued that psychoanalysis works for intelligent, articulate adult neurotics who can talk out, and not act out, their unconscious (and, in particular, their id) impulses. The typical juvenile delinquent is often inarticulate, unintelligent, and someone who acts out desires. Psychoanalysis would introduce even more unconscious desires into the client's consciousness, and thereby compound his or her problems. Schoenfeld noted also that psychoanalysis is time-consuming and expensive. Furthermore, there are few trained psychoanalysts available to work with offenders. Thus, psychoanalysis is not a practical alternative for most criminals or delinquents.

Recent meta-analyses of correctional treatment programs appear to confirm the unsuitability of psychoanalysis or other insight-oriented therapies for offender populations (Andrews et al., 1990; Lipsey, 1992). These reviews suggest that the behavioral, cognitive behavioral, and social learning models, presented in the following chapters, are far more effective with delinquent and adult offender populations.

While stopping far short of a full endorsement of psychoanalysis for offenders, there are nevertheless some valuable vestiges of psychoanalytic theory and practice that can be a part of good counseling or social service. First, counselors should know what defense mechanisms are and that many come from deep-seated anxiety. If, in our current rush to correct skill deficits and behavioral problems in the "here and now," we ignore long-standing feelings, unexpressed fears, and unresolved issues; we are likely to find that these unresolved issues will continue to block or divert us from other endeavors, such as education, skills development, or cognitive therapy (Palmer, 1994). In response to Schoenfeld, then, some offenders are highly anxious, even neurotic. And neurotic offenders usually get into trouble through a dynamic that is highly relevant to their anxiety. Recent research confirms that neurotic offenders, as classified by the Jesness Inventory (Jesness, 1996) (see Chapter 6, Diagnosis and Assessment of Criminal Offenders), had higher long-term recidivism rates than other offenders, experienced more stress in prison, and did not respond well to a highly regarded cognitive behavioral intervention (Listwan et al., 2004). These offenders do not improve on their own (Warren, 1983), and in one program in which their anxiety was addressed, they achieved more successful correctional outcomes than other types of offenders (Palmer, 1974; 2003).

Second, even though most counselors are not trained to interpret transference for their clients' benefit, there is some value to recognizing transference when it occurs. Indeed, transference occurs in day-to-day living as well as in treatment settings. The counselor who recognizes that the client is treating him or her as a "stand-in" from the past is far less likely to be confused by the client's accusations or attachments. For example, the abused delinquent who has a long-standing distrust of authority is not really reacting to us, and our response will be better if we do not take his or her behavior personally. Whatever else we might say about psychoanalysis, counselors and other social service workers are still being trained to recognize transference. Moreover, there is a special need for workers, particularly in corrections, to be aware of their own tendencies toward **countertransference**. Countertransference occurs when a client pushes the worker's "buttons" to the extent that the resulting anger, retaliation, or disinterest on the part of the counselor interferes with a more objective understanding of the client. And when we fail to see through our own irrational reactions (countertransference), we are in no position to participate in an experience that will facilitate the client's growth (Adler, 1982).

Third, self-control has re-emerged as a key component of recent criminological theory (Gottfredson & Hirschi, 1990). While many would argue that lack of control and impulsivity can be targeted through a number of alternative counseling strategies (Andrews & Bonta, 2003), one must agree that the psychoanalytic paradigm had much to say about the notion of control, particularly **ego control**. Poor self-control is essentially the ego's inability to balance the demands of the superego, or the impulses of the id. The implication is that the ego must be strengthened.

In their work with delinquents, for example, psychoanalysts such as August Aichorn (1935), and later Kurt Eissler (1949), attempted to strengthen delinquent egos and superegos through the process of transference. For delinquents, this is not possible unless an initial or preparatory phase occurs. The goal in this initial phase is to establish transference between the delinquent and the psychoanalyst. For delinquents who are narcissistic or psychopathic and incapable of having positive feelings toward others, this requires a special kind of psychoanalyst, one who is able to relinquish moral standards easily, and one who seems omnipotent to the delinquent— he or she, in other words, is even more cunning or clever than the delinquent (Wulach, 1983). The delinquent must also feel that the psychoanalyst's omnipotent power will be used only for his own benefit. He or she must see the psychoanalyst as benign.

The therapist also shows responsibility and concern for others. If the psychoanalyst remains nonjudgmental and helps to resolve the problems presented by the patient, the positive transference will begin to build up. Eissler (1949) believed that this process recapitulates for the delinquent a traumatic experience from his childhood in which the parents failed him or her. The psychoanalyst, if successful, carries the delinquent through this recapitulation without causing further trauma. In this way, the early trauma loses some of its compelling effect, and the delinquent begins to trust authority figures.

Eissler noted that delinquents continually seek the new and the novel. In his opinion, this is to help them avoid awareness of their internal thoughts; it is a defense. Delinquents are sensitive and flee from boredom, so the psychoanalyst must continually try to provide the delinquent with surprises in order to stimulate him or her. The analyst must not be predictable. This taxes the psychoanalyst's ingenuity. With the psychoanalyst also showing concern for others, and the identified client showing increasing trust in the therapist, a number of therapeutic gains may be accomplished (Eissler, 1949).

Today, there are shorter approaches to developing ego control than those discussed in the work of Aichorn and Eissler. In fact, psychology is no longer wedded to the notion that psychoanalytic therapy must occur several times a week for many years. The current model is generally shorter (Arlow & Brenner, 1988). One very short approach to strengthening ego controls was shown recently in Arcaya's training of police mediators to manage crisis situations involving emotionally disturbed persons. Here, police mediators were encouraged to improve the ego's contact with reality by: (1) assessing whether the crisis is precipitated by the ego's inability to manage superego ideals, as with individuals suffering from excessive guilt or demonstrating self-injurious behaviors; or (2) determining whether the crisis is motivated by impulses of an aggressive or sexual nature (or by id impulses). In the case of the former, mediators are instructed to "make the ego aware of how its judgment is being distorted by guilt and disparagement" (Arcaya, 1989). In the case of the latter, clients may be less agitated but less verbal as well. The mediators are directed to verbally identify the person's intentions, for example, "You look like you are ready to fight; is that true?" Both approaches assume that the ego has lost its ability to be rational; the mediator's role, then, is to give reality back to the ego.

Finally, recognizing the role of trauma and other adversities in precipitating some forms of aggression, substance abuse, and sex offenses, psychodynamic therapy with offenders actually continues to be practiced in some settings. One such setting involved the treatment of assaultive patients assigned to a United States veterans' hospital. Improvements on psychological assessments of aggression were greater for the veterans in the psychodynamic group than those in a cognitive behavioral group (Lanza et al., 2002). Research on a considerably larger sample of men who batter found that psychodynamic therapy worked better for men with dependent personalities and cognitive behavior approaches were more effective among the men with antisocial thought patterns (Saunders, 1996). Additional work with substance abusers started therapy with cognitive-behavioral approaches to coping with abstinence and relapse prevention, and then moved to psychodynamic therapy with some offenders working to resolve underlying conflicts associated with substance abuse (Herman, 2000). With these offenders, psychodynamic therapy *alone* (without the cognitive-behavioral and relapse prevention component) did not work. Outcomes for psychodynamic approaches also vary according to the quality of the therapeutic alliance (Horvath & Symonds, 1991).

The tenacity of psychodynamic therapy has an important perspective on the effects of trauma, particularly early trauma. The psychoanalysts observed that unresolved traumas continue to visit us—in the form of reenactments, or, in the extreme form (post-traumatic stress disorder), or in their ability to serve as subconscious motivators of future behavior, such as when we choose the spouse who resembles an abusive parent. Here again, transference with a trusted therapist is a useful vehicle for change. When the client and the psychoanalyst discuss an event or relationship from the past, the therapeutic relationship (transference) allows the past to be "rehearsed, sorted out, coped with, and (ultimately) set aside" (Redl & Toch, 1979). Sources disagree on the necessity or purpose of reliving the past (Foa et al., 1993; Liebert & Spiegler, 1994), but it remains in use as a psychotherapeutic approach for victims of trauma.

Conclusion

As we stated at the beginning of this chapter, Freud's psychoanalytic theory is both the first major theory of the human mind and the first major technique for psychotherapy. Because of its status in the field of psychology, it has been subjected to more analysis (and criticism) than perhaps any other theory. Indeed, there are many ways of presenting the basic theory, and the ideas presented in this chapter are an attempt to present a clear approach to the fundamentals of the theory.

Psychoanalytic theory provides an excellent and relatively comprehensive method for understanding the criminal. Based on the theory, we can propose a number of generalizations about the motivations and causes of crime.

However, to understand a particular criminal requires a great deal of information about the person, his or her thoughts, and his or her past. Superficial knowledge about the client allows only questionable speculation.

As a technique of therapy, the time involved in even the shorter forms of psychoanalysis is a major drawback. The time required for and cost of such treatment is prohibitive. Few non-offenders actually undergo or can afford psychoanalysis; it follows that its practice among offenders is nearly nonexistent.

Notes

[1]   The presentation of psychoanalytic theory in this chapter is not based entirely on Sigmund Freud's original description of his theory. Instead, the presentation is based on a more recent, rational approach to the theory proposed by Walter Toman (1960).

[2]   The terms *psychodynamic* and *psychoanalytic* are often used interchangeably; however, more recent versions of psychoanalytic thought and practice are usually referred to as psychodynamic. In contrast to the earlier psychoanalytic approaches, psychodynamic models place more of a focus on ego development and object relations.

Key Concepts and Terms

anxiety	free association
become conscious of unconscious desires	id
countertransference	interprets
defense mechanisms	object relations
delinquent superego	principle of psychic determinism
displacement	projection
ego	projective identifications
ego control	psychodynamic therapy
ego deficits	reaction formation
ego failures	superego
ego ideal	therapeutic alliance
ego psychology	transference
ego strengths	windows to the unconscious

Discussion Questions

1.   Can you think of any evidence that the unconscious exists? Have you ever been convinced that you have an unconscious? What evidence can you list?

2.   Is psychoanalysis a reasonable procedure to use with criminals? Why or why not? Can you argue both points of view?

3. Describe the essential characteristics of the delinquent children studied by Redl and Wineman.

4. Have you ever had criminal desires, thoughts, or fantasies? What stopped you from satisfying those desires? Can you relate the desires and the inhibiting factors to Freudian concepts?

5. Describe the basic techniques used in psychoanalytic therapy.

6. What sorts of lessons can be borrowed from psychoanalytic/psychodynamic theories and used in our daily work with offenders? Which aspects of these theories should not be used by those untrained in psychoanalysis?

Chapter 4

Radical Behavioral Interventions

David Lester, Michael Braswell,
and Patricia Van Voorhis

Behavior modification, or behavior therapy, stands in stark contrast to the psychoanalytical, insight-oriented strategies discussed in the previous chapter. Perhaps the most important difference concerns the effectiveness of the behavior strategies in contrast to the traditional psychoanalytical model; the research is now showing us that our best chances of achieving success with offenders rests with the radical behavior strategies presented in this chapter, and with related cognitive, cognitive-behavioral, and social learning methods discussed in the next two chapters (see Andrews et al., 1990; Andrews & Bonta, 2003; Antonowicz & Ross, 1994; Garrett, 1985; Gottschalk et al., 1987; Izzo & Ross, 1990; Lipsey, 1992; Pearson et al., 2002; Sherman et al., 1997).

The behavior models also differ markedly from the psychoanalytical models in their approach and assumptions. Most notably, behavior approaches deal with the present, the **here and now**, whereas the psychoanalytical models devote considerable time to uncovering, understanding, and healing the past. Behavior approaches attempt to increase or decrease specific target behaviors. In contrast to the traditional counseling approaches, behavior therapists devote little attention to the emotional sources of problematic behaviors; instead, their work focuses upon identifying the present conditions that are maintaining or discouraging these behaviors. In fact, radical behavior interventions may occur with no interaction at all between the therapist and the client, because the vehicle for change is not the counseling relationship but rather the therapist's manipulation of stimuli, rewards, and punishments—the mechanisms that instigate and maintain behavior.

Finally, behaviorists do not focus on pathology or illness that may be causing dysfunctional behavior. In the learning perspective, problematic behavior is no different from normal behavior. Both are learned in the same way and can be explained using the same models for learning.

Much of the success of the behavior approaches may have to do with the nature of offenders and the criminal behaviors they commit. To illustrate, Vicky MacIntyre Agee (1995) identifies a number of ways in which traditional therapies simply may not fit the specialized nature of juvenile offender populations. Her observations are pertinent to adults, as well. They include:

1. Traditional treatment fails to engage the involuntary, noncompliant juvenile who resists treatment, denies his or her problems, and is engaged in aggressive, ritualized, and addictive behaviors.

2. Traditional psychotherapeutic techniques of insight-oriented therapy have practical and theoretical limitations for juveniles with characteristic deficits in social cognitive skills (such as low empathy, poor means-ends reasoning, and concrete thinking).

3. Traditional techniques such as "venting" anger are inappropriate for juveniles who characteristically have difficulty controlling their aggression.

4. Traditional, nondirective techniques do not provide the intensive supervision, confrontation, limit-setting, and directive guidance in learning socially acceptable behaviors that are required by a population that is often aggressively noncompliant and victimizes others.

5. The traditional approach of focusing on early childhood experiences allows juveniles to shift the focus away from personal accountability in the present. This tends to encourage externalization of blame to dysfunctional families, staff, and society and provides juveniles with more justification to victimize others.

6. The traditional emphasis on one-to-one therapy is contrary to the peer-based group therapy, which is seen as the most effective form of intervention.

7. Traditional approaches tend to direct services toward problems not predictive of recidivism, such as anxiety, depression, fitness, self-esteem, and moral development.

Behavior therapy is the outgrowth of the enormous amount of work carried out by early physiologists trying to understand how animals acquire behavior. These scientific studies, conducted at the beginning of the twentieth century, led to the formulation of a number of laws of learning. Ivan Pavlov's (1927) work on classical conditioning is considered one of the earliest systematic accounts of how behavior is learned.

The next step was to see whether these models could be applied to humans. Psychologists John Watson, Mary Cover Jones, Hobart and Willie Mowrer, and others found that much human behavior could be learned in the same way that animals learned behaviors in the laboratory. Eventually, theories of how problematic behaviors could be learned were proposed and, as an outgrowth of these theories, this same group devised the earliest behavior treatment techniques (Spiegler & Guevremont, 1993). By the 1950s, the psychological community was beginning to voice doubts about the widespread efficacy of psychoanalysis, and behavior therapies were becoming more widely accepted (Eysenck, 1952).

By this time, a second behavioral approach, operant conditioning, had emerged from Edward Thorndike's early studies (1913) and B.F. Skinner's (1953) refinements in the 1950s. The two approaches, classical (or respondent) conditioning and operant conditioning, come under the heading of **radical behavioral approaches**, because they mechanistically target behavior with a more direct training approach using observable reinforcements, punishment, and stimuli. At the same time, they minimize the importance of the thinking processes on which we focus in the cognitive, cognitive-behavioral, and social learning models (Chapters 8 and 9).

Because, according to the behavioral perspective, criminal behavior is learned behavior, it can also be "unlearned." We move now to the various techniques that have been devised to help individuals "relearn."

Classical Conditioning

Classical (respondent) conditioning was first described by a Russian physiologist, Ivan Pavlov (1927). Pavlov's work was primarily concerned with the association between a stimulus and a response as it changed a subject's behavior. The focus was on the stimulus—what occurred "before" the response. By discovering which stimuli elicited which responses, a subject's environment could be manipulated to introduce "new" stimuli that could then "condition" new behaviors. Of course, positive or negative behaviors could be conditioned as demonstrated in Watson's (1916) classic experiment with "Little Albert," diagrammed in Figure 4.1. By repeatedly associating a harmless white rat (conditioned stimulus) with a very loud noise (unconditioned stimulus), Watson was able to condition Albert to fear (conditioned response) the white rat as he would normally fear (unconditioned response) the loud noise, even though he was originally unafraid of the small animal. To reverse Little Albert's negative learning, the behaviorist would have to associate something positive, such as a toy or candy, with the feared white rat.

In the classical conditioning model, the behaviorist identifies two stimuli. The unconditioned stimulus naturally acts as a stimulus to elicit an **unconditioned response**. In most babies, for example, no conditioning is necessary for a very loud noise to cause fear (the unconditioned response). Albert, however, may not have feared the white rat without the behaviorist's conditioning. The repeated pairing of the white rat (**conditioned stimulus**) with the loud noise (**unconditioned stimulus**) caused Albert to associate the rat with the noise. That is how he was conditioned (or learned) to fear the white rat (**conditioned response**).

Figure 4.1

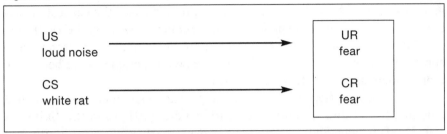

Conditioned stimuli are very important antecedents to behavior. Stimuli prompt us to fear, anger, sex, work, crime, and almost any other behavior we can think of. Some stimuli (e.g., fire sirens and traffic lights) are effective for most people, thus promoting behaviors that are common in society. Others are idiosyncratic, emerging from unique learning environments—specific fears, for example. Still others are problematic, such as an adult's identification of a young child as sexually attractive.

The objectives in radical behavior interventions are to either decelerate an undesirable target behavior, accelerate a desirable target behavior, or both. How can we use classical conditioning to change problematic behaviors? One way to do this is by making such individuals afraid of or upset by objects that once attracted them. We create a **mini-phobia** through a process called **aversion therapy**. In looking at a problem behavior often linked to crime, let us say we have an alcoholic who does not want to be one. He is attracted to alcohol, yet he wants to be able to stop drinking. Aversion therapy sets out to make him feel afraid of it or feel nauseated in its presence. First, we need a stimulus that automatically makes him feel nauseated (i.e., an unconditioned stimulus). We use a drug, such as apomorphine, that makes people feel nauseated and vomit after they receive an injection of it. We then inject our alcoholic with apomorphine, wait until he is just about to feel nauseated and vomit, and then we give him alcohol to drink. He drinks and vomits. We keep repeating this, and eventually he vomits or feels nauseated at the sight, the smell, and even the thought of alcohol. We can diagram this as shown in Figure 4.2.

Figure 4.2

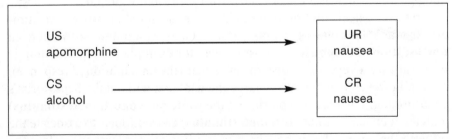

We could treat a number of behaviors in this fashion (e.g., drug abuse, overeating, pedophilia, and smoking). We could treat sex offenders in this way by pairing the preferred sex object (e.g., a picture of a child) with nausea. We could treat addictions to alcohol, drugs, or gambling in this way. In fact, we could treat any clearly observable and discrete behavior in this way. Needless to say, however, such treatment can be quite controversial.

There are three main kinds of this aversive conditioning (or punishment).

1. First, there is drug-induced nausea as utilized in the above example.

2. Occasionally, behavior therapists use electric shocks (usually to the finger or the arm) as aversives. For obvious ethical and legal reasons, this process is used when other methods have failed. Shock therapy is typically reserved for purposes of eliminating dangerous behaviors that have not responded to other, less objectionable alternatives (Kazdin, 1989). Medical applications to stop problems such as chronic sneezing, self-injurious behaviors, or repeated vomiting appear to have been successful in instances in which doctors knew there were no physiological reasons for these behaviors.

3. In **covert sensitization**, the behavior therapist creates a fantasy for the client in which aversive elements are woven into a story involving the desired object. In this case, the client must visualize the conditioned stimulus and the unconditioned stimulus. This can be recorded on tape and the patient can play the tape to him- or herself several times a day, until the formerly desired object is no longer desired.

Examples of aversion therapy can be found in the literature on the addictions and exploitive sexual behaviors. Barker and Miller (1968), for example, have reported on the use of electric shocks as the aversive stimulus in the treatment of compulsive gambling. For one gambler, they brought a slot machine into the laboratory and set it up in a room that simulated the normal atmosphere of a gambling den. While the gambler played it, for up to three hours at a time, he was shocked with up to 70 volts, at one point receiving between 300 and 600 electric shocks in a six-hour period. Eventually, Barker and Miller found that shocking the man only on 50 percent of the gambling trials, with the shocks randomly distributed over the gambling trials, was more effective than shocking him on every trial. They also noted that the treatment aroused strong emotions in the gamblers. One client became sick after three hours of treatment and felt a revulsion toward the slot machine, wanting to throw it out of the window. He also felt quite angry toward the counselor, but he did not terminate treatment. Another client wept during treatment and on several occasions attacked the machine.

In another example, Maletzky (1980) employed a procedure called assisted covert sensitization in the treatment of exhibitionists. Subjects were treated two times per month for 10 to 12 months. Imagery and photos of exhibitionistic scenes were paired with the aversive stimulus of a malodorous substance (valeric acid). These treatments were also conducted in at-home sessions. The behavior treatments were followed by an additional 12 months of psychotherapy for related issues such as marital problems and social anxiety. For an additional year, several "booster" sessions with the aversive therapy were held in the treatment setting and at home. Maletzky reported that 87 percent of the clients learned to eliminate all overt exhibitionist behaviors.

Classical conditioning can also be used to eliminate fears. Let us assume that we have an offender client who demonstrates extreme anxiety regarding job interviews associated with parole. In **systematic desensitization**, a technique devised by Joseph Wolpe (1958), we help the client to relax during these times. We introduce relaxation instructions similar to those used in hypnosis or yoga exercises. We then present him with an innocuous example of the feared object, such as a photo of someone interviewing for a job with an employer, all the time giving him the relaxation instructions. When he can relax completely in the presence of this stimulus, we increase the intensity of the stimulus, eventually having a real employer in the room with him, perhaps eventually having him actually interview for a position. It should be noted that in this situation, the client learns a new response and unlearns an old response. The goal is to replace avoidance with "approach" behavior.

In some cases, the anxiety might have subsided by gradual exposure to employment interviews without the relaxation exercises. If we return for a moment to Figure 4.1, we recall that a conditioned stimulus was created through repeated presentations with an unconditioned stimulus. What happens, then, if we present the conditioned stimulus *without* the unconditioned stimulus for numerous trials? The learned association with the unconditioned stimulus often becomes extinct. Thus, if Little Albert repeatedly experienced the white rat without the loud noise, his fear of the rat could become extinct. This process is referred to as **exposure therapy**. Intense, more prolonged exposure is called **flooding**.

Because classical conditioning is often misunderstood, some clarifications are in order:

1. First, classical conditioning will typically not work if the client is not motivated to change his or her behavior. It is easy to undo the effects. Let us say we have succeeded in making our alcoholic feel nauseated when drinking alcohol. If he does not wish to change his drinking behavior, all that he has to do when he leaves the clinic is to drink. Initially he will feel nauseated, and he may vomit. But very quickly, the learning that he acquired in the clinic will "extinguish," and he will no longer feel nauseated by alcohol. He has to be motivated to use the period of nausea to avoid alcohol and find substitutes. Anthony Burgess's classic novel, *A Clockwork Orange*, may

be good literature, but it is poor psychology. Alex, who was made to feel nauseated by violent behavior, could have undone the effects of the aversive conditioning by getting into several fights. The nausea would eventually be extinguished or pass. He would not have had to commit suicide.

2. Second, to create a mini-phobia is all well and good, but it is not sufficient. While our client is avoiding the formerly attractive object, we must teach him a new, socially acceptable alternative behavior. It is not sufficient merely to eliminate pedophilia. We must also teach dating behaviors and other appropriate social behaviors. Even though an alcoholic becomes sober, we must also deal with the threat of secondary addictions and the other problems that helped to create the need to drink. In addition, we must teach the alcoholic more appropriate ways of responding to stressful situations. Unless we do this, the client is at risk of reverting to the former, undesirable behavior.

3. The unconditioned stimulus in aversive conditioning is called **punishment** in everyday life. Punishment is useful only if we wish to quickly eliminate some undesirable behavior. It is not sufficient in itself to rehabilitate offenders because it does not teach people what to do. It merely creates mini-phobias and fears, or nausea. This is why psychologists say that punishment is not an optimum teaching mechanism. Procedures based on positive reinforcement (see next section) have been found to be much more effective in teaching new, more prosocial behaviors.

Operant Conditioning

Operant conditioning, the development of which is now most clearly associated with B.F. Skinner (1953), involves modifying behavior by the judicious use of rewards. Let us assume that, in the presence of some stimulus (S), a particular behavioral response is made (R). If this response is followed by a reinforcer (a rewarding stimulus), then that behavioral response is more likely to occur in the presence of the stimulus on subsequent occasions. We diagram this as follows:

Figure 4.3

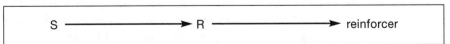

S ⟶ R ⟶ reinforcer

There are two kinds of reinforcers. A **positive reinforcer** is the onset of a pleasing stimulus. Examples would be food, something to drink, affection, or attention. A **negative reinforcer** is the offset of an unpleasant stimulus, for example, a reduction in anxiety or pain. In both instances, the reinforcer is any behavior consequence that increases the likelihood that the target behavior will be repeated. Put differently, rewards or reinforcements are **contingent** upon the client demonstrating the target behavior.

An example of how this process can work in everyday life may help to clarify. A mother puts her child to bed and goes back to the living room of the house. The child is scared of being alone and calls to the mother. The mother ignores the child's calls. Eventually the child begins to cry, and the mother goes to see what is wrong. The stimulus here is being alone in a dark bedroom. The response that the child is making is crying. The reinforcer is a negative reinforcer, the end of discomfort when mother arrives. The mother who does this consistently can eventually shape the behavior of her child so that he or she cries for hours at night before going to sleep.

As an example of positive reinforcers at work, consider how we might teach an autistic child to talk. We make every spoonful of every meal contingent upon the child emitting a desired response. First, we may reward him with a spoonful of food whenever he makes eye contact with us. We may have to wait until he spontaneously makes eye contact with us, or we may turn his head by hand. After many sessions of this, he will make eye contact spontaneously. Now we make the sound "fff." We keep repeating the sound until he makes a rough approximation of the sound. Then we give him a spoonful of his meal. Eventually we demand a better and better approximation of the sound "fff," until we reward him only for close approximations. Then we move on to other sounds, eventually moving to words, and sentences. This process is called **shaping**. We reward approximations to the desired response, gradually instituting stricter and stricter criteria before we reward the child. Note that in order to use classical conditioning, we needed a response that was already in the client's behavioral repertoire. In operant conditioning, we can shape a response and thereby create behaviors that are new to the client.

How else is operant conditioning different from classical conditioning? Operant conditioning modifies behavior by affecting the consequences of the behavior, whereas classical conditioning affects the antecedents or stimuli for specific behaviors. Thus, behavior is influenced by its antecedents and its consequences; the likelihood of a given behavior (e.g., violence) increases in the presence of certain stimuli (e.g., ridicule). Its likelihood of recurring, however, also depends on whether the violent behavior incurs rewarding or punitive consequences. In the operant therapeutic model, the "learner" must first demonstrate the target behavior prior to being reinforced. In classical conditioning the learner can be more passive, experiencing the association between a conditioned and an unconditioned stimulus. The unconditioned stimulus, an electrical shock, will not occur after the target behavior in classical conditioning. It must occur simultaneously with the target behavior.

In operant conditioning, the value of reinforcers is likely to be idiosyncratic. That is, specific reinforcers may be perceived by some learners as rewarding and by others as rather uninteresting, perhaps even unpleasant.

One can envision a number of rather widely acceptable rewards, such as praise, attention, or money, but generally, behavioral therapists must devote considerable attention to identifying the most potent reinforcers for the individual being treated. Accordingly, many programs award tokens or points that can be exchanged for tangible awards, thereby giving the participant an opportunity to choose a desirable reinforcer.

With some (e.g., a severely depressed individual) it may not be possible to find anything that acts as a reward. In such cases, the reinforcers do not have to be results that most would consider to be rewarding. The **Premack Principle** maintains that the target behavior could instead be reinforced by a frequently performed, routine behavior (Masters et al., 1987). If a severely depressed inmate cannot identify enjoyable activities or rewards, for example, we may make a routine, like sitting in a chair and staring out the window, contingent upon his cleaning his cell.

Operant conditioning is employed therapeutically in both individual and group settings. In both settings, therapists adhere to the principles of effective reinforcement. Spiegler and Guevremont (1993) list them as follows:

1. Administration of the reinforcer must be contingent upon the performance of the target behavior.

2. Every effort must be made to ensure that the client understands that the reward is an earned response to the demonstration of the target behavior.

3. The reinforcement should be administered immediately after performing the target behavior.

4. Continuous reinforcement should be used initially, followed by intermittent reinforcement. Ultimately, most clients are phased out of the reinforcement schedule.

5. Reinforcers must keep their incentive value. If a client becomes satiated with repeated use of a reinforcer, therapists may have to change the reinforcer.

6. Use natural reinforcers when possible. These are rewards, such as praise, that the client is likely to experience outside of therapy. This increases the likelihood that a target behavior will be maintained

7. Reinforcers should be administered consistently.

How we administer the reinforcements can vary. Earlier in the chapter, we discussed the process of shaping. In another case, the contingency contract might seem more appropriate. The **contingency contract** specifies the behavior responsibilities of the client and others who are responsible for administering reinforcements. The contract identifies the target behavior as well as the reinforcers for performing the behavior. It should be written in clear, unambiguous terms and, whenever possible, the client should be given the opportunity to assist in negotiating the terms of the contract. In dealing with parent-delinquent interactions, for example, Stuart (1971) devised a plan in which the parents and child sat down together with a behavior therapist and worked out a contract for the family. Stuart worked with a family whose daughter had been referred by a juvenile court for drug abuse and truancy. In exchange for the privilege of going out at 7:00 P.M. one weekend night, Candy had to get a "B" average in all of her classes during the week and return home by 11:30 P.M. In exchange for Candy doing all of her housework chores and keeping her curfew, her parents agreed to pay her a financial reward on the morning after the day that she earned the money. In addition, a system of bonuses and penalties was devised.

The effects of such contracts are often indirect. Often the main effect is to reduce family friction and arguments. The family pattern of interaction then becomes more rewarding for everyone. Stuart noted that backup counseling may be useful, such as training in interpersonal interaction for the parents, and academic and vocational counseling for the youth. One drawback to contingency contracting, however, concerns the number of behaviors that can be targeted through this process. Contingency contracts can become unwieldy when more than a limited number of target behaviors are addressed (Stein & Smith, 1990).

With target behaviors that are new and unfamiliar to clients, it is not enough to contract for the behaviors. Some attention must be given to structuring **prompts** that direct the client to perform certain actions. Prompting or **stimulus control**, as it is also called, aims to ensure that antecedent events are in place to encourage the client to behave in a certain manner. "Check yourself," a familiar refrain in Anger Management and Aggression Replacement Training programs, is a statement that counselors can give to clients, or clients can give to themselves, to control their anger in time to prevent an aggressive episode. A client's self-control can then be reinforced by the therapists (Goldstein, Glick & Gibbs, 1998). Over time, it may be possible to phase out, or **fade,** the prompts. Stimulus control may instead involve encouraging clients to avoid environments that present too many stimuli for the behaviors they are trying to avoid (Masters et al., 1987).

Up to this point, the focus of our discussion on operant conditioning has been on encouraging the development of prosocial, functional behaviors through the use of reinforcement. Yet a good deal of attention in operant conditioning is given to decreasing or decelerating undesirable behaviors. What strategies can be used to decelerate undesirable behaviors? We have already discussed aversion therapy, or punishment, within the classical conditioning paradigm. At this point we present options within the operant conditioning model.

Decreasing Problematic Behaviors

One of the most common strategies used to decrease an undesirable behavior is to cease reinforcing the target behavior. All behaviors are maintained through one reinforcement or another. One direction commonly taken by therapists, then, is to identify what is maintaining the behavior and to eliminate all reinforcers of the behavior they are attempting to decelerate. Sometimes extra social attention, or even a parent or teacher's display of anger or emotion, may serve to reinforce the acting-out behavior of a child. Ignoring inappropriate behavior, in such cases, takes away its reinforcement, and the undesirable behavior may then become extinct. This strategy should not, however, be confused with a general pattern of ignoring the child. Indeed, the practice of ignoring inappropriate behavior is typically used as a part of a larger behavioral treatment package. At another point in time we would expect to find the same parent or teacher praising appropriate behavior.

With children, one of the more common ways to remove positive reinforcements as well as stimuli for inappropriate behavior is through a practice known as **time-out**. Time-out involves removing the child from the location where the acting out occurred to a room or corner where there are no reinforcers for his or her behavior. With children, time-out is for relatively limited periods of time, usually not longer than five minutes. A general rule, in fact, suggests one minute in time-out for each year of the child's age.

The operant model may also employ negative consequences for bad behaviors. Behaviors that result in negative consequences will at some point be avoided. For most of us, for example, enough costly speeding tickets will encourage us to drive at more moderate speeds. In such instances, behaviors decelerate as a result of their **response costs**.

In criminal justice agencies, restitution, fines, and prison sentences may seem to offer response costs to some behaviors, but it is doubtful that these options follow behavioral guidelines for decelerating undesirable behavior. Such guidelines are enumerated by Spiegler and Guevremont (1993) as follows:

1. The negative consequence should occur immediately after the undesirable target behavior.

2. The negative consequence should be consistently administered, after each time the target behavior occurs.

3. The client should be reminded that the response cost is occurring as a result of a specific behavior that was not acceptable.

4. Reinforcement should not closely follow the delivery of the consequence.

5. The client should receive a warning prior to receiving the negative consequence.

6. Alternative, more desirable behaviors, should be developed in place of the undesirable behaviors.

To these guidelines for decelerating behavior, we should also add the suggestion that punishers, aversives, and response costs should not be the mainstay of behavior therapy. As Gendreau and Andrews (2001) note, reinforcers should outnumber punishers by a factor of four to one in the total behavior treatment package. Most of your work, in other words, should utilize reinforcers.

Aversive consequences, another form of punishment, can be administered in operant conditioning. In contrast to the classical conditioning uses of aversive therapy, however, the aversive in operant conditioning is a behavior consequence that is administered after a behavior is demonstrated. When behaviors need to be eliminated quickly, as is the case with self-injurious behaviors committed by severely mentally ill clients, mild electrical shocks can be useful. Alternatives to the shocks could include noxious odors, bitter-tasting substances, bright lights, and other aversive stimuli.

Radical Behavioral Approaches to Early Intervention and Offender Therapy

An example of operant conditioning in practice is seen in the work of Gerald Patterson at the Oregon Social Learning Center. Patterson and his associates developed a successful approach to teaching parents the principles of behavior therapy. The course includes 8 to 14 weeks of highly structured lessons along with homework assignments. They begin by training parents to observe the behavior of their children and then to track and monitor the frequency and circumstances of these behaviors. From such monitoring, a reinforcement system is developed. This is typically a token system in which the child earns points that can later be exchanged for mutually agreed-upon rewards (Patterson, 1982; Patterson & Gullion, 1976). As parents become adept at noticing and reinforcing good behaviors, they are taught how to decrease unwanted behaviors through the appropriate use of punishment (e.g., time out, loss of privileges, and response costs) and by not attending to inappropriate behavior. The model is particularly useful in the families of delinquent children because many of these families have been observed to demonstrate less use of positive reinforcements with children (Patterson, 1982) and to be more likely to misuse aversive responses (Kazdin, 1989).

There are many types of behavioral family programs. They range from those in which a trained therapist works with an individual family to those like Patterson's, in which multiple families are trained to use behavioral principles in child rearing. Many such programs address a variety of family skills, the parents' skills as well as those of the children. The curriculum of the Strengthening Families Program (Kumpfer, DeMarsh & Child, 1989), for example, targets parent, child, and family skills. In the beginning, children and parents attend separate classes. Parents develop skills related to clear communication, use of attention and rewards, effective discipline, substance use education, limit setting, and problem solving. Children work to improve their communication, understand feelings, cope with anger, manage stress, and resist peer pressure. They are also taught the consequences of substance abuse and compliance with parental rules. The remaining sessions work with the family as a unit on many of the same skills as they pertain to actual family problem solving and activities.

Operant conditioning has also been utilized in the treatment of drug abuse. Perhaps the most clear example of this involves the use of monetary reinforcement for drug abstinence (see Higgins & Silverman, 1999). In one example of such a program, Kenneth Silverman and his associates awarded cocaine patients vouchers for abstinence that could be verified by urine screens. Vouchers were used in lieu of money in order to prevent abusers from using the money to purchase drugs. Researchers found that more than half of the patients in such **abstinence reinforcement** programs achieved more than six weeks of continuous abstinence as compared to only five percent of those who did not receive the vouchers (Silverman et al., 1998). The maximum payments in these programs reached a value of $1,155. A more poignant example of the power of monetary-like reinforcement was achieved when the same group studied treatment-resistant, intravenous drug users receiving methadone treatment. For these individuals, the researchers tested the effects of vouchers valued at much higher monetary amounts. In this case, individuals could receive vouchers totaling as much as $3,480. The group receiving the more valuable vouchers achieved a dramatically higher rate of abstinence than those awarded at lower levels, and they remained abstinent for a longer period. The lesson in all of this is that the magnitude of the reinforcement clearly matters.

Stein and Smith (1990) utilized an operant conditioning program in conjunction with cognitive restructuring (Chapter 9) to treat adolescents who had been diagnosed as oppositionally defiant. Prior to beginning the therapy, the youths' parents were asked to compute behavior frequencies, or baselines, for the following target behaviors: room care, personal hygiene, completion of chores, abusive behavior and language, and safety violations. Rules and expectations pertinent to each of the behavior categories were developed, and a child's daily allowance was made contingent upon compliance with the rules. Parents provided food and shelter; an earned allowance had to cover all additional needs such as clothing, car expenses, and recreational pursuits. The allowance was given daily if all rules were followed, and a bonus was given on the weekend for compliance throughout the entire week. Results for the operant conditioning and cognitive restructuring, combined, were far superior to those for the group of similar adolescents who received only cognitive restructuring.

While Stein and Smith achieved commendable results with a direct award of money or an allowance as reinforcement, a more common approach, particularly in treatment programs for delinquents, would be to award tokens or points, which then can be exchanged for more meaningful rewards.

In fact, the token economy is one of the most frequently employed operant conditioning models. The first comprehensive token economy was developed by Teodoro Ayllon and Nathan Azrin (1968) in the early 1960s at the Anna State Hospital for the mentally ill in Illinois. Operant procedures and token reinforcements were used to motivate mentally ill patients to engage in desired behaviors.

The token economies are especially valuable because they can be used with groups of clients. The therapist first sets out a list of desired target behaviors and the rewards (e.g., number of points, tokens, stars) that each behavior will receive. They next identify a list of rewards or reinforcements for which the tokens may be exchanged, such as extra television privileges, a weekend furlough, recreation time, purchases from a store, and other reinforcers. The token economy is governed by a structured system of rules designed to ensure that reinforcers will be administered according the principles listed above. Thus, the token economy may be used to reinforce varied behaviors, such as better study habits, good hygiene, or use of a skill learned through other components of the program.

Token economies can also be used to decelerate behaviors. Usually this involves clients losing tokens or points for behaving inappropriately or for failing to demonstrate expected behaviors. Token economies have become a mainstay of many juvenile correctional programs. One of the more well-known examples, Achievement Place, was run in Lawrence, Kansas, in the 1970s (Phillips et al., 1973) as a family-style residential treatment program for youths referred by juvenile court or welfare agencies. The program had a strong token economy system in which numerous behaviors were rewarded if performed appropriately—manners, academic skills, and personal hygiene habits. The tokens earned by the youths could be exchanged for snacks, permission to go out, money, and use of recreational facilities.

Upon entry into the program, the youths received points on a daily basis. They then moved to a weekly accounting system, and finally to a condition in which privileges were free. If the youth could handle this last stage, he was then prepared to return home. In follow-up studies, youths treated by this program had better school attendance after one year than youths placed in institutions or on probation; they also evidenced lower recidivism rates after two years (19% for the Achievement Place group versus 53% for institutionalized youth and 54% for probationers). By the late 1980s, there were more than 215 residential programs using this model, which came to be called the Teaching Family Model (Wolf, Braukmann & Ramp, 1987).

Some of the most recent applications of radical behaviorism, including the use of token economies, were ushered in with the passage of the 1997 Individuals with Disabilities Education Act Amendments (IDEA, 1997). This act mandates the performance of **functional behavioral assessments** and **positive behavioral supports** and interventions for students in special education situations. The act targets those with developmental disabilities who exhibit challenging behavior. The functional behavioral assessments assumes, first, that problematic student behavior is purposeful and serves some function for the child (e.g., escape from a difficult task, peer attention). Second, such behavior is assumed to be exacerbated or supported by aspects of the environment. Third, identification of such antecedents and supporting consequences of behavior ought to be used to develop interventions and methods for supporting positive behavior (Dunlap et al., 1991). Simply put, it is incumbent upon the school personnel to assess what is stimulating and reinforcing inappropriate behavior and to do so for each student who poses disciplinary problems related to special needs.

Unfortunately, contemporary school environments present many stimuli for disruptive behavior. In a recent survey of nearly 2,000 high school students, for example, Haas (1999) reported disturbingly high proportions of students who indicated exposure to: verbal insults, difficulty reaching goals, aggressive role models, peer pressure, isolation from significant peer groups, school failure, and antagonism from other students. Of these, the frustration of school failure, insults from others, and the difficulty reaching goals proved to be significantly related to aggressive behavior in school. Thus, the mandated functional behavioral analysis of conditions affecting the behavior of individual students would have many qualities of school life to examine.

IDEA 1997 also mandated that schools develop plans to address problems identified in the functional behavioral assessments. The resulting positive behavioral support typically involves the development of a behavioral program for the student, which might include modification of the instructional setting or tasks, improved control of peers, the teaching of new social skills, and changes in the school or classroom reward system. Some programs have resulted in token economies for teaching and rewarding appropriate new behaviors or the development of peer and staff teams to serve in supportive roles to students. In many cases, the positive behavioral support involves the entire school (Scott et al., 2002).

The concept of positive behavioral support emphasizes the importance of reinforcement-based strategies and seeks to discourage overly punitive orientations. Clearly one intent of the law is to encourage schools to be more deliberate in their control of the environmental stimuli and rewards, and clearer about the behaviors they teach and expect of students. This need not be as structured as a token economy, but in response to the law one was recently set up in a correctional educational program for delinquents. Teachers set up a point system that rewarded students for use of appropriate social skills, reduction in specific inappropriate behaviors, and staying on-task. The behavior of the students improved considerably (Feinstein, 2003).

Emerging in both the family and school-based applications of operant and classical conditioning are concerted efforts to develop and test program models that are responsive to families and individuals from diverse ethnic backgrounds and socioeconomic conditions. It is well-known, for example, that cultural attitudes and practices influence parenting (Forehand & Kotichick, 1996). As a result, lessons need to be presented in culturally relevant contexts. Moreover, the adversity of poverty and inner-city life produce stressors that significantly reduce resources available to succeed in school programs or family therapy. School and family support services become very important in this regard.

The Stability of Newly Acquired or Decelerated Behaviors

An important problem with behavior therapies concerns whether the learning acquired through either classical or operant conditioning will persist after the behavior therapy ends. We noted earlier, for example, that behaviors that were decelerated during aversive conditioning could return once the therapy ended, particularly if clients were unmotivated to change. Similarly, if an alternative school teaches children better work habits, and reinforces those habits through a token economy, will the habits persist when the reward structure of the token economy is no longer in place? Put differently, can these newly acquired or newly decelerated behaviors generalize to the person's day-to-day living outside of the program? Is the therapy **generalizable** or will offending behaviors return once offender clients leave the program?

Fortunately, the behavioral models offer some strategies for helping the therapy to generalize to other settings. One recommendation involves the use of **in vivo therapy,** or treatments that approximate the client's day-to-day life rather than a hospital setting. Much of Gerald Patterson's behavioral approaches, for example, take place in the home. Parents are trained to monitor and respond to behaviors in the home setting.

Another contributor to improved generalization can be found in the nature of the reinforcers or punishers. Praise is an example of a reinforcer that may continue, albeit intermittently, after therapy ends. Teaching clients self-reinforcement provides naturalistic reinforcement but also creates a reinforcer that will follow the client beyond the termination of therapy.

Follow-up sessions also have proven to be helpful in improving generalization. In this regard, Maletzky's (1980) work with sex offenders provided for follow-up sessions at regular intervals following the initial therapy. Taken further, **relapse prevention** programs teach clients to recognize the symptoms of relapse to substance abuse or sex offending behaviors.

Programs should phase rewards out over time. Vicky Agee's programs for delinquents at the Closed Adolescent Treatment program in Colorado (1979) and later at the Paint Creek Youth Center in Ohio (1987), for example, started delinquents on a very structured, daily reward schedule. They then graduated to a system of receiving the reinforcements once a week. The final stage was a community reintegration stage in which the token economy schedule was phased out altogether.

Finally, the more meaningful the behavior to the client, the more likely he or she is to be motivated to maintain it after therapy (Spiegler & Guevremont, 1993). People who learn new social skills may find themselves rewarded in ways that are perhaps ultimately more important than the reinforcers administered during therapy (Goldstein et al., 1989). In fact, the cognitive and social skills approach to correctional intervention is becoming a popular and successful correctional treatment approach. While they employ social learning strategies as well as operant conditioning, they are based on the assumption that a youth is a delinquent because he or she does not have the necessary social, academic, and vocational skills to obtain rewards through legitimate means (O'Leary & Wilson, 1975). The treatment then focuses on:

1. Teaching basic academic skills, such as reading;

2. Teaching manners and roles to adopt when relating to parents, supervisors, and peers; and

3. Teaching parents and the youths to interact in ways that permit mutual rewards.

Incidental to these three areas of teaching, the counselor develops a trusting and supportive relationship with the youths (O'Leary & Wilson, 1975). Up to this point, we have contrasted the behavioral approach with counseling, perhaps to a misleading degree. In actual practice, it is not unusual to augment behavioral therapy with counseling. Thus, the individual who is undergoing covert sensitization for pedophilia may be participating in indepth counseling at the same time. In an analogous fashion, we may even look at interactions between behavior therapists and their clients and observe typical counseling behaviors.

Conclusion

Many people have an emotional reaction to behavior modification techniques because the programs seem to be overly manipulative of people. Yet as Skinner (1971) has clearly pointed out, whether we like it or not, our behavior is under the control of rewards and punishments administered to us by our environment and the people in it. The decision is not whether to have such effects or not, but rather whether we shall plan them or not. Skinner would argue that planned rewards and punishments are preferable to unplanned ones.

Figure 4.4
A Case Study: Jason

> This is a good time to introduce readers to Jason. Throughout this book, you will be asked to assume the role of Jason's case manager or counselor. In this capacity you will be asked to: (a) design a contingency contract for Jason (Figure 4.5 in this chapter); (b) think about what certain counseling strategies would look like for Jason; and (c) devise a treatment plan.
>
> But first, let's introduce you to him.
>
> **Jason: A Case Study**
>
> **I. Background and Social History:** Jason or "JT," as he likes to be called, is a 24-year-old male doing three to five years for burglary in his first stint at State Prison. JT first came into contact with the juvenile justice system when he was 14. Truancy, minor school vandalism, and several weeks of being expelled for fighting, or as he referred to it, "standing up for his manhood," had twice placed him on probation. JT had a difficult family life. His mother was a quiet woman with little education. She worked hard on a factory assembly line and seemed to keep the family together, at least financially. Ten-hour days, however, left little energy or time for other parental functions. Jason's father had been married three times before he married JT's mother and had been known for his drinking, gambling, and occasional wife beating. He was often away from home for weeks at a time.
>
> By the time JT was 18, his older brother Joe was doing a five-year stretch for assault and battery, his fourth offense. JT's younger sister, Mary, had taken a different path. Although frequently ridiculed by her father, Mary continued to make the honor roll in high school, dreaming of one day becoming a high school language teacher, a dream that had recently come true. JT and Mary were only two years apart in age and had always been close, although JT disdained her educational goals, claiming that an "an education on the streets" is what it takes to get ahead in this world. JT, Joe, and Mary all were well above average in intelligence, although Mary was the only one who seemed to be trying to take advantage of her abilities.
>
> Jason dropped out of school in the tenth grade. He regrets that decision now, but at the time, he felt that school was boring and he did not like his teachers.
>
> **II. Criminal History:** Although this is Jason's first prison term, it is his fourth adult conviction. His juvenile record shows two adjudications, one for assault and another for vandalism and truancy. At age 19, Jason was convicted of assault and placed on probation. By age 22, Jason had two additional convictions, both for burglary. In all of his past offenses, Jason has acted in the company of associates who also have criminal records.
>
> **III. Current Offense:** Jason was convicted of robbery. With two friends, he robbed a pharmacy in a nearby neighborhood. The trio took $855 in cash from the pharmacist at gunpoint. This is Jason's first offense involving the use of a weapon.
>
> You are JT's prison counselor. His disciplinary reports have consisted of relatively minor infractions such as "mouthing off" at his laundry supervisor and stealing fruit from the kitchen to make a kind of alcoholic beverage. His records indicate that he is in good physical health. The severity of Jason's offending behavior has escalated over time. This is his second violent offense as an adult, and his first involving a weapon. Jason displays some feelings of inferiority but demonstrated a good deal of false bravado during his initial interview.

Figure 4.5
The Case of JT: A Contingency Contract

The contingency contract discussed in this box is based on the case study of Jason, which was presented on page 78. As explained earlier, contingency contracts make a desired privilege contingent upon the demonstration of certain behaviors that correctional staff wish to reinforce. For example:

Treatment Plan—Example:

Goals of the Behavioral Approach (for Jason):

To make more frequent contact with family members.

To strengthen Jason's relationship with Mary.

To demonstrate respect for Mary's accomplishments.

Approach:

Jason will participate in several contingency contracts, in which ultimately home furloughs are made contingent upon: (a) increased contact with family members (phone and letters); (b) requesting visits from family members, particularly Mary; and (c) demonstrating key relationship skills (as taught in the social skills program). These contracts should be set forth in manageable increments of change and self/social responsibility. At first we will not reinforce Jason with home furloughs, but rather with increased library privileges.

Complementary counseling sessions will address: (a) what responsibility to family members means; (b) rejection of irresponsible behaviors; (c) the skills associated with responsible relationships; and (d) reasons for respecting those who attain career accomplishments in prosocial ways.

Approach—Example:

Behavioral contracts, or contingency contracts, typically contain the following elements:

1. Statement of the role of both the client and the counselor.

2. Clear description of the behavior(s) expected from the client.

3. Clear description of the reward(s) associated with such behaviors.

4. Identification of the criteria to be used to determine success or failure in achieving each goal.

5. Criteria for altering the contract.

Figure 4.5—continued

The following is an example of a simple behavioral contract that can be used in a counseling session.

CONTRACT

- -

TASK	REWARD
WHO: _____	**WHO:** _____
TASK: _____	**TASK:** _____
WHEN: _____	**WHEN:** _____
HOW WELL: _____	**HOW MUCH:** _____
_____	_____
_____	_____

- -

SIGNATURE: _____ **DATE:** _____

SIGNATURE: _____ **DATE:** _____

COMMENTS ON AGREED UPON TASK: _____

_____

_____

_____

AGREED UPON REVISIONS TO TASK: _____

_____

_____

_____

Figure 4.5—continued

For this part of Jason's treatment plan, this contract might look like the following:

CONTRACT

TASK	REWARD
WHO: Jason	WHO: Counselor
TASK: Call Mary;	TASK: 1 hr. extra library time per week
WHEN: 15 min., once a week, 3 weeks	WHEN: 3 weeks
HOW WELL:	HOW MUCH:
I will call Mary once a week to see if she will visit me. I have to try at least 3x before I give up for the week.	After Jason calls Mary once a week for 3 weeks. He should try to talk for 10-15 minutes

SIGNATURE: Jason Smith   DATE: 4/20/99

SIGNATURE: Joseph Jones   DATE: 4/20/99

COMMENTS ON AGREED UPON TASK: _____

_____

_____

_____

AGREED UPON REVISIONS TO TASK: Task will be revised
if Mary is unavailable to answer her calls.

_____

_____

Indeed, there are ways in which nonbehavioral counseling strategies use behavioral reinforcements. In life as well as in therapy, reinforcers can be overt or covert. In overt reinforcement (most uses of the behavioral model), the client is aware of the reinforcers and when they are being applied. In covert reinforcement, the client may be unaware of the reinforcer. For example, when we talk to someone, our listener may occasionally say "um-hmm" or nod his or her head. We may not notice this, but these responses shape what we are saying. Behaviorists would argue that it is ethically preferable to permit the client to be aware of the reinforcers to which he or she is subjected.

One of the attractive features of behavior therapy (especially token economy systems) is that it is less expensive to treat clients with this technique than with conventional counseling. The staff using the techniques need less training, and many would argue that there are benefits to treating observable behaviors—especially in corrections. Also, the token economy systems can be used to treat a greater number of clients for a given financial outlay. Notwithstanding the efficiency of these programs, staff must be carefully trained and supervised. The programs will not work if rewards are dispensed inconsistently, inappropriately, or unethically. To prevent such abuses, it is imperative to have qualified professionals, even clinical directors, overseeing the treatment program and offering staff adequate training in the principles of the behavioral therapy.

In later chapters we will see that many of the strategies of classical and operant conditioning are components of newer treatment strategies such as social learning and cognitive behavioral models. Relapse prevention approaches to substance abuse treatment, for example, clearly recognize the value of stimulus control and reinforcement. These later therapies recognize that humans learn in ways that go beyond the learning models proposed by the radical behavioral models. They learn vicariously, by observing the behavior of others, particularly role models (see Chapter 8). Delinquents, for example, will model their behavior on that of the staff or their peers. They will learn by watching other offenders interact with the staff. It is important to be aware that this learning takes place. Clearly, when correctional officers are not good role models, they often undermine the efforts of correctional treatment programs.

Humans also learn beliefs, perceptions, attitudes and values, which can have a profound effect on their behavior (see Chapter 9, Cognitive Therapies). Some of these are criminogenic, as when a criminal blames the victim of a crime. We can also learn reinforcing thoughts or cognitive stimuli. All of these become the treatment targets of later social learning and cognitive behavioral approaches, which will be discussed in later chapters.

Finally, regardless of the preferred style of correctional intervention, all correctional staff should be familiar with the appropriate use of punishment and reinforcement. Correctional settings in which punishments are misused or reinforcements are not forthcoming in an appropriate manner are seldom successful.

Key Concepts and Terms

abstinence reinforcement
aversion therapy
aversive consequences
classical (respondent) conditioning
conditioned response
conditioned stimulus
contingency contract
contingent
covert sensitization
exposure therapy
fade
flooding
functional behavioral assessment
generalizable
here and now
in vivo therapy
mini-phobia

negative reinforcer
operant conditioning
positive behavioral support
positive reinforcer
Premack Principle
prompts
punishment
radical behavioral approaches
relapse prevention
response costs
shaping
stimulus control
systematic desensitization
token economy
time-out
unconditioned response
unconditioned stimulus

Discussion Questions

1. Describe classical conditioning.

2. How is operant conditioning different from classical conditioning?

3. Can you think of behaviors that your parents modeled that shaped your behavior? For what behaviors did they reward you, and what kinds of general rewards did they use?

4. What are the criticisms of behavior therapy versus traditional counseling as a way of changing people's behavior?

5. How can behavior therapy be abused and what steps can be taken to guard against such abuse?

6. What steps might be taken to improve the prospects of generalizing the results of behavioral therapy to day-to-day life?

7. What role does monitoring play in the construction of an operant conditioning program?

8. How might a parent-training program not be culturally sensitive?

Chapter 5

Early Approaches to Group and Milieu Therapy

David Lester and Patricia Van Voorhis

Most correctional counseling occurs in groups. In fact, the modalities discussed in the three chapters about social learning, cognitive behavioral, and family therapy all take place primarily in group settings. In this chapter, however, we take time to set forth some of the basic principles of group therapy and to discuss models that preceded the growth of social learning and cognitive behavioral approaches in corrections. In their time, many of these were famous, many are discussed to this day, and a few are still used in some correctional settings. Our focus in this chapter is in keeping with the previous chapters on psychoanalysis and radical behaviorism; we wish to leave the reader with a sense of the foundations of contemporary correctional counseling and therapy.

Obviously, the crucial difference between group and individual counseling is the presence of the other clients. Usually between five and 10 clients meet once or twice a week for about 90 minutes with one counselor, or co-counselors, to discuss problems or work on behavioral or attitudinal change. It is important to stress, even before we discuss specific modalities of group therapy, that the very presence of a group is itself considered to be a vehicle for change. That is, groups offer some therapeutic tools that are not available in individual therapy. Yalom (1995) discussed some of the curative properties of group counseling.

1. **Imparting information**. Both the counselor and the other clients impart information to one another. They advise and suggest and give direct guidance about problems in living. This advising may be implicit, with the information being picked up incidentally, or it may be a planned part of the program of

counseling. Because all participating members offer different perspectives on an issue, there are more opportunities for learning than one might see in individual counseling.

2. **Instilling hope**. Groups serve to model and impart hope, which is crucial if any kind of counseling is to have an impact on clients. Groups do this by putting the new client in a group with someone who is further along in treatment and who has survived crises. It fosters the attitude, "If he can do it, so can I."

3. **Universality**. Clients frequently feel unique and alone with their problems, as if they alone grieve, suffer, use drugs, or commit crimes. Their social isolation usually heightens these feelings. It is curative to hear other clients report similar thoughts and feelings and to see them work through similar issues.

4. **Altruism**. During group counseling, clients help one another. They support, suggest, reassure, offer insights, share similar problems, and point out each other's strengths. This helps to lessen the morbid self-absorption that clients sometimes experience and so sets healing forces in motion. In some cases, this support may continue after the group therapy ends.

5. **Corrective recapitulation of the primary family group**. Often clients have had bad experiences with their families— parents, spouse, and children. The group provides a partial family in which better social relationships are worked out. The clients transfer their feelings toward their own family members to members of the group, but, with the counselor's guidance, a better resolution of the interpersonal problems is achieved.

6. **Development of social skills**. Group counseling provides opportunities for social learning (see Chapter 8). It is hoped that these new social skills will generalize to the client's relationships outside of therapy—to families, friends, and employers—in ways that will improve the client's life.

7. **Imitative behavior**. Social learning is facilitated by the tendency of clients to model themselves on the other group members and on the counselor. Furthermore, vicarious (or spectator) counseling takes place as the members watch other clients receive therapeutic attention from the group and the counselor. Clients can also experiment with new behaviors in the group before trying them in the outside world. This change process is further facilitated by the fact that the group members are peers. Especially with adolescents, peers can be a potent force for change.

8. **Interpersonal learning**. Related to these factors, the group is itself a social microcosm. Group members interact and form relationships. They learn about their strengths, limita-

tions, distortions, maladaptive behavior, and other significant aspects of their interpersonal behavior. They receive feedback on how they act toward others.

9. **Catharsis.** The interactions in the group often bring up emotions and the group members can express these emotions in the group setting, supported by a trained counselor. This catharsis is good, and the more emotional the transactions, the more potent the impact can be.

10. **Group cohesiveness.** In effective group therapy settings, clients in the group accept one another, they share, they belong and they come to mean a great deal to one another. The group becomes a haven from the stress of life. This group cohesiveness and social support facilitates self-acceptance, self-esteem, the expression of emotions, and other therapeutic events.

Under what conditions are these benefits most likely to be achieved? Experts in group dynamics maintain that group size is an important factor. Group therapy to an auditorium full of clients does not achieve the benefits enumerated above! Ideally, groups should be in the range of 8 to 10 individuals. Sources recommend starting with a larger group—12 to 14, because some members will drop out or not even appear for the first meeting. In corrections, of course, members can be transferred to other settings or incur new offenses. Groups larger than 12 may have a difficult time developing trust or "jelling" as a group. They also afford opportunities for some members to avoid participating by deferring to more dominant members. At the same time, small groups (less than eight people) can create too much pressure on members along with discomfort and self-consciousness. In a recent evaluation of a cognitive-behavioral program for parolees, for example, Van Voorhis and associates (2002) found that groups smaller than eight members were far less effective in reducing offender recidivism than larger groups.

Membership structure is another consideration. Should groups be closed-ended with all members beginning and ending at the same time, or should they be open, admitting new members at any point? This issue is not as clear as the matter of group size; each model has its own strengths and weaknesses (see Strordeur & Stille, 1989). In halfway houses and jails, where commitments are short, closed-ended groups may mean that fewer offenders actually get referred to the groups. Their term expires before a new group has the opportunity to start. In contrast, open-ended groups can serve more clients and afford opportunities for new members to work with more experienced members. Even so, closed-ended groups are more likely to be more cohesive than groups that experience changing memberships. Finally, some types of programs have carefully sequenced curricula; new members simply could not be brought "up to speed" in an efficient manner. Simply put, we do not have a clear answer about whether a group should be open-ended or closed-ended.

There is a large body of literature that discusses the use of group counseling with offenders. Two clear advantages have encouraged the use of group counseling with such clients. First, it is more economical, and the financial aspect has had a great deal to do with its value to corrections. A dozen or so clients can be treated by one counselor at a time, and a given number of staff can treat more clients. Second, group counseling subjects the offender to input from his or her group. Offenders are frequently not motivated to change. They are resistant to treatment. They may even deny their need for treatment. Offenders who have committed similar crimes sometimes break through this denial and resistance where professional counselors fail (Myers & Jackson, 2002; Walters, 2001). Finally, group therapy can be as effective as individual therapy. Meta-analyses comparing the reductions in recidivism for offenders in individual therapy, as compared to those in group therapy, find no difference. They are equally effective (Andrews et al., 1990; Lipsey, 1992).

Since the 1950s, the literature on group therapy has focused on how a specific theory or modality of psychotherapy might be applied to group counseling. The modalities discussed throughout this book, the psychodynamic, behavioral, social learning, and cognitive behavioral approaches, have each been written about extensively as the basis for group counseling. In this chapter, we will mention six additional systems of psychotherapy—Person-Centered Therapy, Transactional Analysis, Psychodrama, Milieu Therapy, Guided Group Interaction, and Reality Therapy—that have not been allotted a chapter in this book and are not grounded in the theories more central to offender therapy. We discuss them in a historical context, because although these approaches once enjoyed considerable attention in corrections, in general they have not withstood the empirical scrutiny of meta-analytic research. They have not, in other words, been found to be as effective with offenders as the modalities discussed in later chapters of this book.

Person-Centered Therapy

Person-Centered Therapy was developed by Carl Rogers (1951), who assumed that clients have within them the potential for positive change and self-actualization if appropriate conditions are present in the therapeutic situation. Person-Centered Therapy is a humanistic approach designed to help clients feel increased self-worth and develop a healthy self-concept. The goal of the Person-Centered therapist is to establish a therapeutic relationship in which these changes can take place. In order to accomplish this, the therapist tries to gain an empathic understanding of the client, gives the client unconditional positive regard, and tries to be and act genuine. The therapeutic approach has an explorative quality to it, in that clients are encouraged to attempt to uncover, understand, and appreciate their emotions and perceptions.

In demonstrating **empathic understanding**, the counselor tries to show the client that he or she has an understanding of what the client is saying and feeling. Empathy does not mean approval, and it is not the same as sympathy. It simply means that the counselor can fully understand the client's mental state, at least for the issues that are being discussed in the counseling situation.

Conditional positive regard means that we like a person only if he or she meets certain conditions. For example, parents who give conditional positive regard to their children approve of and reward them only when they meet certain criteria, perhaps being polite and well-behaved or achieving good grades in school. In contrast, **unconditional positive regard** means that we value a person no matter what they do, say, think, and feel. Therein lies a very clear difference between Person-Centered and behavioral therapy. The behaviorist recognizes many instances where regard and other positive reinforcements should be contingent upon certain behavioral standards.

To be **genuine,** the counselor must be open and honest in his or her relationship with the client. In this way, the counselor acts as a role model for how the client should be in his or her own interpersonal relationships. **Congruence** is a closely related quality. A congruent human being is one who is honest with himself or herself and others. Very little energy is devoted to putting on façades or appearances or trying to be someone he or she is not. Who others see is pretty much who the person is. Person-Centered Therapy values congruence, both as a therapeutic skill and as an ultimate goal for clients.

Paraphrasing and non-verbal cues of understanding, such as nodding the head, are also employed. In giving clients verbal and non-verbal messages of understanding and acceptance, the client is encouraged to greater self-understanding and self-acceptance.

In recent years, Person-Centered Therapy has ceased to be a system all by itself, although some counselors continue to follow its rules and styles. Rather, the prevailing view is that a Person-Centered counseling style embodies skills that every counselor ought to develop, no matter what system of counseling he or she follows. Not everyone agrees that this is true for offenders, however. Although Person-Centered Therapy is a well-known and highly regarded approach to therapy, there are very few studies finding it to be effective with offenders. In one such study, conducted by Truax, Wargo, and Silber (1966), incarcerated delinquent girls were randomly assigned to treatment and no-treatment conditions. Those given treatment met in groups for 24 sessions spread over three months. The girls who were given Person-Centered group counseling developed a more positive self-image, more conformity to normal values, and spent less time in institutions in the year after release.

Unfortunately, when we examine the larger body of studies on treatment effectiveness, Person-Centered approaches do not fare well. Perhaps examples of alternative client-counselor dialogues will give the best picture of why Person-Centered approaches do not work as well with offenders. Imagine the case of John, who meets with his counselor the day after becoming so angry with his wife that he became violent. The counselor may respond to John in different ways (Van Dieten, 1998). If Person-Centered Therapy is the chosen approach, the counselor must help John to understand his anger toward his wife and the sources of his frustration. In doing so, John may reach an improved level of self-awareness and self-regard.

THE PERSON-CENTERED DIALOGUE:

> JOHN: I had the worst day ever at work. The boss was on my case all day for being late to work and making a mistake on one of the jobs. I didn't deserve it. I knew I was going to blow if anyone got in my face. I just knew my wife was going to mess up dinner and the kids would be screaming. I walked through the door, and there she was, watching TV—no dinner—just some nag about don't slam the door.

> COUNSELOR: So John, it sounds like you were very frustrated. Seems like you want your wife to be more attentive to you.

> JOHN: She didn't even look at me. Then she launches into a discussion about why we don't have more money. I just couldn't take it. She was talking too much and was really asking for it. Before you know it, I just lost it.

> COUNSELOR: So in the face of so much anger and disappointment, you hit your wife. Let's try to explore some of these feelings.

THE COGNITIVE-BEHAVORIAL DIALOGUE:

> JOHN: I had the worst day ever at work. The boss was on my case all day for being late to work and making a mistake on one of the jobs. I didn't deserve it. I knew I was going to blow if anyone got in my face. I just knew that when I got home my wife was going to mess up dinner and the kids would be screaming. I walked through the door, and there she was, watching TV—no dinner— just some nag about don't slam the door. She didn't even look at me. Then she launches into a discussion about why we don't have more money. I just couldn't take it. She was talking too much and was really asking for it. Before you know it I was hitting her. She has to learn that I just can't take it anymore.

> COUNSELOR: John, at the outset, let me say that hitting someone—violence—is not acceptable. The police and your probation officer are correct in citing you for this behavior and securing a restraining order. We will get to discuss your disappointment with your boss and your wife. However, even though you said you had some reasons for hitting your wife, hitting is just not an acceptable response to them.

JOHN: I expect to have more attention when I get home, especially after the really rough days. When, I don't, I get too mad. I don't want to be hitting family members.

COUNSELOR: It's important to look at what you were thinking before you struck her. We can talk about your frustration and feelings about your marriage at a later point in time, but for now I'm concerned about the possibility that your thinking may have an influence on how you behave. Are you suggesting here that this disappointment justifies violent behavior?

We can allow for the possibility that some Person-Centered therapists would have been more directive than the above example, but at some point the therapist would have to portray the strategies of Person-Centered therapy. These strategies, especially unconditional positive regard and paraphrasing, could be interpreted by some offenders as offering tacit approval of their behavior. In the Person-Centered example above, the counselor appears to be reinforcing inappropriate responses to anger, frustration, and disappointment. More importantly, the woman remains in danger, and therapy has not addressed the offender's behavior. The hope in this regard is that a better understanding of John's frustrations will ultimately put an end to the violence. In contrast, the cognitive approach begins on a more preventative level. The counselor first addresses the violent behavior as unacceptable, and then begins to educate the offender as to how his thoughts contributed to the violence. In addition, counseling will work on the accuracy of the thoughts themselves. Later, the cognitive-behavioral therapist will probably portray this situation and others like it as "high risk" situations for this offender. Counseling at that time would set out to develop coping strategies to enable the offender to have better ways of dealing with bad days.

We are not suggesting that respect, understanding, genuineness, and empathy have no place in work with offenders. On countless occasions these counselor skills will be most useful and crucial to developing a therapeutic alliance with the offender. However, in changing the behavior of offenders, there are better treatment goals than self-esteem and positive self-regard (see Chapter 7). Surprisingly, perhaps, low self-esteem has not been found to be a risk factor for future offending. Moreover, unconditional positive regard and agreement can be easily viewed by offenders as a reinforcement of criminal thinking and exploitive behavior.

Figure 5.1
The Case of JT: A Group Therapy Approach

The group therapy approaches discussed in this box are based on the case study of Jason, presented on page 78 of this text.

Treatment Plan—Example:

The Goals of Group Therapy:

To offer Jason increased hope of changing his life.

To assist in understanding the common ground of human behavior.

To assist others in participating in their growth toward health.

To develop group cohesiveness and spirit (Yalom, 1995).

To assist Jason in acknowledging the importance of: (a) feeling worthwhile to self and others; and (b) loving and being loved by others.

To identify behaviors that impede Jason's ability to meet these needs.

To identify alternative, more constructive ways to meet these needs.

Approaches:

Psychodrama, e.g., role reversal, soliloquy, the double, the mirror technique, behind the back, high chair, empty chair, and ideal other.

Reality Therapy as practiced in individual meetings with Jason and in group therapy with other offenders.

Approach—Example:

1. **Psychodrama:**

   The Empty Chair: In Jason's situation, it would be helpful to use the empty chair for a conversation with Jason's father. If he can get a glimpse behind the emptiness of his dad's emotional distance, Jason might experience his own pain in a more meaningful way. The empty chair would allow Jason (the protagonist) to imagine his father (the antagonist) seated in an empty chair and to interact with this imaginary person (his dad).

   Counselor: "Your father is now sitting in the chair opposite you. He is here to talk with you in a way he never could when you were a child. What might be your first thought about sitting here with your father?"

   Jason: "I have never been able to forgive him for the way he treated me as a child."

   Therapist: "Can you say that to him?"

   Jason: "I don't know whether I want to talk to him or hit him!"

   Role reversal could be used in combination with the above. Here Jason pretends to be his father. Ultimately both discussions could tap unexpressed feelings of hatred, rage, guilt, rejection, resentment, grief, and guilt.

Figure 5.1, *continued*

The counselor should focus on the "here and now" as well as on Jason's taking personal responsibility for his thoughts and actions. Finally, Jason's perceptions should be regarded with dignity.

The group should encourage Jason to ask his family for more frequent visits. Letters and phone calls to his family could encourage relationship building among family members who have remained in communication with each other.

At first, Jason should attend a closed group. Later, when he has acquired a more positive way of thinking and behaving, perhaps an open group would prove more beneficial.

2. Reality Therapy offers another group approach that is quite commonly used in corrections. The primary assumption of Reality Therapy is that personal difficulties stem from a basic inability to fulfill essential human needs: (a) the need to feel worthwhile to self and others; and (b) the need to love and to be loved. From this view, Jason is seen as someone who is unable to meet these needs in appropriate ways. Reality Therapy endeavors to show clients how their current behavior impedes their efforts to meet their own needs and to assist them in developing more constructive alternatives.

Corsini (1973) offers eight principles that might guide the types of communications that might ensue during Reality Therapy sessions:

Communicate caring:

Counselor: "Can you tell me what led up to the burglary that got you sent here?"

Jason: "I was drinking after a fight with my girlfriend. I was really hating her, and I was broke. I needed money."

Counselor: "Jason, when you talk about your role in the robbery, I feel that we are getting closer to meeting some of the goals you set for counseling."

Focus on present behavior rather than feelings:

Jason: "I'm really feeling down right now. This place is getting to me."

Counselor: "What are you doing that might contribute to your being depressed?" (Corsini, 1973: 299).

or

Counselor: "Now that I understand how you're feeling, let's examine what you are doing. What are you doing now that might contribute to your being depressed? Let's take a look at that." (Corsini, 1973: 300).

Focus on the present:

Jason: "I hate this place. It sucks!"

Counselor: "Tell me about one thing that you could change right now about your situation."

Figure 5.1, *continued*

Value judgment: ". . . each individual must judge his own behavior and evaluate what he is doing to contribute to his own failure before he can be assisted" (Corsini, 1973:300).

Jason: "I just don't seem to be getting anywhere. It's all a useless game. I'll die here."

Counselor: "Do you believe that participating in these counseling sessions is helping or hurting you?"

Planning: ". . . we help the individual make specific plans to change failure behavior into success behavior."

Jason: "You're the counselor. Make me better, so I can get out of here."

Counselor: What do you think would have to happen to make you better?

or

Counselor: "Tell me what better means."

or

Counselor: "I'll be glad to help you. What should we do first?"

Commitment ". . . it can only come from making and following through with plans that we gain a sense of self-worth and maturity" (Corsini, 1973:302).

Jason: "I'll be on time. Just for you."

Counselor: "I accept your commitment. I'm glad that you see the importance of counseling and our relationship."

No excuses ". . . make it clear to the individual that excuses are unacceptable . . . we believe people know why things go wrong" (Corsini, 1973:303).

Jason: "I would have been on time, but I was late leaving the dining hall."

Counselor: "I see that your earlier commitment to be on time didn't work out. Do we need to make a new plan?"

Eliminate punishment ". . . do not punish patients with critical statements such as, 'I knew you would not do it,' or 'see, you've done it again.' In making such statements the counselor punishes the client and thereby reconfirms his failure identity" (Corsini, 1973:303).

Jason: "The correctional officers are blaming me for some missing books."

Counselor: "Jason, I don't know what happened. I do know that you are trying to quit behaving the way you did when you committed the burglary, and are trying to become a more committed and more positive decision-maker."

Transactional Analysis

Transactional Analysis, developed by Eric Berne (1961), is partly based on Freud's psychoanalytic theory. In the first stage of Transactional Analysis, called structural analysis, Berne simplified Freud's concepts and made them holistic in nature. In particular, rather than talking about id, ego, and superego wishes, Berne talked about the Child, Adult, and Parent ego states. An **ego state** is a coherent system of behavior patterns and the thoughts and feelings that accompany this pattern. The **Child ego state** resembles the way we behaved as a child, and we enter that state, for example, when we have fun at a party or perhaps when we get angry. **The Adult ego state** is the pattern of behavior we show when we are being mature and rational people, such as when we collaborate with co-workers on projects. The **Parent ego state** is when we assume a nurturing or parenting role, often with our children, but occasionally with friends who elicit that role from us. Those in the Parent ego state are usually directive toward others.

These terms are much easier to comprehend and apply than their psychoanalytic/ psychodynamic counterparts. While many people might have difficulty uncovering which unconscious id wishes might be motivating their behavior, they can usually identify when their Child ego state is directing their behavior. The Transactional Analysis terms also seem to arouse less anxiety in people than terms in Freud's psychoanalytic theory. Clients can quickly learn the terminology and identify these ego states in themselves.

After introducing clients to these terms, sometimes in individual counseling and sometimes in group counseling, Berne then helped people explore the ways in which people interact. He taught clients to recognize which ego state each member of the relationship was in during a particular discussion and which ego state each member was addressing. The ideal, in most situations, is to communicate from an adult state to an adult state. If we communicate to a colleague from our Adult ego state, for example, we should not be surprised if he communicates back to us from a Child ego state. Then again, he might just get mad, but anger is also likely to involve one's Child ego state. Instead, both of us would be wise to think about having the conversation on an adult level.

In addition, Berne taught clients that communications between people (their **transactions**) may take place at overt and covert levels simultaneously—a process he called a **game.** For example, two colleagues may appear to be having an Adult-to-Adult conversation about staying after hours to work on a project, but they may also be having a covert Child-to-Child conversation about the possibilities of having a sexual liaison. Again, the terms introduced by Berne and his colleagues proved simple for people to understand and apply to their everyday behavior. The understanding of interactions is greatly facilitated by the clients interacting in a group, and so group counseling became a popular form of Transactional Analysis.

In one of the earliest applications of Transactional Analysis to offenders, Ernst and Keating (1964) switched to the modality after a psychoanalytic approach failed. During the psychoanalytic phase, the group leaders tried to serve as benign and benevolent listeners, directing comments to the group as a whole, trying to promote group cohesion, and believing that the group itself would have a healing effect. Instead, they found that the prisoners took advantage of the group. For example, one group of prisoners ran a protection racket with the other group members' confidences. The prisoners would avoid meaningful topics using a variety of ruses, such as "We covered that last night in the wing, Doc," or they would focus the group activity on one or two weak prisoners, thereby eliminating themselves from treatment.

The group leaders then switched to a Transactional Analysis style. They defined the treatment goals of each prisoner in the first group session, and they used these therapeutic contracts to cut down on the waste of time. They focused the group members on the gross behavioral changes in the men's behaviors, such as voice tone, body postures, and so forth. When any of these behaviors showed changes, the group leaders examined the reasons and implications of these changes. For example:

> Phil, in a low-pitched, clear, confidential manner says to Mac, "Say, Mac, I want to tell you something for your own good. You talk about good manners but you interrupt other people while they are talking. Now I know you might not like this but I'm doing this for your own good." Mac's conversational response had a bouncy quality as he told Phil, "You're sore because I know that you ain't so pure, besides you're trying to impress the doctor" (Ernst & Keating, 1964:977). At this point Phil lost his temper and shouted at Mac. Focusing on his voice change, Phil recalled that his first voice tone was modeled on the highly respected director of the orphanage he had lived in until he was 16 years of age. The second voice was that of his childhood temper tantrums. As Phil worked this out, he modeled for the other group members an Adult ego state in operation. Most of the inmates could identify their Child, Adult, and Parent ego states, and the act of analyzing the transactions strengthened their Adult ego states, and eventually the groups moved on to analyzing the games that they played.

Jesness (1975) reported on the Youth Center Research Project in California, in which one school for delinquent youths was set up with a Transactional Analysis program while another school was set up with a behavior modification program. Boys ages 15 to 17 were randomly assigned to the two schools and their subsequent progress was monitored.

In the Transactional Analysis program, the youths were given books to read on the theory of Transactional Analysis, and they were encouraged to make specific behavioral contracts with the counselors. Most of the counseling was conducted in group sessions. In the behavior modification program, a token economy system was set up with rewards for academic behaviors and convenience behaviors, such as being quiet after lights-out. The token economy also involved punishment of antisocial behavior.

Jesness noted that after treatment, the two groups showed identical parole revocation rates, with about 32 percent being revoked during the first year. Although there was no **treatment effect** between the two groups, these rates were less than other schools in the California correctional system and lower than the rates for the target schools before the new treatment programs were begun. Thus, both programs had some beneficial effect. Jesness also noted that during the treatment program, the staff became less likely to move the youths to security quarters in response to disruptive behavior. In learning to run the programs, it appeared that staff became more skilled and flexible in their approach to disciplinary problems.

To some extent, the success of these boys depended upon their personality characteristics. For example, Jesness classified the youths using Warren's I-level system (Warren, 1983) and found that unsocialized passive delinquents of level I_2 did better in the behavior modification program, while the manipulators of level I_3 did better in the Transactional Analysis program. Thus, effective assignment of a delinquent youth to a treatment program may well depend upon having a sound classification system for delinquent youths. These findings will receive additional attention in the chapter on correctional classification as we discuss the notion of offender responsivity (Chapter 7, Overview of Offender Classification Systems).

The behavior modification program had a greater effect on the youths' behavior, while the Transactional Analysis program had a greater effect on the youths' attitudes and self-report data. After treatment, the youths in the Transactional Analysis program were more likely to show positive regard for the staff, which had a favorable impact on their parole success.

Program quality also mattered. For example, there was some evidence that parole success was related to the competence of the counselors in the Transactional Analysis program, but not for the behavior modification program. Furthermore, success in the Transactional Analysis program was related to the degree of the youths' participation in the program. Thus, a behavior modification program may work better with counselors with less training and with less motivated youths.

The Youth Center Research Study discovered some important patterns that have been found in other correctional evaluations. First, a program seldom works with all offenders. Instead, it typically works with some better than others. Simply put, there are no "magic bullets" (Palmer, 1992). Second, program quality matters. The "state of the art program" does not work if it is poorly delivered. Finally, with offenders, group participation rather than group listening is crucial (Van Voorhis et al., 2002).

In another study, Krauft (1974) placed sixth-grade boys with behavioral problems into one of three groups: 16 weeks of Transactional Analysis, 16 weeks of independent study, or 16 weeks of the normal school program. He found no differential effects for the three treatment programs. Transactional Analysis did not appear to be of much use with these boys. However, Santsaver (1975) put boys of a similar age into a treatment program in which Transactional Analysis was combined with behavior modification. Each child was taught the basics of structural analysis, and they were awarded points for maintaining an Adult ego state when interacting with others. In addition, specific behavior goals were set and contracts made, such as "I want to stop throwing paper in Mr. Brown's class," and the boys were awarded points for succeeding in attaining the goals. Each Friday, the points earned were cashed in for material goods. Almost all of the boys showed improvement in their behavior.

Psychodrama

Psychodrama (see Greenberg, 1974; Rutan & Stone, 1984; Yablonsky, 1976) is a form of group counseling devised by J.L. Moreno (1934). Psychodrama involves giving the client an opportunity to act out and thereby experience various aspects of his or her life situation in front of an audience. In doing so, the client creates a drama in which he or she is the protagonist, the other members of the group are the other actors, and the counselor is the director.

For Moreno, spontaneity was an important component of mental health, and participation in psychodramatic experiences encouraged spontaneity. The client was the central figure in a drama with other clients who were playing the roles of significant others in his or her life. Rather than sitting and verbalizing about his or her feelings toward these significant others, the patient had to act and react to them, and this forced a greater degree of spontaneity. The aim of this psychodramatic experience was to create a **catharsis** (an emotional purging) and insight. It was assumed that psychodrama would achieve this more readily because it came closer than other forms of counseling to producing the actual scenarios of people in their everyday lives. Therefore, additional discussions of these insights were unnecessary, because the client experienced them in action.

There are three phases to a psychodrama session. First, there is a warm-up session, in which the group discusses issues that concern the members in their personal lives. Out of this discussion, the counselor chooses a client to be the protagonist, or main character, and the problem that he or she will work on.

The second phase involves the primary action in the drama. Typically, psychodrama uses a real stage, as in a theater, with an audience, but psychodramatic techniques can be used in conventional group counseling sessions as well. The counselor is at the same time the producer of the drama, the director, and the social analyst. The client is called the protagonist in the drama. Clients are not to act, but to accurately portray scenes and incidents from their lives. There are a number of special techniques to aid this dramatic portrayal.

1. **Role reversal**. One group member may be playing the role of a significant other in the protagonist's life, for example, a spouse. In role reversal, the director interrupts the action and has the two actors switch roles. The protagonist then has to play the spouse in the drama while the other group member plays the protagonist. This enables the protagonist to see himself or herself through the eyes of the significant others.

2. **Soliloquy**. The protagonist is helped to work through a psychological state by airing his or her feelings or thoughts as in a dramatic soliloquy. Often this is encouraged by having the protagonist walk while talking, because it appears that muscular movement facilitates the flowing of speech. This resembles free association, but the aim is to facilitate the dramatic action. Soliloquies may be combined with the next technique, the double.

3. **The double**. If the protagonist is having difficulty holding his or her own against the other actors, the director chooses another group member to play the protagonist with him, so that there are two individuals having the role of the protagonist. The double can also try to verbalize the protagonist's feelings and thoughts that are not being expressed, thereby enlarging the dramatic experience.

4. **The mirror technique**. In this technique, the protagonist sits down in the audience or group and watches another group member play himself or herself on stage. The protagonist can then see himself or herself as others see him or her.

5. **Behind the back**. Here, the protagonist sits with his or her back to the other group members or audience, and the counselor leads a discussion about the client.

6. **High chair**. The protagonist sits on a chair that is on a raised platform, higher than the other group members. This is assumed to increase feelings of power, which might be necessary to deal effectively with enemies.

7. **Empty chair.** Here, the protagonist imagines his or her antagonist seated in an empty chair and interacts with this imaginary person. Role reversal can be used in combination with this.

8. **Ideal other.** Here the protagonist is permitted to interact with a group member playing a significant other as the protagonist would like him or her to act. This is a very rewarding experience and often reduces tension at the end of a psychodramatic session.

The counselor-director of a psychodrama can be creative and devise new methods as appropriate to facilitate the dramatic action. It is important that the director be spontaneous and creative in this role.

The other actors, also called auxiliary egos, can be selected by the protagonist or the director. Often they, too, learn from their experience in the drama. The audience can also learn from identifying with the roles portrayed in the drama, and they provide useful feedback in the third and final phase of a psychodrama, the post-discussion.

The post-discussion is when the audience and persons who portrayed auxiliary egos share their experiences with the protagonist. They relate similar incidents from their lives that parallel or develop the action just seen in the psychodrama. In the post-discussion, the group identifies with the protagonist. This facilitates group insight, increases cohesion, and enlarges interpersonal perceptions. Analysis of the protagonist's behavior is not part of this phase.

A psychodrama is in the here-and-now. Even when a past situation is reenacted or a future situation is anticipated, the action takes place in the present. The actual experience is not relived; the here-and-now memory of it is produced. The director keeps the session in the present. For example, were a group member to say "When I was young, I hated my father," the director would have him or her say instead, "I am young and I hate my father." Furthermore, a psychodrama accepts as real the protagonist's view of significant others. Protagonists have complete control over the truth as they see it. Their perceptions of others in their lives are acted out. Even if the protagonist is hallucinating, the others in the psychodrama would, during the action, join in the distortion.

Psychodrama has been used to prepare offenders for specific anticipated experiences or to assume new roles (Haskell & Weeks, 1960). For example, Eliasoph (1955) used psychodrama to help addicts prepare to face peer pressure to use drugs when they were once again out on the street. Yablonsky (1955) used the technique to prepare parolees for roles that they would have to play in their lives, while working or when reporting to their parole officer.

Early uses of psychodrama also sought to educate others about offenders' lives. Miller (1960), for example, used psychodramatic techniques in his work with a juvenile court to help parents understand the problems of their children by having them watch the children in their psychodramas. He also had the judge, probation officers, and other court personnel watch the psychodramas in order to come to a better understanding of the family situations. At a boys' village, Miller had the boys play the roles of the staff while the staff watched the drama. The psychodrama provided an excellent means of confronting the staff with their behaviors, thus helping them to change.

More recently, psychodrama was used to help: (a) inmates cope with the stresses of prison life (Schrumski et al., 1984); inmates develop educational skills (Melnick, 1984) and child abusers to learn appropriate parenting skills (Gaudin & Kurtz, 1985). Even so, the modality, like some of the others reviewed in this chapter, did not fare well in comparison to behavioral and cognitive-behavioral approaches to offender therapy (Andrews et al., 1990).

Milieu Therapy

Traditional institutions, both psychiatric and correctional, have certain common customs (Goffman, 1999; Sykes, 1958). One of their goals is to ensure that the inmates are kept away from the rest of society, and thus they have custodial functions. Admission to the institution is often frightening, humiliating, and demoralizing. When in the institution, the inmates depend entirely upon the staff for determinations of what they can do. Communication with the outside world is restricted, and the inmate's sense of personal identity is weakened by the institution's routines. The institutional environment often provides isolation; a highly simplified, rigid life; an authoritarian atmosphere; and impersonal staff. The institution typically rewards conformity and passivity and creates dependency rather than self-sufficiency.

The concept of the **therapeutic community** (sometimes referred to as **milieu therapy**) was developed by Maxwell Jones and others after World War II, as a result of their attempts to rehabilitate repatriated prisoners of war. The development of the design was also facilitated by the increasing effectiveness of medications in controlling symptoms of disturbed inmates, so that they became less intimidating to staff and more amenable to treatment. A third stimulus for the development of the therapeutic community was the increasing number of inmates and the relative shortage of trained counselors (Jones, 1968, 1973).

There is a great deal of variation in how therapeutic communities are run. Essential to their functioning is the principle that all members of the institution provide therapeutic experiences: the professional staff, the nonprofessional staff, and the inmates. All must come together to form a community where all have an active role in helping to change inmate behavior. Typically, group procedures are employed. Group counseling is often led by the trained professional staff, but sometimes the inmates themselves lead these sessions. In many therapeutic communities, the inmates have a great deal of influence on decisions that are made about the administration of the program. New inmates to the institution may be interviewed and screened by the current inmates in addition to the professional staff. In some therapeutic communities, the inmates can veto the entrance of new members to the community. In correctional institutions, this may mean that an offender is sent to a custodial setting rather than to the therapeutic community. There may be opportunities for individual counseling, social activities, and inmate-staff meetings to discuss the running of the community. The introduction of a therapeutic community into an institution changes the whole social structure of the institution. The staff, in particular, must switch from authoritarian to more democratic procedures. The line staff may also require special training programs so that they understand and apply the principles of the overall treatment philosophy.

The functioning of a therapeutic community is clearly more similar to the lives of inmates in the outside world. Thus, participation in a therapeutic community may better prepare the inmates for release than settings that

take away individual autonomy. Furthermore, therapeutic communities provide treatment 24 hours a day. The inmates are always in a therapeutic situation, because even a trivial conflict between two inmates may eventually
involve their friends and may be discussed the next day at one of the group
meetings. There is social learning in the here-and-now for the inmates.

Therapeutic communities vary according to the treatment modalities they
use. A therapeutic community located within the Federal Correctional Institution in Oxford, Wisconsin, for example, was based primarily on Transactional Analysis, as modified by Martin Groder (see Erskine et al., 1988). At
the Ventura School for Girls in California, William Glasser (1965) set up a
community based on Reality Therapy. Still others (actually most) use a
more confrontational approach, such as Guided Group Interaction or Positive Peer Culture.

Because we cannot divorce the effect of the milieu from the treatment
modality used within the milieu, and because therapeutic communities
vary in terms of the treatment modality used within them, it is difficult to
summarize their effectiveness. Earlier meta-analyses, for example, indicated
that milieu therapy failed to reduce offender recidivism. (Andrews et al.,
1990; Garrett, 1985). However, more recently, several evaluations of therapeutic communities for drug offenders find commendable outcomes, especially if accompanied by aftercare in the community (Griffith et al., 1999;
Knight et al., 1999; Lipton, 1996; Martin et al., 1999; Wexler et al., 1999).
The answer to the question of effectiveness really depends upon the quality
of the therapeutic community and the treatment offered within it.

Guided Group Interaction

Guided Group Interaction (GGI) was first described by Abrahams and
McCorkle (1946, 1947) in their work with military offenders at Fort Knox
in Kentucky. These offenders met in groups of 15 to 35 men for about 50 minutes daily. Following their individual and group efforts, about 40 percent of
the men were restored to duty, and their recidivism rate was in the range of
six to 10 percent. McCorkle did not call the group work Guided Group Interaction at that time. Later, Bixby and McCorkle (1951) reported on their use
of GGI in a New Jersey correctional institution. The delinquents were in a
therapeutic community in which one component offered group counseling.
These groups were led by an active leader and the leader and group members tended to be very confrontational with each other—a characteristic that
has become the hallmark of GGI.

GGI was designed to harness the power of peer pressure and support,
which is key to adolescent motivation. As such, staff leaders had to avoid taking over the group and had to allow the group members to do most of the
work. Staff were responsible for setting up the group, putting forward and
enforcing certain ground rules, and identifying the values, behaviors, and atti-

tudes that would be valued in the group. This meant that after setting up the ground rules and expectations for the group, staff were expected to become non-authoritarian and democratic. The leader could also be a role model and a catalyst for the group, but he or she had to allow the group members to be the agents of change. Group members were encouraged to confront each other's rationalizations and thinking errors. Often, group members would not help another member unless they were satisfied that the individual had "come clean" about their behavior. When new delinquents entered the institution, more experienced group members lead the attack on the new member's rationalizations. Precautions were taken to keep the confrontations within appropriate boundaries. Staff were trained to identify and deal with abusive confrontations and those that appeared to be made for purposes of attaining power over other members. They could not, however, overprotect certain members or create a situation in which a member could take problems to a chosen staff member rather than to the group. The group's potential for change was considered stronger when members expected to have to work through most matters in the groups than when problems were "taken care of" in private one-on-one counseling sessions.

Here is how a typical juvenile detention center might describe its program:

> It is a community-based, residential rehabilitation program for delinquent adolescents. The therapeutic modality is Guided Group Interaction, which is a sociological therapy designed specifically to utilize peer pressure to modify delinquent behavior and minimize institutional living problems. These tasks are accomplished by assigning the supervisory and therapeutic responsibilities to residents of the program. They are guided through their daily activities, which include a therapy session, by staff skilled in creating situations in which residents' values, decision-making skills, motives, and temperament are questioned. Residents are then selectively rewarded, principally by their peers, for making decisions that will enhance their opportunities for becoming productive citizens. Guided Group Interaction, combined with our employment, educational, and physical education components, enables more than 75 percent of our residents to return successfully to the community and remain free of any further delinquent activity. This is accomplished in a nonincarcerative and nonpunitive environment. There are no bars or locked doors. There are no guards or supervisors forcing residents to do various tasks. The status system based on "might makes right" does not prevail as in other reformatories and prisons. Young men are given the opportunity to change their behavior in a dignified and humane environment at a cost of approximately one-third that of the expense incurred by an inmate in a correctional institution.

GGI programs often excluded many types of delinquents, such as hardened delinquents, the psychiatrically ill, sex offenders, drug users, mentally retarded youths and serious runaways. Indeed, studies have shown that not all offenders benefit from confrontation delivered in such programs. The act-ing-out behaviors of highly anxious offenders, for example, tend to increase when they are exposed to confrontation (Listwan et al., 2004).

GGI programs were initially set up for delinquents and then became com-mon to therapeutic communities for adult substance abusers. In both cases, the principles of GGI are used to shape all aspects of the residential program. More recent adaptations of the principles of the therapeutic community and GGI programs are programs called **Positive Peer Cultures**. An early eval-uation of the Positive Peer Culture revealed a substantial reduction in recidi-vism rates (Vorrath & Brentro, 1985). More recent evaluations have blended the Positive Peer Culture elements with cognitive behavioral programs to improve moral reasoning and reduce criminal thinking. The EQUIP program is an example of this (Gibbs, Potter & Goldstein, 1995). Here, program staff worked diligently to assure that the culture and the groups were not simply confrontational. Rather, members were taught how to be positive toward one another, and to encourage each others' efforts to live prosocial lives, thereby emphasizing the importance of "mutual self-help." Results for the EQUIP program were favorable. Thus, GGI and PPC programs demonstrated unfa-vorable results in early meta-analyses (Andrews et al., 1990; Garrett, 1985), but more recent evaluations show much stronger treatment effects, especially in the context of therapeutic communities for substance abuse (Griffith et al., 1999; Lipton, 1996; Martin et al., 1999; Wexler et al., 1999).

Reality Therapy

Reality Therapy is a counseling technique introduced by William Glasser. Glasser (1965) argued that everyone who seeks psychotherapy suffers from the same basic inadequacy—an inability to fulfill his or her essential needs. The more severe the symptoms of the client, the more deprived those essential needs are.

Herein lies the "reality" in reality therapy: the most basic human needs are the need to love and be loved and the need to feel that we are worthwhile to our-selves and to others. The only way that these needs can be satisfied is through involvement with at least one other person and by maintaining a satisfactory standard of behavior. We must correct ourselves when we break the rules of soci-ety and praise ourselves when we follow them. When we fulfill our needs, we must take care not to deprive others of their ability to fulfill their needs. If we do all this, we are responsible. If we do not follow these guidelines, we are irre-sponsible. The bottom line is that we must be realistic about what we are actually doing and about the true consequences of our behavioral choices.

Most people make attempts to fulfill needs to love, be loved, and feel worthwhile, but when these attempts are unsuccessful, it is primarily because they denied the impact of their behavior on their personal relationships and their sense of self-worth. They may not have contemplated the consequences of their behavior, or they may have had irrational ideas about the likely consequences of their behavior. In order for counseling to be successful, people have to recognize and accept reality and try to fulfill their needs within the framework of reality.

The Techniques of Reality Therapy

Reality Therapy recommends that counselors work within three core procedures:

> **Involvement.** The counselor must become involved with the client, setting up a relationship that involves caring and respect. While doing this, the counselor must also act responsibly. He or she must be tough, but also interested, human, and sensitive. Counselors may talk about themselves and their own struggles to be responsible. They must not be aloof or superior. They also must act as a good role model for the client to follow.

> **Rejection of Irresponsible Behavior.** Counselors must reject the unrealistic and irresponsible behavior of the client. Yet at the same time they must accept the client and maintain their involvement with him or her. In other words, they should reject the client's irresponsible behavior while accepting him or her as a person. The emphasis is on behavior. The counselor praises the client for responsible behavior and disapproves of irresponsible behavior. Even better is when the client judges his or her own behavior and categorizes it as responsible or irresponsible. Counseling is directed toward making the client behave responsibly, not necessarily toward making him or her happy. However, if behaviors become more responsible, self-regard is likely to follow.

> **Teaching.** The counselor teaches the client better ways to fulfill his or her needs within the limits set by reality. The counselor focuses on the client's present life, his or her behavior, interests, hopes, fears, opinions, values, and personal ideas of right and wrong. The counselor will talk about new horizons, try to expand the client's range of interests, and try to make him or her aware of life beyond his or her difficulties.

Any topic may be discussed: work, sports, books, movies, hobbies, finances, health, marriage, sex, or religion. The aim is to let the client test his or her ideas against those of the counselor and thereby learn what is responsible. The debates with a counselor who occasionally admits that he or she is wrong and who changes his or her opinions set a good model for the client to follow.

The counselor looks for the client's strong points and responsible behaviors and tries to expand these areas. The counselor never allows the client to make excuses. In doing so, the counselor focuses on the present. The past cannot be changed and is all too often used as an excuse by clients.

The counselor prefers to ask *what* the client is doing rather than *why* he or she is acting in this manner. The reasons for behavior are not important. The reality of what the client is doing and its consequences, however, are crucial. The client must learn to consider how this action will help him or her.

After clients have admitted their responsibility, and after they have learned responsible ways, their symptoms and problems should abate. They are now fulfilling their needs responsibly. To hold a client to a responsible course of action may make him or her angry, just as children get angry with their parents. But closeness to others through love and discipline helps them to gain self-respect. Discipline means love. It tells the individual, "I care enough about you to force you to act in a better way." Children who have laissez-faire parents, for example, often grow up feeling unloved. We learn to be responsible through our involvements with other responsible people, preferably loving parents who love us, discipline us, and permit us to try out our newly acquired responsibilities as soon as we feel able. The counselor tries to play a similar role.

Reality Therapy can be used for individual or group counseling. It has been used in private practice, with children, with delinquents and psychiatric patients, and with schoolchildren in the classroom. When it is used in institutions, the program must be total. The staff must be involved in the program and educated in Reality Therapy, and this means the professional staff as well as the custodial staff—everyone. Education, privileges, and all the other components of the institutional program must be tied into the Reality Therapy program.

The Techniques in Action

Cohen and Sordo (1984) presented several vignettes of Reality Therapy in action. Here are just a few:

> **Involvement**. David was arrested for stealing a car. He admitted to his probation officer that he had stolen the car, driven without a license, and wrecked the vehicle. He stressed that he had learned his lesson. He was married and had a baby daughter, and he pledged to begin a new life, stay away from criminal involvement, and get a steady job. The probation officer took out a pad and began to write down David's words, asking him to repeat them and speak more slowly. David was suspicious, but the probation officer explained that they would eventually work out a treatment plan and that it was very important that they both remember exactly how David had stated his goals. At the next meeting, the probation officer read out the goals as stated by David at the earlier session. David was curious, and, in response to David's questions, the probation officer began to explain the principles of Reality Therapy. The involvement process was underway.

Rejection of Irresponsible Behavior. Jacqueline was 24 years old and unmarried, with an eight-year-old daughter. She was a successful prostitute with a high-level clientele. During each counseling session, Jacqueline defended her lifestyle. She viewed her work as a type of social work, helping the lonely and providing a sexual outlet to frustrated men. She never used drugs or alcohol. The counselor noted that she came regularly to the counseling sessions, but he had been unable to get her to reevaluate her behavior and lifestyle. Finally at one session, he said that if it was so good to be a prostitute, then he assumed she would like her daughter to become one. At that point she broke down and cried. She could not continue the session, and the counselor walked outside with her where she hailed a taxi. At the next session, she was ready to begin planning a different life.

Joseph was 18 years of age. He talked about his father's death in a car crash before he was born, the series of foster homes he had been placed in, and the three years he spent in an institution for the retarded despite his above-average intelligence. What could the social worker expect of him? The social worker spoke toughly but warmly. He explained that he was not prepared to treat Joseph as an unfortunate child, even though his childhood had been terrible. He would limit their conversations to what was happening now and what could happen in the future. Joseph would have to find others to talk to about his past. The past had happened. The future could be improved. By the end of the session, Joseph had agreed to a plan for change.

Commitment to the Plan. Danny had just been released from his third prison term for burglary and was meeting with his parole officer, with whom he already had a good relationship. They agreed to work on three aspects of life: work, family, and abiding by the law. They drew up formal contracts. Danny would begin work at an appliance repair shop, even though he was not pleased with it. He agreed not to leave the job unless he found a better one. He agreed to spend his spare time with his wife except to play basketball at a community center. Finally, Danny would try to develop friendly relations with the local police. The three tasks were detailed and weekly contracts drawn up. The parole officer visited Danny's employer and his wife and the local police station regularly. The parole officer praised Danny to his employer and his wife when he fulfilled the contracts, which increased Danny's self-esteem. He began to be proud of his success. Danny honored his commitments for two years, during which time they were extended to other areas of his life. Eventually, Danny was given an early discharge from parole.

The classic application of Reality Therapy was set up by Glasser (1965) at the Ventura School for Girls in California. Girls committed to this institution had a history of delinquency and had failed in less restrictive juvenile probation placements. The Ventura School was the last stop before commitment to an adult prison, and the school represented their last chance for rehabilitation. The girls generally stayed at the school for six to eight months, a year at the most.

The school had three programs. The custodial program ensured that the girls could not escape. The treatment program was based on Reality Therapy. The counselors who were responsible for the treatment also worked with the other staff of the school to train them in the principles of Reality Therapy to ensure that everyone at the school was consistent with the philosophy. The school program organized academic, vocational, and recreational programs.

All girls had a full daily schedule. Because everyone at the school was trained in Reality Therapy and was concerned with the girls' progress, the treatment program was a total one. For example, all of the staff discouraged irresponsible behavior. They provided warmth and affection, together with discipline. If a girl improved enough to be released, she returned to the community. If not, she was transferred to another institution.

In line with the tenets of Reality Therapy, the staff showed no interest in the history of the girls, only in the present. The girls were held responsible for their behavior. Throughout their stay at the school, they were kept informed of the evaluations of them that were made by the staff. Girls who acted irresponsibly were excluded from the program and housed in a special discipline cottage, which had its own daily program. Of the 400 girls at the school, typically one or two girls were in the discipline cottage at any one time for long periods (several months) and a dozen or so were there temporarily (a couple of days to a couple of weeks).

One can hardly miss the element of **confrontation** in these various examples, and Reality Therapy certainly allows for that. However, the model also stressed involvement and respect for clients, a quality that has sometimes been overlooked in correctional uses of both Reality Therapy and GGI. The skill of knowing when and how to confront is a delicate one. Counselors must confront in ways that do not destroy client trust or self-respect. Unfortunately, the history of corrections offers too many examples of programs that took the prerogative to confront to abusive extremes. Certain instances of Reality Therapy-like strategies and GGI (e.g., Synanon and Daytop Village during the late 1970s) are now more likely to be presented as case studies of ethically flawed approaches to treatment than as models of "best practice." Verbal attack sessions were perhaps most poignant, in sessions referred to as "the game" or "the haircut"—two practices that have since been called into question (see Deitch & Zweben, 1984). None of this is to say that counselors avoid confrontation in corrections—they do not. But there are correct and incorrect uses of confrontation. As noted above, more recent models have rewritten these approaches to place more emphasis on "mutual self help" and cognitive skills, and to assure that counselors and peers use confrontation in an appropriate manner (Wexler, 1995).

Evaluations of the effectiveness of Reality Therapy in corrections were equivocal and programs at Ventura and Synanon were never adequately evaluated. Currently, most of the writing on Reality Therapy pertains to its use in educational rather than correctional settings. Moreover, the strategy has evolved somewhat since the 1960s (Lennon, 2000) with contemporary approaches focusing more on the choices made between behavioral options and the choice process itself (Glasser, 2000).

Conclusion

Group and milieu therapy have grown in popularity as the preferred mode of treatment for offenders. There are several benefits. First, they are economical. In times when funding for agencies and institutions is kept to a minimum, the psychological services are often among the first programs to be cut. Treating offenders in groups permits a counselor to assist more offenders in a limited time span than does individual treatment.

Group and milieu therapy have certain advantages for the treatment of offenders. As we pointed out, counselors sometimes struggle to completely understand the mindset and attitude of the offender. Other offenders can supplement the counselor's knowledge. Offenders who are further along in treatment often have an accurate awareness of what the newly admitted offender is thinking and feeling, and they can encourage his or her movement into the next stages of the treatment process.

Furthermore, it makes good sense to extend the treatment part of institutionalization beyond a mere hour or two each week. If an offender goes to see a counselor for one session each week, what happens to him or her during the rest of the week? Typically he or she interacts with other offenders and institutional staff in ways that are not supportive of the counseling goals and that may often be antagonistic to those goals. Milieu therapy and therapeutic communities ensure that the total environment is structured in ways that support rehabilitative goals and processes. We would expect, therefore, a greater impact on the offender than time-limited counseling carried out for an hour or so each week.

As a result, in group and milieu counseling, pragmatic and counseling aims may come together to support the best rehabilitation programs that have been established.

We should note, however, that there are dangers in such programs. As long as those who organize and supervise these programs have decided on appropriate goals and have hired and trained competent staff to implement these goals, then the programs will probably be reasonably effective. But group and milieu therapy can become oppressive, forcing people to conform to goals and ideals that are not their own. When used in these contexts, the programs may be called "re-education" by the totalitarian staff and "brainwashing" by their opponents. Thus, in looking at programs using some forms of group and milieu therapy, we must be alert for staff members who may have subverted the original goals of the program and introduced non-therapeutic elements.

Key Concepts and Terms

Adult ego state	paraphrasing
catharsis	Parent ego state
Child ego state	Person-Centered Therapy
conditional positive regard	Positive Peer Cultures
confrontation	psychodrama
congruence	Reality Therapy
ego state	therapeutic community
empathic understanding	transactions
game	Transactional Analysis
genuine	treatment effect
Guided Group Interaction	unconditional positive regard
milieu therapy	

Discussion Questions

1. Why is group counseling successful, and how does it differ from individual counseling?

2. What are the disadvantages of group counseling? That is, what can you get from individual counseling that you cannot get from group counseling?

3. What is meant by a curative property of group counseling? What are some examples of curative properties?

4. Define psychodrama. How would this technique be applied and on whom do you think it would be the most successful?

5. Describe the treatment process used by Guided Group Interaction.

6. Explain the purpose of therapeutic communities/milieu therapy.

7. Why does reality therapy focus on responsibility and behavior as a means for helping clients to meet core needs in their lives?

8. Why is it important for Reality Therapy to encourage clients to acknowledge core needs?

9. Should correctional clients ever be confronted? If so, when, and under what conditions?

10. How does one decide whether or not a given counseling program will work with offenders? Do we need to follow hunches?

Part Three

Offender Assessment, Diagnosis, and Classification

This book endeavors to present a wide array of individual and group correctional treatment strategies. Yet none of the strategies or techniques presented in this book will work with all offenders all of the time. Juvenile and adult offenders represent a highly heterogeneous group of individuals who differ from one other according to their needs, the danger they pose to others, their ability to cope with certain correctional environments, their amenability to specific counseling styles, their willingness to participate in correctional treatment programs, and their ability to relate to others. Failure to identify and to plan for these differences can be both dangerous and expensive to correctional agencies.

It is dangerous, for example, to fail to identify potentially violent correctional clients prior to their committing harmful acts against others. Often, agencies that do not classify for dangerousness can address the problem only after the fact, after an inmate has attacked a staff member or another inmate. In the face of such potentially violent conditions, a number of correctional systems have been under court mandates to classify inmate populations appropriately.

The next two chapters will discuss how this can be achieved by: (1) clinical identification of mentally ill offenders; and (2) systematic testing or screening of all correctional clients for risk potential.

Chapter 6 presents an important overview of the major categories of mental illness and mental retardation. In recent years correctional agencies have had to deal with a growing proportion of mentally retarded and mentally ill offenders. Such offenders can pose a serious threat to others if they are dangerous, or conversely may themselves be highly vulnerable to being victimized by other inmates. Often a mental health-related diagnosis will be a major factor in determining correctional placement. Carbonell and Perkins point out that although mental illness assessments and diagnoses must be formulated by licensed psychologists or psychiatrists, it is, nevertheless, extremely important for correctional staff to be trained to recognize symptoms. Otherwise, referrals to appropriate services do not occur in time to prevent tragedies or other problems.

A second strategy of identifying potentially dangerous or vulnerable inmates is discussed in Chapter 7. In contrast to the methods discussed in Chapter 6, Chapter 7 discusses classification strategies that are administered to all members of a correctional setting, usually upon admission. Risk assessment instruments, for example, are administered shortly after conviction and classify offenders according to high, medium, and low potential for absconding, violating conditions, and committing acts of aggression. Another method, psychological classification, separates inmates into groups that differ according to personality criteria. Some types are described as aggressive, some anxious, some vulnerable, and some are believed to be relatively trouble-free.

As noted above, failure to utilize appropriate classification strategies can result in higher costs to correctional agencies. Not all probationers, for example, need to be monitored on a weekly basis. Only high-risk offenders need intensive supervision. Others need not receive undue amounts of scarce staff resources. Similarly, neurotic inmates may respond differently to therapy than do aggressive, committed criminals. Van Voorhis observes that it makes good sense to assign clients to the treatment options that best fit their needs and psychological characteristics. The alternative, treating offenders as if they are all alike, often creates a situation in which the program is not as successful as it could be. Simply put, the successes of clients who are assigned correctly may be canceled out by failures of the clients who are incorrectly assigned, but who nevertheless might have succeeded in another type of program.

Chapter 6

Diagnosis and Assessment of Criminal Offenders

Joyce L. Carbonell and Robin Perkins

Introduction

Mental health assessments attempt to answer questions about how and why people think, feel, and behave in different ways. Such assessments try to describe how an individual copes with stress, perceives a stimulus or event, how he or she may feel emotionally at the present time, what kinds of concerns or interests he or she may have, his or her ability to pay attention or concentrate on a given task, his or her ability to remember different events that have occurred recently or in the past, how he or she relates to other people, and his or her ability to solve problems or think about different issues. While these are the general purposes of assessments, they are very similar to the diagnosis and assessment issues that arise when dealing with criminal offenders. An offender may be assessed before trial, after trial, while incarcerated, or when on parole. The questions range from traditional issues concerning intellect and emotional functioning that are relevant to an offender's functioning while incarcerated, to psycho-legal issues such as insanity and competency.

Assessments, no matter what the purpose, are snapshots of an individual at a given time. While assessments can provide information about an individual's underlying personality or intelligence, which is less subject to change over time, they can also reflect how the individual is thinking, feeling, and functioning at the time that he or she takes the test.

Think about a snapshot that shows a smiling young man dressed in prison garb. By looking at the picture we can say that the man appeared happy at the time the picture was taken, although we do not know why he was happy. In a similar way, an assessment can tell you that individuals may feel distressed, depressed, anxious, fearful, or angry at the time that they were assessed, but it might not apply to how they felt the week prior to or after the assessment. Such assessments are considered to be **dynamic**. That is, they can change over time.

Other assessments, however, are more stable. For example, if the photo shows that the man has a beard, it would probably be safe to say that he had a beard before the picture was taken. Depending on the length of his beard, we may feel comfortable making a statement regarding how long he had the beard. Similarly, if he has green eyes, we would assume that his eyes were green before and after the picture. In the same manner, some assessments provide information regarding an individual's underlying style of relating to the world, including such things as how this person relates to society as a whole, his or her tendency to abuse drugs or alcohol, his or her style of solving problems, and other issues concerning this person's basic personality style. These assessments are called **static assessments,** because they do not change much, if at all, over time.

If the one snapshot of the young man can tell us something about that moment in time, then it is easy to see how actually knowing the man might provide even more information. For example, if you knew him you could tell the photographer that the reason behind his happiness was that he had just been granted early release. Thus, the daily information that you observe, combined with the evaluation performed by the mental health professional, can give a more complete picture than either would alone.

In summary, assessments by mental health professionals attempt to answer questions about how and why people think, feel, and behave in different ways. They do this by providing information about how the individual being tested was feeling, thinking, and functioning at the time that the assessment was administered and by integrating this information with the daily observations provided by the correctional counselor or other staff.

Many problems that occur in correctional settings may actually increase the need of a mentally disturbed person for mental health services (American Bar Association, 1989). It is important for correctional counselors, case managers, and other staff to be able to recognize certain signs and symptoms and to use this information to make appropriate referrals. Although not all types of mental illness can be discussed in this chapter, we will cover the major categories and use three case examples to illustrate. As we move through the chapter we will refer to these inmates as we explain how assessment works. The three inmates are:

> James, a 19-year-old white male who burglarized a bakery with several other slightly older males, is serving his sentence in a state institution. Other than some minor driving violations, this is his first encounter with the criminal justice system. James appears to others to be very quiet and mostly a loner. He does not ask many questions and answers others with brief replies. He has frequent

minor rule infractions and has trouble adjusting when the prison routine changes. He is often the subject of practical jokes and at times lashes out at others.

Marianna, a 30-year-old Hispanic female, is in jail. She and her husband have been accused of importing cocaine into the country. The jail staff notes that she has not been eating and seems depressed. Her attorney has raised questions regarding her competency to stand trial.

Horace is a 45-year-old black male who is in his fourth year of imprisonment, having been convicted of second-degree murder. He is viewed as "strange" by the other inmates and staff, and he believes that he has special powers. Although he is not generally a management problem, he does become testy whenever the prison routine is altered for any reason.

The Role of the Correctional Staff

Correctional staff can play an important role in the assessment of inmates and probationers by serving as sources of information for the mental health professional. As noted earlier, the mental health professional may see the offender for only a brief period, compared to the correctional staff or probation officers who may see the offender numerous times over the course of many months. They will know important things about the inmate that will aid in a mental health assessment and they may be the first person who suspects that the offender needs assessment and possibly treatment. Thus, it is the observation and intervention of correctional personnel that frequently lead to assessment and treatment for the offender. In deciding to refer an offender for a mental health assessment, it is important to start with what you already know, and what you know is what you have observed.

Correctional staff members are in a unique position to observe inmate behavior, because they have the opportunity to interact with and see the inmate in a variety of situations and contexts. This opportunity to observe allows the correctional staff to gather important information about the inmate's behavior that can assist mental health professionals in making a mental health assessment. Correctional officials play a crucial role, and their ability to observe and communicate accurately is of great importance. They must know what is important information to communicate to the mental health professional and how to communicate that information.

A common problem with observation is that observers tend to make assumptions about what they see and report their assumptions rather than the behavior of the person observed (Eysenck & Eysenck, 1983). Another way of thinking about this is to realize that many people report their interpretation of events, rather than describe the event itself. In addition, people tend to merge information from an event they witnessed with information they learned later, thus making their final report less reliable (Loftus & Palmer, 1974). When asked to report on what they observed, the information that is reported is a combination of the observed information and the subsequent information.

Inmate James, who was described earlier, does not make eye contact. One staff member describes him as sullen, and another staff member reports that he is shy and withdrawn. Both have seen the same behavior, but they are reporting their interpretation of the behavior, not the behavior itself. At the same time, the person who describes James as sullen because he does not make eye contact may overhear someone else indicate that James does not pay attention to instructions, and the officer may add this to his or her description even though it is not a behavior the officer has observed. It is the description of observed behavior that is the most important to communicate to the mental health professional.

A description of Horace would be more useful if it described the things that he did and said, rather than simply stating that he is strange, because this does not convey any specific information. In fact, labels sometimes tell us more about the person using them than they do about the person being labeled. Although you might believe that Marianna is depressed, it is important to note what she is doing or not doing that has led you to that belief.

In general, it is better to provide too much information rather than leave out pieces that might be important. So when in doubt, pass on the information. Be as specific as possible about what you have observed. Ask yourself the following questions about the behavior that you wish to describe:

1. How often does the behavior occur? Is it a daily event or does it only occur several times a week?

2. Does it occur only in certain contexts, like at work or in the housing unit?

3. Does it involve only certain people, such as other inmates or staff?

4. When does it occur? Does it happen only after phone calls or visits? Does it happen at other times, too?

Reporting your specific observations is the most helpful approach. In the case of James, reporting that James does not make eye contact, instead of reporting that James does not pay attention when addressed, is a more accurate report of what you have actually seen. With Marianna it would be helpful to describe her crying in terms of how often and when, and report her statements regarding her wish to die. For Horace, rather than noting that he is strange, you could describe his statements about aliens and obtain copies of the writings he has been doing regarding his alien friends.

Because there is such a wide variety of behavior possible, it will help to know something about the major diagnostic categories that are used by mental health professionals. The next section will describe a few of the major categories that are listed in the *Diagnostic and Statistical Manual of Mental Disorders*, Fourth Edition, Text Revision, generally known as the DSM-IV-TR (American Psychiatric Association, 2000).

The DSM-IV-TR

The **DSM-IV-TR** is the "bible" of mental health diagnostics. Although the correctional counselor or case manager is not expected to diagnose, it helps to know basic information about the major mental health categories. The DSM-IV-TR begins with a cautionary statement, noting that the criteria are offered as guidelines and that to use the criteria properly requires "specialized clinical training that provides both a body of knowledge and clinical skills" (2000:xxxvii). Although armchair diagnoses are common, they are frequently incorrect. Mislabeling may cause numerous problems in the correctional setting for both the offender and the staff.

In addition, it is important to remember that although the DSM-IV-TR allows mental health personnel to use labels to put people into categories, there is a great deal of overlap between categories, and many people have multiple diagnoses. Because there are numerous criteria for each diagnosis and a person does not have to meet all of the criteria to be diagnosed as having a certain problem, people with the same diagnoses may look quite different from one another. For example, if a person must have three of nine symptoms to be diagnosed with the disorder, two different people could each have three of the symptoms, but have completely different symptoms. In spite of these problems, diagnostic categories provide important information and assist in developing treatment plans.

There are 16 major diagnostic classes in the DSM-IV-TR, but only a few will be covered here. In addition, there is a category for "other conditions that may be a focus of clinical attention." The DSM-IV-TR is a multiaxial system in which people are diagnosed along several different dimensions, or axes. Axis I, for example describes clinical disorders and Axis II describes personality disorders and mental retardation. The other axes relate to general medical conditions and social and environmental stressors. Although there is not room to discuss all of the categories of mental disorders, those described here will be those that are of most importance in correctional settings because they are the most common, or because they are the most disruptive to the management and security of a correctional setting. Keep in mind that many people will have more than one diagnosis, and that in spite of diagnostic criteria, there can still be disagreement about what diagnosis best fits a person.

Mood Disorders

Mood disorders are the common cold of mental health, but can range in intensity from mild to severe. While it is common for people to experience feelings of depression at times and elation at other times, in a mood disorder, these feelings are more intense and disrupt daily functioning for a longer period. These disorders include the depressive disorders, such as major depression and dysthymia, manic disorders, and the bipolar disorders.

A person with **major depressive disorder** experiences a depressed mood nearly every day; episodes of crying; lack of interest or pleasure in almost all activities nearly every day; a lack of appetite or significant weight loss (or gain) without an attempt to diet; an inability to sleep or a constant desire for sleep; agitation or feelings of fatigue and lethargy; feelings of worthlessness or guilt; problems with thinking, concentration, attention, and memory; and recurrent thoughts of death or suicidal ideation. Some individuals who experience a severe episode of major depression may also experience some symptoms of psychosis.

A **dysthymic disorder** is also a depressive disorder but tends to be more chronic in duration. A person with dysthymia will appear to be chronically depressed and irritable, but not at the level of severity required for a diagnosis of depression. People who are dysthymic may complain of trouble sleeping, loss of appetite, problems with concentration and decision making, and low self-esteem.

While a depressive disorder is characterized by an experience of intense depression, a **manic disorder** is characterized by an experience of intense elation or sometimes an irritable mood. During a manic episode the individual experiences a period of elevated or irritable mood that lasts at least one week. The individual may experience feelings of grandiosity, a decreased need for sleep, pressured speech, a feeling that his or her thoughts are racing, difficulties with attention, physical or mental agitation, and an overinvolvement in activities that are experienced as pleasurable without regard to any risk involved. A **bipolar disorder** is one characterized by the occurrence of manic episodes and depressive episodes in alternation. It is easy to see, from this description, how an individual with a manic disorder or in a manic phase could become involved with the criminal justice system or have difficulties coping with incarceration.

Depression is a common mental health problem in correctional settings. Feelings of depression are frequently associated with losses, and incarceration generally involves a series of losses for the inmate. While some inmates will experience brief episodes of depression that will dissipate without intervention, any inmate who appears to have depressed or elevated moods that are more prolonged than is typical should be referred for mental health assessment. Marianna, who was discussed earlier, is an example of an inmate who should be referred for evaluation.

In Marianna's case, the correctional counselor noticed that she has not been eating and has appeared to be sad. This prompted further observation, which included checking on her sleeping habits and talking with her. The correctional staff on night shift reported that Marianna was awake most of the night crying. When the correctional counselor asked her how she was doing, she became very tearful and stated that she felt hopeless about her current situation. Although Marianna denied feeling suicidal, she stated that she wished she were dead. A referral was made to the mental health staff for further evaluation. The referral included what the inmate had said and what the counselor had observed, as well as what the correctional staff had observed.

Psychotic Disorders

Unlike mood disorders, some of which may occur in response to environmental variables, **psychotic disorders** are almost always pre-existing, although they may be exacerbated by the conditions of incarceration. Additionally, people on medication to control the symptoms of a psychotic disorder may not reveal this at the time of their arrest, and thus may come to a correctional setting without having had their medication for some time. An additional difference between psychotic and mood disorders is that mood disorders can be seen as extending along a continuum from a normal mood change to a pathological mood change, but psychoses are qualitatively, not quantitatively, different from normal behavior and feelings. Thus, while you may be able to describe a person as mildly depressed or severely depressed, you would not describe a person as "just a little psychotic."

Psychotic disorders are those in which the person has an impaired sense of reality. **Schizophrenia**, for example, is a psychotic disorder and one with which most people are familiar. Because many of the other psychotic disorders have symptoms in common with schizophrenia, schizophrenia will be used as the example for psychotic disorders. When they hear the term "schizophrenia," most people think of hallucinations (seeing, hearing, smelling, or feeling things that are not there) or delusions (having erroneous beliefs that involve a misinterpretation of an event or experience). These are called "positive" symptoms of schizophrenia and include other symptoms, such as disorganization in speech and behavior. The "negative" symptoms of schizophrenia include having flat affect; impairments in the ability to produce speech and thoughts; and what is called *avolition*, or problems in initiating activities. A person who is schizophrenic may have loose associations and thus may relate words or concepts that to others do not seem to be connected. They may engage in ritual-like behaviors, and their emotional responses may be incongruous to the situation. Although schizophrenics may be able to get along with others, it is difficult for them to establish relationships with others. Counselors and other inmates may not feel rapport or empathy with them. But in spite of the unusual nature of some of their behavior and symptoms, their behavior can vary greatly. While at times they may be incapable of carrying on a rational conversation, later they may be quite capable of writing a reasonable and well-written request for medical service (Kaplan & Sadock, 2000).

Horace is a good example of a person with schizophrenia who is in a correctional setting. Others see him as strange, and while he is not openly disliked, there is no one who is close to Horace. He is easily upset by small changes in routine because he has many small rituals each day that may go unnoticed by other people, but have great significance to Horace. Many of his requests and demands are incomprehensible to the staff because they involve his delusional beliefs about aliens and his own special powers. He is socially withdrawn and is frequently seen talking to himself or looking off into space, both of which may be the result of hallucinations. Most of Horace's problems occur when his schedule is disrupted or he interprets an action or incident in a delusional fashion, causing him to behave erratically in the eyes of others. Yet Horace is able to follow a schedule reasonably well, and at times has relatively normal conversations with his case manager. His case manager is aware of the problems he creates and took the opportunity to refer Horace during a relatively calm time when he was amenable to the referral.

It is important to be aware that a person who is psychotic acts on information that is not shared by others. As a result, he or she is seen as unpredictable. It is not useful to challenge their beliefs or their perceptual distortions. People who are delusional or psychotic are frequently frightened and suspicious of others. Perhaps the best approach is to neither confirm nor deny, but to listen and recognize what impact those beliefs or distortions may have on the inmate's behavior. If you make the mistake of pretending to believe the delusions or hallucinations, you then may be challenged as to why you are not acting on them. If you try to argue about such matters, you will only lose the cooperation of the inmate. As with Horace, it is easier to make the referral when the inmate is less overtly disturbed and more likely to cooperate. As the correctional counselor or case manager, you can provide the mental health staff with the description of the behaviors that have led to your concern. Because such behaviors are intermittent in nature, your ability to describe and report the actual behaviors is essential.

Mental Retardation

Mental retardation is not so much a specific disease as it is a concept (Gregory, 1987). Although mental retardation was traditionally thought of as having an intelligence quotient (IQ) score below a certain level, definitions today involve not only the IQ score, but include deficits in adaptive behavior and require that the retardation was apparent in the developmental years (APA, 2000; Grossman, 1983). For a person to be considered mentally retarded, their IQ score must be about 70 or below and be accompanied by deficits in adaptive behavior. A person with an IQ of 73 could be considered retarded if adaptive functioning is also poor, but a person with an IQ of 70 might not be described as retarded if his or her adaptive functioning is good. Because adaptive functioning refers to how effectively individuals cope with common life demands and how well they meet the standards of personal independence expected of someone in their age group, sociocultural background, and community setting (APA, 2000), a person with intellectual deficits will have difficulty coping with the demands of a correctional setting, be it jail, prison, or probation. This is complicated by the fact that most mentally retarded criminal defendants or inmates do not wish to be labeled as "stupid" and may develop ways of trying to hide their intellectual and adaptive deficits. A mentally retarded inmate may learn to survive in prison by being aggressive, because he or she cannot cope in other ways, having failed to master social and cognitive skills (Conley, Luckasson & Bouthilet, 1992).

The largest group of incarcerated people with retardation is likely to be in the mild mental retardation range. This category constitutes the largest group of people with mental retardation. At the high end of this range, people can generally learn basic literacy and vocational skills, while at the low end they may have more difficulty with learning basic academic and job skills. Even at the high end of this range, people with mental retardation will need support and guidance, particularly when their environment is stressful. Although some studies indicate that only about two percent of inmates are mentally retarded, others indicate that the prevalence of mental retardation in the prison population is approximately 10 percent (Smith et al., 1990). Even if the number of mentally retarded inmates in a given institution is small, the mentally retarded require more staff attention than other inmates and are more likely to be victimized (Denkowski & Denkowski, 1985). In addition to the two percent of those of who are mentally retarded, there is a larger group of inmates who fall into a category that has been called "marginally competent" (Gregory, 1987) and that are classified as having **borderline intellectual functioning** (APA, 2000). Borderline intellectual functioning is listed in the DSM-IV-TR as one of the "other conditions that may be a focus of clinical attention." These people may have significant adjustment problems, although their IQ scores do not identify them as retarded. As Gregory (1987) pointed out, in the past an IQ below 85 was considered mentally retarded, but the cutoff point was lowered to avoid stigmatizing many people who were able to make an adequate adjustment.

Given the problems that mental retardation can cause for both the offender and the staff, it is essential for correctional staff to identify inmates who may be retarded or marginally competent and are not receiving appropriate services. Identification of those with mental retardation is difficult because there is no specific personality or physical feature that always occurs with mental retardation. Some people functioning in the mentally retarded range are placid and others are aggressive and impulsive because they have poor communication skills and are unable to make their needs known (APA, 2000).

Although there are no personality characteristics that always identify a mentally retarded person, there are behavioral clues. Mentally retarded offenders may indicate that they understand a question or a command, but will be unable to repeat it back in their own words; they may have poor reading skills and use only simple words when communicating (Bowker, 1994). They may have trouble following complex directions or understanding abstract concepts, and they are more likely to be impressionable and thus be more easily victimized and manipulated. They may be slow to adjust to the routine of the institution and slow to adjust to any changes in the institutional routine.

James, whose case was described earlier, is an example of an inmate whose intellectual functioning should be evaluated. He has trouble following directions and does not verbalize well or frequently. He is the object of practical jokes, to which he responds with anger. As with many inmates who are mildly retarded, James is unlikely to reveal to his case counselor that he has a history of special education or that he has trouble reading. His poor writing skills make it difficult for him to make written requests, thus increasing his sense of frustration. Referring James for assessment would determine whether he is functioning at a low level and might assist in referring him to appropriate educational services that would enhance his ability to cope.

Personality Disorders

Personality can be thought of as an individual's ongoing style of relating to the world. This involves how an individual perceives events, relates to self and others, and copes with stress. The DSM-IV-TR defines **personality disorders** as ". . . an enduring pattern of inner experience and behavior that deviates markedly from the expectations of the individual's culture . . . This enduring pattern is inflexible and pervasive across a broad range of personal and social situations" (APA, 2000:686). Personality disorders begin in adolescence or early adulthood and lead to an impairment in functioning.

There are 11 different personality disorders, each with its own set of diagnostic criteria. These disorders are grouped into clusters based on common dimensions. Cluster A, the odd-eccentric cluster, contains the personality disorders of **paranoid personality disorder, schizoid personality disorder**, and **schizotypal personality disorder**. These disorders are characterized by a pervasive mistrust of others, a preference for isolation over social relationships, an inability to experience or display a wide range of emotions, a pervasive tendency to distort perceptions and information, odd and/or magical thinking, an unusual appearance, and behaviors that are eccentric or bizarre.

Cluster B, which covers the dramatic-emotional dimension, contains the diagnoses of **antisocial personality disorder, borderline personality disorder, histrionic personality disorder**, and **narcissistic personality dis-**

order. In general, these disorders are marked by a disregard for the normal expectations of society or social relationships; a lack of empathy for others, or an inability to take on the perspective of another; impulsivity; irritability or mood swings; irresponsible behaviors; deceitfulness; interpersonal relationships that are very intense, unstable, and frequently violent; substance abuse; difficulties with controlling emotions or modulating emotional displays; a tendency to engage in self-destructive behaviors; a desire to be the center of attention at all times; and a sense of low self-worth that gets communicated as either grandiosity or as self-degradation.

The last cluster, C, which covers the anxious-fearful dimension, includes the personality disorders of **avoidant personality disorder, dependent personality disorder,** and **obsessive-compulsive personality disorder**. These disorders have common features that include social inhibition, feelings of inadequacy, fear of rejection or ridicule, an excessive need to be taken care of, difficulty with making autonomous decisions or independent actions, fear of abandonment or being alone, a preoccupation with details or organization, a tendency to be inflexible in values, and a desire for perfectionism that interferes with an ability to perform.

Inmates with personality disorders present many problems in institutional settings. People with personality disorders may be incarcerated due to their difficulties with societal expectations and with making good decisions, and the same behaviors that led to their incarceration are likely to be repeated in the institutional setting. In general, their ability to cope with stressful events is very poor and their judgment tends to worsen as their stress levels increase. Inmates with personality disorders may be manipulative, impulsive, and may actually harm themselves or make a suicidal gesture when angry or unable to cope with stress. Frequently, these inmates come to the attention of correctional staff when they break the rules or harm themselves out of anger or an attempt to manipulate for some privilege. When these types of behaviors are present with a persistent pattern, or any time an inmate is in danger of harming self or others, a referral to a mental health professional is warranted. It is useful to keep in mind that people with personality disorders are very difficult and frustrating to deal with. While it is common to find this group of people frustrating, this frustration should not stand in the way of referral to a mental health professional for assessment.

Substance Abuse and Dependence

Substance abuse and dependence is a broad category that can include abuse of alcohol, prescription drugs, or street drugs. A person is considered **substance dependent** if he or she continues to use a substance in spite of significant problems related to its use. The DSM-IV-TR describes the criteria for substance dependence as having developed tolerance for the substance and needing more of the substance to achieve the desired effect, having withdrawal associated with cessation of use, being unable to cut down on use, and taking the substance in larger amounts over time than was intended. In addition, substance dependence leads to a decrease in other social, occupational, and recreational activities, as well as an increase in the amount of time spent in activities surrounding obtaining the drug.

A person can abuse substances without becoming dependent, and in that case they are considered under the category of **substance abuse** rather than dependence. Although they may not meet the criteria for dependence because they have not had withdrawal or developed tolerance, people with substance abuse problems use substances in dangerous situations and continue to use substances in spite of persistent problems caused by such use. Having repetitive substance-related legal problems is also considered one of the symptoms of substance abuse. Although the DSM-IV-TR divides substance-related disorders by the type of substance being abused, many people abuse more than one substance and may also have another disorder in addition to their substance abuse. One substance may be used to counteract the effect of others. Regardless of whether the person is considered dependent or an abuser, the long-term use of some substances can cause serious medical problems and may cause organic brain damage, leading to more problems with day-to-day functioning. Thus, a substance abuser who has ceased using drugs may still be affected by previous use.

The Bureau of Justice Statistics (2003) indicates that drug users have a greater involvement in crime than nondrug users, and that they are unlikely to have received treatment. Heavy alcohol use is also common among arrestees. Thus, a correctional counselor or case manager will face a large number of inmates with histories of drug use and a low likelihood of having received treatment for that drug abuse. Because of the profound impact of substance abuse and dependence on an offender's behavior, it is important for correctional counselors and other staff to be aware of the various signs of use of different drugs and the types of behaviors that are associated with each. Although treatment of substance disorders is difficult, structured programs are of help to some abusers and referrals for evaluation should be made for those who appear to be current abusers or those who have histories of drug abuse and appear to be adversely affected by the long-term effects of their abuse.

Suicide

Suicide is not a diagnostic category, but it is an important issue for correctional counselors because of the increased incidence of suicide in correctional settings. Suicide can be associated with almost any category of mental disturbance, including substance abuse. Some categories of mental disorder may increase the probability of suicide, but one cannot rule out the possibility of suicide based on the presence or absence of a particular disorder.

Suicide is of particular concern in jails. Synopses of studies of jail suicides indicate that it is the number one cause of death in jails and that the suicide rate in jails is considerably higher than in the general population (Carr, Hinkle & Ingram, 1991; Winkler, 1992). The rate of suicide in prisons also seems to be higher than that in the general population, but not as disproportionately high as it is in jails, and it may vary depending on whether the prison is state or federal (Kennedy, 1984). Kennedy (1984) suggests that suicide may be a reaction to the depression and anxiety that accompany incarceration and suggests that the anxiety surrounding impending release may also be a risk factor.

While there is no single indicator that always will alert the mental health professional to suicide, most people who commit suicide have spoken about it to someone. Statements regarding feeling hopeless and helpless should be a cause for concern and referral for evaluation. In addition, some offenders will give away possessions before a suicide and will attempt to put their affairs in order. The initial period of incarceration appears to be the time of the highest risk, particularly for first-time offenders and for intoxicated inmates. In prisons, loss of a relationship, such as a divorce or a break-up, is also associated with suicide (Arboleda-Florez & Holley, 1989).

All suicidal statements and attempts should be taken seriously. Although some argue that suicide attempts and statements are manipulative actions, they can have serious consequences because people can die accidentally or deliberately kill themselves. Perhaps it is useful to remember that someone who is willing to risk injury and death to get attention is in need of intervention. Although depressed people are at risk for suicide, so are many people who do not show signs of depression. Given the potential seriousness of a suicide attempt or a completed suicide, it is essential to refer for assessment those who have expressed suicidal ideation either through verbalizations or behavior.

Techniques of Assessment and Diagnosis

Once the offender is referred to a mental health professional, a variety of techniques may be used to evaluate the problem. The nature of the problem, the characteristics of the inmate (e.g., reading and attention span), and the training of the mental health professional dictate what type of assessment will be done. A psychiatrist is likely to conduct an interview and take a history. A clinical psychologist is also likely to conduct an interview and take a history. Psychologists are also likely to use a variety of assessment instruments, depending on the nature of the presenting problem. Two of the major categories of testing instruments used are those that evaluate intelligence and those that evaluate personality characteristics. The interpretation of most assessment instruments depends on information collected during the interview, so interviews will be discussed first.

Interviews

The interview is the basic method for collecting background information about a person. How the interview is conducted depends on the orientation of the interviewer (e.g., behavioral, psychoanalytic) and the purpose of the interview. Interviews, although they vary greatly, generally elicit biographical information, information about current life experiences, symptom information, and social history, thus helping the examiner place the test results in the context of the offender's life. Although very useful, interviews are generally nonstandardized and thus different interviewers might elicit different information from the same interviewee. To help alleviate this problem, several structured interviews have been developed and are used to aid in diagnosis. These structured interviews are sometimes structured around the diagnostic system and lead to a diagnosis. For example, the Structured Clinical Interview for DSM-IV (SCID) (First et al., 1997) gives detailed instructions to the interviewer about what to ask and indicates what additional questions to ask, depending on the answer to the previous question. In addition to the SCID, there are other structured interviews, such as the Schedule for Affective Disorders (SADS) (Endicott & Spitzer, 1978).

Intelligence Testing

Intelligence is a concept that has long been debated and opinions range from those who believe that it is a measure of genetic potential to those who believe that it is simply a measure of acculturation. David Wechsler, who developed one of the most widely used intelligence tests, believed that that intelligence is "global in nature and represents a part of the greater whole of personality" (Groth-Marnat, 2003). Evaluations to determine an IQ score take many different forms and range from group-administered tests that may not require any writing or reading, to an individually administered test. It is important to remember that the tests alone do not classify a person as mentally retarded, because there must also be a deficit in adaptive functioning. Although there are measures of adaptive functioning available, they are generally of little use in correctional settings because the behaviors assessed are not relevant to life in an institution.

The "group" tests such as the Revised Beta Examination: Second Edition (1978) and the Shipley Institute for Living Scale (Shipley, 1983) are useful for screening, but do not tell us many specifics about an offender. An individual test gives the examiner more opportunity to observe the inmate and it may help the examiner to understand why the inmate has performed in a certain way. Does the offender work slowly or experience difficulty in comprehending the instructions? Was the offender ill on the day the test was taken and not functioning well? Or was the offender just unwilling to cooperate? However, in spite of these issues, group tests serve an important function and provide a good estimate of intelligence scores for most inmates.

Individual tests of intelligence are more costly to administer, but provide more information about an individual. The **Wechsler Adult Intelligence Scales—III (WAIS-III)** (Wechsler, 1997) is the standard assessment instrument for adults. It is a multidimensional test and assesses many different abilities. It takes an hour or more to administer, but provides the examiner with a detailed picture of a person's strengths and weaknesses. A person's score on the WAIS—III compares the individual to the average person and gives us a picture of how that individual looks compared to others in the same age group. Information about an offender's skills and weaknesses can help correctional staff in finding the appropriate vocational, counseling, and job placements for the offender.

Intelligence tests do not measure the person's academic achievement, and in many institutions, academic testing is given by the education service when inmates enter the prison. The intelligence score is a useful piece of information to use in conjunction with the academic testing, because it helps to predict what the person's academic achievement could be with the appropriate educational assistance.

Personality Tests

Personality tests are usually divided into two major categories—projective and objective tests. **Projective tests**, such as the Rorschach (Exner, 1993), are not as commonly used as objective personality tests, like the **Minnesota Multiphasic Personality Inventory 2 (MMPI-2)** (Butcher et al., 1989; Graham, 2000) because they are time-consuming to administer, score, and interpret. Projective tests must be administered individually and scored individually, making them less attractive in settings where large numbers of people need to be evaluated or screened. Because there are valid and reliable group-administered instruments for personality, projective tests are not common in institutional settings where large numbers of people may need to be evaluated. There are many other projective tests, such as the **Thematic Apperception Test (TAT)**, projective drawings (Groth-Marnat, 1990), and a variety of incomplete sentence blanks. All of them are considered projective because they present the subject with an ambiguous stimulus upon which he or she must "project" an idea or an image.

The MMPI-2 is the most commonly used objective test instrument. The MMPI-2 has 567 true/false questions and requires that an offender be able to read at the sixth grade level or comprehend the material when presented on audiotape. It has 13 basic scales, three of which assess validity and 10 of which are clinical indices. In addition, it has many supplementary scales to evaluate such factors as drug and alcohol abuse. The MMPI-2 and its predecessor, the MMPI, have been widely used in correctional settings. A typology was developed for use on inmates based on the MMPI (Megargee & Bohn, 1979). It has been updated for the MMPI-2 (Megargee et al., 2001). The typology has enjoyed widespread use and success in correctional settings. It provides an efficient means of classifying offenders into groups that provide information about their institutional and personal adjustment.

Finally, the **Millon Multiaxial Clinical Inventory (MMCI-III)** (Millon, 1997) is a brief self-report inventory of 175 questions. However, it is designed to be used exclusively with populations that exhibit psychological symptoms or are actively involved in therapy. Thus, it is not useful as a screening instrument.

Legal Issues and Mental Health Assessment

The purpose of a mental health assessment is to provide a picture of a person's mental state and his or her current level of functioning. While these assessments are useful, they do not always relate directly to what could be called psycho-legal issues—issues where psychology and the law overlap. Decisions about legal issues such as competency to stand trial, insanity, and diminished responsibility almost always involve the input of mental health professionals, but simply diagnosing an offender does not necessarily provide an adequate answer for questions concerning these issues. In fact, a diagnosis may provide little useful information. There is an imperfect "fit" between legal issues and diagnostic issues. As noted in the DSM-IV-TR:

> In most situations, the clinical diagnosis of a DSM-IV mental disorder is not sufficient to establish the existence for legal purposes of a "mental disorder," "mental disability," "mental disease," or "mental defect." In determining whether an individual meets a specified legal standard (e.g., for competence, criminal responsibility, or disability) additional information is usually required beyond that contained in the DSM-IV diagnosis. This might include information about the individual's functional impairments and how these impairments affect the particular abilities in question. It is precisely because impairments, abilities, and disabilities vary widely within each diagnostic category that assignment of a particular diagnosis does not imply a specific level of impairment or disability (APA, 2000:xxxiii).

In spite of this imperfect fit, mental health and the law are inextricably intertwined. The **insanity defense**, although frequently discussed and frequently the subject of television movies, is rare and is used in only about one of every 200 cases, and it is rarely successful (Wrightsman, 1991). To be found **not guilty by reason of insanity (NGRI)** one must meet specific criteria, and those criteria vary from state to state. However, the general notion behind NGRI is that the offender lacks the appropriate mental state to be convicted, because he or she has not chosen to do wrong; the offender has done so as a result of mental illness. Guidelines for NGRI generally specify that the person must be unable to appreciate the wrongfulness of the act or could not conform his or her conduct to the requirements of the law. Thus, a diagnosis alone does not answer this question. The mental health professional can, however, offer information about a person's functioning and how that person might react in various situations that, combined with the diagnostic information, can assist the court in reaching an appropriate decision.

Because the notion of NGRI is disturbing to many people, other psycho-legal remedies have been offered. In spite of the rarity and lack of success of the NGRI defense, highly publicized cases may make the general public believe that many "guilty" people (people who committed acts but without the appropriate mental state) go free. A solution to this concern is the **guilty but mentally ill** verdict, in which a person can be found guilty in spite of his or her mental state, but also receive treatment in a prison or forensic hospital. It is a compromise position that allows the offender to be found guilty, while, in theory, maximizes the probability that this person will receive treatment. This issue may be of more concern to correctional staff, because people with a guilty but mentally ill verdict will, in many cases, be sent to a prison setting, where their mental illness may be a barrier to adjustment.

The other major issue in the psycho-legal arena is **competency to stand trial**. The issue in competency is basically whether the defendant can understand the charges and the proceedings well enough to assist in his or her own defense. A person who cannot assist in his or her own defense cannot be tried because of the possibility of not receiving a fair trial. Because a person cannot be tried in his or her absence, a person who is "mentally absent" from the proceedings cannot be tried either. There are many diagnoses that are relevant to this issue, including retardation and psychotic disorders, but once again they only provide information about the diagnosis and functioning level. The final decision on these psycho-legal issues is always in the hands of the judge or the jury.

While NGRI refers to the mental state of the defendant at the time of the crime, competency refers to mental state at the time of the trial. In addition, NGRI has the finality of an acquittal, whereas competency can be reassessed. It is possible, in other words, for a defendant to be assessed as incompetent at one point and competent at another point, as with the case of a schizophrenic individual who becomes stabilized after receiving appropriate medications.

Overall, it is important to remember that insanity and competency are legal terms, and not mental health concepts. A person can be mentally ill and still be considered sane and competent. Although the converse could also be true, it is much less likely.

Conclusion

In summary, correctional personnel play an essential role in the timely and appropriate referral of offenders to mental health resources. The correctional counselor, the probation officer, and other correctional staff provide information about the inmate's day-to-day functioning and behavior, thus providing an important and necessary context in light of which the mental health professional can interpret the results of their assessment. By becoming familiar with the various diagnoses and their manifestations, correctional staff will be able to assist offenders in obtaining the appropriate services and provide valuable input to the mental health professional.

In addition to making referrals, the correctional counselor and others can use their understanding of the assessment process and the results to assist the offender in developing a better level of adjustment while incarcerated or on probation. Correctional counselors and staff are in a unique position to assist in the evaluation process and to use the results of that assessment. In summary, mental health evaluations are used to make decisions about offender placement, need for treatment, need for medication, and legal status, but they would be incomplete without the input of the correctional counselors and other staff who provide the context for the evaluation.

Key Concepts and Terms

antisocial personality disorder
avoidant personality disorder
bipolar disorder
borderline intellectual functioning
borderline personality disorder
competency to stand trial
dependent personality disorder
DSM-IV-TR
dynamic assesssments
dysthymic disorder
guilty but mentally ill
histrionic personality disorder
insanity defense
major depressive disorder
manic disorder
mental retardation
Millon Multiaxial Clinical Inventory-III
Minnesota Multiphasic Personality
    Inventory 2

mood disorders
narcissistic personality disorder
not guilty by reason of insanity (NGRI)
obsessive-compulsive personality
    disorder
paranoid personality disorder
personality disorders
projective tests
psychotic disorders
schizoid personality disorder
schizophrenia
schizotypal personality disorder
static assessments
substance abuse
substance dependent
Thematic Apperception Test
Wechsler Adult Intelligence Scales—III

Discussion Questions

1. Why is it important for correctional staff to have some knowledge of mental illness?

2. What is the difference between a static assessment and a dynamic assessment?

3. What types of problem behaviors warrant the referral of a correctional client to a psychologist/psychiatrist or mental health unit?

4. What types of mistakes should we seek to avoid in observing and reporting a correctional client's behavior to mental health officials?

5. What procedures are typically followed in diagnosing mental illness?

6. What behavioral symptoms indicate that an individual may be contemplating suicide?

7. Why is a diagnosis of mental illness not enough to secure a verdict of NGRI?

8. How is incompetence different from NGRI?

Chapter 7

An Overview of Offender Classification Systems

Patricia Van Voorhis

The previous chapter discussed the need to identify or diagnose mentally ill offenders in time to appropriately provide for their supervision and needs. In cases in which mental illness or mental retardation is suspected, offenders are referred to psychologists or psychiatrists or to a mental health unit for an in-depth assessment. In this chapter we again discuss offender assessments, but here we focus on assessment and classification procedures that are administered to all offenders within a given correctional unit.

To understand the need for such assessments, we must first appreciate that correctional clients are a highly heterogeneous group, with diverse treatment needs and security considerations. The task of classifying offenders according to risk factors, treatment needs, and other special considerations (e.g., mental and physical health) begins as soon as the offender begins to serve his or her sentence.

In recent years, **correctional classification** has been greatly aided by systematic assessment and testing procedures. Prior to the advent of agency-wide or program-wide classification, correctional classification was primarily a clinical process in which counselors and case managers based decisions on their professional judgment of an offender's dangerousness, treatment needs, treatment amenability, or likelihood of escaping or absconding. While their assessments sometimes may have been correct, critics faulted this process as time-consuming, inequitable, subjective, and discretionary (Bonta, 1996; MacKenzie, 1989). We also have learned that professional opinion alone is not as accurate as professional opinion supported by properly constructed and validated tests (Grove & Meehl, 1996).

Structured tests and procedures for classifying adult and juvenile offenders offer an alternative to the more subjective and open-ended use of professional judgment. A variety of correctional classification systems are available for security, custody, and treatment purposes. The administrative procedures and formats for each system are equally varied, ranging from behavioral checklists that staff complete after a brief period of observation to semi-structured interviews and paper-and-pencil tests.

The common points among all of the classification systems are:

1. They are usually administered to all offenders in a correctional institution or program, usually at the point of intake and at regular intervals thereafter;

2. They form the basis of a typology of offenders in the program, in which each "type" on the typology categorizes offenders according to similar needs or risk levels;

3. Some level of staff training is required to administer the system; and

4. The classification process is governed by agency policies that set forth uniform and efficient procedures, applying the same criteria to all offenders in an expeditious way.

Thus, offenders are classified into subgroups on a **typology**, and each subgroup is relatively homogeneous, whereas the institution or program population as a whole is heterogeneous. With the population now classified into homogeneous subgroups, correctional practitioners have a much-needed tool to assist them in predicting future behaviors, identifying needs, and planning treatment.

Purposes and Principles of Effective Classification

The systems described in this chapter were designed for a variety of organizational needs, and the purposes met by each classification system differ somewhat from system to system. Unfortunately, it is not unusual to find agencies using systems for the wrong purpose. For example, institutional systems typically do not predict new offenses in the community. "What do you want the classification system to do?" is a question that needs to be answered prior to selecting or constructing a classification system (Hardyman, Austin & Peyton, 2004).

Careful attention to some principles of classification and treatment will help to sort out some of this confusion and allow us to use correctional classification systems effectively (Andrews & Bonta, 2003). In summarizing a number of classification studies, Andrews, Bonta, and Hoge (1990) put forward the following principles of classification, which we will refer to frequently throughout this chapter.

The Risk Principle

At first glance, the **risk principle** speaks to a fundamental purpose of corrections: to protect society and to manage safe correctional populations. This, of course, is achieved by separating the dangerous from the vulnerable elements of a correctional population or assigning offenders to minimum-, medium-, or maximum-security institutions or community supervision levels on the basis of their predicted likelihood of recidivism, escape, or other misconduct (Clear, 1988; Levinson, 1988). Because few people cause more concern for the criminal justice system than the inmate who escapes, the parolee who commits a new offense, or the arrestee who fails to show for trial, we have a clear need to identify high-risk offenders. Public safety is widely perceived to be the most important purpose of correctional classification (Feeley & Simon, 1992; Van Voorhis & Presser, 2001).

In more recent years, however, the risk principle has come to have important implications for correctional rehabilitation as well. Research shows us that intensive correctional treatment programs are more successful with high- and medium-risk offenders than with low risk offenders. That is, in intensive treatment programs, higher-risk offenders are more likely to show greater reductions in recidivism (as a group) than less serious, low-risk offenders (Andrews et al., 1990; Bonta, Wallace-Capretta & Rooney, 2000; Lowenkamp & Latessa, 2002).

Your response to this observation might be, "Well of course, high-risk offenders have more 'room' for improvement!" But this is only part of the picture. The risk principle also notes that low-risk offenders tend to do more poorly in intensive treatment than if they had not been assigned to an intensive correctional intervention. Why is this the case? First, low-risk offenders have many prosocial attributes. Premature introductions to intensive correctional programming only serve to introduce them to antisocial role models who model criminal attitudes and behaviors. Especially in the case of institutional programs, such treatment also interferes with many of the very characteristics that makes these individuals low risk—family, education, employment, and prosocial associates.

Thus, the treatment implications of the risk principle are:

1. Identify high-, medium-, and low-risk offenders;

2. Direct intensive treatment efforts (not just intensive security) to high- and medium-risk offenders.

3. Think carefully about institutional placements (e.g., boot camps) or intensive treatment interventions for low-risk offenders.

The Needs Principle

In corrections, we have an ethical responsibility to address the basic needs of offenders. And in most correctional agencies, we view addressing a broad array of needs as a routine task of case management and counseling. Effective counselors or case managers will seek to determine what services an offender should receive, relative to housing, substance abuse services, job development, education, medical assistance, and mental health. Often they use objective needs assessments to identify such needs on an offender-by-offender basis.

Andrews and Bonta (2003) remind us, however, that this process often omits a second question: Which needs are associated with this offender's criminal behavior? Are we recognizing and treating the needs that are most likely to get this offender into trouble again? The **needs principle** maintains that needs related to future offending should receive high priority as we match offenders to programs. Such needs are also risk factors and have come to be called **criminogenic needs**. The three most important criminogenic needs are antisocial associates, antisocial personality characteristics (e.g., impulsivity, restlessness), and antisocial values, beliefs, and attitudes (Andrews & Bonta, 2003; Gendreau, Little & Goggin, 1996). In risk assessment research, these needs show the highest correlation with recidivism. Moreover, if we focus our programming efforts on reducing these needs, we stand a good chance of reducing future criminal behavior. Other criminogenic needs, though not as potent as the three listed above, include: substance abuse, emotional health, financial problems, underemployment, educational limitations, family concerns, and antisocial living arrangements. Programs that focus on criminogenic needs are far more effective than those that do not attend to them with a systematic view toward preventing future offenses (Andrews et al., 1990; Lowenkamp & Latessa, 2002).

The Responsivity Principle

Even when we have classified according to risk and criminogenic need and have then proceeded to target our intervention to the criminogenic needs, we will notice that important considerations remain. These differences will affect how well an offender will be able to respond to his or her treatment plan (Andrews et al., 1990). Clearly, factors such as intelligence, anxiety, ethnicity, cognitive maturity, personality, attention deficit disorder, housing, learning style, childcare, transportation, and other considerations will translate into **treatment amenability** or an offender's likelihood of achieving success in our program. The **responsivity principle** maintains that programs should consider offender characteristics and situations that are likely to become barriers to success in a given correctional program.

Most responsivity characteristics are not risk factors. But they are as important to counselors and case managers as risk factors are, because if responsivity characteristics are not addressed, we never get an opportunity to address the risk factors. Consider the following example:

> After completing an intake interview and a risk assessment, Cassandra's probation officer learned that she has been abusing drugs and alcohol for several years. In addition, she does not have a high school education. A reasonable conclusion would be to require attendance in a substance abuse program and the receipt of a G.E.D. while Cassandra is on probation. However, Cassandra, a single parent, does not have access to adequate transportation and child care. She cannot afford a car, and her children are far too young to leave home alone. Neither child care nor transportation is a risk factor for future criminal behavior. However, without addressing these two issues, Cassandra will not be able to attend substance abuse therapy or G.E.D. classes. She will not, in other words, have access to services that will help her change in ways that make her less likely to re-offend.

The importance of the responsivity principle is not new to corrections. Several programs in the 1960s and early 1970s worked successfully with the notion of **differential treatment or matching** (see, for example, Palmer, 1974, 2002; Reitsma-Street & Leschied, 1988; Warren, 1971, 1983). It is surprising, however, that responsivity is seldom incorporated into correctional treatment or evaluations of correctional programs. In failing to consider the notion of responsivity, we routinely "mask" the treatment effect (Van Voorhis, 1987). We repeatedly hear of programs that "failed," when in fact they probably succeeded with certain types of offenders and failed with others—for the group as a whole, then, the successes were canceled by the failures.

For example, in a recent evaluation of a popular cognitive-behavioral program, Van Voorhis and her associates employed the Jesness Inventory (Jesness, 1996) to classify adult male parolees into the following four personality styles:

> **Asocial aggressive:** Offenders with internalized antisocial values, beliefs, and attitudes. Crime is a lifestyle.
>
> **Neurotic:** Highly anxious offenders, whose criminal behavior represents the acting-out of an internal crisis. Crime for these offenders often has more of a personal meaning than an instrument meaning. Dysfunctional, self-defeating coping responses play a role in getting these individuals into trouble.
>
> **Dependent:** These offenders tend to be immature and easily led. They get into trouble through their own naiveté and in the course of being too easily led by other offenders.

Situational offenders: These offenders have prosocial values and less extensive criminal careers. They get into criminal behavior on a situational basis, when they are unable to cope with certain life events, or through substance abuse.

When these parolees were assigned to Ross and Fabiano's (1985) cognitive skills program (Reasoning and Rehabilitation) some types were clearly more successful than others (see Figure 7.1) (Van Voorhis et al., 2002).

Figure 7.1
Percent Returning to Prison Following Cognitive Skills Programming by Specific Personality Types (Van Voorhis et al., 2002).

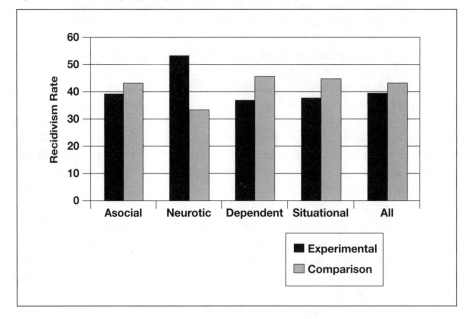

Figure 7.1 also shows that the cognitive skills program was most appropriate for immature and situational offenders. Neurotic program participants, on the other hand, fared worse than members of the comparison group who did not participate in the program. Notice also that the program did not appear to be very successful with the group as a whole. However, a more accurate picture is that it worked with some offenders but not with others. We do not know why high-anxiety offenders performed so poorly. According to their pre-program assessments, they needed the program, but they just could not succeed in it. Perhaps there was too much confrontation. Similar findings were observed with an early GGI program (Empey & Lubeck, 1971). By definition, such offenders are more likely to act-out when confronted. Or perhaps in some self-defeating manner they did not take full advantage of the programmatic opportunity offered to them.

In the future, this program could refer neurotic offenders to a program more suitable to their needs. Such a practice would involve practitioners in doing exactly what the classification system was designed to do—matching offenders to programs they can benefit from. Alternatively, the cognitive program could be altered to better accommodate or work with high-anxiety offenders. Perhaps some facilitators were a bit too confrontational.

We could identify additional purposes of classification. Correctional administrators, for example, use classification to help allocate such resources as staff, treatment options, and bed space. A classification system might separate probationers who need intensive supervision from those who do not, thus avoiding the mistake of devoting too much of a probation officer's time to a low-risk probationer. Classification also streamlines decision making, so we can assign individuals to institutions, living units, case managers, and treatment options in an efficient manner. Finally, many correctional officials appreciate the uniformity of systematic classification systems. Classification helps us to make decisions in an equitable manner because a classification model essentially applies the same test or classification criteria to all who come through the door. For purposes of correctional treatment and counseling, however, the three principles discussed above are the most important.

As we review different types of commonly used classification systems, we will revisit these principles frequently. Readers will notice, however, that sometimes a classification model can meet more than one of the three principles. For example, a criminogenic need is typically also a predictor of future criminal behavior, so it is a risk factor as well as a need. Thus, the program that targets antisocial attitudes would be using both the needs principle and the risk principle simultaneously.

Types of Commonly Used Classification Systems

The choice of a classification system depends on the purpose for which it is being chosen. Generally, the array of correctional classification systems available can be grouped into the categories shown in Figure 7.2:

Risk Assessment Systems

The earliest and most commonly used instruments for classifying offenders were **risk assessments**, designed to predict new offenses or prison misconduct. As early as the 1970s, the U.S. Parole Commission was employing the Salient Factor Score (SFS) to classify parolees into high, medium, and low levels of risk of re-offending (Hoffman, 1983). Institutions were using custody classification systems models based on the National Institute of Corrections Model Prisons Project (NIC, 1979) to classify incarcerated offenders to maximum, medium, and minimum custody.

Figure 7.2
An Overview of Correctional Classification Approaches

Type of System	Purpose: Institutional Corrections	Purpose: Community Corrections
Risk Assessments	Predict institutional misconduct for assignment to maximum-, medium-, and minimum-custody institutions	Predict new offenses for assignment to high-, medium-, and low-risk case loads.
Needs Assessments	Identify offender needs for programming referrals	Identify offender needs for programming referrals
Risk/Needs Assessments	Seldom used in institutions	Predict new offenses with needs that are also risk factors
Responsivity Assessments	Assessments of IQ, maturity, personality, and other attributes likely to interfere with an offender's ability to participate in certain programs.	Assessments of IQ, maturity, personality, and other attributes likely to interfere with an offender's ability to participate in certain programs.

The factors considered in the NIC institutional classification systems appear in Figure 7.3. A host of validation studies found such systems, including their later versions, to be predictive of institutional misconduct, particularly serious misconduct (Hardyman, Austin & Tulloch, 2002). Individual states have modified these systems somewhat, but the basic structure of the NIC model has stayed intact, and it is the most common system in institutional use today.

This classification instrument is administered to all inmates upon admission and then re-administered every six months to one year thereafter. Classification specialists score each item, add the scores, and consult guidelines to determine what institutional custody level matches the score. It is noteworthy that most of the factors listed in Figure 7.3 are **static factors**—they do not change over time. Reclassification assessments attempt to correct for this. Items such as prison misconduct, time to serve, and accomplishments in institutional treatment programs can reduce or increase one's custody assignment. Similarly, some systems change scores or weights on the static items for purposes of reclassification. With the item not counting for as many points on the reclassification instrument as it does on the intake classification system, custody assignments can drop.

Institutional custody classification systems offer no recommendations for programming and correctional treatment. Similarly, they do not predict recidivism in the community. Therefore, it would not be entirely correct to assume that offenders classified at minimum custody are the best candidates for work release, early release, or furloughs. Community risk assessment instruments are needed for this purpose.

Figure 7.3
Factors Considered in Institutional Custody Classification Systems

Intake Classification System	Reclassification
Past institutional violence	Past institutional violence
Severity of current offense	Severity of current offense
Severity of prior convictions	Severity of prior convictions
Escape history	Escape history
Prior felonies	Prior felonies
Stability (age, education, employment)	Stability (age, education, employment)
Time to release	Prison misconduct
	Program/work performance
	Time to release

During the early 1970s, the U.S. Parole Commission implemented the Salient Factor Score (SFS) (Hoffman, 1983). Items are shown in Figure 7.4. SFS items are entirely static, meaning that an offender scored as a poor risk is unlikely to be reclassified as low-risk, or even medium-risk, at a later date. Again, the SFS has little information to offer practitioners about treatment needs. Just the same, it has been revalidated and found to be valid with both male and female offenders (Hoffman, 1994). Over time, new risk assessment instruments have emerged with more dynamic variables such as substance abuse, education, and employment (Baird et al., 1979; Baird et al., 1989).

Figure 7.4
The Salient Factor Score (Hoffman, 1994)

- Prior convictions/adjudications
- Prior commitment(s) > 30 days
- Age at current offense
- Commitments during past three years
- Correctional escape
- Heroin/opiate dependence

Agencies using these two models find them useful in classifying offenders according to risk. They inform what is widely considered to be the most important function of corrections—community and institutional safety. Furthermore, institutional and community risk assessment systems are useful tools in reducing disparity in institutional placement and sentencing (Austin & McGinnis, 2004). Even without additional tools to inform treatment or responsivity considerations, these models, particularly the community risk models, have changed the face of correctional practice (Feeley & Simon, 1992; Van Voorhis & Brown, 1996) and made programs such as intensive probation, a host of intermediate sanctions, and alternatives to incarceration possible.

Most static risk assessment instruments can be completed fairly quickly if staff have a complete presentence report and can interview the offender. Thus, with very little effort or time, the agency can determine the offender's likelihood of failure, committing a new offense, or becoming involved in a serious altercation within an institution. Once a risk classification is completed, the agency knows whether to place an incarcerated offender in a maximum-, medium-, or minimum-custody facility, or a probationer in a high-, medium-, or low-risk caseload.

Needs Assessment Systems

Classifying offenders into separate institutional custody levels or community supervision levels on the basis of risk alone would not convey enough information to guide decisions pertinent to treatment, adjustment to prison, and community re-entry. **Needs assessment systems** attempt to offer such treatment-relevant information. Figure 7.5 shows an example of a needs assessment form, similar to those used in many probation settings (Baird et al., 1979). This form is used to record staff assessments of the offender's problems as well as the magnitude of those problems. These models were originally developed as a supplement to community risk assessment and institutional custody models. Institutional needs assessment forms differ somewhat from Figure 7.5 by including needs related to prison adjustment, such as social adjustment, hygiene, and level of family support.

Needs assessments provide: (a) systematic and objective identification of offender needs; (b) information needed to link offenders to services that promote behavioral change and prevent physical, psychological, or social deterioration; (c) a tool for individualized case planning; and (d) information needed to allocate agency and programming resources. (Clements, McKee & Jones, 1984). At the same time, needs assessments are absolutely essential to emerging prisoner re-entry programs (Austin & McGinnis, 2004; Hardyman & Van Voorhis, 2004; Parent & Barnett, 2003). When used in institutional settings, needs assessments conform to what Levinson termed **"internal classification"** (Levinson, 1988; see also Hardyman et al., 2002). The external system in this case would be the custody classification, and needs assessments classify individuals within a single custody level.

Needs most likely to be identified by these instruments include health, intellectual ability, mental health, education, employment, and drug and alcohol abuse. Like risk assessment models, needs assessments are designed to be administered at intake and at regular intervals throughout the correctional terms. It is important to note that these assessments were never designed to be the final assessment of a serious problem such as mental or physical health; instead, they are intended to triage offenders, identifying those who need more intensive assessments.

Figure 7.5
Assessment of Client Needs

INITIAL INMATE CLASSIFICATION
ASSESSMENT OF NEEDS

NAME _____   **NUMBER** _____
            Last   First   MI

CLASSIFICATION CHAIRMAN _____   **DATE** _____ / _____ / _____

TEST SCORES: _____
                                                                                            I.Q.

                                                                                            _____
                                                                                            Reading

                                                                                            _____
                                                                                            Math

NEEDS ASSESSMENT: Select the answer that best describes the inmate.

HEALTH:
1 Sound physical health, seldom ill   **2** Handicap or illness that   **3** Serious handicap or chronic illness,   _____
                                              interferes with functioning on   needs frequent medical care   **code**
                                              a recurring basis

INTELLECTUAL ABILITY:
1 Normal intellectual ability, able   **2** Mild retardation, some need   **3** Moderate retardation, independent   _____
    to function independently   for assistance   functioning severely limited   **code**

BEHAVIORAL/EMOTIONAL PROBLEMS:
1 Exhibits appropriate emotional   **2** Symptoms limit adequate   **3** Symptoms prohibit adequate   _____
    responses   functioning, requires   functioning, requires significant   **code**
                                              counseling, may require   intervention, may require
                                              medication   medication or separate housing

ALCOHOL ABUSE:
1 No alcohol problem   **2** Occasional abuse, some   **3** Frequent abuse, serious disruption,   _____
                                              disruption of functioning   needs treatment   **code**

DRUG ABUSE:
1 No drug problem   **2** Occasional abuse, some   **3** Frequent abuse, serious disruption,   _____
                                              disruption of functioning   needs treatment   **code**

EDUCATIONAL STATUS:
1 Has high school diploma or GED   **2** Some deficits, but potential   **3** Major deficits in math and/or   _____
                                              for high school diploma   reading, needs remedial programs   **code**
                                              or GED

VOCATIONAL STATUS:
1 Has sufficient skills to obtain   **2** Minimal skill level, needs   **3** Virtually unemployable, needs   _____
    and hold satisfactory   enhancement   training   **code**
    employment

The most common forms of needs assessment ask a correctional case manager or counselor to rate each need according to the extent to which, if any, the problem interferes with daily functioning. In response to the alcohol abuse item, for example, a case manager might be prompted to indicate where there is: (a) no alcohol abuse; (b) occasional abuse, some disruption of functioning; or (c) frequent abuse, serious disruption, needs treatment. Understandably, some have faulted such items as requiring too much subjectivity and being likely to lead to problems with the **reliability** of the instrument.

More acceptable approaches would more closely follow guidelines established by the American Correctional Association, which emphasize the importance of providing objective criteria for each level of need and informing determinations with the best available information (e.g., assessments, presentence investigations, medical reports, and psychological evaluations) (Clements et al., 1984; Hardyman et al., 2004; Hardyman & Van Voorhis, 2004). Alternatively, many agencies use established screens, especially for mental health, substance abuse, and education. Substance abuse, for example, may be assessed by instruments such as: (a) Substance Abuse Subtle Screening Inventory (SASSI) (Miller, 1985); (b) Adult Substance Use Survey (ASUS) (Wanberg, 1993; Wanberg & Milkman, 1998); (c) the Addiction Severity Index (McLellan et al., 1985); (d) Drug Abuse Screening Test (DAST) (Center for Addiction and Mental Health, 1999); or (e) Michigan Alcohol Screening Test (Selzer, 1971). Mental health screenings often utilize the Minnesota Multiphasic Personality Inventory-2 (MMPI-2) (Butcher et al., 1989), the Symptom Checklist 90 (SCL90) (Derogatis, 1994), or the MMCI III (Millon, 1998), to name just a few.

Another alternative is discussed in unpublished agency documents and involves the use of algorithms or scoring rules for combining an assessment with behavioral indicators such as mental health-related incidents, or positive urine screens. The Colorado Department of Corrections, for example, developed scoring rules for combining results of the MCMI III with indicators pertaining to past hospitalization, medications, past treatment, and history of self-destructive behavior to indicate whether the offender is low-, moderate-, or high-need for mental health services. Taking this a step further, the State of Texas links similar need categories to treatment/programming recommendations. For some needs, such as employment, scores also consider an inmate's time to release; inmates close to release are rated as having the highest priority for employment-related services.

What we do with the needs assessment probably is more important than the assessment itself. Unfortunately, many assessments sit in files and are not used. That is, the offender never gets to the service or program the assessment says he or she needs. Observe, for example, the results of a recent evaluation of a community correctional work-release program (Figure 7.6). The first column shows the proportion of offenders in the program who were assessed by the LSI-R as having antisocial beliefs, values, and attitudes. The second column shows the proportion of offenders with criminal attitudes who were placed in a program for criminal thinking and cognitive skills prior to their release. The third column shows the proportion of offenders who were in such a program, but had not been assessed as needing the program. The final column shows the proportion of offenders who needed the program and actually completed it. Figure 7.6 shows quite clearly that this agency did not (or could not) use the needs assessment to **match** offenders to the cognitive skills program. Unfortunately, this is a common problem. In many agencies, assessments are administered and then ignored.

Figure 7.6
**Matching of Offenders to Financial Skills Programming
(Van Voorhis & Spiropoulis, 2003)**

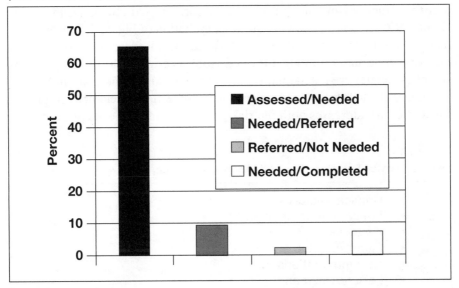

Does this matter in terms of effectiveness? Yes, it does. In a recent statewide study of halfway houses, for example, Lowenkamp and Latessa (2002) reported that those halfway houses which matched offenders to programs on the basis of sound needs assessments achieved much greater reductions in recidivism than those which did not.

Risk/Needs Assessments

Needs assessment systems, such as those discussed above, should not be confused with the needs principle (Andrews, Bonta & Hoge, 1990). This is because the commonly used needs assessments do not by design identify all of the important criminogenic needs.

In a growing number of community correctional agencies, however, risk and needs assessments are being combined into a single instrument. In contrast to the SFS (see Figure 7.4), these instruments contain dynamic items;

scores can change over time. Such classification models constitute what Bonta referred to as the third and most recent generation of correctional classification (Bonta, 1996). The most widely adopted system of this kind is the Level of Service Inventory-Revised (LSI-R). The Correctional Offender Management Profiling for Alternative Sanctions (COMPAS) is another model, which includes both the assessment of risk and needs. In contrast to the needs assessments discussed above, **risk/needs assessments** include only those needs that are also **risk factors**. This is to enable case managers and counselors to make sure that they give focused attention to reducing criminogenic needs, thereby increasing the likelihood that they will also reduce recidivism.

The LSI, shown in Figure 7.7, was designed by Don Andrews in the early 1980s (Andrews, 1982). Subsequent research has found it to be highly predictive of recidivism among a variety of correctional clients (Andrews & Bonta, 1995; Simourd, 2004). A quick examination of Figure 7.7 reveals that many of the LSI items are **dynamic risk factors**. Readers may also recognize that important criminogenic needs such as criminal attitudes and antisocial associates are listed on the LSI. As noted earlier, these are important individual characteristics to try to change in correctional treatment programs. Thus, the LSI addresses both the risk principle and the needs principle.

Figure 7.7
Level of Service Inventory-Revised (Andrews & Bonta, 1995)

- Criminal History
- Education/Employment
- Financial
- Family/Marital
- Accommodations
- Leisure/Recreation
- Companions
- Alcohol/Drug
- Emotional/Personal
- Criminal Sentiments

The LSI-R is administered by case managers and counselors. The assessment process requires a semi-structured interview (Andrews & Bonta, 1995). As with other dynamic risk assessment instruments, the LSI provides for reassessments of an offender's risk score. Reassessment is important, because as offenders change (hopefully for the better) old LSI scores lose their accuracy. Reassessments also make more accurate risk predictions (Brown, 1990; Law, 2004).

It should also be noted that the LSI-R fits a rather specific type of treatment model. Attitudes, criminal history, and associates, the most important correlates of criminal behavior, are also cited by social learning theories of crime (see Akers, 1973; Andrews & Bonta, 2003; Bandura, 1973). As a classification strategy, the LSI best fits programs that are grounded in behavioral, social learning, and cognitive-behavioral treatment strategies such as those discussed in Chapters 4, 8 and 9 of this text. This is not a criticism of the LSI, because it is also noted by Smith, Gendreau, and Goggin (in Chapter 13) that behavioral, cognitive-behavioral, and social learning approaches are the most effective treatment programs for offenders (see Andrews et al., 1990; Garrett, 1985; Gendreau, 1995; Lipsey, 1992; Palmer, 1992). In other words, the LSI-R targets important criminogenic needs in a way that can be used by the types of programs known to be most effective with offenders.

Assessing Responsivity

As noted earlier, being responsive to treatment means that we are able to participate in a given correctional program or setting. That is, it fits our learning styles, intellectual and emotional capabilities, and we have no insurmountable barriers to succeeding in the program. Individual situations and characteristics that are barriers to correctional adjustment and success in correctional interventions are referred to as **responsivity characteristics.** When we do not address these, some offenders will be set up to fail.

Some responsivity factors do not have to be assessed. For example, we will not need to find a test to determine whether a single mother needs childcare in order to attend a substance abuse program, or if a victim of ongoing spouse abuse needs safe housing in order to comply with the conditions of probation.

Other situations will require assessments. For example, programs that require offenders to prepare written homework assignments and recognize the connection between their thoughts and their behavior will need to assess intelligence, because low-functioning individuals have difficulty succeeding in such situations. Intelligence screens such as the Culture Fair Test (Cattell & Cattell, 1973), the Shipley Institute for Living Scale (Shipley, 1983) or the Revised Beta Examination, Second Edition (1978) are frequently used for this purpose. Educational programs will need to determine an offender's reading level. Increasingly, we are noticing that correctional programs that engage in confrontation of offenders may not succeed with highly anxious offenders (e.g., see Listwan et al., 2004). A personality assessment, such as any of those discussed below, will help identify such an offender.

The earliest form of assessments for responsivity involved assessments of offender personality characteristics. During the 1970s and 1980s, a number of correctional psychologists worked to develop psychological assessments to facilitate the notion of differential treatment (Megargee & Bohn, 1979; Quay, 1984; Quay & Parsons, 1972; Warren, 1971, 1983; Jesness and Wedge, 1983). Grounded, as all classification research is, in the notion that offenders are not all alike (Palmer, 1978, 2002), the assessments developed by these scholars classified offenders according to personality

(Megargee & Bohn, 1979; Warren, 1983; Jesness and Wedge, 1983; Quay & Parsons, 1972; Quay, 1984) or conceptual/cognitive maturity (Warren, 1983; Jesness and Wedge, 1983). These and later studies found that different "types" made different adjustments to prison (Bohn, 1979; Megargee & Bohn, 1979; Megargee et al., 2001; Quay, 1984; Van Voorhis, 1994) and different responses to specific types of correctional interventions (Heide, 1983; Warren, 1983; Palmer, 1974, 2002; Van Voorhis et al., 2002).

This section offers three examples of **psychological classification systems** that have been used in offender settings. These systems were first developed for juveniles and later for adults (Van Voorhis, 1994). In order to furnish a broad overview of different types of systems, this section introduces: Interpersonal Maturity Level (I-level) (Jesness & Wedge, 1983; Warren et al., 1966); Quay's Adult Internal Management System (Quay, 1984); and the Megargee MMPI-based Typology (Megargee & Bohn, 1979; Megargee et al., 2001). These systems also fit the notion of "internal classification" discussed in the needs assessment section above.

The three systems differ in terms of the types of psychological characteristics and criteria that form the basis of the respective typologies. Some are developmental typologies, and others are personality-based. One, Megargee's MMPI-based Typology, includes categories for psychologically disturbed inmates. Some of the systems tap a combination of factors (e.g., maturity, personality, pathology). The systems also differ in their methodology of administration, including such varied techniques as interviews, tests, and staff observation forms. The time required for staff to administer the instrument also varies from system to system. I-level interviews can take from 45 minutes to two hours, but there is a shortened version available through the Jesness Inventory (Jesness, 1996, 2003). The original MMPI contained 566 questions; the MMPI-2 has 567 items.

Interpersonal Maturity (I-level) (Jesness & Wedge, 1983; Warren et al., 1966) began with the theoretical work of Sullivan, Grant, and Grant (1957). During the 1960s and 1970s it developed into a classification system for use with juvenile offenders in the California Youth Authority (Warren et al., 1966; Warren 1983). Interpersonal Maturity, or I-level, is a classification system and treatment model based on the ways in which people view themselves and others, as well as the ways in which they interact with others. The original I-level system required practitioners to administer and clinically rate a semi-structured interview. This process was viewed as time-consuming and vulnerable to complications in the assessment process (Harris, 1988). Current uses of the I-level classifications use an actuarial measure of I-level, which is a part of the Jesness Inventory (Jesness, 2003). Because it contains only 160 true/false items, it is easier to administer than the interview. This test was developed for adolescents, but may now be used with both adults and adolescents (Jesness, 2003; Van Voorhis, 1994).

The classification scheme consists of four levels that characterize individuals on a cognitive developmental sequence pertaining to self and interpersonal perspectives. In addition to the four levels, the offender classification system also has personality subtypes within the levels. Therefore, the psychological characteristics tapped by the classification system are: (1) cognitive development or interpersonal maturity and (2) personality. We will present each in turn.

The developmental component of I-level shares assumptions common to several other ego and cognitive developmental (stage) theories as set forth by Loevinger (1966), Piaget (1948), Kohlberg (1976), and others. These theories maintain that cognitive development:

1. involves changes in qualitative thought processes that describe *how* one thinks (not *what* one thinks);

2. occurs through a developmental sequence of stages that are the same for all persons;

3. occurs in the direction of increasing complexity (i.e., one's thinking becomes more complex with development);

4. represents an underlying logic at each developmental stage that appears to be consistent across situations; and

5. occurs through stages that are hierarchical integrations that enable individuals to comprehend all stages below and one stage above their diagnosed stage of reasoning.

Because development can cease at any point along the continuum, a cross section of the population, theoretically, would show a distribution of persons at all stages.

The levels of interpersonal development range from the least mature stage of the newborn infant (I_1) to a theoretically ideal stage of interpersonal maturity that is rarely attained (I_7). A description of the socio-perceptual frame of reference that characterizes each level shows how individual perceptions of and reactions to others and the environment change with the development of the personality. Warren (1983) refers to the frame of reference embodied in each level as a "relatively consistent set of expectations and attitudes, a kind of interpreting and working philosophy of life." This way of making sense of one's environment, then, is relatively consistent across situations until the individual matures into the next level, where a new frame of reference is integrated with previous experiences and perspectives.

Although seven levels have been set forth in the theoretical work of Sullivan, Grant, and Grant (1957), only four levels apply to delinquent and offender populations. Phil Harris' (1988) abbreviated description of levels 2 (I_2), 3 (I_3), 4 (I_4), and 5 (I_5) follows.

I_2 is a stage typical of very young children. Major concerns center on differentiating persons from objects. Other persons are viewed solely as sources of gratification (e.g., as "givers" and "takers," evidencing no understanding of others nor an ability to predict or influence the behavior of others).

I_3 youths have learned that they have power; their behaviors affect the responses they receive from others. Much of their activity centers around learning how power is structured. They tend to apply stereotyped rules and simple formulas when interacting with others.

I_4 youths operate from a set of internalized values. They are aware of feelings and motives in themselves and in others and their relevance to communication and relationships with others. They tend to be rigid in their application of rules and to be concerned with their own uniqueness.

I_5 individuals are considerably less rigid in their application of rules than are (persons) at I_4; they tend to see grey areas in situations and are tolerant of viewpoints different from their own. Role conflict is a major concern of such (persons). The most distinguishing characteristic of this stage is empathy—the capacity to experience the world from the perspective of another person.

An overview of these characteristics presents a compelling case for differential expectations and responses to the correctional clients under our supervision. One would not, for example, expect an I_3 delinquent to readily understand what it was like to be "in the shoes of" the dorm mate whose cigarettes he stole last night. Similarly, an I_4 delinquent may be defensive about any failure on his part to measure up to his expectations of himself. These expectations may be either prosocial or antisocial, but by knowing his I-level diagnosis, we would predict the youth to be holding on to these values in a somewhat rigid manner.

The I-level system offers a subtype diagnosis in addition to the I-level classification. The subtypes are neither theoretically derived nor developmental, but rather empirically identified personality-based subtypes of the four levels described above. They might also be termed the personality-based adaptations found to be evidenced at each of these levels. Harris's (1988) descriptions are as follows:

I_2: Asocial Passive: Responds to unmet demands by withdrawing, whining, or complaining.

Asocial Aggressive: Responds to unmet needs with open aggression.

I_3: Immature Conformist: Conforms to whomever has the power at the moment and sees self as less powerful than others.

Cultural Conformist: Conforms exclusively to a specific group of peers.

Manipulator: Counteractive to any source of power, adult, or peer. Extremely distrustful of others.

I_4:   Neurotic Acting-Out: Internally conflicted due to negative self-image. Responds to internal conflict by putting up a façade of superadequacy and maintaining a high level of activity. Attempts to keep others at a distance through distracting behavior or verbal attack, even though he or she may be very sociable.

Neurotic Anxious: Also internally conflicted due to a negative self-image. Responds to internal conflict with guilt, anxiety, or depression. Tends to be introspective and frequently attempts to engage others in gaining self-understanding. Self-analysis is not genuine; it is an attempt to reduce anxiety while preserving both positive and negative parts of self-identity.

Cultural Identifier: As part of his or her socialization process, certain values were internalized that permit a range of delinquent acts.

Situational-Emotional Reaction: Responds to a current crisis, situation, or an emotional change that is recent in origin.

I_5:   The subtypes of this group are identical to those found at I_4.

The treatment applications of I-level involve classifying offenders and then assigning them to case managers and counselors who have been specially trained to work with that "type" of individual. I-level diagnoses are also helpful in determining an appropriate treatment strategy and living environment. The California Youth Authority experimented with this method of differential treatment during the 1960s and 1970s with some degree of success. Clearly, the most important finding of this study was that responses to treatment were differential, depending both upon the type of delinquent and the type of treatment received (Palmer, 1974, 2002; Warren, 1971, 1983).

The Behavioral Classification System for Adult Offenders (Quay, 1983), also referred to as the **Adult Internal Management System (AIMS)** (Quay, 1984), differs from all of the other systems, because the diagnosis does not directly involve input from the offender. Instead, staff complete two behavior observational checklists. The first, the Life Histories Checklist, consists of 27 items designed to be answered after a review of the offender's background reports and perhaps a brief interview. The second instrument, the Correctional Adjustment Checklist (CAC), is completed by a staff member and is based on staff observation of the offender over a brief period in the correctional setting. It contains 41 items.

Scores on the two checklists are combined, and the offender is classified into one of five personality types:

1. Aggressive-Psychopathic
2. Inadequate-Dependent

3. Neurotic-Anxious

4. Manipulative

5. Situational

Names have since been changed to the less descriptive Alpha I, Alpha II, Sigma I, Sigma II, and Kappa, and correspond to their respective rates of institutional misconduct. A similar system exists for use with juveniles (Quay & Parsons, 1972). The AIMS manual identifies a number of treatment issues for each type, but the most common application of the system has been for separation of inmates into housing units, especially separating predatory inmates from vulnerable inmates. For this purpose, the system is more aptly termed a management rather than a treatment tool. Van Voorhis (1994), however, noted numerous correlations between the Quay types and treatment-related and institutional adjustment variables. In addition, three studies of the effectiveness of the system have been conducted, and all report reduced disciplinary infractions (Bohn, 1979; Levinson, 1988; Quay, 1984). The system is used in the Federal Bureau of Prisons and institutional settings in South Dakota, South Carolina, Ohio, and Missouri.

The **Megargee MMPI-based Typology** (Megargee & Bohn, 1979; Megargee et al., 2001) was developed for use with youth and adult offenders. As the title implies, the classifications are obtained from results of the Minnesota Multiphasic Personality Inventory (MMPI). The classification system was developed by Edwin I. Megargee and his associates at Florida State University as a means of classifying large correctional populations. It involves separating MMPI profiles into 10 categories on the bases of profile configurations, slopes, shapes, and elevations. The scoring rules for doing this are available in a book titled *Classifying Criminal Offenders with the MMPI-2: The Megargee System* (Megargee et al., 2001).

The 10 types are described below along with a brief description of the MMPI profile associated with each type. Megargee gave each type a nondescript name (e.g., Able, Baker, Charlie, etc.) in order to allow an empirical process of identifying the behavioral characteristics of each type, thereby discouraging any biasing effects from preconceived labels. Zager's (1988) description of each of the types, in order from least to most disturbed, follows:

> Item: The (MMPI) profile lacks elevation with scales generally under 70. Items are described as a generally stable, well-adjusted group with minimal problems or conflicts with authorities.

> Easy: The profile has low elevations with the top scale below 80 and often below 70. Scales that often are elevated are 4 and 3 (of the MMPI profile) and the profile slopes down to the right. Easys are described as bright, stable, with good adjustment, personal resources, and interpersonal relationships. Many are underachievers.

Baker: The profile has moderate elevations, with typical elevations on scales 4 and 2 and sloping down to the right. Bakers are described as inadequate, anxious, constricted, and dogmatic, with a tendency to abuse alcohol.

Able: The profile has moderate elevations, typically on scales 4 and 0. Ables are described as charming, impulsive, and manipulative. They are achievement-oriented and often adjust well to incarceration.

George: The profile has moderate elevations similar to Baker, but scales 1, 2, and 3 are more elevated. Georges are described as hard-working, submissive, and anxious, with learned criminal values. They often take advantage of educational and vocational programs.

Delta: The profile has moderate to high elevation on scale 4, with other scales below 70. Deltas are described as amoral, hedonistic, egocentric, manipulative, and bright. They are impulsive sensation-seekers who have poor relations with peers and authorities.

Jupiter: The profile has moderate to high elevations sloping up to the right with elevations typically on scales 8, 9, and 7. Jupiters are described as overcoming deprived backgrounds to do better than expected in prison and upon release.

Foxtrot: The profile has high elevations with the top scale over 80 and others over 70. It slopes up to the right with scales 8, 9, and 4, the top three scales. Foxtrots are described as tough, streetwise, cynical, and antisocial. They have deficits in most areas, extensive criminal histories, and poor prison adjustment.

Charlie: The profile has high elevations with the highest scale above 80 and several scales above 70, typically peaking on scales 8, 6, 4, and sloping to the right. Charlies are described as hostile, misanthropic, alienated, aggressive, and antisocial. They have extensive histories of poor adjustment, criminal convictions, and mixed substance abuse.

How: The profile has very high elevations with at least three scales above a T-score of 70. Hows are described as unstable, agitated, and disturbed mental health cases. They have extensive needs and function ineffectively in major areas.

The MMPI-based system offers a means of efficiently identifying offenders who exhibit certain forms of psychological disturbance. Inmates classified as "How," for example, are noted to be disturbed and often warrant a mental health placement. One could not, of course, substitute this classification for a more thorough assessment similar to the one described in Chapter 6 by Carbonell and Perkins, but the MMPI results are useful in supporting such diagnostic work. In this sense, the Megargee System serves as both a classification function for all inmates and as a tool in further assessing inmates who appear to be suffering from more serious forms of mental illness.

The psychological systems are sometimes criticized as being too complicated to administer and use. There are many types within most of the systems and the administration process has been noted to be cumbersome. However, the most recent research on psychological classification has resulted in a commendable simplification of the administration and assessment procedures. In addition, a recent comparison study of the three systems described above found that the numerous types could probably be distilled down to four among adult males (Van Voorhis, 1994). They are the four types listed on page 137-138.

To understand how these systems address responsivity, imagine two adults on your caseload. One has been classified as neurotic, the other as an asocial agressive (with antisocial beliefs, values, and attitudes), see page 137. We will notice fairly quickly that the man classified as neurotic cannot tolerate criticism well, is highly defensive, and seems to have more difficulty trusting us than the man classified as a committed criminal. He is quick to misunderstand our discussions and intentions. We may even notice that any type of criticism of the neurotic offender results in an increase rather than a decrease in his acting-out behavior. The committed criminal, on the other hand, needs to know that we are "not buying" criminal thinking and needs to hear from us when we notice his criminal attitudes getting him into trouble. Simply put, what works for one backfires with the other. A similar phenomenon may occur as we make treatment referrals. A certain type of treatment program may work for the neurotic offender but may be exploited by the more manipulative offender.

Future Directions in Correctional Classification

Correctional classification and assessment is an area that continues to evolve. Three new directions are particularly noteworthy. The first involves a more studied look at the classification of women offenders. The second concerns the development of risk models for specific types of offenders, e.g., sex offenders, psychopaths, and substance abusers. The third is the development of seamless classification systems in which the same assessment is used across probation, institutional, and parole assignments—sometimes even pretrial.

First, at both national and state levels, agencies have voiced concern for the validity of classification systems among women offenders. In fact, a recent nation-wide survey of state directors of classification revealed that 36 states still had not validated their custody classification systems on women offenders (Van Voorhis & Presser, 2001). Efforts to do so in several states discovered that the existing systems were either invalid for women and/or overclassified them, thereby placing them at higher custody levels than warranted on the basis of their ultimate prison adjustment (Hardyman & Van Voorhis, 2004). There is no point in defending this; the use of invalid classification systems is highly unethical (ACA, 1995; APA, 1992; AAPSC, 2000). In addition to the core issue of validity, researchers are asking whether risk means the same thing for women as it does for men. Do high-risk women, in other words, have the same follow-up rate of recidivism as high-risk men? Another question concerns whether similar risk factors (e.g., family, associates, financial considerations) mean the same thing for men and women, or could we describe these factors in a more gender-responsive manner that then leads to better programming for women? Finally, has the current generation of risk/needs assessments tapped the most important needs for women, or are there others that would be lead to more beneficial programs and services (see Bloom, Owen & Covington, 2003; Van Voorhis, Pealer & Spiroupolis, 2001)?

Validity and Reliability: What Do We Mean?

Throughout this chapter we frequently use the terms *validity* and *reliability*. Perhaps we should discuss what is meant when we say "A classification system is not valid" or "Is this really a *reliable* way to secure this classification?" Because these concepts are essential to the task of treating offenders fairly, let us take a few minutes to assure that readers have a reasonable understanding of these terms.

When Is a Classification System Valid?

A classification system is valid when it measures what it promises to measure. Correctional risk assessments, for example, promise to predict recidivism or prison misconduct—depending on the system. Offenders are placed in high, medium, or low risk levels according to their prediction score. If the prediction score or levels are accurate, those who are classified as high risk should incur more new offenses than those who are classified at low risk. This is called **predictive validity**. To determine if this is the case, a researcher will take data from a sample of offenders and follow them for at least 12 to 24 months, keeping track of any new offenses during that period. When the data have been analyzed, we should see something like this:

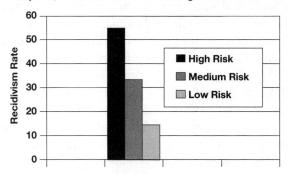

In other words, high-risk offenders really were at greater risk of committing new offenses than low-risk offenders. If we saw something different, such as columns showing that each group had the same rate of recidivism or something other than the "descending stairs," we would conclude that the system was invalid.

Validity also requires that the system correlates or reaches a similar classification as another measure of the same construct—in this case risk. This second form of validity is called **construct validity**. We would have construct validity, for example, if, in a sample of offenders classified according to both the LSI-R and the SFS, most offenders achieved the same classification on both assessments. If the LSI-R gave a different risk classification than the SFS for many offenders, we would conclude that the instrument did not have construct validity.

Why do we frequently discuss validity as an ethical consideration? In corrections, the lives of offenders can be profoundly affected by their correctional classification. Individuals facing trial, for example, can either be released on their own recognizance or jailed, depending the results of a risk assessment instrument. Risk assessments sometimes also determine early prison release or whether a probationer will be placed on electronic monitoring. Similarly, prison classification systems determine whether an inmate will be placed in a minimum-custody facility or in a medium- or maximum-custody facility with less freedom of movement and fewer privileges.

When Is a Classification System Reliable?

A classification system is reliable when two tests of the same individual produce the same classification. This could be when one individual takes a test twice or when one or two individuals administer an assessment on two separate occasions. We want similar results. We are especially concerned with questions that ask for too much judgment on the part of an interviewer. This chapter, for example, refers to a question that asks interviewers to determine whether an offender's substance abuse is causing minor levels of disruption or major levels of disruption. Would two interviewers score that item the same? To check on the reliability of an assessment, draw a random sample of 50 offenders who agree to be assessed twice by two independent counselors or case managers. Take the assessments and count the number of cases in which the assessment results were the same for each assessment. There will be 50 pairs of assessments here; at a very minimum, 80 percent of them should show the same classification regardless of the person administering the assessment.

Second, the studies of specific types of offenders, such as psychopaths and sex offenders and of specific criminogenic needs have produced numerous additional assessments to support the case management and supervision of these individuals. These include, for example: (a) the Hare Psychopathy Checklist-Revised (Hare, 2004); (b) the Sex Offender Needs Assessment Rating (SONAR) (Hanson & Harris, 2000); (c) The Static 99 (Hanson & Thornton, 1999); (d) the Spousal Assault Risk Assessment Guide (SARA) (Kropp et al., 1997); and (e) the Criminal Sentiments Scale (Simourd, 1997). Assessments for substance abuse were listed earlier in this chapter.

Finally, **seamless classification systems** could one day replace the use of separate systems for community and institutional agencies. For example, an instrument like the LSI-R or the COMPAS could be administered at a presentence point and readministered at regular intervals thereafter. It would follow the offender into a correctional facility and back out to parole. As circumstances change, such as when programs are completed or abstinence is achieved, the dynamic risk/needs scores would be readministered. The value of such a model is particularly relevant to new prisoner re-entry and transition programs designed to address the needs of record numbers of prison inmates who are now returning to their communities (Petersilia, 2003). Suggestions such as those recently formulated in the NIC Transitions Model (Parent & Barnett, 2003) include using such assessments to: (a) begin planning for release as soon as inmates are admitted to prison, and (b) assure continuity of care throughout the correctional term and beyond.

Conclusion

The systems discussed above do not exhaust all classification options, but rather exemplify the types of systems that are available. In addition, research and development of classification technology is a major area of criminological study that promises to produce numerous advances in the years ahead.

In the meantime, classification has already become a valuable tool of correctional management and treatment. Indeed, research has shown that the implementation of a classification model can enhance treatment effects (Andrews & Bonta, 2003; Palmer, 2002), is highly relevant to institutional adjustment (Van Voorhis, 1994), reduces recidivism in correctional settings (Bohn, 1979; Levinson, 1988; Quay, 1984), and guides case managers and counselors to the programs that are most likely to change offender behavior.

This is not to suggest, however, that correctional classification efforts have always been successful, or that systems can be implemented easily. In fact, future consumers of these systems should be alerted to the reality of some very serious mistakes that have been made with systems that appeared, at least on paper, to be easily implemented. A **myth of efficiency** appears to have marred many attempts to classify correctional populations. The myth of efficiency works on the desire to find a classification system that can be completed so easily that the agency does not need to concern itself with overburdening an already overworked staff. The myth might hold, for example, that the probation officer who has a caseload of 100 probationers need not complain about being required to complete a risk assessment instrument because it only takes three minutes to fill out the form. Indeed, the risk assessment instrument shown in Figure 7.4 appears to be clear and easy to complete. Why would an agency have problems with it when the questions are so straightforward? Yet this level of simplicity can also be a system's shortcoming, because the form can be filled out so quickly that staff need not give it *any* thought. Unfortunately, even these simple systems have incurred problems with inaccuracy (Austin, 1986; Buchanan et al., 1986).

In addition to the issue of reliable assessment, researchers are noting many cases in which classifications and assessments simply are not used for their intended purpose, such as when offenders are not matched to programs (Lowenkamp, 2004) or custody levels (Van Voorhis & Presser, 1971) on the basis of the classification tool available to them.

Potential users of these systems should also be warned of the problems in borrowing a risk assessment instrument from one jurisdiction and implementing it in another with no consideration for how well it fits (Clear, 1988; Jones, 1996). Researchers have warned that the weights or scores for each item may change substantially across settings. Thus, in order for a prediction instrument to be as accurate as possible, it must be validated to each new location (Wright et al., 1984). Cut-off points separating risk levels are also unique to each jurisdiction. Surprisingly, a number of agencies have been flooded with more offenders than they have resources for because of a failure to project how many offenders would ultimately be assigned to each category. More troubling, as is being learned in a series of studies on women offenders, the system may be completely invalid and inaccurately assigning inmates to unnecessarily austere correctional settings (Hardyman & Van Voorhis, 2004).

In conclusion, classification appears to make good sense from both a management and a treatment perspective. But as with any program strategy, treatment integrity is an issue. All of the systems listed above have carefully established guidelines regarding their use, and problems have resulted from not adhering to them. Yet there have also been numerous instances of successful implementation, which have served to improve the functioning of correctional programs.

Figure 7.8
A Case Study

In this and the previous chapter, we presented a number of tools for achieving a good understanding of correctional clients. If a need is indicated, for example, mental health diagnoses from psychologists or assessments from other health care providers offer counselors valuable insights into a client's challenges and strengths. Correctional classification tools help us to identify risk, needs, and responsivity characteristics that also must be considered in the treatment plan.

Prior to referring clients to appropriate interventions, correctional case managers and counselors must first decide upon treatment goals and a course of planned intervention. This involves reviewing a client's social and criminal history as well as any classification scores, mental health reports, or educational assessments. These form the bases of a treatment plan, the foundation upon which key client needs are set forward and goals of supervision and counseling are determined. Treatment plans typically contain the following components:

I. Background and social history
II. Criminal history and dynamics of criminal incidents
III. Description of the current offense
IV. Classifications, assessments, and mental health history, focusing upon criminogenic needs
V. Treatment goals
VI. Treatment approaches for addressing client needs

Jason is an avid reader, especially of sports and adventure stories.
Assume that you are asked to develop a treatment plan for Jason, one that will hopefully point him in a more positive and meaningful direction. In addition to accounting for Jason's social and criminal history (above) the treatment plan will furnish any rel-

Figure 7.8, continued

---

evant mental health and classification information and detail the criminogenic needs that you plan to have addressed during Jason's prison term. In this case, you have not observed any behaviors that would prompt you to refer Jason to the prison's mental health unit for an interview and assessments. He did, however, complete several assessments offered through the correctional system's classification unit. These included a Level of Service Inventory (LSI-R) (Andrews & Bonta, 1995), an IQ assessment, and a Jesness Inventory (Jesness, 1996). Results of these assessments are as follows:

Classification and Assessment: Jason's score on the LSI-R indicated that he was at a medium-high risk of reoffending. This risk classification makes Jason appropriate for the institution he is in and also suggests that Jason is a candidate for many of the types of intensive treatment programs targeted to criminogenic needs. In addition, the LSI-R serves as a case management tool, because it prioritizes the criminogenic needs that should be targeted while Jason is incarcerated. Jason's main criminogenic needs are: (a) criminal associates; (b) criminal attitudes; (c) limited work skills; (d) educational limitations; and (e) problematic family relationships.

The Jesness Inventory classified Jason as a CFC (Cultural Conformist). CFCs are described as offenders who: (a) see little reason to question their way of life or change their behavior; and (b) rarely admit to having serious personal problems. When they *do* admit to personal problems, they blame them on others (e.g., police, schools, and lawyers). CFCs are oriented to their peers for social approval and satisfaction of needs. They often possess antisocial values that are highly supportive of their criminal behavior.

Jason's IQ score on the Culture Fair Test (Cattell and Cattell, 1998) was 118, clearly above average.

To staff in the classification unit, Jason did not appear to be a candidate for any substance abuse interventions. On further observation, however, this may need to be re-evaluated. You have just learned, for example, that Jason received a disciplinary citation for stealing fruit to make an alcoholic beverage. Your concern leads you to a plan to further discuss Jason's drug and alcohol use, perhaps even to administer a substance abuse screening instrument. It is not uncommon for offenders to misrepresent their substance abuse in intake interviews, and for treatment practitioners to learn of the problem later.

At present, you decide to focus on the following criminogenic needs:

Criminal attitudes, supportive of antisocial and criminal behavior,

Limited cognitive skills, e.g, poor problem-solving and decision-making skills,

Limited educational attainments or job skills,

Aggressive attitudes and behavior,

Orientation to criminal rather than to prosocial peers or family members.

While these may not represent all of the criminogenic needs identified by the LSI-R, they are your priorities at the present time. These may change over time, as Jason improves, or as different criminogenic needs (such as substance abuse) become apparent.

You also note that Jason has the following strengths:

Above average intelligence,

Good physical health,

Affirmation from his sister,

Enjoyment of reading and remorse over his failure to complete high school.

Figure 7.8, continued

Thus, you write the following treatment goals:

V. Treatment Goals:

1. To reduce criminogenic thought patterns;
2. To build problem-solving and decision-making skills;
3. To build skills for managing anger;
4. To encourage Jason's relationship with prosocial individuals (e.g., his sister, key correctional staff, and inmates who model anti-criminogenic behaviors);
5. To complete the GED and some college-level courses.

Key Concepts and Terms

Adult Internal Management System (AIMS)
correctional classification
criminogenic needs
differential treatment
dynamic risk factors
internal classification
Interpersonal Maturity Level (I-level)
matching
Megargee MMPI-based typology
myth of efficiency
needs assessment systems
needs principle
psychological classification systems

reliability
responsivity principle
responsivity assessment
reponsivity characteristics
risk assessment
risk factors
risk/needs assessment
risk principle
seamless classification systems
static risk factors
treatment amenability
typology
validity

Discussion Questions

1. What are the common points of the classification systems discussed by Van Voorhis?

2. What purposes are served by correctional classification?

3. Which of the systems is the most popular for classifying offenders? Why?

4. What does Van Voorhis mean when referring to the "myth of efficiency?"

5. Distinguish among the risk principle, the needs principle, and the responsivity principle. How is each important to correctional treatment efforts?

6. How might an accurate correctional classification system make a correctional treatment program more effective?

7. What is meant by the statement that a classification system should be valid and reliable?

8. Why is it unethical to use a classification system that is not known to be valid?

Part Four

Contemporary Approaches to Correctional Counseling and Treatment

---

The three counseling and treatment approaches presented in this section form a core set of modalities that are known to reduce offender recidivism if they are delivered correctly.

Social learning models (observational learning approaches) are discussed in Chapter 8. The chapter maintains that observational learning is the most common form of human learning. Learning from this perspective, however, is most likely when careful attention is given to providing: (a) role models with good relationship skills; (b) opportunities to practice newly learned skills and behaviors; (c) specific performance feedback; and (d) client reinforcement for learning the new behaviors. Social learning theory provides the theoretical foundation for popular skills development programs.

The cognitive therapies build on the social learning approach but focus on "thinking processes" (Chapter 9). These strategies target dysfunctional perceptions, attitudes, and beliefs that, in turn, support and encourage dysfunctional behavior. In correctional settings, cognitive restructuring programs seek to change characteristic offender "thinking errors" that support criminal behavior. Another approach works on cognitive skills, maintaining that delinquent and adult offenders often demonstrate deficient thinking skills that can be improved in treatment settings.

Finally, family therapy models look to the family system as a vehicle for reforming offenders. In Chapter 10, Van Voorhis and Braswell observe that family treatment programs may be the most appropriate response to offenders who come from dysfunctional family systems. Chapter 10 introduces the notion of systems theory and discusses how it works in both the development of family problems and in the therapies that work to address these problems. Systems therapy, as exemplified by the Structural, Communication, Strategic, and Conjoint Family Therapy approaches, operates from a noticeably different paradigm than the more linear approaches discussed in previous chapters. The most recent family therapy model for offenders is Multisystemic Therapy (MST). MST borrows from the earlier models of family therapy, but also provides wraparound services to offenders and their families.

Fortunately, the models presented in this section are also becoming increasingly popular in corrections.

Chapter 8

Social Learning Models

Patricia Van Voorhis and Emily Salisbury

Classical conditioning and operant conditioning, presented in Chapter 4, are not the only models of human learning. In fact, direct learning (operant conditioning) is not even the *predominant* mode of human learning. According to Albert Bandura (1977), most of the learning achieved by human beings occurs through a process of **observational learning**. That is, notwithstanding the importance of reinforcement, punishment, and stimuli to learning, most of what we have learned over the course of our lifetimes has been learned vicariously, through observing and imitating others. From this perspective, **role models** and the process of **modeling** are crucial (Bandura, 1977). Social learning approaches integrate a number of the learning concepts discussed in Chapter 4, but the emphasis is on modeling. Modeling provide a means for clients to observe and imitate the behaviors, or **goal behaviors**, that the therapy is designed to teach.

Social learning programs dominate correctional rehabilitation endeavors. Their popularity is largely due to their efficiency and their cost-effectiveness, but their effectiveness cannot be overlooked. The meta-analyses, discussed in the previous chapter, reveals that social learning models, especially when combined with cognitive-behavior models (Chapter 9, Cognitive Therapies), are among the most effective treatment approaches (Andrews & Bonta, 2003; Andrews et al., 1990; Antonowicz & Ross, 1994; Dowden & Andrews, 2000; Lipsey, 1992, 1999; Losel, 1995). Indeed, high-quality social learning/cognitive-behavioral treatment approaches have achieved reductions in recidivism as high as 20 to 30 percent (Andrews & Bonta, 2003).

To understand the importance of modeling to learning, we need only think for a minute about our own learning experiences. To have learned directly, or solely through rewards and punishments, even through a gradual process of shaping, would have been extremely inefficient. We did not pick up our skills, be they athletic, verbal, social, or occupational, through such a process of trial and error. We observed other athletes or writing styles that we especially appreciated, or we remembered the social skills of those whom we perceived as popular. Then we imitated the skills of these role models and, through practice and reinforcement, we became increasingly proficient in using them.

The modeling provided by others facilitates our own learning in several ways, by:

1. Demonstrating how to perform a new behavior—an invaluable assistance to the acquisition of totally new techniques and skills;

2. Prompting or showing us how to use the behavior at the appropriate times;

3. Motivating us, or increasing our desire to use a new skill or behavior—especially when the model is reinforced for his or her skill; and

4. Disinhibiting us—modeled behavior reduces our anxiety and fear about using totally new behaviors, thereby reducing tendencies to avoid rather than practice the new skill (Masters et al., 1987; Spiegler & Guevremont, 1998).

Alternatively, models who are punished for certain behaviors usually dissuade us from imitating their behaviors. The notion of deterrence, for example, is based on the assumption that, as we view others being punished, we will avoid committing the same behaviors that led to their fate.

We might recognize that we did not imitate *everyone* we met, or even many of the people we met. Instead, we imitated the behavior of people who appeared competent, attractive, and those who were rewarded. This was a highly idiosyncratic process. You may have sought to imitate the attractive athlete, for example, while the student across from you was impressed with the knowledge demonstrated by her math teacher, and the student in front of her thought that the person in the front row of the class had a special flair for dress and style. Simply put, not everyone is a good role model, and those who are important role models for others may not be for us and vice versa. We will devote considerable attention in this chapter to the qualities needed to be an effective role model to juvenile and adult offenders.

Unfortunately, modeling also promotes the learning of criminal behavior. Indeed, having antisocial associates (or role models), is one of the strongest and most recognized risk factors for delinquent and criminal behavior (Akers, 2001; Andrews & Bonta, 2003; Elliot, Huizinga & Ageton, 1985). Poor parental modeling is strongly associated with antisocial behavior (Patterson, 1982; Patterson, Reid & Dishion, 1992), and modeling of aggressive behavior leads to aggression and hostility in those who view aggression (Bandura, 1973; Kirby et al., 2003; Patterson, 1982).

This chapter shows how modeling can be used to reverse antisocial behavior and to foster prosocial behaviors, social skills, and responsible attitudes. The successes of this approach with delinquent and adult offenders have been many. Prior to the advent of its use with children, modeling therapies achieved proven success in dealing with such matters as: assertiveness, depression, medical and dental phobias, substance abuse, self control/impulsivity, anxiety, parenting skills, sexual dysfunctions, social skills, and a wide range of phobias (Masters et al., 1987).

Environments are also important to the social learning paradigm. **Therapeutic communities**, a popular treatment strategy in both correctional and mental health settings, emphasize the importance of all aspects of the environment in the treatment of clients. In traditional therapeutic communities, for example, both staff and inmates are trained to act as appropriate role models (see Chapter 5, Early Approaches to Group and Milieu Therapy). All staff members, not just the treatment staff, are considered potential models. In order to model fair and respectful relationship styles, an effort is made to substitute authoritarian roles and policies with fairer modes of communication and decision making. Administrators also endeavor to remove the oppressive trappings of institutional living and to replicate, as much as possible, life outside the institution (Burdon et al., 2002). A therapeutic community may even remove some of the architectural and design features of the traditional prison, reasoning that the program cannot teach offenders how to function democratically and fairly in an environment that creates even the appearance of authoritarianism.

In contrast to some of the earlier forms of milieu therapy, contemporary therapeutic communities based upon a social learning model show clear signs of success. One such program, the Amity prison-based drug treatment therapeutic community in California, found that participants in the treatment group were significantly less likely than those in the control group to be returned to prison following release. This difference, however, was no longer significant after three years (Wexler, De Leon, Kressel & Peters, 1999; Wexler, Melnick, Lowe & Peters, 1999). Just the same, those in the treatment group who completed the therapeutic community treatment and aftercare group were significantly less likely to return to prison compared to those who: (1) dropped out of treatment, or (2) completed treatment but not aftercare (Prendergast et al., 2004).

Social learning interventions also take cognitive processes (i.e., one's thoughts, beliefs, values, and perceptions) into account. Indeed, much of our learning involves the thoughts that prompt and support our behavior or those that appraise the stimuli that are presented to us (Bandura, 1977). Cognitive-behavioral approaches recognize that the effectiveness of rewards, punishments, role models, and almost all other environmental factors are highly dependent upon how the client perceives these factors. They also more deliberately target thoughts and thought processes. A more detailed account of cognitive behavioral approaches for offenders is presented in Chapter 9, Cognitive Therapies.

Who Makes a Good Role Model?

As noted earlier, only certain individuals function as effective role models. A growing body of research shows us the qualities of good role modeling. For example, the early research by Albert Bandura and his associates (Bandura, 1965, 1977; Bandura et al., 1963; Bandura & Walters, 1963) found that the following factors affect whether or not a person will be imitated:

1. Attractiveness;

2. Competence; and

3. Extent to which the person is rewarded.

Early research by Donald Andrews (1980) focused on how offenders learn prosocial attitudes and behavior. Note that Andrews' term for prosocial attitudes is "anticriminal sentiments." In a series of studies, Andrews manipulated learning environments, examining each in turn, in order to identify optimal modeling styles for teaching offenders prosocial sentiments and behaviors. Andrews found that it was not enough to simply be exposed to anticriminal individuals; one also needed to participate in a process that involved discussion of the prosocial values in order to experience attitudinal change. Thus, opportunities to view modeled interactions *and to practice* or respond to others, facilitated offenders' learning.

Additional findings spoke to the relationship qualities of the role models. Andrews found that individuals who were skilled in interpersonal relationships, those who were more open, warm, and understanding of the viewpoints of others, effected more learning than those who were less skilled in these relationship qualities. In one study he reported that the type of probation officer whose clients had the least recidivism after the program was one who modeled anticriminal behaviors and sentiments, but also possessed good relationship skills (Andrews, 1980).

As shown in Figure 8.1, officers who scored low on relationship skills and who even tacitly modeled criminal sentiments tended to have clients whose behavior did not change over time. Interestingly, the clients of officers who had good relationship skills and but demonstrated criminal modeling were found to have higher recidivism rates. The clients of officers with good relationship styles who also modeled anticriminal behaviors showed lower recidivism rates. The importance of the relationship skills of the role model is also seen in the final group. Officers who were low in relationship skills but strong on anticriminal modeling did not effect the desired recidivism reductions. Simply put, models with warm interpersonal styles were much more effective than those with more detached modes of relating to clients. The relationship skills and interpersonal sensitivity of role models is crucial. Without it, the modeled behaviors often are not learned. However, we must remember that role models with advanced relationship skills will facilitate the learned transfer of whatever behaviors they are modeling. If an interpersonally warm counselor or peer models antisocial behavior, that is what will be learned.

Figure 8.1
Relationship Style vs. The Message: What Do Offenders Learn? (Andrews, 1980)

		Firm, Fair, Warm	Distant
Content of Probation Officer's Message	**Prosocial**	Prosocial values, beliefs, and behaviors	No behavioral change
	Antisocial	Antisocial values, beliefs, attitudes, and behaviors	No behavioral change

In later writings, Andrews and Bonta further defined the qualities of effective modeling. Good role models, according to Andrews and Bonta (2003), are noted to be enthusiastic, open, and flexible, and they afford their clients the freedom to express their opinions and feelings. This does not mean that the counselor or correctional worker never expresses disapproval, and always says what clients want to hear. At times, good relationship skills may also require that correctional counselors express disapproval toward clients. This must be done without threatening the clients' psychological sense of well-being. If a client has missed an appointment or returned late from a weekend furlough, for example, we cannot afford the luxury of ignoring the behavior. We can and should be honest about our concern and should do so by limiting our comments to the behavior and its consequences—consequences to the offender and to us as his or her supervisor. In this way, we critique the behavior, but not the person. We retain a belief in the client's ability to succeed and in his or her inherent worth as an individual. The relationship qualities of good role modeling also involve maintaining an environment of mutual liking, respect, and caring, in which openness, warmth, and understanding are offered within the limits of appropriate interpersonal boundaries. As noted in Chapter 1, these qualities serve most counseling relationships well.

In addition to relationship qualities, correctional counselors must give considerable attention to the manner in which prosocial behavior is modeled and antisocial behavior is discouraged. In demonstrations of behaviors, for example, role models must be clear. If possible, the model should indicate, even if this has to be done verbally, that he or she is rewarded for using the behavior being modeled. In turn, the counselor must attend to rewarding or praising the client for demonstrating new behaviors. As discussed in the next section, reinforcement, a primary component of the operant conditioning paradigm, is also a key to social learning interventions. Clients must work in a reinforcing and encouraging environment. Moreover, if new behaviors or skills are difficult or fear-inducing, counselors should empathize with the client's fear. Where appropriate, counselors may also relate a time when they had, but overcame, a similar fear.

We might also give some attention to techniques of reinforcement and disapproval. Reinforcement often takes the form of praise. Andrews and Bonta (2003) recommend that such praise be strong, emphatic, and immediate statements of approval, support, and agreement with the client's statements or behavior. Nonverbal expressions such as eye contact, smiles, or a sharing of experiences are also sound techniques of approval. Additionally, some time should be given to a cogent statement of why approval of the client's actions is being offered—what is good about the behavior? Reactions of this nature, of course, should be strong enough to distinguish the counselor's responses as a reinforcement rather than a pleasant manner of behavior.

Andrews and Bonta (2003) recognize the occasional need to disapprove of a client's behavior in effective ways. Indeed, the probation officers studied in Andrews' earlier research, those who had good relationship skills, nevertheless did not make reinforcing comments indiscriminately; they did so in a contingent manner (Andrews, 1980). Correctional counselors are advised to make clear, emphatic, and immediate statements of disapproval or disagreement. These reactions should follow the behavior or the counselor's knowledge of the behavior in a close time proximity—not several days later. Clients must receive a clear explanation of the counselor's reasons for disapproval. This might also include a suggestion of a prosocial alternative to the attitude or behavior to which the counselor objects. Disapproval should stand in stark contrast to a counselor's more satisfying relationship with the client (or else it will not be recognized as disapproval). Finally, the relationship should return to more positive regard once the client again demonstrates prosocial behavior.

In summary, Andrews and Bonta (2003) suggest that "anticriminal modeling" include the following:

1. Learn to recognize criminal thinking patterns and be able to differentiate them from anticriminal modes of thinking (see Chapter 9 for criminal thinking errors). Recognize also that specific offenses, for example, sex offenses, violent sex offenses, spouse abuse, hate crimes, and more general forms of violence have their own cognitions and supporting language (e.g., "She was coming on to me"). Do not show tacit approval of these orientations.

2. Correct any negative attitudes toward police, courts, and correctional agencies.

3. Do not tolerate or become lax toward rule-breaking behaviors or "ends justify the means" orientations.

4. The pro-criminal expressions of case managers may promote the recidivism of their clients. Be attentive to your own anti-social expressions (e.g., cynicism regarding the criminal justice system).

5. Don't attempt "con talk" in an effort to become closer to clients.

6. Model "anticriminal expressions": (1) emphasize negative consequences of criminal behavior; (2) reject criminal cognitions (see Chapter 9); and (3) identify the "risks" of associating with criminal others or of accepting the belief systems of criminal others.

7. Encourage association with "prosocial others."

8. Encourage clients to avoid "high-risk" situations.

9. Model good self-management skills: examining one's own conduct, thinking before acting, thinking about the consequences of one's own behavior, setting realistic standards for oneself, and working on avoidance and denial patterns.

10. Insist on attendance and the completion of assignments listed in the treatment plan.

11. Focus on criminogenic expressions and behavior and the behaviors that may lead to recidivism, rather than the behaviors that are simply irritating (e.g., loud mannerisms).

12. Reinforce anticriminal expressions, for example, responsible work habits.

This section has portrayed modeling as an essential therapeutic skill. Without too much thought, one could imagine a number of behaviors that counselors or other staff could engage in that would serve just the opposite function—subtly reinforcing offenders for their antisocial acts. Imagine, for example, the halfway house case manager who wants too much to be liked by the residents of the institution, who smiles at a resident's use of aggressive language, who espouses the "boys will be boys" orientation, and who fails to react to language and behaviors that are exploitive of women. Picture the counselor who supports a weekend furlough for a resident who has "had a bad week," all the while ignoring the fact that the resident has failed to accomplish any of his or her goals for the week. Imagine the probation officer who jokes about "beating the system," or tells the client, "just keep the judge happy," instead of supporting the prosocial value of the conditions of probation. How about the group home adviser who gives little thought to the criminal peers with whom the client is allowed to congregate or allies with the client against other staff members? Unfortunately, these behaviors are not uncommon in correctional settings and neither is the reinforcement of such acts. Some criminogenic orientations may even be well-supported in our culture.

For some, the approaches recommended in this section may seem too structured, perhaps too rigid. The costs of modeling antisocial behavior, however, are high, even when our behavior seems inadvertent. And the need for consistency is greater for offenders than it might be for more responsible individuals. Perhaps we can afford occasional lapses with children who typically demonstrate prosocial thinking and behavior, but with conduct-disordered children or children with other behavioral difficulties we cannot afford to be inconsistent (Samenow, 1989). With delinquent or adult offenders, the outcome is equally certain—antisocial modeling on our part, no matter how subtle—is likely to perpetuate or encourage antisocial attitudes or behavior.

The Process of Observational Learning

Notwithstanding its importance, the skill of the role model is only one of the factors influencing observational learning. Learning is a process, and social learning is a more complex process than we observed with the classical and operant models. To illustrate this process, Albert Bandura (1977) set forth the sequence of factors affecting the success of observational learning.

Figure 8.2 assumes that a goal behavior has already been modeled. It goes without saying, perhaps, that the behavior will not be learned if the observer pays no attention to the modeled event. Thus, the first box in Figure 8.2 shows that such attention depends on the qualities of the modeling and the characteristics of the observer. Modeling stimuli must be **distinctive**. That is, the model has to be noticed. At the same time, the model cannot be so different from the observer as to be a novelty. We are more likely to **imitate** people who we want to be like; clowns, or many other types of entertainment, are likely to be viewed for their entertainment value rather than imitated. **Affective valence** refers to the emotional reaction to the behavior being demonstrated. If the modeled behaviors invoke fear or anxiety, they are less likely to be imitated than behaviors that appear to be enjoyable. We might, for example, be more interested in modeling our behavior after a tennis instructor than the model who is preparing us to cope with an upcoming dental procedure.

Similarly, **complex goal behaviors** will be approached with less enthusiasm than a task for which we have a high degree of **self-efficacy** or confidence in our ability to perform. Conversely, if we undermine self-efficacy, as when we tell girls they are not good in math, we should not be surprised when our modeling of a solution to a math problem produces anxiety or avoidance.

Figure 8.2
The Process of Observational Learning (Bandura, 1977)

Modeled Goal Behaviors

I. ATTENTIONAL PROCESS

A. Modeling Stimuli

Distinctiveness
Affective Valence
Complexity
Prevalence
Functional Value

B. Observer Characteristics

Sensory Capacities
Arousal Level
Perceptual Set
Past Reinforcement

II. RETENTION PROCESS

Symbolic Coding
Cognitive Organization
Symbolic Rehearsal
Motor Rehearsal

III. MOTOR REPRODUCTION PROCESS

Physical Capabilities
Availability of Responses
Self-Observation
Accurate Feedback

IV. MOTIVATIONAL PROCESS

External Reinforcement
Vicarious Reinforcement
Self-Reinforcement

Future Demonstrations of Goal Behaviors

The word "prevalence" in Figure 8.2 refers to the **prevalence of role models**. Ideally, we would hope that our clients will see goal behaviors modeled outside of our treatment groups as well as within them. Environments are extremely important in this regard. Indeed, treatment efforts are often discouraged by:

1. Parents and family members who model behaviors that oppose those that we are trying teach (e.g., aggressive behaviors);

2. Institutional staff who are not trained to reinforce or serve as models for the goal behaviors or (worse yet) those who model the very antisocial behaviors and attitudes that we are trying to prevent; and

3. Peers who encourage delinquents to revisit criminal behavior.

Finally, the higher the **functional value** or usefulness of the modeled goal behavior, the more likely it is to be adopted. How valuable, for example, will better behavior and new skills be?

Whether an observer pays attention to a modeled goal behavior also has a lot to do with the characteristics of the observer. At a minimum, observers need to have the **sensory capacities** to see and hear the model. Just the same, observational learning has been used in mental health settings in which patients evidence intellectual, neurological, and other physical and mental impediments to attentiveness. Such difficulties must be planned for, however, because **arousal levels** also affect learning; both hyperaroused or inattentive, lethargic clients will have difficulty attending to the modeled behaviors. Moreover, the client's attitude or **perceptual set** toward the model, the behavior being modeled, the other clients in the program, and the whole idea of participating in this particular treatment program need to be considered. Have similar experiences been reinforced in the past, or were they onerous ordeals that affected the client's desire to participate in the present experience? Bad attitudes and expectations on the part of learners will interfere with even the best of learning situations. Clients who bring with them negative stereotypes of teachers and fellow students have a difficult time learning.

If all goes well, and the client has paid attention to the modeling, he or she still must remember or mentally retain the experience. The event must be mentally organized in an individual's mind in order to be retained sufficiently in memory. Can the individual verbally describe the skill/goal behavior? **Symbolic coding** refers to any of a number of strategies for translating an observed behavior into memory. Certainly, translating the behavior into words and remembering the words is one way. We are also likely to retain visual imagery. **Cognitive organization** will also occur as we relate the event to others or we evaluate certain qualities of the event (e.g., the tone of the role model's voice, style of dress, etc.), and assess our interest in the entire matter.

Practicing the modeled goal behavior is an important task; behavior rehearsal or practice is essential to the process of observational learning. Rehearsal can occur *symbolically*, such as when clients review modeled events in their imagination. Clients should also have the opportunity to actually demonstrate and practice the behaviors in treatment (**motor rehearsal**). The most common form of motor rehearsal is **role-playing**, in which clients are given the opportunity to repeat the goal behaviors, while counselors and sometimes other clients assume complementary roles for the purpose of practicing the behaviors.

The success of this practice phase of learning is highly dependent on the factors listed in the third component of Bandura's model (Figure 8.2). It goes without saying, perhaps, that the client must be physically (and mentally) capable of performing the behavior. If he or she does not possess the physical capabilities to replicate the entire behavior exactly, he or she should be capable of **component responses** so that approximations to the behavior can be demonstrated. One seldom perfectly duplicates a golf instructor's swing on the first attempt, for example, but there ought to be some attempt at a swing that the instructor and the student can then react to with **accurate feedback** and accurate **self-observation**. Hopefully, such feedback and additional practice will improve the golf swing over time.

Bandura's scheme also deals with a client's motivation for using the behavior in the future. As discussed in Chapter 4, operant conditioning theory maintains that reinforced behaviors are more likely to be repeated than those that are not reinforced or those that are punished. Reinforcement in this case can come in many forms. The counselor's praise, or **external reinforcement**, should occur in most situations. Observers of the role model will receive **vicarious reinforcement** as they note the role model's reinforcement and will come to expect similar rewards from their own demonstrations of the behavior. **Self-reinforcement** is extremely important. Especially when the goal behavior is valued behavior or has a good deal of functional utility, clients are likely to feel a strong sense of pride and satisfaction in accomplishing the new behavior. Some learned behaviors are likely to serve as reinforcements in themselves, for example, new athletic skills, assertiveness, improvements in study habits, or improved parental effectiveness.

Figure 8.2 omits some key issues. First, it says very little about the nature of the modeling process, which can be quite varied. Modeled behavior can involve a **live model** or a **symbolic model**, such as one we might observe in a film, a book, or in our imagination. Some social learning processes also make use of **covert modeling**, a process that encourages clients to visualize their performance of the behaviors they want to perform. Role models can also engage in **participant modeling**, in which they perform the target behavior with the client.

An important consideration not yet addressed is the process of repeating the behaviors outside the learning environment. As with other learning models, clients need to **generalize** the newly acquired behaviors outside of their therapy, in day-to-day living. Often **general imitation** as well as **specific imitation** of behaviors is desired. If, for example, a client is taught to avoid a specific high-risk situation, such as his friends at a local bar (specific imitation), the counselor will hope that he will learn to identify other high-risk situations and avoid those as well (general imitation). Generalization of learned skills is often a function of environmental considerations (Goldstein et al., 1989) or what is happening in the homes and neighborhoods of our clients. Will parents model and reinforce the goal behaviors, for example, or will they model dysfunctional alternatives?

Our overview of the structure of an observational learning process, or the social learning paradigm, should make a compelling case for treatment and program planning. Many of the correctional treatment settings we work in will be using this paradigm, but when is modeling being used effectively, and when is it not? In this regard, program planners and practitioners must ask a number of questions:

1. Are they employing and training skilled role models?

2. Are they identifying goal behaviors that their clients are able to perform, and if not, are they breaking complicated goal behaviors down into manageable components?

3. Are there sufficient opportunities for role-playing and practice?

4. Are staff reinforcing client behaviors and teaching clients to feel pride in their newfound skills?

5. Are staff in other areas of the correctional environment modeling the goal behaviors and reinforcing clients in using the new goal behaviors?

6. Have we made provisions for facilitating the generalization of newly learned behaviors to settings outside of the correctional environment?

Social Learning Interventions in Corrections and Prevention

As a program in itself and as a component of other programs, social learning and modeling forms the mainstay of many correctional treatment endeavors. We could offer numerous examples, but for purposes of illustration, we focus on two: Parent Management Training (Kazdin, 2000; Reid, Patterson & Snyder, 2003) and Structured Learning Training, also called Skill Streaming (Goldstein et al., 1989).[1]

Parent Management Training

Parent Management Training (PMT) is a treatment strategy for dealing with children and adolescents who exhibit conduct problems. The strategy was developed at the Oregon Social Learning Center (see Patterson, 1974; 1982), but has since been widely adopted and researched throughout the United States and internationally. PMT employs a social learning approach to train parents to alter their children's behavior at home. Most of this work has focused on children with oppositional defiant disorder, conduct disorder, and juvenile offenders, but the approach has also been used with children diagnosed with autism, attention-deficit/hyperactivity disorder, mental retardation, and other diagnoses.

Research on PMT has shown how poor parental discipline contributes to child behavioral problems (e.g., Patterson, Reid & Dishion, 1992) and how good parenting skills can prevent such problems (Kazdin, 2000; Reid et al., 2003). Keeping with the social learning paradigm, that behavior is learned through observation, modeling, shaping, reinforcement and punishment, child behavioral problems surely can be fostered by poor parental discipline. Specifically, parents (1) allow children to escape punishment; (2) ignore (do not reinforce) good behavior, (3) do not monitor their children well enough to observe the behaviors that should be reinforced or punished, (4) do not set limits, and (5) punish inconsistently and coercively. When the child's aversive behavior escalates, parents demonstrate inappropriate levels of anger and aggression, which are then modeled to the child. This package of events then causes child behavioral problems to become more intense over time and begins to cause other problems in the child's life, including problems with academics, peer relationships, delinquency, and substance abuse.

Treatment for these behaviors begins with the parents; often one parent or a single parent attend either individual sessions or sessions with other parents. They are taught to identify antecedents or stimuli for prosocial behaviors they hope to teach their children. These may include verbal prompts and instructions and modeling. PMT seeks to develop positive behaviors in order to reduce the need for antisocial negative behaviors (Kazdin, 2000). It is necessary to show parents the importance of reinforcing good behaviors through the use of social reinforcement (e.g., praise), token reinforcements, or the process of making privileges contingent upon desired behavior. Reinforcement schedules are developed and maintained. Parents must also work to reduce undesired behavior, using brief time-outs, or loss of privileges, but the preference is for rewards and the fostering of positive behavior. Other strategies of operant conditioning are also taught to parents, including shaping, extinction, and how not to inadvertently reinforce inappropriate behavior.

The parents themselves may engage in role-play with the therapist or other group members as they work to learn new ways to set limits, praise, and interact with their children. They must learn to identify and observe their children's behavior over time, and to adhere to specific reinforcement schedules, especially early in the treatment process. This typically involves some degree of record-keeping. Later these schedules may become more intermittent and ultimately may be phased out. The therapy will also target the child's behavior in school, including classroom deportment, relationships with peers, and homework. School officials and teachers may become partners in the behavioral program.

The duration of treatment depends largely upon the severity of the child's behavioral problems. For milder cases, therapy can range from six to eight weeks; programs for more disturbed children last from 12 to 25 weeks (Kazdin, 1997). As noted earlier, PMT has been evaluated in many controlled studies and found to be effective in reducing behavioral problems in schools and homes (see Patterson et al., 1993; Serketich & Dumas, 1996). Reductions in delinquency have also been observed (Bank et al., 1991; Dishion & Andrews, 1995). Evaluations have also documented improvements in parenting skills. The strategy, however, is somewhat time-consuming and demanding. Understandably, families dealing with poverty, limited social support, parental histories of antisocial behavior, single parenting, and high levels of stress from other problems are at high risk for dropping out of the program (Kazdin, Mazurick & Siegel, 1994).

Structured Learning Training/Skill Streaming

An example of a structured approach to social skills training is seen in Arnold Goldstein's **Structured Learning Training** (Goldstein et al., 1989), later called **Skill Streaming** (Goldstein & Glick, 1999). Skill Streaming is also one of three components of a treatment package called Aggression Replacement Training (Goldstein, Glick & Gibbs, 1998) and part of a peer-helping approach referred to as EQUIP (Gibbs, Potter & Goldstein, 1995) (see Chapter 9). Working on the assumption that delinquents, especially aggressive delinquents, possess fewer social skills than nondelinquents, Goldstein and his associates set out a list of 50 essential social skills. These are shown in Figure 8.3. Structured Learning Training/Skill Streaming endeavors to teach these skills.

Consistent with the social learning model, the staff use the teaching strategies of (1) modeling, (2) role playing, (3) performance feedback, and (4) generalization training. The latter, generalization training, encourages the youths to practice newly learned skills in a variety of settings. In addition, each skill is broken down into several steps. Youths being taught negotiating skills (Skill 4,d), for example, proceed through the following six steps:

1. Decide if you and the other person are having a difference of opinion.

2. Tell the other person what you think of the problem.

Figure 8.3
Example of Structured Learning Skills for Adolescents

Group 1.   *Beginning Social Skills*

   a. Listening
   b. Starting a conversation
   c. Having a conversation
   d. Asking a question
   e. Saying thank you
   f. Introducing yourself
   g. Introducing other people
   h. Giving a compliment

Group 2.   *Advanced Social Skills*

   a. Asking for help
   b. Joining in
   c. Giving instructions
   d. Following instructions
   e. Apologizing
   f. Convincing others

Group 3.   *Skills for Dealing with Feelings*

   a. Knowing your feelings
   b. Expressing your feelings
   c. Understanding the feelings of
      others
   d. Dealing with someone else's
      anger
   e. Expressing affection
   f. Dealing with fear
   g. Rewarding yourself

Group 4.   *Skill Alternatives to Aggression*

   a. Asking permission
   b. Sharing something
   c. Helping others

   d. Negotiation
   e. Using self-control
   f. Standing up for your rights
   g. Responding to testing
   h. Avoiding trouble with others
   i. Keeping out of fights

Group 5.   *Skills for Dealing with Stress*

   a. Making a complaint
   b. Answering a complaint
   c. Sportsmanship after the game
   d. Dealing with embarrassment
   e. Dealing with being left out
   f. Standing up for a friend
   g. Responding to persuasion
   h. Responding to failure
   i. Dealing with contradictory
      messages
   j. Dealing with an accusation
   k. Getting ready for a difficult
      conversation
   l. Dealing with group pressure

Group 6.   *Planning Skills*

   a. Deciding on something to do
   b. Deciding on what caused a
      problem
   c. Setting a goal
   d. Deciding on your abilities
   e. Gathering information
   f. Ranking problems by
      importance
   g. Making a decision
   h Concentrating on a task

Source: Goldstein, A., Glick, B., Irwin, M., Pask-McCartney, C. & Rubama, I. (1989). *Reducing Delinquency: Intervention in the Community*. New York: Pergamon Press.

   3.   Ask the other person about what he or she thinks about the problem.

   4.   Listen openly to his or her answer.

   5.   Think about why the other person might feel this way.

   6.   Suggest a compromise.

   Similarly, youths learning to deal with group pressure (Skill 5,1) engage in the following four steps:

   1.   Think about what the group wants to do and why.

   2.   Decide what you want to do.

3. Decide how to tell the group what you want to do.

4. Tell the group what you have decided.

Most of the writings of Arnold Goldstein and his frequent coauthor Barry Glick stress the importance of the stages of social learning. Modeling, for example, should employ either live role models or videotapes of models demonstrating each of the skill steps. Moreover, the modeling should occur in a variety of settings in order to assure the transfer or generalization of the skill to real-life experiences outside of the correctional environment.

Role playing provides an opportunity to practice or rehearse the skill immediately after it has been modeled. In role-playing, youth participants choose co-actors to play the role of a significant other who might be relevant to the youth's use of the skill in real life. Before engaging in the role-play, the main actor must describe how the skill would actually be used in his or her life, and that becomes the scenario for role-playing. Trainers must, of course, assure that the main actor and co-actor do not, for some reason, discontinue the role-playing prematurely, prior to covering all of the steps to the skill. Each group member must engage in role-playing each skill taught and must identify a situation relevant to his or her home environment.

Performance feedback is an essential follow-up to each of the role-playing exercises. Whenever possible, trainers must offer praise and encouragement. The feedback, however, is highly structured, and much attention is devoted to commenting on whether specific steps were actually demonstrated to an effective degree. Trainers, in other words, cannot limit their comments to general evaluative remarks; for example, "That was nice, Joe" is not sufficient.

The written accounts of Aggression Replacement Training and Structured Learning Training devote considerable attention to techniques for assuring that the newly learned skills are generalized outside the training settings. The program designers warn of the many flawed program efforts in which youth demonstrated new behaviors in correctional settings, but failed to use them upon returning home. Thus, transfer training identifies a number of techniques for encouraging the endurance of new prosocial skills. One strategy involves overlearning, or the use of more learning trials than those needed to obtain an initial indication of the skill. Participants find themselves learning a single skill in a variety of ways, including role-playing in different situations, observing the practice of others, writing the skill steps, and engaging in multiple homework assignments. In addition, the training attempts to replicate life situations similar to those experienced in the home environments of the group participants.

New behaviors are difficult to sustain when program participants return to environments that either fail to reinforce prosocial behaviors or reinforce the antisocial behaviors that the program sought to discontinue. Therefore, Goldstein and his associates attempted to show parents and family members the various skills taught to youth and to impress upon them the need to support their teachings in home settings. In one evaluation of a program that used skill streaming, the family program did not increase the effectiveness of the overall programs over what the program had achieved for the delinquents alone (Goldstein et al., 1989). In part, this may have been due to the difficulty in securing full participation of the families. Written accounts of the program suggested that families were overburdened with adversity; securing their participation may have required more effort than conducting the family program itself.

Figure 8.4
The Case of JT: A Social Learning Approach

The social learning approaches discussed in this box are based on the case study of Jason, presented on page 78. The essence of a social learning intervention is the strategy of anti-criminal modeling coupled with opportunities for practice and appropriate use of reinforcement and punishment (Andrews & Bonta, 1998). These techniques should take place in structured group sessions as well as in day-to-day interactions with correctional staff.

Treatment Plan—Example:

The Goals of a Social Learning Approach (for Jason):

To develop appropriate conflict management skills.

To understand and identify high-risk situations.

To associate with prosocial individuals and avoid antisocial individuals.

Approaches:

Jason will take part in a social skills course, in which he will focus on skills of conflict management and avoiding antisocial individuals.

Goals will also be approached through staff's ongoing adherence to the techniques of anti-criminal modeling.

Approach—Example:

As noted above, Jason will participate in a social skills course (see Goldstein & Glick, 1999). He will receive instruction in a variety of social skills, but will focus on those pertaining to conflict management and association with positive, prosocial people. The following exemplifies a class session in which Jason and other group members are taught the skill of compromising.

1. Modeling: *Co-leaders model a discussion between two persons in conflict.*

   Counselor A (Jason): When you change the channel in the TV room, without asking me, I get very angry. Sometimes you interrupt shows that I am really interested in, and then I don't get to see what happened.

   Counselor B (Horace): I guess it is hard to miss a favorite show. I know I don't like it when someone does that to me. However, you are often watching TV, Jason. Whenever, a big show comes on, like a big game, or great movie, you are already in the room watching something else. I've missed some great shows this year.

Figure 8.4, *continued*

> *Counselor A: (Jason): Listens to Horace's concerns and indicates that he hears them.* Well, I like to watch TV a lot, and you do seem to like sports more than I. Maybe we can work this out in a dorm meeting. Maybe, at the beginning of the week, we could talk about what really good shows are coming up. And then let the group vote on what shows they want to schedule the TV for. If a show is not on the schedule, and I am watching something else, I get to continue to watch my show. But you could talk to me about changing, like tell me what is on and ask if you can change it. But if I'm there first, I don't have to say yes.
>
> *Counselor B (Horace):* That sounds ok. Let's talk to others about it tonight.

2. Role Play (Practice): *Jason practices role playing a similar conflict with another group member. They attempt to demonstrate the skills of: (a) expressing anger; (b) listening to the perspective of the other person; (c) relating their understanding of the other's position; and (d) suggesting mutually beneficial alternatives.*

3. Receiving Feedback: *Group leaders and other group members comment on the role playing. They offer praise when possible and suggestions when warranted (e.g., try not to use blaming language, speak to your own feelings, and do not make assumptions about the motives of other people, etc.).*

4. Generalization Training: *Group leaders give members homework. In this case, for example, they might ask Jason and other group members to practice similar conflict resolution strategies outside of the group. Over time, the members should practice these lessons in increasing levels of difficulty.*

5. Feedback on Homework Assignments: *At the next meeting, group members discuss their practice outside of the group. Leaders and group members provide feedback.*

In addition to the social skills classes, staff use the techniques of good role modeling and appropriate use of reinforcements and punishments (see Andrews & Bonta, 1998). In Jason's case, these might involve:

> Staff refusing to reinforce any antisocial comments that Jason might offer *(e.g., "That lady was insured for that TV")*. Staff should also indicate to Jason that such communications are inappropriate and likely to be contributing to his troubles.
>
> Insisting on Jason's compliance with prison rules as well as his conformity to the rules of group participation. Staff should not allow the enforcement of rules to drift and become inconsistent.
>
> The staff should model prosocial behaviors in their interactions with inmates. They also should not imitate or smile at Jason's criminogenic expressions, or indicate that they too sometimes "go over the line."
>
> Encourage Jason's association with prosocial individuals—his sister, perhaps. Point out that his association with antisocial individuals is high-risk behavior and usually leads him to trouble.
>
> Offer Jason praise and encouragement when he accomplishes important tasks (e.g., responsible work habits or a new social skill).

Conclusion

We began our presentation of learning therapies in Chapter 4, with accounts of the radical behavioral interventions of classical conditioning and operant conditioning. In this chapter, learning is shown as a process that can occur vicariously as we observe the experiences of others. We learn, in other words, from role models in our environment. In recent years, correctional programs have made wide use of this learning paradigm. And when the social learning models have been delivered according to design, they are among the most successful programming options currently available. This chapter has stressed that programs based on social learning theory evidence a high degree of treatment integrity when they employ effective role models who possess good relationship skills, provide ample opportunities for role playing, offer feedback toward refining initial attempts, reinforce accomplishments, and generalize learned behaviors to real-life situations.

We continue the discussion of learning strategies in the next chapter. There we discuss the role our thoughts play in determining how we perceive events and persons around us, as well as how cognitions serve to support our own behavior. Our thoughts or cognitive processes and how we use them are also learned; at the same time, cognitions can be changed by learning.

Note

[1] We chose these two examples because they present an especially clear example of the social learning model at work. In the next chapter, however, we will see that social skills training (modeling applied to the task of learning social skills) is often combined with a cognitive component. The cognitive component teaches participants to change their thinking about their own behavior. These cognitive changes then influence the behavioral changes.

Key Concepts and Terms

accurate feedback

affective valence

arousal levels

cognitive organization

complex goal behaviors

component responses

covert modeling

distinctive

external reinforcement

functional value

general imitation versus specific
    imitation

generalize

goal behaviors

imitate

live model

modeling

motor rehearsal

observational learning

participant modeling

perceptual set

prevalence of role models

role model

role-playing

self-efficacy

self-observation

self-reinforcement

sensory capacities

Structured Learning Training/
Skill Streaming

symbolic coding

symbolic model

symbolic rehearsal

therapeutic communities

vicarious reinforcement

Discussion Questions

1. What relationship skills must a person possess in order to be an effective role model?

2. Think for a minute about the most effective teachers you have had over the years. In what ways did their classes demonstrate the principles of effective modeling? How did they utilize the various steps of the social learning process?

3. What is the rationale behind teaching the skills listed in Figure 8.2 to offenders?

4. Identify the important components or steps of the social learning process.

5. What is meant by "anticriminal modeling?" In what ways do case managers or counselors sometimes inadvertently demonstrate criminal modeling?

6. According to PMT, what are the skills of good parenting?

Chapter 9

Cognitive Therapies

Patricia Van Voorhis and David Lester

Cognitive therapies focus on the ways in which people think. Thinking, of course, entails a broad array of processes and skills, including problem-solving skills, the ability to plan for the future, the ability to empathize with others, flexibility (whether we see our world in concrete, absolute terms or are more open to a range of possible interpretations), accepting responsibility, and anticipating the consequences of our actions. **Cognitive** also refers to what we think, our attitudes, beliefs, values, and the relatively stable manner in which we make sense of our surroundings. As Donald Meichenbaum, a well-known cognitive psychologist, once explained to a group of college students: "Our thoughts often operate as cognitive templates that can be carried from situation to situation" (1986). If we believe, for example, that stealing from our next-door neighbor is wrong, we probably will refrain from stealing at other times when the possibility is presented.

Most of us do not need to be reminded of how our thoughts sometimes serve to dramatically exacerbate difficult situations. Cognitions, however, are also known to play a major role in psychological problems, such as depression (Beck et al., 1979), anxiety disorders (Beck & Emory, 1985), and other forms of mental illness. Importantly, those who commit crimes on a repeated basis also are known to think irrationally, evidencing irresponsible "thinking errors" (Barriga et al., 2000; Elliot & Verdeyen, 2002; Walters, 1990; Samenow, 1984; Yochelson & Samenow, 1976), displaying numerous internalized antisocial values (Jennings, Kilkinney & Kohlberg, 1983; Kohlberg, 1976), and possessing very limited problem-solving and other cognitive skills (Andrews & Bonta, 2003; Gendreau, Little & Goggin, 1996; Ross & Fabiano, 1985).

Cognitive therapies are not as intensive as the analytic therapies discussed in Chapter 3, and there is more counselor-client involvement than we might observe in the radical behavioral interventions (Chapter 4). With the cognitive approaches, counselors work with individuals or groups to change irrational thinking and to develop more adequate thinking processes.

During the past decade, the cognitive treatment modalities have become a preferred approach to counseling and therapy. This is especially true in our current climate of health care reform and the advent of "managed care," in which recipients of mental health services are encouraged by insurance providers to remedy problems in as few sessions as possible. Cognitive therapies are viewed as "here and now" approaches that are among the most efficient and expedient therapies available.

The growing interest in cognitive therapies for juvenile and adult offender populations is equally understandable. First, cognitive counseling strategies, like the behavioral strategies discussed in Chapters 4 and 8, deal with observable client characteristics—thinking and behavior. Thus, cognitive strategies are easier to use because these characteristics are clearer than the unconscious motives, fears, and anxieties targeted by psychoanalysis and other methods. Second, because most correctional agencies can afford to hire only a few psychologists or clinical social workers, many correctional counseling, case management, and group facilitation functions are conducted by non-clinicians who must receive systematic training. Cognitive methods have proven to be quite valuable in this regard. Agencies have found that they can efficiently train non-clinically trained staff to use the cognitive methods. This is especially true in the case of the cognitive skills programs, in which the training of case managers, probation officers, and others is often conducted through in-service training sessions. Programs delivered by non-clinicians, however, look more like classrooms than therapy sessions. They follow structured, often scripted, manuals and leave little to therapy.

A third reason for the popularity of cognitive-behavioral programs has to do with the nature of offenders. Offenders differ from non-offenders in the obvious manner in which their behaviors and the thinking that generates their behaviors have hurt others. Confronting these harmful behaviors and dysfunctional thought patterns makes good sense if the confrontation can be performed in a professional and appropriate manner. The cognitive strategies provide a framework for doing so.

Finally, many recent evaluations of cognitive interventions with juvenile and adult offenders have shown the programs to be highly effective (Andrews et al., 1990; Antonowicz & Ross, 1994; Garrett, 1985; Izzo & Ross, 1990; Lipsey, 1992), including three recent meta-analyses devoted solely to cognitive-behavioral programs (Lipsey, Chapman & Landenberger, 2001; Pearson et al., 2002; Wilson, Allen & MacKenzie, 2000). In fact, one of the most recent meta-analyses found the cognitive-behavioral methods to be more effective than radical behavioral models (Pearson et al., 2002). It would be difficult to fault the efficiency, clarity, and effectiveness of these methods.

While cognitive and cognitive-behavioral approaches have proliferated in corrections, they generally fit into one of two models: **cognitive restructuring**, in which interventions endeavor to change the content of beliefs, values, and attitudes; and **cognitive skills**, in which interventions seek to improve cognitive processes—the structure and form of reasoning (i.e., *how* we think) rather than its content. The division is not always clear. Some programs target both content and process. Cognitive skills programs, developed by Ross and Fabiano (1985); Goldstein, Glick, and Gibbs (1998); and Bush, Taymans, and Glick (1998), to name just a few, target both cognitive processes and criminal thinking errors.

We begin with the cognitive restructuring approach, moving from the foundational work of Albert Ellis's (1973) Rational Emotive Therapy, a model designed for general use, to Yochelson and Samenow's (1976) focus on criminal thinking errors, an approach designed for offenders.

Cognitive Restructuring Approaches

Rational Emotive Therapy

Rational Emotive Therapy (RET), devised by Ellis (1973) is widely recognized as the foundation of cognitive restructuring. RET is concerned with emotions and thoughts that impair our existence. Let us say, for example, that the client experiences an unpleasant occurrence, a failure, or a rejection. RET refers this as an **activating experience** and seeks to assess how the client makes sense of this experience.

In the unhealthy thought sequence, an **irrational belief** follows the activating event: "Isn't it awful that she rejected me? I am worthless. No desirable woman will ever accept me. I deserve to be punished for my ineptness." Several troubling emotional states result from this irrational belief. The patient feels anxiety, depression, worthlessness, or hostility as a consequence. In the healthy thought sequence, however, the activating experience is followed by a **rational belief**. "Isn't it unfortunate, annoying, or a pity that she rejected me?" Following this rational belief are the emotional states of rejection, disappointment, and annoyance, but these states are far more manageable and transient that those that build from irrational beliefs.

According to Ellis, rational beliefs increase positive feelings and minimize pain. They are accurately related to real (not imagined) events. Irrational beliefs decrease happiness and maximize pain. In most cases, irrational beliefs are distorted perceptions of the activating event. They prevent the client from fulfilling his or her desires in the future.

RET teaches the client that emotional states are not a result of the activating experiences, but rather the result of irrational beliefs. That is, these beliefs are often more damaging than the activating event. The client must be taught to dispute the irrational beliefs. Why is it awful? How am I worth-

e evidence that no one will ever love me? Why should I have
b? By what law do I deserve to be punished? Once the
ute rational beliefs for irrational beliefs, he or she will be
ld make more appropriate decisions.

ein, Burns (1980) listed some common irrational ways of
thinking. In **all-or-nothing thinking**, for example, things are viewed as black
or white. A less-than-perfect performance is a failure. In **overgeneralization**,
one negative event is seen as a never-ending pattern of defeat. In **mental filter**, individuals dwell on negative details and filter out the positive aspects,
and in **disqualifying the positive,** positive experiences are re-labeled as "not
counting" for one reason or another. In **magnification** or **catastrophizing**,
individuals exaggerate the importance of something. For example, a person
says, "This is the worst thing that could have happened to me," when it is far
from the worst thing. They label themselves or others, which leads to name-
calling. "I am a jerk or a loser. You are a fool or an evil person." These labels
are distortions, but serve to create irrational emotions. In **jumping to conclusions**, individuals assume that they know what another person is thinking but fail to check with that person, or predict the future outcome negatively
and so do not bother to attempt the task. In **shoulding**, individuals try to motivate themselves by saying "I must . . ." or "I ought . . ." and so feel guilty when
they do not. It is preferable to say "It would be nice if I . . ."

All-or-nothing thinking has been noted by counselors to be particularly
characteristic of alcoholism, drug addiction, bulimia, and other addictive disorders (van Wormer, 1988). Alcoholics Anonymous members refer to such
irrational thought processes as **"stinking thinking."** Burns (1980) and others note that irrational thoughts are not only self-defeating, they are set-ups
for personal failure. In many instances, all-or-nothing, perfectionistic
approaches to life also set the stage for a need to escape or medicate feelings of failure. Thus, the addict seeks the substance that causes those feelings to go away, albeit temporarily.

The Techniques of Rational Emotive Therapy

The RET counselor is active, persuasive, educational, directive, and, at least
in the Ellis model, hardheaded. The counselor teaches the simple basic theory of RET. Therapy involves disputing the client's irrational beliefs. There are
no "shoulds" or "musts." "Awful" is an indefinable term. The counselor
shows how these irrational beliefs generalize to other aspects of the client's
life, affecting many future decisions and emotional states. The counselor
points out that the causes of disturbed behavior are current and observable. The
client must be taught to continually observe and challenge his or her own belief
system. RET does not deal with the client's early history, unconscious thoughts
and desires, nonverbal behavior, dreams, or any transference that occurs in the
counseling situation. According to RET, such early experiences affect clients
in the present only because the clients themselves perpetuated them.

The counselor teaches the theory, points out irrational beliefs, interprets quickly and with no pretense that the interpretation may be easy to accept. The counselor may seem confrontational, but in being confrontational, he or she confronts the beliefs, not the client. Of course, good counseling skills are important in drawing out the client's beliefs, values, and attitudes.

The counselor will use a variety of techniques to aid in this task: role-playing, modeling, bibliotherapy, stories, behavior therapy techniques, philosophic discussion, or audiovisual aids. **Role-playing** (see Chapter 8) involves practicing new behaviors (roles) in the counseling situation before trying these behaviors in other situations. **Modeling** (Chapter 8) involves copying behaviors demonstrated by the counselor or others. Bibliotherapy involves reading useful books, especially self-help texts. The counselor also stresses homework assignments, in which the client practices the lessons of counseling. The client must be encouraged to act and to experiment: "Meet three new people this week. Attend your most difficult class, instead of avoiding it. Initiate social engagements." This helps the client take risks, gain new experiences, interrupt dysfunctional habits, and change philosophies.

Ellis states that the goals of Rational Emotive Therapy are to leave clients with a minimum of anxiety (self-blame) and hostility (blaming others), and to give them methods of self-observation and self-assessment that will ensure that they continue to be minimally anxious and hostile.

Applications to Offenders

Most of Ellis's work was with non-offenders, but in his early writing, Ellis (1979) discussed the case of an exhibitionist he had treated. The client was a 28-year-old social worker who exposed himself several times a year. He had been arrested twice and was on the verge of ruining his professional career. He had been married for eight years, had two children, and functioned well at his job. He had come to counseling under duress because the court had ordered him to seek counseling or be sentenced to jail.

Ellis was able to demonstrate the client's irrational thinking to him. First, the client believed that he must perform well in his sexual and general life, that he had to win the approval of his significant others, and that he must not do anything stupid, especially because he was a professional. The demands that he made upon himself led him to feel inadequate when he failed to satisfy his wife sexually. For Ellis, demands that we make upon ourselves are irrational. It would be nice if we always performed well in our lives. It would be rewarding and pleasant. But it is not necessary, and failing to always perform well is not a catastrophe.

Second, the client believed that his wife must not be so critical of him and ought not to deprive him sexually. He thought that she was horrible for being so mean and frustrating. He also thought that other women ought to give in to his sexual advances. Again, such thinking is irrational. It would be convenient if others did what we wanted them to do. But there is no rational reason they should. And they are not horrible people for not doing what we want. They are ordinary people, like ourselves, simply trying to cope with and survive the events of everyday living. Third, he believed that life ought not to be such a hassle and that he could not stand the difficulties that life presented to him. In point of fact, he could stand the difficulties, as can most of us, all the while as we say to ourselves "I can't stand this!"

These irrational beliefs led him to experience emotions such as self-pity, depression, and anger. Ellis would often diagram the impact of beliefs on emotions and behavior according to what he referred to as the A (action), B (belief), C (consequence) Model of Rational Emotive Therapy. Using this model, the client's irrational thinking could be mapped as follows:

ACTION [A]:	The client fails in some endeavor.
BELIEFS—IRRATIONAL [B]:	I always fail. I'll never succeed. I am a worthless person.
CONSEQUENCE [C]:	Depression/self-pity.

After challenging the irrational belief, a healthier sequence occurs:

ACTION [A]:	The client fails in some endeavor.
BELIEFS—RATIONAL [B]:	Where is the evidence that I always fail? Just because I failed at this task does not mean that I will always fail in the future. I am not a worthless person; I'm an ordinary person who failed at this particular task.
CONSEQUENCE [C]:	Mild annoyance and disappointment.

Thus, Ellis treated the client by pointing out his irrational thinking and helping him to challenge each of its components. The client realized that he wanted certain outcomes (such as getting more approval from his wife), but he also realized that he did not have to obtain them. As he surrendered his "shoulds" and "oughts," and substituted preferences and wishes, his behavior became less compulsive and he felt better able to control his antisocial sexual behavior.

Ellis accepted the client, while rejecting the behavior. He helped him get in touch with his hostility and depression, thereby reducing their intensity. He helped him acknowledge his behavior without denigrating himself. Later he gave the client homework assignments of meeting other women and risking rejection. He taught him relaxation techniques. Treatment lasted about seven months. Four years later, the man had not returned to his pattern of exhibitionism. He had arranged to divorce his wife and was meeting other women.

Criminal Personality Groups

It is important at this point to discuss cognitive restructuring strategies that have been developed to specifically target the dysfunctional cognitive patterns of offenders. A number of explanations for criminal behavior suggest that offenders demonstrate characteristically criminal orientations, such as blaming victims, asserting their entitlement to the property and personal safety of others, and other thinking styles that serve to support their criminal behavior. Yochelson and Samenow (1976) and later Samenow (1984; 2001) identified more than 50 such **"thinking errors"** in their work with offenders at St. Elizabeth's Hospital. Criminals, according to Yochelson and Samenow, demonstrate the following:

1. They blame others for their criminal behavior, maintaining, for example, that they "couldn't help it," or that "someone else made them do it."

2. They develop an "I can't" attitude toward their own responsibilities.

3. They often fail to understand the concept of injury to others.

4. They fail to empathize or put themselves in the place of another person, particularly their victims.

5. They fail to put forward enough effort to accomplish necessary goals. Sometimes they seem to not know how much effort is enough.

6. They refuse to accept responsibility.

7. They assume an attitude of ownership or entitlement to the property of others, treating others' property as if it already belonged to them.

8. They do not appear to understand what constitutes trustworthy behavior.

9. They often expect others to "fall into line" to accommodate their own wishes.

10. They make decisions irresponsibly by not gathering enough facts, making assumptions, and blaming others.

11.   Pride is more important than acknowledging their mistakes or allowing others to get a point across.

12.   They demonstrate a flawed definition of success and the time it takes to succeed; believing, for example, that they should be a success overnight.

13.   Many offenders cannot seem to accept criticism.

14.   They deny their own fear and fail to recognize that fear can be constructive.

15.   They use anger to control others and fail to acknowledge their anger in appropriate ways.

16.   They overzealously attempt to obtain power, demonstrating "power thrusts" in inappropriate ways.

Others have identified somewhat similar cognitive patterns among offenders (e.g., see Barriga et al., 2000; Elliot & Verdeyen, 2002; Ross & Fabiano, 1985; Sykes & Matza, 1957; Walters, 1990), but Yochelson and Samenow's work is especially useful to counselors for the number of thinking errors identified and the suggestions offered to counselors for correcting these errors. The job of the counselor, according to Yochelson and Samenow, is to correct these thinking errors, and the task of the correctional treatment facility is to provide an environment in which such errors can be corrected by both treatment and custodial staff and by inmates in group work or day-to-day institutional life. Staff and inmates are taught to identify and to correct these thinking errors in themselves and in others. The correction techniques substitute rational thinking for the errors identified above. Examples of some of these corrections follow:

1.   Accept no excuses for irresponsible attitudes or behaviors.

2.   Do not allow the offenders to shift the focus of responsibility from themselves.

3.   Point out how the offender is hurting others, and instill a sense of what it is like to be hurt.

4.   Teach the offender the process of role-taking, or taking the perspective of others.

5.   Socialize offenders to what is a sufficient amount of effort for given tasks. Show them that responsibility sometimes means doing what we don't want to do and that failure to expend effort can have adverse consequences.

6.   Point out ways in which the offender may be refusing to accept responsibility.

7.   Visualize reversals of the offender's irresponsibility (for example, what it would be like if others failed to meet their responsibilities to the offender).

8. Teach offenders that trust must be earned and call attention to instances in which the offender is betraying the trust of others.

9. Teach offenders to communicate expectations openly, to evaluate whether they may be asking for too much, and to deal with disappointment.

10. Teach principles of good decision making.

11. Teach them to accept mistakes and the fact that we all make them, and have to admit to them.

12. Show offenders that they need to plan ahead and accept a gradual sequence of stages toward the accomplishment of goals. Discourage notions of fast catch-ups to the status of others.

13. Teach that criticism is something we learn from, if it is merited. If it is unwarranted, ignore it.

14. Reassure offenders about the important role of fear in our lives and how to differentiate healthy fears from unhealthy fears.

15. Teach appropriate skills of anger management.

16. Call attention to, and do not accept, "power thrusts."

Paint Creek Youth Center, a facility developed by Vicky Agee during the mid-1980s, incorporated Yochelson and Samenow's principles into the facility's token economy or point system (see Chapter 4). Points were rewarded for, among other behaviors, a youth's refraining from the use of thinking errors. These points could then be exchanged for privileges. The Paint Creek program employed several other program modules, such as family therapy, a sex offenders' program, and victim awareness groups. Evaluation results of the program were favorable when conclusions were limited to only the youths who completed the program in its entirety (Greenwood & Turner, 1993).

What we have seen in both examples of cognitive restructuring is that counseling, from these perspectives, targets and seeks to change irrational, erroneous, and faulty thinking. The types of irrational thoughts identified by rational emotive therapy are those that can lead to generalized unhappiness and depression. The criminal personality groups, on the other hand, correct criminal thinking errors. These clearly are not errors that make offenders unhappy, but they serve to support, excuse, and sometimes reinforce criminal behavior. Use of such errors releases inhibitions one might have toward committing a crime, thereby "freeing" one to behave in a criminal manner.

Notwithstanding the popularity of these programs, some precautions are warranted. What happens, for example, if offenders who do not evidence criminal thinking are admitted to the offender-based cognitive-behavioral program? There are many such offenders. Offenders who possess prosocial values and are less prone to criminal thinking should not be participating in these cognitive restructuring groups. Doing so only serves to teach criminal thinking. Traditional, offender-based, cognitive-restructuring groups should also be re-evaluated for women offenders (Bloom, Owen & Covington, 2003). Researchers have noted, for example, that women offenders are less likely than men to possess the prototypical criminal thinking mentioned above (Barriga et al., 2001; Erez, 1988). This is not to say that cognitive-behavioral interventions are not likely to work with women, but rather that the "one size fits all" approach does not seem appropriate. Cognitive restructuring programs may need to be tailored to the dysfunctional thinking that characterizes a more gender-responsive set of thought processes.

Cognitive Skills Approaches

Where cognitive restructuring seeks to change the content of reasoning, cognitive skills programs seek primarily to change the structure or form of one's reasoning. In order to fully understand the cognitive skills programs, it is important to understand the distinction between structure and content. Impulsivity, for example, has a characteristic cognitive process or structure regardless of whether one is being impulsive in the way one drives one's car or in the way one seeks to obtain desired property. For one thing, very little thought is given to the consequences of the behavior. Similarly, both individuals demonstrate limited awareness of alternatives to these antisocial behaviors. From this view, cognitive skills programs place greater emphasis on what clients are *not thinking* than on what they *are thinking*.

Donald Meichenbaum is widely credited with the seminal work on cognitive skills. Meichenbaum developed cognitive-behavioral coping skills through **self-instructional training** and later stress inoculation (Meichenbaum & Jaremko, 1982). Self-instructional training teaches clients how to talk to themselves or **"self-talk"** through difficult situations. The process begins with the counselor talking his or her way through a task or situation, and includes behavioral tasks as well as admonitions to "go slowly," "concentrate," and other helpful reminders, including self-praise. Next, the client works through the same process with the counselor, again verbalizing these tasks aloud. The third stage finds the client performing the tasks by himself or herself, but again verbally discussing the process. Final stages encourage clients to perform tasks alone, but with covert self-instruction, saying the instructions to themselves. These approaches were used successfully with school-age and pre-school children, schizophrenic patients, the elderly, and others.

Stress inoculation training is similar to self-instructional training, except clients are instructed to encourage and reinforce themselves (e.g., "I know how to handle this"; "I am in control") while engaging in the self-talk pertinent to coping skills. The encouragement offered to oneself during difficult situations helps to promote a sense of **self-efficacy** (or self-confidence), a human trait that is associated with success. Stress inoculation was initially applied to helping clients cope with pain, anxiety, and fear, but in recent years, we have observed successful approaches with victims of trauma, including rape and child abuse (Meichenbaum & Deffenbacher, 1988).

Self-instruction and stress inoculation attend to behavior as well as cognition. Indeed, many cognitive models are also called **cognitive-behavioral approaches**, because they recognize that: (1) cognitions, as well as behaviors, are learned; and (2) behavior is prompted, supported, mediated, and reinforced by cognitions (Bandura, 1973). In addition, one sees considerable use of modeling and role-playing (the tools of the **social learning** approach presented in Chapter 8) in the practice of cognitive-behavioral psychology. Today, cognitive-behavioral approaches are widely recognized as a subfield, if not a major component, of behavior therapy.

Cognitive Skills Programs for Offenders

As noted above, for many offenders, criminal behavior follows impulsive thinking. Simply put, many offenders make impulsive decisions when they might have engaged in constructive problem solving. Improving the processes used to think though and act on a problem is the goal of many cognitive-behavioral programs for offenders.

An excellent example of a cognitive-behavioral program that targets a distinct cognitive skill is seen in Taymans and Parese's (1998) curriculum, titled Problem Solving. This program is shorter than most offender-based cognitive programs. While most programs require 30 to 40 sessions, Problem Solving is completed in four or five sessions. In this program, participants are given two important tools. The first is an understanding of the "conflict cycle," or how one's thinking can lead to good or bad consequences. This is shown in Figure 9.1, below.

Figure 9.1
The Conflict Cycle (Long & Morse, 1995)

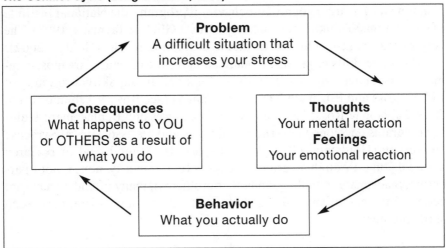

After repeating several exercises that show the impact of thoughts on behavior and its consequences, offenders are introduced to the second tool, The Problem Solving Steps:

1. **Stop and Think:** Be quiet, get space, and calm down.

2. **Define the Problem and Determine Goals for Its Resolution:** What is really wrong? What do I want?

3. **Gather Information and Insight about the Problem:** Be sure to differentiate facts from opinions.

4. **Identify Alternative Courses of Action:** What are my choices and what are the likely consequences of each choice?

5. **Choose a Course of Action:** What is the best choice? What is my plan?

6. **Evaluate the Results:** Did I achieve my goal? What have I learned?

Instructors are trained to teach both skill acquisition and skill application. To generalize these problem-solving tools to a variety of situations, instructors vary the "problems" and give homework assignments, which require offenders to use the skills in their day-to-day lives. Of course, the program requires use of behavioral strategies of modeling, role-playing, feedback, and generalization training to teach these rather concrete steps to problem solving.

A recent quasi-experimental evaluation of Problem Solving, conducted for the Virginia Department of Correctional Education, found that the program reduced disciplinary infractions committed by both community and institutionalized participants (Spiropoulis, Spruance & Van Voorhis, forthcoming). These reductions occurred in four of five research sites, and in some settings write-ups were as much as 20 percent lower for the Problem Solving group than the comparison group. Problem Solving later became a component of a larger cognitive-behavioral program, the National Institute of Corrections' Thinking for a Change (Bush, Glick & Taymans, 1998). The larger program also achieved favorable evaluation results (Golden, 2002).

Cognitive skills programs for adult and juvenile offenders are most commonly associated with the cognitive skills and living skills programs of Robert Ross and Elizabeth Fabiano in Canada (see Ross & Fabiano, 1985; Ross, Fabiano & Ross, 1989) and with the Aggression Replacement Training programs developed by Arnold Goldstein and his associates at Syracuse University (Goldstein, Glick & Gibbs, 1998). A good deal of research shows us that, through a variety of causes (e.g., poverty, abuse, poor parenting, inadequate schooling, and other problems), many offenders have not acquired the cognitive skills needed for effective social adaptation. Such skills include:

1. self-control;

2. an ability to take the perspective of others (empathy);

3. problem-solving;

4. formulating short-term and long-term plans;

5. avoiding high-risk situations;

6. anticipating the consequences of one's behavior;

7. decision making;

8. coping;

9. flexible rather than rigid thinking strategies, and others.

In response to these problems, one comprehensive cognitive-behavioral program, Reasoning and Rehabilitation (Ross et al., 1989) offers modules addressing:

1. social skills;

2. interpersonal problem-solving;

3. cognitive style;

4. social perspective taking;

5. critical reasoning;

6. values;

7. meta-cognition; and

8. self-control.

Treatment processes in the cognitive skills programs involve a number of different strategies, including games, journal activities, reasoning exercises, didactic teaching methods, audiovisual aids, and group discussions. Offenders are afforded the opportunity to talk though various situations or case studies and are taught new skills for controlling impulsive behaviors. For example, one module of a cognitive skills program developed for the National Institute of Corrections teaches the skill of "self-talk" to help offenders stop old thinking patterns and practice new thinking skills (Bush & Bilodeau, 1993). Group leaders instruct offenders in the following perspectives regarding high-risk situations:

1. "My part" asks participants to think about the part of a situation for which they might be responsible;

2. "Their shoes" devotes some time to imagining what it is like to be the other person in this situation, or to imagine what that other person is thinking;

3. "Respect" directs offenders to change any dehumanizing thoughts they might have regarding others in the situation into "humanizing" ones;

4. "Consequences" asks the offender to identify other situations like this, which produced negative consequences for the offender;

5. "New person" asks the offender to remind himself or herself of the new person he or she wants to become; and

6. "Decent sentiment" trains offenders to identify the more favorable attitudes and sentiments that they routinely cut off or suppress.

Cognitive skills programs begin with strong attention to group rules regarding cooperation between group leaders and participants. Participants are encouraged to "think before they talk," to avoid domination of the group, to be on time, and to attend regularly. In the beginning, they are always taught the importance of cognitions, for example, "what we do in our minds controls what we do in our lives." Throughout the sessions, they are taught to keep "thinking reports" (Bush & Bilodeau, 1993; Bush, Glick & Taymans, 1998: Ross et al., 1989) or "hassle logs" (Goldstein et al., 1998) that describe an event that occurred between sessions. In doing so, offenders are expected to give special attention to the types of thoughts they had about the event. These are discussed in the group sessions, with special attention to the types of thinking patterns that could lead to violent or criminal behavior. Subsequent sessions might begin with a short video or role-play around an event that provoked anger, such as being unjustly accused of something or disagreeing with someone. Group members work through these scenarios, using such developing or newly formed skills as:

1. attempting to see the viewpoints of others;

2. controlling feelings of anger;

3. asserting your own position in a nonviolent manner; and

4. examining belief patterns about the situation and whether they are true.

In later sessions, they may learn skills for preventing adverse outcomes to provoking situations. These may include:

1. stopping dysfunctional thoughts;

2. setting new goals;

3. making and carrying out plans;

4. self-talking one's way through the new plan;

5. practicing new thinking; and

6. reminding oneself of the consequences of incorrect courses of action and thought.

In recent years, the Canadian cognitive skills programs expanded to include **Living Skills**. In these programs, offenders participated in the cognitive skills program to form a foundation for later modules such as:

1. living without violence;

2. parenting skills;

3. community reintegration;

4. managing finances, and others.

Some of the living skills, particularly those in the community reintegration model, are not, strictly speaking, cognitive skills. Such skills as finding and keeping a job, writing a résumé, budgeting, and money management become much more solid, however, when they are built on the foundation of sound cognitive skills. For example, money management (e.g., budgeting, saving, borrowing/financing) becomes clearer once offenders have addressed problems with impulsivity. As noted in the previous chapter, some of these skills can be taught through role-playing and modeling, through the social learning approach, and then used in combination with the cognitive models (Hollin, 1990). In fact, we will conclude this chapter with two programs that combine social learning, moral education, and cognitive skills models.

The most recent cognitive skills curricula are tailored specifically to female offenders. It is unfortunate that most correctional programs and assessments were developed for men and applied to women with few concerns for their appropriateness (Belknap & Holsinger, 1998; Bloom et al., 2003; Chesney-Lind, 1998), but women have clearly been an afterthought. In fact, most studies cited throughout this chapter and this book, including the meta-analyses, were conducted on male offenders. As a result, we do not have a clear picture of what works with female offenders.

Moving On, a cognitive curriculum developed by Marilyn Van Dieten (1999) utilizes many of the cognitive-behavioral strategies discussed above, but alters the treatment targets to be more responsive to women offenders. The extensive curriculum addresses skills pertinent to problem solving, communication, and assertiveness, and helps women to recognize and change negative "self-talk." Considerable attention is devoted to the development of healthy, safe relationships and skills for connecting with their community and building strategies for satisfying personal changes. The program begins with a module pertaining to women in culture, which examines harmful societal images of women, as well as gender-role stereotypes and their impact on women. This work is consistent with emerging research on women's pathways to crime, the Guiding Principles for a Gender-Responsive Criminal Justice System (Bloom et al., 2003) and with several initiatives on female offenders offered through the National Institute of Corrections.

Moral Education Approaches

Some would argue that moral education does not belong in a section on cognitive skills. However, in placing it here, we focus on the developmental changes in reasoning structures that human beings experience over the life course. Humans, according to Piaget (1948), Kohlberg (1976), Warren (1983), and others, progress from the relatively concrete cognitive reasoning structures of children to the more flexible thinking of adults. If our learning environment affords the experience to make such developmental progressions, we are likely to become "more skilled" than one who continues to engage in absolute, concrete forms of reasoning. Immature forms of reasoning create situations in which answers are either "yes" or "no," problems are viewed from single rather than multiple perspectives, one's capacity to understand the perspectives of others is seriously constrained, and moral decisions depend solely on concerns about external rewards and punishments.

Lawrence Kohlberg's **Stages of Moral Judgment** (Kohlberg et al., 1979) form a cognitive developmental classification system that classifies individuals according to the ways in which they think about justice, fairness, and "right" courses of action. As with other cognitive approaches, the six Stages of Moral Judgment pertain to the form or process of reasoning rather than to actual choices that the reasoning might support. The classification process and the treatment model that follow involve assigning an individual to one of the stages on this developmental continuum of cognitive complexity.

Moral Judgment Theory shares assumptions common to several other ego and cognitive developmental theories as set forth by Loevinger (1966); Piaget (1948); Sullivan, Grant, and Grant (1957); and others. These theories maintain that cognitive development:

1. involves changes in qualitative thought process that describe *the way* one thinks (not *what* one thinks);

2. occurs through a developmental sequence of stages that is the same for all people;

3. occurs in the direction of increasing complexity (i.e., one's thinking becomes more complex with development);

4. represents an underlying logic at each developmental stage that appears to be consistent across situations; and

5. occurs through stages that are hierarchical integrations that enable individuals to comprehend all stages below and one stage above their diagnosed stage of moral reasoning.

Because development can cease at any point along the continuum, a cross section of the population, theoretically, would show a distribution of persons at all stages.

There are three levels of reasoning in the moral development continuum: preconventional, conventional, and postconventional. Each level is comprised of two stages. A brief overview of the stage characteristics follows:

I. **Preconventional Reasoning:**

Stage 1: Moral decision making involves blind obedience to authority in order to avoid punishment, defer to power or prestige, and avoid trouble. The interests of other individuals are not recognized.

Stage 2: A "right" course of action at this stage is predicated upon such instrumental considerations as the avoidance of punishment and the furtherance of one's own self-interests. The attainment of these objectives, however, engages one in exchanges and deals with other persons. Thus, others are important in an instrumental sense, as parties to such a deal.

II. **Conventional Reasoning:**

Stage 3: Moral reasoning is internally motivated by loyalty to other people and by a desire to live up to what is expected by significant others. Reasoning at this stage reflects an application of the "Golden Rule" philosophy.

Stage 4: Decisions reflect a desire to maintain such social institutions as the family, the community, and the country as social systems. The roles and rules of these systems are salient.

III. **Postconventional Reasoning**:

Stage 5: Moral reasoning adheres to the utilitarian notion of a social contract or the need to weigh certain rights, values, and legal principles against the greatest good for the greatest number of people.

Stage 6: Such ethical principles of justice as the right to life and respect for the dignity of other persons as ends rather than means are used to generate moral decisions. These principles are maintained to exist in a consistent and universal manner that is exclusive of laws or circumstances.

In delinquent and adult populations, we seldom observe the individuals who are reasoning at either Stage 1 or Stage 6. These are extreme cases. Stage-specific reasoning is perhaps clearer with an example for each of the stages. Let our example be of Tim, a boy who is deciding whether or not to steal a bicycle that he finds unlocked outside in a school playground. It is important to remember that Tim's stage of moral judgment is not determined by his choice to steal the bike or not steal it. Instead, it is his thought process, or reasons for his choice, that determines his stage of moral development. In fact, there are stage-specific reasons for or against stealing. For example:

> If Tim was diagnosed at Stage 2, we might hear him say that he stole the bike because he wanted one, and no one was around, so he knew he wouldn't get caught. If he decided not to steal the bike, he might say that he was afraid of getting caught and being punished.
>
> If Tim was classified as Stage 3, relationships with others would be an important consideration in resolving this moral dilemma. He might decide to steal the bike, for example, so that he could be with his other friends who had bicycles. He might decide not to steal the bike out of concern for the bike owner who would be hurt by losing it. A "Golden Rule" mentality may be heard as he relates his reasoning. That is, because Tim knows that he would not like to have his own property stolen, he chooses not to steal another's bicycle.
>
> At Stage 4, an individual places priority on the importance of maintaining social systems. Laws, of course, help in this regard. It is hard to find a Stage 4 decision that would justify stealing the bike. But a Stage 4 decision not to steal the bike would place priority on obeying laws, not to avoid punishment or the disappointment of others, but rather because laws are important to maintaining social order. Tim might consider what would happen if everyone just stole whatever they wanted to steal.
>
> Finally, a Stage 5 decision against stealing the bike would focus on universal rights that should exist exclusive of laws or circumstances. Property is one such right. Thus, Tim might reason that the owner of the bicycle has a right to keep it, regardless of the laws or opinions of others, or for that matter, what might happen to Tim if he gets caught.

As we observe Kohlberg's developmental sequence of cognitive reasoning, we can also observe some developmental gates where some earlier noted cognitive difficulties would probably cease to exist. Stage 2 individuals, for example, demonstrate an external locus of control—a right course of action is determined by what is occurring in the external environment, where the individual scans the situation to determine whether he or she will be rewarded or punished. By Stage 3, however, the individual thinks about his or her relationships with others, an internalized notion. Similarly, the Stage 3 individual is capable of empathizing with others who are like him or her. And by Stage 5, empathy is afforded to those who are not like the self. Recall that empathy and internal locus of control were among the cognitive skills addressed in other cognitive behavioral models.

In correctional treatment programs that emerge from Kohlberg's Stages of Moral Judgment, the most important goal is to try to achieve growth from Stage 2, preconventional reasoning, to the conventional reasoning of at least Stage 3. This is because prosocial, empathic orientations begin at Stage 3, as does the notion of an internalized value system or conscience. Imagine, for example, the child whose decision to cheat or not to cheat on a test is predicated upon an externalized consideration of whether the teacher is in the room (a Stage 2 decision), versus the child who bases the decision not to cheat on an internalized belief that cheating is wrong. In fact, research on Moral Judgment and delinquency reports that Moral Judgment stages are significantly lower among delinquents than among nondelinquents (Jennings et al., 1983). Typically, a significantly higher proportion of delinquents are diagnosed at Stage 2 than nondelinquents. Thus, the goal of facilitating development to Stage 3 appears to be well-founded.

The interventions designed to do that, **moral education programs**, assume that growth in moral judgment is most likely to occur when an individual interacts with prosocial environmental factors that encourage growth. Specifically, Kohlberg has maintained that exposure to fair and participatory environments promotes moral development. The moral education groups expose participants to **moral dilemmas** that are then discussed in groups of individuals who are cognitively processing the various issues at different stages of moral judgment. It is hoped that, over time, the moral conflict, its discussion, and its resolution will advance individuals to the higher levels of reasoning demonstrated by their peers in the group. Day-to-day decision making can also be used to generate "moral discussions." In the Cheshire Reformatory and the Niantic State Farm for Women, for example, Kohlberg and his associates developed intervention strategies based on the moral judgment stages and assessments of the institutional environments. Their strategies consisted of offering inmates some responsibility for decision making in the governance of their living units (Hickey & Scharf, 1980). Most of Kohlberg's work, however, was with schoolchildren in programs referred to as the Just Community.

As will be seen in the next section, current applications of moral education use the moral discussion groups and the Kohlberg developmental theory in multimodal approaches, combined with other cognitive-behavioral or social learning components. Growing interest is also being shown in a program called Moral Reconation Therapy (MRT) (Little & Robinson, 1986). MRT uses several group and workbook exercises designed to develop and improve moral reasoning through 16 graded moral and cognitive stages. MRT can be divided into shorter components, but is somewhat less structured than other cognitive-behavioral curricula. Although MRT is growing in popularity, evaluation results are not impressive (Armstrong, 2003; Finn, 1998).

Aggression Replacement Training (ART)

Employing moral education in conjunction with other approaches recognizes that the moral education groups add an important values-based component to the cognitive skills and cognitive restructuring programs. Values, after all, are internalized and with us on a consistent basis. Learned behaviors and cognitions, on the other hand, are vulnerable to the competing rewards associated with criminal behavior; because crime is so rewarding, one might be more likely to use a new prosocial skill if it is supported by an internalized moral argument (or conscience) (Goldstein & Glick, 1995a). Goldstein and his associates at Syracuse University apply this concept in a cognitive-behavioral program called **Aggression Replacement Training (ART)** (Goldstein et al., 1998).

ART consists of three components:

1. **Skill Streaming**, which teaches a wide range of social skills through a social learning approach (see Chapter 8);

2. **Anger Control Training (ACT),** a cognitive-behavioral approach to teaching juvenile and adult offenders skills for controlling anger;

3. **Moral Education** groups that utilize the discussion groups and dilemmas developed by Kohlberg.

The program's use of moral education is similar to Kohlberg's original model. Offenders discuss and attempt to resolve moral dilemmas. Some of the dilemmas are standard to the Kohlberg model (e.g., the man who steals a drug to save his dying wife, or the "lifeboat dilemma"); Others dilemmas tap issues that may come up within the group or the correctional environment. Because we have already discussed moral education in the previous section and Skill Streaming in Chapter 8, we turn now to a description of the Anger Control Training model.

Borrowing from earlier work on anger control (Novaco, 1979) and stress inoculation (Meichenbaum, 1977), ACT teaches delinquent, aggressive, and conduct-disordered youths to identify and deal with the sources of their anger. ACT uses a five-step approach to anger management:

1. The first step involves helping youths to identify the external events and internal self-statements that most often **"trigger"** their anger.

2. Having identified what provokes them, the second step is to help youths to recognize the **physiological clues** that will alert them to their feelings of anger (e.g., tense jaw, flushed face, clenched hands, stomach feelings, etc.). The intent of the first two steps is to teach the juveniles to recognize their

anger in time to control it. Because both the triggers and the cues are idiosyncratic, counselors must be prepared to individualize their approach to some extent.

3. Next, youth are taught some techniques for dealing with the identified anger. These consist of **"self-statements"** designed to lower anger arousal, such as "chill out," "calm down," "cool off," and other calming phrases.

4. **Reducers** are also taught as a means of helping individuals reduce levels of anger. These include such strategies as the visualization of peaceful scenes, deep breathing, thinking about the consequences of acting out anger, and counting backward.

5. The final step teaches youths to evaluate how well they controlled their anger, and to praise themselves if they performed effectively.

Of course, many of the situations that create anger for us in our daily lives cannot simply be walked away from. They require, instead, our attempts to problem solve and to respond in an honest and appropriate manner. These instances require social skills of expressing feelings, answering a complaint, negotiating resolutions to disputes, and other skills that are taught in the Skill Streaming component of Aggression Replacement Training. Evaluation studies of ART find it to be an effective approach (Goldstein & Glick, 1995b; Goldstein et al., 1998).

A similar program model was implemented in Ohio with juvenile offenders. The EQUIP program utilized a model quite similar to ART but combined cognitive skills, anger management, and moral education with a group approach known as the Positive Peer Culture (Vorrath & Brentro, 1985) (see Chapter 5). The Positive Peer Culture (PPC) meetings endeavor to serve as a mutual help group with the goal of motivating youths to help each other and to act responsibly. Meetings known as EQUIP meetings were interspersed throughout the PPC meetings. These sessions worked on social skills, anger management, and moral development. Results for the EQUIP program were also favorable (Gibbs, Potter & Goldstein, 1995).

Cognitive-Behavioral Programs and their Effectiveness— Much Depends on Program Integrity

Throughout this chapter, we have presented much evidence of the effectiveness of cognitive-behavioral programs for offenders. This optimism pertains to offenders as a whole as well as to specific types of offenders, e.g., sex offenders (Nagayama Hall, 1995) and substance abusers (Pearson & Lipton, 1999). In response, the implementation of cognitive-behavioral programs and their curricula has been widespread. Yet two meta-analyses of cognitive-behavioral programs note that the most effective treatment programs were small demonstration projects, studied, in some cases, by the very individuals who developed the curricula. When the programs were expanded to entire agencies and evaluated by outside researchers, however, the treatment effect diminished considerably (see Lipsey et al., 2001; Wilson et al., 2000).

The likely explanation for such findings faults the treatment integrity of the expanded programs. During the pilot phase of these programs, facilitators were probably carefully trained and monitored. Most importantly, the small demonstration sites were able to keep close tabs on program quality. Understandably some of the initial focus on quality was lost when these programs were implemented agency-wide to larger groups of participants.

How does this take happen? If an agency wants to implement a given cognitive-behavioral program, they invest in extensive staff training, purchase manuals, and start delivering the program. But does this assure that trained facilitators understand the training, keep to the basic program design, maintain good relationships with the participants, or are adept at using the core skills of the cognitive-behavioral and social learning approaches (e.g., modeling, practice, feedback, and reinforcement)? Will staff be retrained if they have not retained these skills?

To illustrate, a recent evaluation of Reasoning and Rehabilitation found no significant difference between the program participants and members of the comparison group. As shown in Figure 9.2, the 12-month recidivism rates (rearrest) for those in Reasoning and Rehabilitation was 36 percent as compared to 38 percent for the comparison group (Van Voorhis et al., 2002). Further examination of Figure 9.2, however, finds that some of the Reasoning and Rehabilitation programs worked better than others. Groups in which leaders maintained good classroom control (structure) achieved recidivism rates of 19 percent instead of the 36 percent achieved by all of the participants. Additionally, use of appropriate cognitive-behavioral techniques (practice and feedback) increased the effectiveness of the program. Groups in which participants had the opportunity to practice in all of the sessions evidenced a recidivism rate of 24 percent instead of 36 percent. It is not clear what was occurring in the less successful programs, but less participation suggests that perhaps the group leader was doing most of the talking rather than helping offenders try out new ways of thinking and behaving. Understandably, those who completed the program also had much lower recidivism rates (25%). In sum, while policy makers and practitioners are optimistic about the cognitive-behavioral approach, much needs to be done to assure that the programs are delivered according to their design.

Figure 9.2
Effects of Program Quality on Offender Outcomes (Van Voorhis et al., 2002)

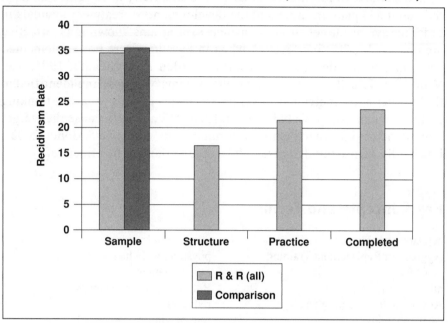

Conclusion

Cognitive and cognitive-behavioral therapies have achieved much respect among mental health and correctional practitioners. They are among the most successful treatment models currently available. Correctional agencies have discovered that they can train correctional treatment staff, including some who may not have clinical degrees, to use the models effectively. In part, this may be attributable to the fact that cognitive therapy is a demystified system of therapy, in comparison to an approach such as psychoanalysis. Indeed, many of the popular "self-help" books currently in print are based on cognitive therapy techniques. At the same time, many of the in-service training opportunities for correctional treatment practitioners emphasize cognitive therapy and cognitive counseling. Program materials (e.g., treatment manuals, lesson plans, assessments, and training modules) are more readily available for these than for other approaches discussed in this book. The counseling techniques and groups can be short-term, although treatment can take up to two years in some cases.

These comments are not intended to oversimplify the cognitive approach. Cognitive therapies require active and directive counselors who challenge and confront the irrational thoughts and irresponsible behaviors of their clients, while continuing to value the clients as persons.

Finally, agencies could incur serious problems with treatment integrity if, in the course of relying too much on the simplicity of cognitive therapy, they omit adequate training and the development of treatment manuals in order to save resources. In such instances, programs known to be effective are observed to be "ineffective" when in fact they were not implemented according to the design (Van Voorhis, Cullen & Applegate, 1995; Van Voorhis et al., 2002). Just the same, the systems of counseling identified in this chapter have tremendous potential to change the inappropriate thinking patterns and maladaptive behavior styles of offenders. Because they target a set of factors known to be highly criminogenic (Andrews & Bonta, 2003), it is hardly surprising that research has found them to be effective.

Key Concepts and Terms

activating experience
Aggression Replacement Training
   (ART)
all-or-nothing thinking
Anger Control Training (ACT)
catastrophizing
cognitive
cognitive-behavioral approaches
cognitive restructuring
cognitive skills
criminal personality groups
disqualifying the positive
gender-responsive programming
irrational belief
jumping to conclusions
Living Skills
magnification
mental filter
modeling
moral education programs
moral dilemmas

overgeneralization
physiological clues
rational belief
Rational Emotive Therapy
reducers
role-playing
self-efficacy
self-instructional training
self-statements
self-talk
shoulding
Skill Streaming
social learning
Stages of Moral Judgment:
   Preconventional Reasoning
   Conventional Reasoning
   Postconventional Reasoning
stress inoculation training
stinking thinking
thinking errors
trigger

Discussion Questions

1. What is the theory behind the cognitive therapies?

2. Why do you think these therapies are so popular today?

3. Think of occasions when you have been angry, depressed, or had some other strong emotion. Can you recall what thoughts went through your mind? Write them down. Can you dispute them—that is, point out the irrational elements in them and change them to rational therapy?

4. Describe the theory and techniques of moral education interventions.

5. Explain the difference between a cognitive restructuring program and a cognitive skills program.

6. What role do criminal thinking errors play in crime causation?

7. How effective are cognitive-behavioral programs with female offenders?

8. How do correctional programs lose their integrity?

Chapter 10

Family Therapy

Patricia Van Voorhis and Michael Braswell

Family environments and the quality of family life are often cited in the development of criminal behavior. Families play a role in producing criminal behavior in a variety of ways, including the failure to form adequate parent-child attachments (Baumrind, 1985; Bowlby, 1988), exposing children to violence in the home (Thornberry et al., 1994), excessive conflict (Katz & Gottman, 1993), inadequate child socialization and parenting skills (Larzelere & Patterson, 1990; Loeber & Dishion, 1983; Patterson & Dishion, 1985), and dysfunctional styles of interaction. From a systemic perspective, a delinquent or criminal member may be a symptom of a very troubled family system (e.g., Haley, 1976; Vogel & Bell, 1960). In such cases, problem behavior serves functional purposes for the family, such as when delinquency takes the family's attention away from a faltering marriage (Henggeler, 1982; Minuchin, 1985). The relevance of the family to criminal behavior is perhaps most poignantly evident when members commit acts of violence against each other as demonstrated in child and spouse abuse.

Concerns for family issues also must extend beyond the etiology of criminal behavior to concern for what happens *after* a conviction or adjudication of a family member. Often by necessity, the day-to-day business of criminal justice agencies does much to threaten the stability of families. Criminal and family courts separate hundreds of families each day. Juvenile justice agencies have been criticized both for prematurely separating children from their biological families and for prematurely returning institutionalized youth to families that cannot offer a better alternative to the institution. Institutions further aggravate the problem when they limit visitations, forbid contact visits, fail to place inmates in close geographical proximity to their families, and neglect family issues in the course of treatment. In a recent survey of incarcerated parents, more than 60 percent reported being incarcerated more than 100 miles from their home. Moreover, 57 percent of fathers and 54 percent of mothers reported having no visits from their children (Mumala, 2000). For mothers especially, retaining custody after a period of incarceration has become more difficult in recent years. The Adoption and Safe Families Act of 1997 terminates parental custody after a child has been in foster care for at least 15 of the past 22 months. The law affects incarcerated parents as well as those in treatment for some forms of mental illness or substance abuse (Bloom, Owen & Covington, 2003).

Ironically, when the period of incarceration and separation is over, the offender's chances of returning to a normal life often depends on how well the family is functioning by the end of the ordeal (Hairston, 2002) and how much support the family is able to offer the inmate (Nelson, Deess & Allen, 1999). Given the observation that many marriages dissolve after two years of incarceration (Brodsky, 1975), and that contacts with family members diminish over time incarcerated (Lynch & Sabol, 2001), we can expect that many long-term inmates will not be returning to supportive family settings. Even in cases that do not result in separation, the stresses of police and court proceedings usually prove to be a severe jolt to most families. In all of the examples cited above, it is clear that much is expected of the families involved with juvenile delinquents and adult offenders. It is hoped that effective family therapy programs, along with emerging prisoner re-entry policies and some of the family-strengthening programs mentioned toward the end of this chapter, can assist families in need.

The prospect of an offender's return to a law-abiding life is even more complicated than the issue of whether the family adjusts to his or her arrest and disposition. Success may also depend upon the offender's participation in some form of treatment, the quality of family life prior to treatment, and the nature of the family's involvement in the treatment process. In many cases, the policy of treating the criminal or delinquent family member while ignoring the family's problems wastes time and money. Correctional counselors and case managers frequently express the frustrating claim that their clients improve during treatment only to get worse upon returning to families lacking affection, adequate supervision of children, support, and open communication (Janeksela, 1979; Klein, Alexander & Parsons, 1977). Early writings on family therapy note similar results among other problem clients, including schizophrenics (Bateson et al., 1956), drug addicts (Hirsch & Imhof, 1975; Stanton, 1994), anorexics (Minuchin, Rosman & Baker, 1978), and alcoholics (Meeks & Kelly, 1970; Steinglass, 1994).

The treatment of a troubled family member can have an unfavorable impact on the family as well. Problem members often play an important role in maintaining familiar but unhealthy patterns of interaction between family members (Hoffman, 1981). As a result, if the troubled member becomes well, the **family system** may be threatened unless other members have participated in the change process. Family members may want to return to a less painful status quo arrangement of living together in discord rather than risking a move beyond familiar traditions to greater personal and interpersonal growth. The family therapy literature presents numerous examples of instances in which the improved behavior of the problem member shocked families into unhealthy compensating behaviors, such as identifying new family **"scapegoats"** or withdrawing from therapy (Napier & Whitaker, 1980; Sameroff, 1989). The family system has a reality that is more than the sum total of member characteristics. If the family system is at fault, it is futile to treat only one symptom of its problems.

The following case study demonstrates the power of the family system:

Joe, a 14-year-old-male, and his parents were referred for counseling as a result of his increasing acting-out behavior, particularly at school. Until recently, the teenager apparently had been a reasonably well-behaved and productive student. During the last several weeks, however, both his parents and school officials became alarmed. Verbal disrespect to teachers, plummeting grades and finally joyriding with several of his friends in a stolen car brought him and his family to the attention of the juvenile court.

Joe's family consisted of a mother, father, older sister, and younger brother. Joe's father was an assistant manager at a department store. Severe economic deprivation as a child had resulted in his becoming a "workaholic"; always being prepared for the possible return of "hard times." He was caught between his genuine concern for his son and his compulsive need for greater economic security. Joe's mother was at home, spending the majority of her time caring for Joe's younger brother who was severely retarded. Joe's older sister, who was a senior in high school, seemed less affected by the current family dilemma. She and Joe apparently had very little to do with each other.

Joe indicated he both loved and hated his younger brother. He felt guilty—that perhaps it should have been him rather than his brother who was severely retarded. Just the same, he resented the disproportionate amount of attention his brother received, yet knew it was necessary. Being in the middle, he felt extra pressure to help with his brother's care, but being in the middle also meant that there was little time and attention left for him from his parents. Joe particularly felt neglected by his father.

As counseling began to include Joe and his parents, communication between them improved. Joe and his father grew closer and began to schedule "special" time together. When this initially occurred, Joe's mother began to experience anxiety. Focusing on her need for special time appeared to resolve her feelings of being more isolated from Joe and his father. Subsequent follow-up counseling sessions seemed to indicate that the family was functioning effectively. Joe's grades and behavior had improved. Three months later an urgent telephone call from his mother revealed that Joe had struck one of his teachers and had been suspended from school. During the last several weeks, Joe's behavior had deteriorated rapidly, coinciding with his father's move to another state to take a more economically secure position. The family was to join him at Christmas in their new home.

Joe's prospects seemed bleak. His father was absent from the family in an attempt to improve their economic position with a new job. His absence left a void in Joe's need for relationship with him and at the same time placed additional pressure on an already overtaxed mother. In the father's absence, the family system had to adjust and realign itself, a situation that did not lend itself to Joe's continued improvement.

The field of family therapy considers individual modes of therapy to be too narrow and inattentive to the impact of relationships, families, and their respective systems on family members. Family therapy approaches are consistent with the major tenets of social psychology and, more recently, community psychology, environmental psychology, and social ecology, which assert that individuals cannot be understood apart from their interactions with group, social, and cultural forces in their environments (Bronfenbrenner, 1979). From this view, behavioral problems are seen as having multiple causes that involve families, schools, neighborhoods, workplaces, and peer groups (Zigler, Taussig & Black, 1992). Traditional therapies are also faulted for their failure to recognize the potency of group change, especially at the level of the family system. The family is often the key to long-term change, because in most instances it exercises its influence over the entire life span (Larzelere & Patterson, 1990; Loeber & Dishion, 1983; Sampson & Laub, 1993). While the growing awareness of the family's role in the etiology and treatment of criminal behavior is reflected in recent treatment developments that involve families in the correctional process, the criminal justice system's use of this approach is perhaps not what it should be. This is unfortunate in view of the growing number of favorable evaluation results. In fact, the effectiveness of family therapy is underscored in several recent reviews of the treatment evaluation literature (Andrews et al., 1993; Hazelrigg, Cooper & Borduin, 1987; Kazdin, 1987; Loeber & Hay, 1994; Patterson, Dishion & Chamberlain, 1993; Shadish et al., 1993). At a time when correctional treatment has generally been maligned as ineffective, evaluations of family interventions are showing positive effects on both recidivism rates and family functioning.

History and Overview of Family Therapy

The history of family therapy, as a field, spans a brief 30 years (Nichols & Schwartz, 1998). Until recently, in fact, family involvement in individual therapy was discouraged by such major figures as Freud, Rogers, and oth-

ers as likely to contaminate the client-therapist relationship. Presumably, neurotic conflicts with other family members or perhaps a conscious or unconscious desire to win their approval would cause clients unwittingly to deny
and distort their true feelings and impulses.

The earliest approaches to family therapy were problem-centered efforts
to cure illnesses, particularly schizophrenia, by treating the family through
group counseling techniques (Nichols & Schwartz, 1998). Initially,
researchers attempted to identify prototypical patterns of family interaction
in order to characterize each problem. But efforts to describe the "schizo-
phrenogenic family" or the "alcoholic marriage" proved to be oversimpli-
fied. It soon became clear that family issues were not necessarily specific
to the presenting problem. The common elements among such problem-centered families were more generally: (a) their presenting problem; and (b) the
fact that the family functioned in a dysfunctional manner that served to perpetuate the presenting problem (Russell et al., 1983). The exact nature of the
dysfunction, however, varied from family to family.

Later years witnessed the development of several distinct treatment
models. Notwithstanding their different approaches, each model held several fundamental assumptions regarding the importance of the systems
within which we love, play, and work.

More recently, some authors fault family therapy itself for being too narrow. These critics assert that family systems should not be the sole target of
therapeutic intervention, because families are comprised of individuals
who possess varied individual strengths and problems, and some of these may
affect family functioning more than others. They also observe that families
exist in reciprocal relationships with extra-family systems such as schools,
work settings, and neighborhoods. Any one of these outside systems may significantly influence the quality of family life or impede the progress of family therapy (Henggeler & Borduin, 1990). Such concerns launched
Multisystemic Therapy (Henggeler & Borduin, 1990), an eclectic approach
that combines several of the family therapy models, discussed below, with:
(a) individual approaches for a troubled family member (if needed); and (b)
other community services (e.g., childcare and school advocacy).

Family therapy is viewed today as a significant field of mental health. Services that address a diverse array of problems are available through many private and public mental health programs. The term *family therapy* would be
misleading, however, if it suggested that these services are obtained solely
by intact nuclear families. Family therapy is more accurately viewed as a treatment modality designed to address the problems that result from the manner
in which individuals perceive and manage their relationships. Such services
may be retained by a variety of living units, including single-parent homes,
gay and cohabiting couples, single people, and reconstituted families.

Good approaches to family therapy must also modify their approach to
reflect ethnic diversity. This is not just because the criminal justice system
deals with much diversity, but because the context of the family differs so

dramatically across ethnic groups. Ethnicity affects role expectations, family values, concepts of morality, religiosity, needs, and perceptions of life events. Although most of the writing on family therapy addresses the needs of the white, middle-class family living in the general, not criminal, population, the move to ethically responsive approaches is beginning to take shape (Ho, 1987; Kumpfer, 1999).

Schools of family therapy differ primarily in their treatment focus, or the type of family problem that is addressed in therapy. In organizing the complex array of methods, Guerin (1976) divides strategies into two basic schools: psychodynamic and systems-based technologies. The psychodynamic approaches include the individual, group, and experiential therapies of Ackerman (1966), Zuk (1975), Whitaker (1976), and others. Systems-based approaches encompass the communications (or strategic) methods of Haley (1976) and Satir (1972), as well as the structural strategies developed by Minuchin (1974) and Bowen (1978). Absent from Guerin's early classification scheme are social learning models, e.g., the work of such behaviorists as Alexander and Parsons (1982); Patterson (1974, 1982); Gordon and Arbuthnot (1987); Gordon and associates (1988), and Kumpfer, DeMarsh, and Child (1989); and the multisystemic treatments of Henggeler and Borduin (1990). These will also be discussed in this chapter.

Despite the uniqueness of each of the family therapy models identified above, many share in varying degrees the belief that the family should be viewed as a system. A number of concepts that have emerged from early studies of the family as a system continue to be viewed as fundamental to family therapy today. Families are seen as having a unity that is greater than the sum of the individual personalities comprising the system. As a result, when a family approaches therapy with a troubled member, it is the family system rather than the individual that is assumed to be in need of the most help.

Treatment of a system follows from a different causal paradigm than that used in the individual, nonsystemic therapies summarized earlier. Nonsystemic models employ a linear approach to therapy. In other words, they assume that problem behaviors follow a simple cause-and-effect relationship. The assumption is that if we intervene with the cause of a problem, we will alleviate the resulting problem. Systems therapies, in contrast, view problem behaviors as circular, reciprocal, and interrelated. Symptoms are part of a multicausal relationship system (Nichols & Schwartz, 1998). It is not simply that a child's behavior problem adversely affects other family members; other family members also affect the child.

In understanding systems therapies, it is important to understand the qualities of systems. Patricia Minuchin (1985) summarizes these as follows:

1. **Any system is an organized whole, and elements within the system are necessarily interdependent**. Because of their interdependency, the system cannot be fully understood by assessing only an individual member of the system. The sys-

tem is more than the sum of its parts; the behaviors of members of the system exist in a context.

2. **Patterns in a system are circular rather than linear**. The behaviors of members, in other words, exist in larger chains of circular, reciprocal, and spiraling interactions. This picture argues against blaming individual family members for the family's problems.

3. **Systems have homeostatic features** that maintain the stability of their patterns. Over time, behaviors of system members can become consistent and predictable. Systems appear to prefer this steady state, and may experience stress when change is needed. In a variety of ways, systems may also seek to resist change.

4. **Evolution and change are inherent in open systems**. Systems need to change over time. The family system that raises small children, for example, needs to be different than the system than sends these same children to high school. Open systems are more likely to grow and change than closed, isolated systems. Open systems exchange information with the environment outside the system. In doing so, they become more adaptive. Closed systems appear to experience more psychosocial difficulties such as abuse or incest (Alexander, 1973). Because there is no opportunity to question abusive or other dysfunctional behaviors (the family is not interacting sufficiently with the outside environment), these behaviors may also come to be viewed by family members as normal or justifiable.

5. **Complex systems are composed of subsystems**. These subsystems carry out distinct roles within the system. The roles of the parental subsystem, for example, are different from those of the sibling subsystem.

6. **The subsystems within a larger system are separated by boundaries, and interactions across these boundaries are governed by implicit rules and patterns**. Some of these rules are socially prescribed. Most societies require that parents supervise children. Other rules may be developed within the system, e.g., "we don't talk to anyone about family matters." Boundaries are discussed further in the section on structural family therapy, but for now they refer to the borders that differentiate one system from other systems. Likewise, they are the borders that differentiate the system's various subsystems (e.g., parents, children, and various dyads). We refer to these boundaries as open, closed, or semi-permeable. As will be seen shortly, the appropriateness of a given boundary, rule, or pattern depends on the nature of the subsystem.

What can a system do to bring about difficulties for one or more of its members? Any number of things. In striving for "**homeostasis**," or a balanced, steady state of equilibrium, family systems "elect" (although not necessarily consciously) members to help stabilize the system in its ongoing patterns (Sameroff, 1989). One case history of a family's experience in therapy, for example, describes David and Carolyn Brice's desperate attempts to cope with their oldest daughter's acting-out behaviors (Napier & Whitaker, 1980). Claudia's extreme unhappiness with her parents was shown in her constant battles with her mother, late and long disappearances from home, sexually acting-out, and a frightening preoccupation with death. Fairly early in therapy, co-therapists helped the parents to see that Claudia's behavior functioned to keep the Brice family together. The Brices' marriage had cooled down several years prior to the onset of Claudia's problems and had ceased to meet the needs of either partner. Claudia's dramatic behavior served to emotionally unite her parents in their concern for her, while conveniently allowing them to escape the problems of their marriage. Claudia's behavior, in this case, maintained a certain degree of homeostasis in a dysfunctional system. Oddly, as Claudia's behavior improved after this revelation, the Brices' son, Don, began acting out. Dysfunctional systems often unconsciously defend against the cure of one of their members by electing another scapegoat, or by taking the family or individual members out of therapy in order to maintain homeostasis. As might be expected, Don's behavior also improved rather quickly, but resolution of the marital difficulties consumed the remainder of the therapy process.

Much of our knowledge of family systems was advanced by Murray Bowen (1978). Bowen maintained that troubled families create dysfunctional system boundaries and communication processes. Members may become "fused" into an undifferentiated mass. In this sense of "stuck-togetherness," individuals lose their sense of uniqueness. Such fused or enmeshed individuals function in emotionally reactive, as opposed to rational, ways. Poor boundaries between individuals, in this case, make it difficult for individuals to understand themselves. It becomes difficult for members to be aware of where they leave off and other family members begin. In other words, I may have a strong sense of "who we are" as a family, but little or no idea of "who I am" as an individual. Such a system may become closed, blocking outside sources of information and maintaining a distorted sense of reality. Members also may communicate through a process of "triangulation," in which emotions cease to be a two-way exchange. Instead, a three-person system is formed. The wife, for example, may tell her daughter, rather than her husband, about the frustrations of her marriage. While this process may succeed in ventilating emotions, it fails to resolve conflicts and is not healthy for the daughter.

The perspective of the family as a system represents a new paradigm in psychotherapy, a dramatic shift from linear to circular causality in which the individual can no longer be viewed as an individual personality formed by discrete events from his or her past. According to the systems paradigm, individual behavior is largely the result of the social context that is often dominated by the family. The causes are ongoing and circular, the turbulent products of all of the interlocking relationships, **roles**, rules, communication patterns, boundaries, and habits that families develop.

The following sections provide brief overviews of five major family therapy models:

1. Psychodynamic

2. Communications

3. Structural

4. Social learning approaches

5. Multisystemic Family Therapy

While this discussion of pure approaches may serve to clarify the various models, they may also offer a distorted view of the typical therapeutic process. Most applications are eclectic. In day-to-day practice, therapists often borrow techniques and perspectives from several models. Moreover, the models themselves are not mutually exclusive. Even in the vast literature on families and family therapy, these lines are becoming blurred, as authorities present more and more models that represent a blending of the somewhat artificial distinctions listed above.

Psychodynamic Family Therapy

The earliest forms of family therapy were conducted from a psychodynamic perspective. These models had their origins in the work of Freud and Adler, but credit for theoretical and treatment developments pertinent to family therapy is directed to the later work of Ackerman (1966), Framo (1970), Boszormenyi-Nagy and Ulrich (1981), Stierlin (1977), Sullivan (1953), and Dicks (1963). Although psychodynamic therapists do not dismiss systems theory entirely, they adhere primarily to traditional perspectives on unconscious forces.

The most important focus in **psychodynamic family therapy** is on **object relations**. Object in this case refers to the person and his or her relationships with others, particularly intimate others. Object relations is defined by Westen (1991) as "a set of cognitive and affective processes that mediate interpersonal functioning in close relationships." Object relations theory maintains that components of family life, especially those relevant to the child's relationship with his or her mother, are internalized. Throughout the course of a lifetime, internalized parent-child interactions are then held to influence the functioning of one's interpersonal relationships as well as one's perception of self. The form of these representations changes over time, moving from infantile dependence or merger with the mother, to independence, to interdependency with others, to an ideal of mutual exchange (Liebert & Spiegler, 1994). Healthy development requires that people move away from the dependence of childhood to the interdependence of adulthood, or to **individuate**. In addition, intimate relationships of adults often reflect repetitions of issues affecting past relationships as well as the adequacy with which children separate, or individuate, from parents. Problems with object relations may be manifested in a variety of dysfunctional patterns, including difficulties with:

1. failure to individuate or separate from parents (e.g., intense dependency);

2. conflict management;

3. formation of trusting relationships;

4. ability to delay gratification;

5. tolerance of closeness or separation;

6. confidence; and

7. self-esteem.

People may also carry over an inaccurate sense of themselves and others into new relationships. The repetition of dysfunctional scripts from the "home of origin" (Barnhill & Longo, 1978), projective identification, or transference of parental characteristics onto others (Boszormenyi-Nagy and Ulrich, 1981) can mar adult relationships.

As with individual psychodynamic approaches, psychodynamic family therapists strive to uncover, clarify, and interpret unconscious material from the past. Once this material is brought into consciousness, therapists can help clients to **"work through"** or translate their newfound understanding into productive, more functional behaviors. The identification of unconscious material may occur more efficiently in family therapy than in individual therapy. In individual therapy, clues from the unconscious areas of the personality emerge from observations of a client's free associations, defense mechanisms, dream therapy, and from transference (see Chapter 3). Transference occurs when aspects of past relationships and transactions are transferred to the therapist during therapy. The transference can then be observed and interpreted for the client. In family therapy, however, transference may occur among family members as well to the therapist. Family members may also direct projective identifications onto other members. Some of these projections may encourage delinquent behavior. A father, for example, may gratify his own aggressive instincts and fantasies through the aggressive behaviors of his son. Such projections and other defenses are likely to be more frequent in family therapy than in individual therapy (Nichols & Schwartz, 1998).

Psychodynamic therapists may have to attend to the history of each family member in order to discover the sources of family difficulties. The "working through" process may also be more complex, but somewhat faster, because there are more opportunities for it to occur in the family therapy setting than in individual therapy.

Although psychodynamic family therapy boasts a rich theoretical literature and numerous case studies, evaluations have not found the psychodynamic approach to be as effective as other models (Andrews et al., 1993; Shadish et al., 1993). We also recognize that the object relations perspective of the psychodynamic approach is criticized by many, particularly feminists, as placing too much blame on mothers. Whether we focus on the "mother blaming" problem or not, psychodynamic interventions stand apart from more modern approaches to family therapy, which recognize a wider range of factors at work in contributing to delinquent and criminal behaviors (Pardeck, 1989).

Communications Family Therapy

Interest in the communications of families began as research (rather than as therapy) with the work of Gregory Bateson (Bateson et al., 1956), Donald Jackson (1967), Jay Haley (1976), and Virginia Satir (1967). As the term suggests, communications therapists help families by studying and improving upon the manner in which members communicate with each other. This has involved not only a study of the words transmitted in family communication but **"metacommunication"** as well. Metacommunication refers to a second level of communication that can convey as much information as the verbal content of a conversation. Words say one thing, and other factors, such as voice tone and body language, say another. Family therapists have learned that metacommunication can complicate family interactions in ways that can create problems for a family system.

Early therapy with schizophrenics, for example, noted numerous instances in which family members would convey one thought verbally (e.g., "I love you") and just the opposite nonverbally (e.g., non-emotive tone, lack of physical contact, etc.). This phenomenon is known as the **"double bind."** For example, Bateson and associates (1956) relate the story of a mother's visit with her son who was recovering from a schizophrenic episode. The mother stiffened when the young boy put his arm around her, but when he withdrew, she asked, "Don't you love me anymore?" When he blushed, she quipped, "Dear, you must not be so easily embarrassed and afraid of your feelings." The visit resulted in the patient's becoming upset and assaultive later in the day. Similar confusion is caused by a process called **"mystification,"** in which family members distort the experiences of other members by denial or relabeling. For example, a parent may say to a child, "You must be tired," rather than "You're feeling angry." In such environments, children are not trained to communicate or to recognize feelings.

Communications therapy, and the strategic therapies that evolved from the communications model, typically work from a systems perspective. Therapists believe that they cannot understand family interactions until they understand the family's role patterns, stability, levels of communication, and governing processes from a systems perspective. Such processes are generally believed to maintain homeostasis in the family (Jackson, 1967). As a result, therapists are very sensitive to both the processes and form of information exchange rather than to the specific content of interaction.

The goals of communication therapy require therapists to take deliberate actions to modify poor patterns of communication and interaction, especially regarding the patterns that serve to maintain destructive behavioral or psychological symptoms in one or more of the family members. Therapists view such actions as a type of covert message that is symptomatic of other family problems (Jackson, 1961). The therapist first seeks to identify the messages and then to interfere with their feedback loop by substituting new patterns of interaction for the patterns that seem to encourage displays of the symptom. Therapists intervene by changing the rules of communication, identifying problematic communications, or by beating the system at its own game by breaking problem communication in a manipulative manner.

The most direct approach to alerting family members to dysfunctional communication styles is seen in the treatment techniques of Virginia Satir (1967). Her strategy typically involved identifying and clarifying the numerous complicated and tangled messages of her clients. After identifying the sources of confusion, she corrected patterns by modeling clearer messages, and encouraging communication of personal statements ("I" rather than "you" or "we"), differentiation of opinion from fact or principle, and direct communication to other members rather than about other members. The communication material most frequently identified by Satir concerns emotions and affect. She maintained that being in touch with feelings and communicating them in a clear manner (and allowing others to do the same) is a key to healthy family life as well as to the self-esteem of family members.

To understand how our discussion of thoughts and emotions may affect our sense of self, listen to the following two ways in which a father might communicate anger toward his son:

Without "I statements":

> "You know, you can really get angry with a kid who is too lazy to study or go out and get a job."

With "I statements":

> "My son's lack of motivation makes me angry. He is too lazy to study or go out and get a job. This is frustrating to me, because I'd like to think he is better than that."

What do we hear from the remark which uses the "I statement"? We hear more ownership of the feelings of frustration and anger. The "you statement" pushes the anger aside; perhaps it reflects some belief that the father is not entitled to feel angry. In using the "I statement," however, the father is more likely to own and acknowledge his anger, and to give himself permission to feel angry. Perhaps he will also face the fact that his son is having diffi-culty taking responsibility for his school and work. Denying the frustration, however, is not going to be helpful.

Haley (1976) later criticized the directness of Satir and others as inef-fective and naive. Families and individuals, he maintains, are often resist-ant to change and they are not able to change on the basis of information alone. They get "stuck" in dysfunctional patterns. What does it mean to be stuck? Well, imagine the same situation in which a college-aged child does little else besides sitting at the computer, watching television, or partying with friends. There may have been several family fights over the situation, and many counseling sessions, but still the youth continues to sit and let his parents support him.

Haley's approach in such a situation involved changing the rules, games, and power basis at work in the family system. He is known for his use of the **"therapeutic paradox,"** or the technique of prescribing (or demanding) the symptom that catches patients in the bind of either performing the symptom (e.g., hearing voices) and thereby admitting that the symptom is not voluntary, or not hearing voices, thereby admitting that they are not crazy. For exam-ple, if instead of allowing a client to repeatedly offer an excuse, a counselor simply agrees with the excuse (e.g., client: "I am not smart enough to get through college"; counselor: "Gee, maybe you aren't."), the client is placed in a bind between agreeing that he is incompetent or admitting that with some changes (like going to class and reading the required texts), he really could handle the job. Because many clients in this situation would refuse to actu-ally believe that they are incompetent, they are left with the realization that "I can't handle this job or this course" was an excuse that allowed them to stay stuck, and to avoid finding a less challenging job or college program. This strategy gains some power for the therapist, which Haley found was needed in order to encourage clients' use of problem-solving rather than destructive, blaming, or rationalizing behaviors.

Haley also relabeled or **reframed** the motivations of family members in an attempt to portray specific family members in more acceptable terms (e.g., a parent's checking on a child's progress is a reflection of love and concern, rather than nagging). In recent years, Haley's work has been termed **Strate-gic Family Therapy** and currently is viewed as an offshoot of communica-tions therapy.

Structural Family Therapy

Salvador Minuchin's **Structural Family Therapy** (Minuchin, 1974) began with the families of delinquent boys at Wiltwyck School. Later, as Director of the Philadelphia Child Guidance Clinic, the model expanded to address a more diverse array of families (Minuchin, Rosman & Baker, 1978). This work has since devote a good deal of time to Hispanic families

(Kurtines & Szapocznik, 1996) and to families living in poverty (Minuchin, Colapinto & Minuchin, 1998).

Borrowing heavily from systems theory, the goal of structural family therapy is to alter the patterns of family **subsystems** and their boundaries. **Family structure** is a term pertaining to the stable and enduring interactions that occur in family settings. Over time, according to Minuchin, families develop habitually utilized rules and patterns of interaction. The husband who encourages his wife to "tell the story about whatever" and then proceeds to interrupt her with corrections of petty, peripheral details is a fitting example. Such an interaction has happened before and bored listeners may be subjected to several repeat performances in a single evening unless they wisely extricate themselves from the situation. Some structures are universal (e.g., parents protect children), and others are uniquely characteristic of specific families (e.g., Mom controls).

Structural Family Therapy also targets **boundaries** within the family system. The nature of family subsystems and their boundaries is a treatment target that has not been discussed elsewhere in this book. Just the same, it is an extremely important problem to address. There are numerous subsystems within a family, including individuals, parents, children, spouses, specific **dyads**, and alliances or conspiracies. Figure 10.1 shows just a few of these. Family boundaries dictate the roles of members and the terms of their participation. The **permeability** of subsystem boundaries is one concern of the structural therapist. What those boundaries should look like depends on the nature of the system. Intimate relationships, for example share a good deal of space, but not all aspects of one's personhood. As shown in Figure 10.1 the "healthy couple" has shared space and separate space. **Rigid boundaries** between subsystems indicate that the subsystems are extremely independent of each other (see Figure 10.1). Such subsystems are also considered disengaged. **Disengaged boundaries** are highly appropriate to some situations—when strangers sit together on a bus, perhaps. In fact, how do you feel when an individual shares the most personal aspects of his or her life with you during a first meeting? It is usually somewhat uncomfortable. An element of disengagement, at least at first, is more comfortable. But in the context of intimate relationships, disengagement often seems hurtful to at least one of the partners, because it seems to indicate a lack of interest on the part of the other partner. Of course, it may also indicate that both of them are uninterested. The husband who regularly shows no concern for his wife's grief exemplifies "disengagement." In disengaged families or subsystems, then, members may also appear oblivious to the effects of their behaviors on other members. Add children to the mix, as shown in the second column in Figure 10.1, and the system is probably evidencing elements of neglect. All members are very independent, but that is not the appropriate relationship between parents and young children.

Figure 10.1
Family Subsystems

Structure	Couples	Families
Healthy		
Disengaged		
Enmeshed		
Dysfunctional Dyads and Alliances		

The **enmeshed system**, on the other hand, displays a high degree of support, interdependence, warmth, affection (or quasi-affection), and control—too much. Boundaries between subsystems are diffuse—not very clear. Often, this discourages the independence of members of the subsystem and adversely affects their abilities to cope with difficulties outside of the subsystem. Enmeshed systems also may interfere with the individuation of children. Members sound, feel, and act alike. Over time, individuals may not have a separate sense for their own feelings and responsibilities. As a result, they may have a poor sense of how to cope with their own feelings, needs, desires, and stresses. Neither type of boundary configuration (disengaged or enmeshed) solves family problems well, because neither is flexible enough to sustain change, explore alternatives, or support the growth of individual members.

Finally, there is the issue of who is allied with whom and the appropriateness of those alliances. The last diagram in Figure 10.1 shows a child sharing intimate space with an adult, while the age-appropriate adult partner is disengaged. This figure depicts a situation of physical or emotional incest. In contrast, the family diagram at the top, showing a more healthy system, shows adult partners sharing intimate space, but giving children some degree of space in a relationship that is affectionate, protective, and parental.

Structural Therapy endeavors to reorder dysfunctional family structures in a manner that:

1. Establishes a clear generational distinction between parents and children (e.g., the children and parents are not peers);

2. Realigns dysfunctional subsystems (e.g., a parent-child dyad working against the other parent); and

3. Develops semipermeable, flexible boundaries that are neither enmeshed nor disengaged.

The therapist proceeds through the following stages:

1. "Joining" the family system to form a new therapeutic system with the family. The therapist is a member of this system, but respects the authority of the parents, accommodates individual reactions to others and the therapeutic situation, and demonstrates acceptance and understanding;

2. Encouraging enactments of family interactions and observing spontaneous episodes of interactions;

3. Diagnosing structure, subsystems, and boundary configurations (e.g., who says what to whom and in what way?);

4. Realigning the structures as a participant (e.g., shaping the competence of a family member, enabling subsystems to assume appropriate roles); and

5. Realigning subsystems and boundaries (e.g., strengthening boundaries between parents and children, loosening boundaries between spouses, encouraging open discussion of difficulties, etc.).

One can observe an example of Structural Therapy at work with the parents of neglected children in Philadelphia. Here Polansky and his colleagues endeavored to foster an improved balance among family roles—one that did not neglect children (Polansky et al., 1981). The therapists worked to establish clear parental roles of supervision and nurturance. They reframed parents' dysfunctional perceptions of themselves and their children and encouraged parents to reassume leadership and responsibility for children, thus altering subsystem boundaries. In this and in other structural family therapy approaches, the goal is to make the family system more functional, so that individuals have a healthier sense of belonging within the family, as well as a healthy sense of their own individuality (Minuchin, 1974; 1985; Minuchin & Fishman, 1981).

In a study by Szapocznik and associates (1989), structural family therapy was found to be more effective than individual therapies for 69 Hispanic boys with behavioral and emotional problems. Their work also achieved reductions in drug use among adolescent family members. It is important to note that the Szapocznik and associates study is part of an emerging literature that seeks to explore whether traditional therapies are relevant across diverse ethnic groups. Prior to beginning the therapeutic programs, however, Szapocznik and associates devoted considerable attention to learning about the Hispanic clients' expectations of family therapy and identifying the most therapeutically relevant family issues.

Structural Family Therapy also has been integrated into social learning approaches in Alexander and Parsons' (1982) Functional Family Therapy approach, and into Henggeler and Borduin's (1990) Multisystemic Family Therapy. Both are discussed below.

Behavioral and Social Learning Models

Authorities recognize numerous behavioral differences between delinquent and nondelinquent families. Alexander and his colleagues, for example, note that delinquent families in comparison to nondelinquent families are less talkative, utilize fewer positive interruptions, are more defensive and less supportive, and are less active (Alexander & Parsons, 1982). In addition, delinquent homes appear to set too many rules that are enforced inconsistently. Conflict management in such families is often unsatisfactory and characterized by an inability to negotiate resolutions, or to differentiate rules from requests. Patterson and his colleagues note such additional behaviors as a parental tendency to reinforce deviant ("coercive") behaviors, to punish in an inconsistent manner, or neglect to monitor children's behavior (Patterson, 1982; Patterson & Fleischman, 1979).

Accounts of applications of family therapy to delinquent families widely recognize social learning and behavioral programs as promising strategies in the prevention and treatment of delinquent behavior (e.g., see Andrews et al., 1990; Andrews et al., 1993; Gendreau & Ross, 1987; Kumpfer, 1999; Olson, Russell & Sprenkle, 1980). These programs are grounded in theories of social learning and operant conditioning (Chapters 4 and 8). Their interventions, for the most part, target observable behavioral problems that occur in the family setting and appear to be related to the delinquent or antisocial behavior of the children in the family. These include: (a) communication problems; (b) poor parenting skills (e.g., monitoring and appropriate use of rewards and punishments); (c) problems with conflict management; and (d) day-to-day home management skills.

The treatment goal for Patterson and his associates at the Oregon Social Learning Center is to improve the parenting skills of parents of children with conduct problems. Most important in this regard is strengthening the parents' ability to use appropriate methods of operant conditioning or contingency management. Parents of such children are often observed to: (a) insufficiently monitor/track children's behavior; (b) spend little time with children; (c) not back up threats and admonitions; (d) punish in an inconsistent manner, e.g., only when they are in a bad mood; (e) have poor control over their own anger; (f) be inconsistent with each other; (g) nag; (h) be overly permissive; and (i) fail to make rewards contingent upon good behavior.

Programs at the Oregon Social Learning Center teach parents to define, record, and monitor coercive behaviors. Parents are encouraged to discontinue negative reinforcement of coercive behaviors (e.g., giving in to the child's whining), to administer rewards contingent upon prosocial behaviors, and to administer appropriate and effective punishments in response to coercive behaviors. Therapists endeavor to reduce the overall number of punitive responses while improving their effectiveness. Punishment is considered necessary, but family members are trained to reduce their tendency to punish with anger, and learn to make greater use of techniques such as time-outs, withdrawal of privileges, allowance reductions, and increased work assignments. Parents are also instructed in more general principles of child management to identify normative child behaviors and to utilize effective tactics of negotiation and compromise (Patterson, Chamberlain & Reid, 1982). The results of these interventions have been favorable, even among high-risk youth (Bank et al., 1991; Dishion & Andrews, 1995). The OSLC model has also been developed for foster care parents (Chamberlain & Reid, 1991).

In another behavioral approach, Karol Kumpfer and associates developed the Strengthening Families Program (Kumpfer, 1999), an approach that strengthens the skills of parents, children, and the family as a whole. SFP is conducted in a 14-week program that was initially designed for drug abuse prevention with 6- to 12-year-old children of substance-abusing parents. It is now considered to be appropriate for troubled families regardless of whether substance abuse is an issue. The model has since been tailored to rural and urban African-American families (Kumpfer, 1999), and to Hispanic and Asian families. Modifications have also resulted in a shorter program, a school-based program, and a program for low-income parents.

The program builds skills related to family relationships, parenting skills, and social and life skills. Skills taught to parents in a separated module include strategies of child reinforcement and attention, communication, substance use education, problem solving, and limit-setting. Children are taught skills of communication, understanding feelings, social skills, problem solving, resisting peer pressure, compliance with parents, and developmentally appropriate substance abuse education. The family sessions address problems, plan recreation, and reinforce positive behavior. SPF has been found to be effective with substance-abusing parents as well as ethnically diverse parents.

A third example, Functional Family Therapy, is more broadly targeted to the operations of the family as a system (Alexander & Parsons, 1973; 1982; Alexander et al., 1988). FFT is one of the first family therapy approaches for antisocial children and it is still in practice. We place it within a behavioral category of family therapy because most meta-analyses do, and because the program works with family skills and targets specific family behaviors.

Even so, there are some decidedly eclectic qualities to this program. For example, concerns for the family as a system are clear. Generally speaking, the goal of this short-term behavioral family intervention program is to improve the functioning of the system by fostering reciprocity among family members, developing effective communication skills and reducing negativity, and by teaching family members how to effectively deal with circumstances that bring about family conflict and delinquent behaviors. Family therapists model, prompt, and reinforce such behaviors as clear communication of feelings, differentiation of rules from requests, use of negotiation strategies, especially as they pertain to delinquent-relevant issues (e.g., curfew, choice of friends, etc.), and the development of solution-oriented communication styles (e.g., interrupting for clarification, additional information, or feedback).

Functional Family Therapy is primarily grounded in social learning theory but borrows from the Structural Family Therapy approach. Consistent with Structural Family Therapy, time in therapy is also devoted to understanding what function problem behaviors have in the family system. Many of the behaviors that are treated are those that fit into a larger family systemic context; once their function is understood, therapy seeks to find an appropriate alternative. In addition, an operant model is employed, especially with families that have young children and adolescents. Short-term and long-term effects on family interaction styles and on recidivism have been favorable (e.g., see Alexander & Parsons, 1982; Klein, Alexander & Parsons, 1977; Barton et al., 1985; and later by Gordon et al., 1988). Treatment gains for the group studied by Gordon and his associates, however, were diminished over a longer follow-up period (Gordon, Graves & Arbuthnot, 1995).

This approach has also been modified to be responsive to poor, multicultural families, and to address a variety of behavioral problems, including delinquency, aggression, and substance abuse.

Multisystemic Treatment

Multisystemic Treatment (MST) (Henggeler & Borduin, 1990) emphasizes the importance of assessing and treating child and adolescent conduct disorders by addressing a broad spectrum of family problems. Treatment of family systems from this approach must consider all factors that contribute to the child's behavioral problems, including the problems of specific individuals as well as the influence of extrafamily systems. Proponents of the Multisystemic approach believe that traditional forms of family therapy are too simplistic. That is, the approaches described above: (a) fail to consider the importance of the problems of individual family members and extrafamily systems (e.g., schools, peers, neighbors, and workplaces); (b) fail to consider individual developmental issues (e.g., the cognitive maturity of children); and (c) are to reluctant to borrow, when appropriate, from the individual treatment models. In contrast to the family systems paradigm, MST maintains that the family system may not always be the sole cause of the dysfunctional behaviors of individuals within the system. Moreover, there may be a need to use multiple family therapy approaches, including structural family therapy (Minuchin, 1974) and behavioral parent training (Patterson, 1982), while at the same time treating some family members for their individual problems (e.g., delinquent peers, poor social skills, substance abuse, and mental health). In this way, MST continues to value the notion of a family system, but sees the family as part of a wider array of systems that also affect the family system. Moreover, a family member with severe behavioral, health, or other difficulties can affect the family system so seriously that it makes sense to devote most of the therapeutic attention to that individual member of the system.

In sum, MST offers multiple modalities of treatment. Nine principles guide the MST approach (Henggeler et al., 1998):

1. Understand the family's identified problems within a broader systemic context.

2. Understand the family's positive and systemic strengths use them as levers for change.

3. Encourage responsible behavior and discourage irresponsible behavior among family members.

4. Keep interventions present-oriented and action-oriented, targeting specific and well-defined problems.

5. Target sequences of behaviors that contribute to the identified problems. Consider behavioral sequences that occur within the family system and with the multiple systems that interact with the family (e.g., school, extended family, neighborhood).

6. Keep interventions appropriate to the developmental level and needs of young family members.

7. Require daily or weekly intervention-based efforts from family members.

8. Continuously evaluate the effectiveness of the interventions from multiple perspectives. Assure that service providers assume accountability for overcoming barriers to successful outcomes.

9. Promote treatment generalization beyond the period of treatment to long-term maintenance of therapeutic change. Empower caregivers to address family members' needs across multiple systemic contexts.

The Multisystemic approach occurs over the following sequence of strategies:

1. **An Initial Assessment** is conducted with the child's parents or parent. This interview results in a description of the child's behavior in the context of the strengths and weaknesses of the child as well as the child's environment. This includes a description of the strengths and weaknesses of the: (a) school; (b) child's abilities; (c) parents' marriage; (d) peer and social network; (e) siblings; (f) parenting skills; and (g) quality of the interrelationship between these entities.

2. **A treatment plan** that sets a system of interventions in place that builds on existing strengths of the child and the other systems.

3. **Goals of treatment**: Where other family therapies may recommend additional treatments such as assessments for attention deficit disorder, or substance abuse treatment for one family member, Multisystemic Treatment is likely to involve the family therapist in these aspects of the treatment plan as opposed to referring the clients to other providers.

MST seeks to be flexible and recognizes that different combinations of risk factors are at work with different families. Interventions are individualized. In some cases, treatment may appear to be little more than problem-solving, such as when a plan is developed to see that children are supervised after school. In other instances, the treatment may include therapeutic meetings with the entire family, marital therapy with the parents, or a parenting skills class. Finally, treatment plans may involve a number of outside community services that are not therapeutic in nature, such as child care, transportation, recreation centers, school interventions, or job development.

In most cases, the intervention is intensive, lasting four to six months, where service is available to the family for 24 hours a day, seven days a week. The family is assisted by a professional masters- or doctoral-level therapist and a case worker. Both are supervised by a psychologist or psychiatrist. The intervention is not tied to any standard modality of family therapy; strategic family therapy, structural family therapy, and cognitive behavioral therapy have all been used, depending upon the family's needs.

Clearly, MST is held in high regard. Licensed MST programs exist throughout the United States and internationally. Evaluations of MST also show that this approach is effective for treating serious and chronic juvenile offenders (Borduin et al., 1995; Henggeler, Melton & Smith, 1992; Mann et al., 1990), even in inner-city, lower-class, high-crime neighborhoods (Henggeler et al., 1986). Its use with delinquency and anti-social behavior has been well-tested.

MST was initially used with the families of children with behavioral problems. Later applications found MST to be a useful treatment for other clinical problems (Henggler & Lee, 2003), including substance abuse (Henggeler et al., 1996; Randall et al., 2001), juvenile sex offending (Borduin et al., 1990), and child abuse (parents) (Brunk, Henggeler & Whelan, 1987).

In contrast to the other family therapy models discussed in this section, MST offers a distinct focus on case coordination as well as therapy. "Intervention with other systems" is really an academic way of saying that MST gets needed help to the family, helping it to resolve crises with schools, financial well-being, mental health, substance abuse, and so on. There is no pretense that family therapy alone will resolve the other hardships faced by these families or that families can even participate in family therapy if more competing threats are present. In this regard, MST is consistent with the well-known family preservation approaches (Nelson, 1991) that seek to keep problem children out of the juvenile justice and foster care systems. Homebuilders is perhaps the most well-know model of this type (Haapala & Kinney, 1988). The service time is limited (4-6 weeks) with caseworkers coordinating concrete services such as food, transportation, and child care. Counseling from a variety of modalities is also available (e.g., cognitive-behavioral, communications). Most of the counseling and case worker services are provided in the home, or scheduled in a nearby office or neighborhood during a time that is convenient to the family (Kinney et al., 1991).

Particularly for families flooded by adversity, the "wraparound" services model makes good sense. In these models, families participating in family counseling or substance abuse treatment (or not), are less likely to be overwhelmed by having to find their own way to meet other essential needs. In some cases, the need for wraparound services may be chronic, needed off and on for the duration of a lifetime, as with some forms of mental illness, mental retardation, and advanced forms of drug and alcohol addiction. This is a note of caution. The writings on the multi-service programs often read as if service and therapy are linear—they have a beginning (when the client or clients are in crises), a middle (when counseling or services are delivered), and an end (when everyone gets better). Many families in such situations, however, do not get better and cannot be dropped at the end of the prescribed "short-term" intervention. They may become stabilized for periods of time, but require services again at a later time. In such cases, the partners must plan for ongoing services.

Family Therapy and Criminal Justice Applications

Involving family members in the rehabilitation or reintegration of an offender appears to be especially appropriate:

1. whenever we observe the family to be intertwined in the etiology of offending behavior (which occurs frequently);

2   in many instances of family violence;[1]

3   when a family member is abusing drugs or alcohol;

4. when we want to facilitate an institutionalized family member's return to family life.

A view of the family therapies as they address these specific problems offers an improved understanding of criminal justice-related applications of family therapy. One danger in discussing family therapy as an approach to family violence, substance abuse, and criminal behavior, however, is in assuming that there are prototypical family styles and treatment approaches for each problem. In fact, sources discourage thinking in terms of the "alcoholic family," the "violent family," or the "delinquent family." They maintain that it is reasonable to expect dysfunctional interactions in such families, but important to encourage careful observation and diagnosis of each family (Russell et al., 1983; Aldarondo & Strauss, 1994). Because there are many paths to the problems listed above, it is not very helpful to match treatments to problems as if all families with a given symptom encompassed the same treatment issues.

Domestic Violence

Child abuse. In its current eclectic and diverse stage of evolution, family therapy seems to at least partially address, if not cover, the span of family problems that result in child abuse. In response to increasing concern about child abuse, family therapists and researchers have targeted the following focal concerns: (a) dynamics that promote abuse; (b) interactional contributions of the child victim to abusive situations; (c) marital discord; (d) aggressive sibling interactions; (e) alcohol- and drug-related factors; (f) child sexual abuse, including incest; (g) poor self-image of the parents; and (h) parents' psychological vulnerability to stress. Situational stressors also contribute to the problem (see Baird, Wagner & Neuenfeld, 1992; Saunders & Azar, 1989). These include: (a) excessive number of children; (b) employment and economic problems; (c) poor home and financial management skills; (d) young age of the mother; (e) emotional loss resulting from death or separation; (f) chronic illness of a parent; (g) rapid life changes; and (h) social isolation.

Given the wide array of interacting factors at work in child abuse, it is not surprising that the most recent writings suggest that treatment take place on multiple levels (e.g., individual, familial, and community) (Becker et al., 1995). As noted earlier, multisystemic approaches in particular have been tested and found to be an effective means of family preservation (Schoenwald & Henggeler, 1997) and treating abusive parents (Brunk et al., 1987). Even so, most all of the other approaches to family therapy have been found to be appropriate in the treatment of abusive and neglectful families. A portion of the work at the Oregon Social Learning Center, for example, deals with abuse precipitated by explosive behaviors in children and parents' inability to control them. Here, parents are taught more effective parenting practices (Patterson, 1982). Structural and communications therapies also have a history of being effective methods for dealing with child abuse (Minuchin, 1974; Pardeck, 1989).

These results do not necessarily pertain to children who have been sexually abused in incestuous relationships. Here, sources disagree about whether the child should be treated in a family system that includes the abuser. Any use of family therapy in such situations must secure the protection and empowerment of the incest victim relative to the power held by the abuser or perhaps even the parental system (Barrett, Trepper & Fish, 1990). In fact, it is not uncommon to offer family therapy separately to the victim, the perpetrator, and the non-abusing parent (Collins & Collins, 1990), or to treat the perpetrator alone in individual or group therapy.

Spouse abuse. Therapy with partners who batter must address the following types of problems (Saunders & Azar, 1989; Stith & Rosen, 1990): (a) inability to express feelings and emotions; (b) emotional dependence; (c) alcohol and drug abuse; (d) heightened adherence to masculine sex-role stereotypes; (e) lack of assertiveness; (f) social isolation; (g) poor coping skills; and (h) habitual communication and behavioral patterns that escalate into violent interactions.

Often, techniques of crisis management are practiced prior to beginning more long-term therapy. The first goal must always be to stop the violence. In addition, therapists are quick to encourage their clients to use local community support services and programs, such as self-help groups (e.g., Batterers Anonymous, Parents Anonymous), parenting skills workshops, hotlines, marriage enrichment programs, and services that offer relief time for parents (Gaudin et al., 1991).

Without blaming victims for an abuser's decision to use violence, most family therapists recognize that there are reciprocal dynamics to many of the target problems listed above. Thus, even though limits have to be set with perpetrators of violence, couples who wish to stay married are encouraged to address the problems of family violence together, thus taking a systems view to its solution (Chamow, 1990). Indeed, many of the published accounts of family therapy recommend a systemic or an ecosystemic approach (e.g., see Flemons, 1989; Nichols & Schwartz, 1998). This perspective is not necessarily inconsistent with feminist concerns for protecting victims, taking a strong stand against violent behavior, and avoiding victim-blaming (Stith & Rosen, 1990). Interventions target most of the problem areas enumerated above. In addition to addressing many of the sources of family stress (e.g., finances, parental issues), conjoint (structural and strategic family therapy) marital therapy appears to be the predominant approach, assuming, of course, that the couple wishes to stay together. Unfortunately, the effectiveness of family therapy as a response to spouse abuse has not been widely researched (Saunders, 1996).

In light of the dearth of research on the efficacy of family therapy in addressing spouse abuse, we remind readers that an alternative approach of treating only the batterer may also be effective. For example, batterers may benefit from skills training, including anger management (Bedrosian, 1982; Edleson & Grusznski, 1988; Hamberger & Hastings, 1988), other cognitive-

behavioral approaches (Saunders, 1996), and support groups for both victims and batterers (Petrik et al., 1994). In recognizing the relevance of
family therapy as a vehicle for treating family violence, however, one cannot ignore the fact that the safety of family members, as well as their future
well-being, must be given priority over efforts to improve the quality of their
relationships. Often the removal of abusive members from the home, out-of-
home placements, legal aid, career planning for a life without one's spouse,
therapy for the victim, and self-help and support groups provide more
appropriate alternatives (Saunders & Azar, 1989).

Substance Abuse

Numerous authorities implicate the family in the etiology and maintenance of addictive behaviors (Kaufman & Kaufman, 1992; Stanton, Todd &
Associates, 1982). Steinglass et al. (1987) observed that alcohol was often
central to many of the interactions in families of alcoholics. The family, for
example, that saved discussions, arguments, displays of warmth, and complaints for times when drinking was occurring often allowed their interactions to be marred by the effects of drinking. More recent studies have
found that families with an alcoholic parent who are able to maintain family rituals (i.e., dinner time, holiday celebrations, vacations) undisrupted by
the alcoholism, are significantly less likely to have children who become alcoholics (Steinglass et al., 1987). By contrast, families in which such rituals
were disrupted by the alcoholism were far more likely to pass on alcoholic
behavior to the next generation.

In addition, addictions are considered among the behaviors that maintain dysfunctional homeostasis within family systems (Steinglass et al.,
1987). Scapegoating, resistance to therapy, poor communication, family modeling of substance-abusing behavior, problems with late individuation and
separation, and poor parenting practices are not uncommon among such families. Moreover, when family dynamics are at least helping to support an
addiction, counselors and case managers need to pay attention. Case managers, social workers, probation officers, and institutional treatment staff may
unintentionally become entangled in the family's efforts to maintain homeostasis, thereby perpetuating the problem. They may also thwart treatment
efforts by failing to maintain the distance needed to keep from becoming a
member of a family triangle, one involving the therapist, the client, and the
probation officer (Mowatt, Van Deusen & Wilson, 1985).

Accounts of family therapy approaches to alcohol and drug abuse report
some encouraging results, but there have not been many methodologically
sound studies of the effectiveness of family therapy with this population (Liddle & Dakof, 1995). While family treatments seem to span all four strategies discussed above, applications of structural and conjoint approaches (a
combination of structural and strategic therapies) seem most common
(Kaufman & Kaufman, 1992).

Until the early 1970s, family therapy with alcoholics consisted primarily of marital therapy. Then several studies noted that the involvement of the alcoholic's family greatly improved the alcoholic's chances of success (Janzen, 1977). Published accounts describe the use of the conflict management and communication strategies of Satir and Ackerman (Meeks & Kelly, 1970), social learning and behavioral approaches (Cheek et al., 1971), and systems therapy (Berenson, 1986).

Family therapy for families with adolescent abusers appears to be more developed than similar services for adult substance abusers (Liddle & Dakof, 1995). Stanton, Todd, and their associates (1982; Stanton, 1994), however, are credited with conducting one of the most comprehensive studies of the effectiveness of family therapy with adult substance abuse. Testing the effects of a family therapy model that combined structural family therapy with strategic family therapy, the authors found this model to be far more effective in reducing drug use than non-family treatment and family education (a movie). Szapocznik's research with adolescents also found structural family therapy highly effective in reducing drug use and associated behavioral problems (Szapocznik et al., 1983). This program also improved family functioning. As noted above, most of Szapocznik's research is with Hispanic families. Similar findings were noted among non-Hispanic participants, as well (Joanning et al., 1992).

Successes of family therapy are not limited to structural and communication models. Friedman (1989) reports excellent outcomes (reductions in drug use) for functional family therapy with families of adolescent drug abusers (Alexander & Parsons, 1982). Behavioral family therapies have been found effective in several small studies (e.g., Azrin et al., 1994). In addition, we have already noted the success of MST with substance abusers (e.g., Henggeler et al., 1996; Henggeler et al., 1991).

The problem of offenders dropping out of treatment appears to plague many offender-based treatment programs, and substance abuse is no exception. However, a number of studies have found that, for a variety of reasons, family therapy approaches appear to have greater client retention rates than individual therapies (Joanning et al., 1992; Liddle & Dakof, 1995). Additional information on family therapy for substance abuse may be found in Chapter 12.

Finally, skills training approaches emanating from both the social learning and the cognitive behavioral models form a strong foundation for improving the parenting practices of abusive parents. One program, Project 12-Ways, teaches basic home-related skills (e.g., shopping, menu planning, cleaning) to the parents who have been accused of child neglect (Lutzker, 1990). The behavioral skill approaches can also be used in this regard to improve parent-child interactions (McLaren, 1988), problem solving (Howing et al., 1989), and interactional skills of a general nature (Kinney et al., 1991).

When a Family Member Is Incarcerated

Although sources have long maintained that inmates involved with families during incarceration make better parole adjustment than inmates who are separated from their families, programs offering family therapy or family services to prison inmates are fairly recent developments. Undoubtedly, incarceration causes a myriad of problems to inmates and families. In addition to the problem of separation itself, families may be unable to obtain adequate information regarding such matters as the status of legal proceedings, visitation policies, transportation to the institution, results of parole reviews, and other necessary information (Fishman, 1988). Economic problems abound. Emotional stress, guilt, sexual frustration, anger, and depression threaten what may already be unstable relationships. There is a need to redefine the marital relationship in the absence of the inmate, and to decide, unencumbered by self-doubt and denial, whether to continue the marriage. In response to the very thought of a wife's infidelity, inmates may engage in acting-out behavior or depressive withdrawal. Their fear of rejection may prompt them to prematurely reject their spouse or family first. Denial and an intense desire to keep a relationship intact may also result in an unrealistic view of their marriages and families, and avoidance of the difficulties that do exist (Kaslow, 1987). Such views create additional stress on families when inmates are released from prison.

And what about children of incarcerated offenders? As noted above, incarceration periods of greater than 15 months seriously affect a parent's chance of regaining custody upon release unless the children have been with a relative of the parent. Community service providers note, however, that this is no guarantee of a smooth transition back into parenthood upon prison release. For example, tired relatives may be quick to return children to parental custody at a time when the newly released inmate must find safe housing, work, childcare, and abide by a myriad of parole requirements, including participation in treatment programs.

Some, but not all, agencies are doing a good job of helping to maintain family relationships during incarceration. A recent survey of correctional agencies (LIS, 2002), for example, reports that only about 27 states have a policy of considering proximity to family in the assignment of inmates to prison settings and only 16 states offer to assist family visitation efforts by furnishing transportation and lodging. Agencies were much less likely to furnish space for overnight visits with children and spouses. Even fewer agencies provide nurseries where newborns may be with their mothers for a period of time following birth.

Classes designed to strengthen parenting skills, however, are growing in number. The same survey indicated that they were available to women in 95 percent of the agencies surveyed and to men in 85 percent of the agencies surveyed. Most of these are conducted without the children present. However, children's participation is possible, available to women in 61 percent of the agencies and to men in 26 percent of the agencies.

Community services to families received a big boost under the Federal Coming Home Initiative developed by the U.S. Department of Justice. This initiative forms partnerships among several key federal agencies, such as Housing and Urban Development and Health and Human Services. Federal grants to all states now fund state models that in many cases also promote partnerships with state-level agencies, including corrections, substance abuse, housing, employment, and mental health. The National Institute of Corrections has contributed to this effort through its Transition from Prison to Community Initiative (Parent & Barnett, 2003), which provides a model (mostly a case management model) for reintegrating offenders into the community following incarceration. Family issues are not the only service provided under the new initiatives, but is not difficult to see the relevance of programs such as MST, Family Preservation, and other multiservice models.

Conclusion

In conclusion, the vast literature of family therapy suggests that it is one of the interventions that has had some success in reducing offender recidivism and improving family functioning.

In the current funding climate, however, family therapy continues to make only modest inroads toward addressing the needs of criminal offenders. While it is clear that it is relevant to those needs, and that evaluations of its effectiveness generally have been favorable, family therapy does not seem to be readily available nor to be routinely considered by court and correctional officials as a viable component of a treatment plan. Current government and private reimbursement policies offer no encouragement. State policies that result in greater reimbursement for state institutional placements than for community-based options and insurance policies that favor medical treatment over mental health treatment or individual treatment over family treatment serve to discourage the use of family-level interventions.

This chapter does not mean to extol family therapy as the panacea that will work with all individuals who approach family and criminal courts. Certainly, not all offenders are amenable to family therapy. Some families of delinquents may be hostile and defensive to the idea of participating in therapy. In numerous cases, parental concern for their children is either nonexistent or too limited to initiate any work at the family level. In addition, some offenders may have exhausted their families by the time they come to the attention of the criminal justice system. Finally, a significant number of families face stressors that are more intense than the criminality of a family member. Understandably, families attempting to survive the exhausting demands of poverty and unemployment will evidence little motivation for family therapy. However, this still leaves a significant portion of adult and juvenile cases in need of family-level interventions. While family therapy is a more complex and expensive endeavor than individual therapy, it is often the more sensible choice. The alternative is to treat one member of a pathological family for symptoms of a much larger problem.

Note

[1]   Efforts to use therapy in the hope of reuniting a family where abuse of a child or spouse has occurred are viewed as too dangerous in some instances (see Saunders & Azar, 1989).

Key Concepts and Terms

behavioral and social learning models
boundaries
communications therapy
double bind
disengaged boundaries
dyads
enmeshed system
family structure
family system
family therapy
homeostasis
individuate
metacommunication
Multisystemic Treatment

mystification
object relations
permeability
psychodynamic family therapy
reframing
rigid boundaries
roles
scapegoat
Strategic Family Therapy
Structural Family Therapy
subsystems
therapeutic paradox
working through

Discussion Questions

1. Why is the family "system" such a powerful unit? How could such a system contribute to an adolescent becoming delinquent? How could such a system help rehabilitate a delinquent family member?

2. Compare the communications model of family therapy with the structural model. What are the advantages and disadvantages of each? Which do you prefer?

3. What are the advantages of Multisystemic Family Therapies over some of the other models discussed in this chapter?

4. Discuss the use of family therapy interventions with child abuse. What kind of interventions seem to work best with this problem area?

5. How could a family therapy program be useful with incarcerated offenders and their families? What would be some unique aspects and limitations of such a program?

Part Five

Effective Correctional Intervention: What Works?

Up to this point in the book, we have presented a variety of theories and strategies of correctional intervention. How do we sort through this wide array of treatment options? Which are most effective for specific offender behaviors? Which are most effective in general, with broader offender populations? In addition to the approaches themselves, what other correctional practices are most likely to encourage offenders to change? In these final three chapters we address these important questions.

David Lester and Gail Hurst present numerous program strategies specific to sex offenders in Chapter 11. In Chapter 12, Patricia Van Voorhis and Gail Hurst review approaches to the treatment of substance abuse. These chapters are intended to be responsive to policy makers and practitioners who face increasing pressures to address the criminogenic needs of these types of offenders. As we review these strategies, however, it is striking to note that our successes are mostly with the behavioral, social learning, and cognitive-behavioral models, and with cognitive-behavioral approaches to relapse prevention. Thus, even though the programs are uniquely relevant to substance abuse and sex offending behaviors, values, and attitudes, the structure of the most effective models is similar to that for other types of serious offenders: behavioral and cognitive-behavioral approaches, along with sound assessment strategies, appear to work best.

Paula Smith, Paul Gendreau, and Claire Goggin show us in Chapter 14 that we can separate less effective program models from more effective ones; an accumulated body of research points us to the types of programs that work, as well as to the types of practices that should be avoided. This is an impressive knowledge base. In presenting it, the authors rely on the meta-analysis referred to throughout this book. These authors, along with Andrews and Bonta (2003), have incorporated the results of the meta-analysis into the Principles of Effective Intervention. As readers review these, it is noteworthy that these "Principles" have received a good deal of attention in both the literature and in practitioner training forums. It is hoped that we will see more and more programs allowing these research results to guide the design and implementation of new correctional interventions.

Chapter 11

Treating Sexual Offenders

David Lester and Gail Hurst

Deviant sexual behavior and sexual aggression continue to be serious social problems in need of more effective solutions (Hall, 1995). Society is concerned enough about the problem to pass special laws concerning sex offenders, sometimes requiring them to be confined in specialized facilities or requiring evidence that they are no longer a danger to society before being released. In the latter case, because imprisonment alone is incapable of preventing recidivism, treatment is critical for the safe release of sexual offenders back into the community.

In recent years, there has been tremendous growth in articles and books dealing with the characteristics, etiology, and treatment of sex offenders. A perusal of this vast literature indicates little evidence of trends in the treatment of sex offenders. Instead, practitioners from a variety of orientations (such as medication, behavior therapy, and psychotherapy) are all exploring the value of their treatment techniques for sex offenders. Case studies are common, as are evaluations of treatment programs for large numbers of sex offenders.

The Role of Assessment

As with other forms of criminal behavior, an adequate assessment of the client's needs and readiness to receive treatment must be performed. A thorough assessment gains pertinent information concerning several areas of the offender's life, including the degree of offending as well as other problems in the offender's life that may contribute to his or her dysfunction.

When assessing sex offenders, the information gained can be grouped into four areas:

1. **Social history** (i.e., employment history; hobbies and interests; family relationships, composition and structure; and significant life events);

2. **Psychological and social problems** (i.e., substance abuse, emotional difficulties, history of nonsexual offending, and antisocial behavior and psychiatric diagnosis);

3. **Sexual development** (i.e., sexual history and experience, attitudes toward sex, sexual knowledge and preference, sexual dysfunction, age of onset of puberty and adjustment to puberty, sexual and intimate relationships, and history of sexual victimization); and

4. **Sexual patterns of offending** (i.e., history of sexual offending, attitudes toward the victim and the offense, masturbatory and sexual fantasies, use of force and physical aggression, willingness to engage in treatment, and ability to specify treatment goals) (Epps, 1996; Maletzky, 1991).

In particular, masturbatory fantasies (see number 4, above) are critical in determining the prospects for successful treatment. As long as the masturbatory fantasies of the client involve age-appropriate intercourse, there is a greater likelihood that treatment will be successful; if the masturbatory fantasies are exploitive and inappropriate in nature, treatment success is much more difficult to achieve because each masturbatory orgasm strengthens the deviant sexual response.

Maletzky (1991) provides a basic structure of how the assessment of sex offenders should occur.

Initial Interview

A **clinical interview** with the offender should be performed first. It is the technique most frequently used to gain information about the offender. During the interview, evaluators should look for defenses commonly used by sexual offenders, because many offenders often distort the accounts of their offending behavior (Epps, 1996). For example, offenders often minimize their acts by taking responsibility for only parts of their behaviors, or by placing some of the responsibility on others, including the victim (O'Connell, Leberg & Donaldson, 1990; Maletzky, 1991). Moreover, evaluators should look for defenses such as denial, rationalization, and claims of seduction, because treatment cannot begin until these types of defenses are addressed and the offender is dealing with his problems openly and honestly (O'Connell, Leberg & Donaldson, 1990; Maletzky, 1991).

The assessment should not rely solely on an interview with the offender. The clinical interview should be supplemented with interviews with significant others, such as wives, girlfriends, and family members, as well as reports from other experts (O'Connell, Leberg & Donaldson, 1990; Maletzky, 1991). It is also advantageous to review additional records, ranging from prior psychological and medical records to police and victim reports. When examining these records, evaluators should search for patterns of disruptive behavior, antisocial acts, past deviant incidents, use of violence or force during the act, and the duration and frequency of the acts (Maletzky, 1991).

It is also critical to include a thorough psychiatric examination. If the sex offender has a psychiatric disorder, it is important to institute treatment for this psychiatric disorder in addition to treating psychological and behavioral problems associated more specifically with the sexual offense.

Penile Plethysmography

Another assessment option concerns examination of the offender's arousal patterns. Because many sexual offenders have deviant sexual arousal patterns, researchers often use **penile plethysmography** (PPG) (also known as phallometry) as a means of determining the arousal patterns of this particular population (Laws & Osborn, 1983; Maletzky, 1991). The PPG consists of a transducer that detects changes in penile erection, and an electronic recorder that then permanently records these changes (Epps, 1996).

PPG has several problems associated with it. First, it is by no means clear that sexual offenders differ reliably in penile responses to deviant sexual stimuli. For example, Baxter, Barbaree, and Marshall (1986) found no differences between rapists and nonoffenders. Second, there are ethical problems associated with its use because presentation of deviant sexual stimuli may legitimize and encourage deviant sexual tendencies, and the stimuli used degrade women and depict children as sexual objects. This is especially relevant when the techniques are used with adolescent male offenders (Marshall, 1996).

While treatment should begin with a complete assessment of the sex offender, assessment should also be continuous in order to monitor and evaluate the offender's response to therapy. Information gained in assessment should also be used to address such issues as:

1. The degree of dangerousness the offender poses to others;

2. The offender's suitability for treatment; and

3. The degree to which the behavior and attitudes of the offender have changed in response to treatment (Epps, 1996).

Problems in Assessment

One problem in assessment is that the research on sex offenders frequently fails to confirm the existence of traits or characteristics unique to the sex offender. As we noted above, the penile response to deviant sexual stimuli sometimes fails to distinguish sex offenders from nonoffenders. In this case, it is difficult to justify assessing the trait or characteristic. There is better evidence for differences in social skills, intimacy, loneliness, self-esteem, and cognitive distortions, and some tentative evidence for differences in sex steroids and brain dysfunction (Marshall, 1996). Even these, however, identify differences *among* sex offenders (Sperber, 2004). Therefore, the factors differentiating sex offenders from nonoffenders are not especially clear.

In addition, a look at some of the articles on the assessment and evaluation of sexual offenders shows that many provide no connection between the measures they recommend and the type of treatment that would be most effective or with the outcome to be expected from the treatment (e.g., Zussman, 1989). This must be remedied in the future. It is critical that the information obtained from an assessment guide the staff in their choice of treatment options and enable good predictions to be made about outcome.

An additional concern is that sex offenders may lie about their histories and attempt to deceive the staff about their psychological state. Emerick and Dutton (1993) recommended the use of polygraph testing to check the accuracy of the offender's responses and to assist in monitoring the offender's compliance with treatment and probation contracts. In their study of adolescent sex offenders, they found that the information obtained from the offenders about their sexual and assault history depended critically upon the source of information. For example, the mean number of victims age 10 or less identified from official and legal records was 1.52. From the intake interview it was 1.87, and from polygraph confirmatory testing it was 2.85. Polygraph testing changed the data on a variety of factors, including number of assaults, degree of intrusion (oral-genital, vaginal, or rectal), abuse children of both sexes, and degree of force used. Emerick and Dutton concluded that sex offenders deliberately attempt to misrepresent themselves.

Classification

Not all sex offenders are alike, and one critical need for assessment is to devise a useful classification scheme for sex offenders (Lester, 1977). Early schemes were based primarily on clinical intuition. For example, Cohen and associates (1971) proposed the following classification of rapists:

1. **Displaced aggression** ("rape—aggressive aim" in Cohen's terminology), in which the act of rape was an expression of anger originally felt toward a wife, mother, or other close female;

2. **Sexually-motivated** ("rape—sexual aim"), in which the man is trying to find a girlfriend but using force to do so;[1]

3. **Sadistic type** ("rape—sex-aggression defusion"), in which the fighting and resistance of the victim and the rapist's own aggression is sexually exciting.

The displaced aggression rapist has a circumscribed problem—that of expressing his anger in a socially acceptable way to the women in his life who frustrate him, and he is not likely to recidivate if he receives appropriate therapy. The sadistic rapist, however, is going to require intensive therapy in order to eliminate the aggression-sexual excitement link and to replace his pattern of sexual behavior with a normal pattern.

More recently, empirically based classification schemes have been devised. At first, Knight and Prentky (1987) used Cohen's system to classify more than 100 rapists and to explore their characteristics. They found, for example, that displaced-aggression rapists were raised by one parent alone more often than the other types, and were more often adopted or foster children. The sadistic rapists had more sexually deviant family members and more homosexual relationships. The compensatory rapists came from stable families and experienced less neglect and abuse from their parents; they also showed other sexual deviations, such as transvestism more often.

Knight and Prentky (1990) found, however, that it was not easy to classify rapists and child molesters into the categories that Cohen and his colleagues had proposed. They therefore modified Cohen's categories until their judges could assign sex offenders into the categories with reasonable interjudge agreement. For rapists, Knight and Prentky classified the primary motivation as opportunistic, pervasively angry, sexual (sadistic and non-sadistic) and vindictive. Rapists falling into each type were also categorized as high, moderate, or low in social competence.

Classifications such as these need to meet three requirements:

1. They must be useful for research into the causation of sexual offending;

2. They must be useful for helping police identify potential offenders—that is, the circumstances of the crime should suggest characteristics of the offender; and

3. They must be useful for treatment—that is, the characteristics of the offender should suggest treatment strategies.

It is unlikely that one classification system would accomplish all three goals. Future research into the classification of sexual offenders should, therefore, focus on each of these goals separately. At the moment, however, no classification system has been linked directly with the outcome of different treatment strategies.

Treatment Approaches

The major objective in treatment is the cessation of offending (O'Connell, Leberg & Donaldson, 1990). This objective is similar to the objective of decreasing deviant sexual arousal in order to decrease offending (Maletzky, 1991).

Traditionally, it was assumed that all sex offenders suffered from the same problems. Therefore, treatment for this population of offenders was one-dimensional. A standard program was used for all offenders (Schorsch et al., 1990). Currently, those working with sex offenders realize that they are treating a heterogeneous population requiring a multidimensional approach, as well as a wider range of treatment approaches (Maletzky, 1991; Schorsch et al., 1990; Sperber, 2004). Within this multidimensional framework, therapists design treatment programs around individual offenders, as opposed to utilizing a standard treatment program.

Physiological Strategies

Physiological (also called organic or somatic) methods of treatment have historically been used to reduce the deviant drives in sex offenders. The most common of these approaches is biochemical, using antiandrogens, which cause a decrease or complete loss of sexual drive, some of which act peripherally (e.g., depo-Provera), while others act centrally (e.g., Leupron). Other types of somatic treatment include surgical castration and stereotactic brain surgery, which disconnects an area of the brain that controls sexual drives (Schorsch et al., 1990). Some critics have argued that these strategies treat the symptom rather than the cause of deviant sexual behavior, but this criticism is equally valid for behavioral strategies. A stronger criticism is that these strategies are immoral because they inflict bodily harm on offenders when alternative therapeutic strategies are available.

In the past, these treatments were sometimes abused. For example, the brilliant mathematician, Alan Turing, who theorized in the 1930s that computers could be built, was arrested in England in 1952 for being a homosexual and forced to have biochemical treatments for his homosexuality. Turing committed suicide in 1954. England decriminalized homosexuality in the 1960s—too late for Turing.

In most nations that permit chemical or surgical castration, it is carried out only on offenders who volunteer and for those who appear to be good candidates for improvement after the procedures. However, in the United States, judicial decisions have limited the extent to which offenders can volunteer for any activity because, as prisoners, they are under duress, and their decision to volunteer for or participate in treatment is not necessarily made freely.

It should be noted that sex offenders may also suffer from other psychiatric disorders, and the treatment of these disorders, such as depression, with common medications such as the selective serotonin reuptake inhibitors (currently the most popular antidepressants) has been found to help in their treatment (Hill et al., 2003).[2]

Behavioral Strategies

Most of the common behavior strategies are based on classical conditioning. **Aversion therapy** (Chapter 4) is one behavioral model frequently utilized in the treatment of sex offenders. The aim of aversive techniques is to help offenders associate unpleasant stimuli with presently attractive, yet unacceptable, behaviors (Quinsey & Marshall, 1983). An array of physical or overt aversive stimuli have been used to treat sex offenders. Chief among them are electric shock, foul odors and tastes, drugs that temporarily paralyze, and drugs that induce vomiting (Maletzky, 1991; O'Connell, Leberg & Donaldson, 1990; Quinsey & Marshall, 1983). In practice, a verbal description of the deviant act, the actual object involved, or a video of the act is presented and paired with an unpleasant smell, taste, or feeling in order to decrease arousal (Barbaree, 1990).

The use of physically aversive stimuli has been criticized because the stimuli are too aversive, even inhumane. Bohmer (1983) pointed out that their use may be in violation of the Eight Amendment, which guards against cruel and unusual punishment. These ethical issues, and the possibility that aversive therapy is not very effective in treating sex offenders, has resulted in a decline in their use (Epps, 1996).[3]

One of the first uses of aversive therapy was, in fact, with a sex offender. Raymond (1956) treated a fetishist in England who was sexually aroused by handbags and baby carriages, attacking those of strangers as well as those of his wife. He was treated by pairing images of handbags and baby carriages with apomorphine, a medication that induces vomiting. The treatment was given roughly every two hours, day and night, for a week. After this first week, the man was allowed home for a brief respite. Then a second week of treatment commenced, with another week of treatment after six months. The man never committed a sexual offense again, and his sexual desires and behavior became normal.

The result of the publication of this study was the use of aversive therapy for a variety of problems, including sexual offenses and such behaviors as alcoholism. The relapse rate was high. It was many years before therapists realized that Raymond's client was married. During the period when the thought of his former fetish objects made him nauseous, he was having normal heterosexual relations with his wife, which presumably were gratifying. Thus, the man learned a new (for him) and satisfying alternative to deviant sexual behavior. The men treated later by behavior therapists typically had no opportunity to learn a substitute, normal pattern of behavior. Suppose that we treat an exhibitionist with aversion therapy so that the thought of exposing himself makes him nauseous. We send him back out into the community, where he lives alone or with parents, is too shy to date, and has few, if any, female acquaintances. Thus, he has no opportunity to engage in normal sexual behavior.

In *The Clockwork Orange* (Burgess, 1987), Alex, an aggressive thug, is made to vomit to scenes of violence, and he is so distressed by the procedure and the result that he tries to commit suicide. He was foolish to do so. All he had to do was beat up six people in one day. He would have vomited or felt nauseous for the first victim, but fine for the sixth. **Extinction** occurs in aversive therapy, a simple form of classical conditioning, if the unconditioned stimulus (in this case, the drug-induced nausea) is omitted, the newly conditioned response (vomiting to the deviant behavior) becomes weaker and weaker and quickly disappears.

Thus, our exhibitionist, now in the community, will quickly show extinction of the exhibitionism-nausea response. Behavior therapists eventually realized that it was critical to deal with more basic problems of the client while they were feeling nauseous in response to the deviant behavior. Our exhibitionist may be given psychotherapy to improve his self-esteem, to develop interpersonal skills, and to find ways of meeting and relating in an adult manner to available women.

Covert sensitization or **aversive imagery** has been used as a replacement for aversive therapy. With this treatment, developed by Cautela (1967), inappropriate sexual stimuli are paired with imagined—not physically aversive—consequences. Specifically, the offender is told to imagine a scene that is relevant to his offending. The therapist then leads him through a series of unpleasant consequences. Examples of covert sensitization include being arrested and going to prison, or getting caught by a mother, daughter, or wife.

For example, our exhibitionist may be led to imagine that, just as he was exposing himself, some police officers rushed up, threw him to the ground, cuffed him, and dragged him off. Or just as he exposed himself, he looked down and saw that his penis was covered with open sores.

It has been argued that covert sensitization can decrease sexual deviance (Quinsey & Marshall, 1983), but its effectiveness as compared to other treatment strategies is marginal. It has been recommended that covert sensitization be paired with physically aversive stimuli, such as foul odors. For example, when our exhibitionist sees his penis covered with sores, a foul smelling odor could be passed under his nose. However, this approach has not yet been adequately tested.

Masturbatory conditioning introduces positive reinforcements, in which deviant fantasies are replaced with nondeviant fantasies (Epps, 1996). Offenders are required to record typical deviant masturbatory fantasies in a diary. With the aid of the therapist, offenders are helped to create a nondeviant fantasy. A masturbatory schedule is formulated in which the offender switches from deviant to nondeviant fantasy as he approaches orgasm. Over time, the deviant fantasy is withdrawn, and orgasms become contingent upon nondeviant fantasies.

Cognitive Strategies

Cognitive approaches, designed to change errors in an offender's thinking, are also frequently utilized to treat sex offenders (O'Connell, Leberg & Donaldson, 1990). Sex offenders often harbor beliefs and attitudes that serve to maintain their deviant behavior (Marshall & Barbaree, 1988; Auburn & Lee, 2003). Moreover, defenses are often used to justify and reduce responsibility. To illustrate, offenders commonly deny wrongdoing, rationalize their behavior by making inappropriate behavior seem appropriate, or minimize their part in the deviant acts. Cognitive approaches are used to identify and confront these errors in thinking (see Chapter 9) (Buschman & van Beek, 2003). It is recommended that these approaches be somewhat confrontational and challenge the defenses, views, and attitudes presented by offenders.

Murphy (1990) identifies several cognitive strategies designed around challenging offenders' distorted thinking.

Empathy training is a program in which victims and other counselors attend group sessions with clients and discuss the effects that victimization has on survivors. To change errors in thinking, programs may also have offenders read books by sexual abuse survivors and then discuss these books during therapy.

Role-playing can be utilized, with the therapist playing the role of the sexual offender while the offender plays the role of a police officer or family member whose job is to challenge the distortions.

Social skills training has also been found to increase the success of treatment programs. It has been suggested that social skills training occur in the later stages of treatment after deviant behaviors have been addressed (O'Connell, Leberg & Donaldson, 1990). Many sexual offenders have extremely poor social skills and are not able to communicate with their peers, especially female peers (Groth, 1983). Therefore, social skills training is designed to help offenders develop and maintain healthy adult relationships. This can be accomplished in several ways. Offenders may be taught to model appropriate behaviors demonstrated by the therapist or videotapes, or through behavior rehearsal, which allows the offender to practice initiating and maintaining conversations with other adults (Maletzky, 1991).[4]

The preliminary results of Marques and associates' (1994) evaluation of California's **Sex Offender Treatment and Evaluation Project (SOTEP)** found promising results for cognitive-behavioral strategies for sex offenders. In 1981, California legislators mandated that a state hospital test the most effective and promising methods of treatment for sex offenders. As a result, the California Department of Mental Health founded SOTEP. SOTEP is a cognitive-behavioral program that adds relapse prevention to its treatment paradigm. Clients involved in SOTEP come from the state's Department of Corrections and have been sentenced for child molesting or rape. Participants attend a relapse prevention group for four and one-half hours each week, in addition to one hour per week of individual therapy sessions and two hours per week with members of the nursing staff. A series of specialty training is also provided, which includes relaxation techniques, sex education, human sexuality, social skills training, and stress and anger management. After completion of SOTEP, clients spend an additional year in the **Sex Offender Aftercare Program.**

The California mandate called for a "valid experimental design"; therefore, in their evaluation, the researchers were able to match and randomly assign volunteer offenders to treatment and nontreatment groups. Subjects were matched according to age, sex offense, and criminal history. Initial results indicated that:

1. treatment subjects were less likely to commit new sex offenses;

2. early treatment dropouts were at a higher risk of recidivism for a new sex offense as compared to those completing one year or more of the programs; and

3. treated child molesters were less likely to commit other violent offenses.

Relapse Prevention

In the 1990s, **relapse prevention** became a common goal of treatment strategies for criminal offenses. There is now an awareness that many clients do not understand how relapse occurs, and relapse prevention programs are designed to teach clients strategies that are useful in dealing with negative emotions, interpersonal frictions, and other stressors that lead to relapse. These programs typically use cognitive and behavioral strategies to help clients gain greater control during the maintenance stage of recovery.

The primary goals of relapse prevention are:

1. to help the offender maintain and enhance the changes produced by the treatment strategies; and

2. to ensure that offenders continue to use the skills that they have learned after treatment has ended.

Other objectives include aiding clients in managing high-risk situations that require successful coping skills, and aiding clients in the maintenance of a prolonged period of abstinence from sexual offending while in the community.

The strength of relapse prevention lies in its emphasis on helping an offender to understand and recognize the psychological and situational factors that place him or her at risk for reoffending. For example, toward the end of formal treatment, the offender should prepare a list that includes the factors, processes, and situations that place him or her at risk for reoffending; ways to avoid the occurrence of these risk factors; and techniques to effectively deal with these triggers when they cannot be avoided. To prevent relapse, the offender should carry the list with him or her, and copies should also be given to supervising agencies.

For relapse prevention to be successful, effective treatment of sex offenders after they have been released into the community must be accompanied by high-quality supervision by probation officers, and it is critical that therapists and probation officers communicate and collaborate with one another. Jenuwine, Simmons, and Swies (2003) have described an integrative program in Cook County, Illinois, that has attempted to achieve this, as has Balduzzi (2003), who also stressed the necessity of including an employment-oriented program and having community involvement (for example, by setting up a citizen advisory board).

Other Program Components

In the 1960s and 1970s, those involved with treating sexual offenders were primarily interested in exploring the use of particular psychotherapeutic techniques with sexual offenders, presenting either single case studies or studies of one particular tactic on a group of offenders (see Lester, 1982).

For example, in the treatment of exhibitionists, cases were reported involving psychosurgery to remove Cajal's nucleus in the hypothalamus (Jones, 1972), psychoanalysis (Rubins, 1968), transactional analysis (Zechnich, 1976), hypnosis (Ritchie, 1968), systematic desensitization to anxiety over sexual contact with adult women (Wickramasekera, 1968), aversive therapy involving electric shock (Kushner & Sandler, 1966), and shame (by having exhibitionists expose themselves on demand in front of an audience (Jones and Frei, 1977).

In the 1980s and 1990s, more multifaceted and comprehensive treatment programs were devised, which incorporate several treatment strategies and focus on a number of problem areas that may be relevant to sex offenders. For example, Marshall (1996) includes components to raise the level of self-esteem of the offenders; confront the offenders' denial and minimization of their actions; help the offenders understand the harm they have done and increase their empathy for their victims; challenge their attitudes, beliefs, and distortions about women and children; and change their sexual fantasies through covert sensitization and masturbatory reconditioning. Marshall achieves this in a group therapy format, with about 10 offenders in each group, which is co-led by a male and a female therapist. Individual therapy is rare and used only to deal with group issues such as insufficient participation. Marshall integrates elements of relapse prevention into all of these components and includes a final segment of the program on this.

Marshall also addresses the problem of the increasing number of sex offenders in prison, while funds for treatment are limited. Multiyear programs are not feasible. He advocates classifying offenders upon entry into prison into those whose needs are extensive and for whom the risk of recidivism is high versus those with limited needs and whose recidivism risk is low. The former are placed into an intensive six-month program with three three-hour sessions a week, while the latter are placed into an equally intensive three-month program. Marshall also notes the importance of treating adolescent sex offenders so that they can be prevented from entering into a sustained adult criminal career as sex offenders.

It became clear in the early treatment programs for sex offenders that group therapy was more effective than individual therapy, especially in getting the sex offender to overcome his hostility toward authority and his denial. Mathis and Collins (1970a, 1970b) noted that therapists have difficulty breaking through the offender's defense mechanisms of denial, intellectualization, and isolation of affect (in which the emotion is detached from the accompanying thought or behavior). Mathis and Collins found that an open-ended group, with offenders at various stages of treatment, was especially useful because the offenders who have made some progress in their treatment are better at breaking through the defenses of the newly-admitted offender.

Mathis and Collins also urged the use of male and female co-therapists. The female therapist's role is to provide the presence of an understanding and kind woman who is not seductive and rejecting. The male therapist can be more confrontational about the effects of offending on the offenders' lives, while the female therapist can focus more on interpreting the psychological aspects of the offenders' behavior.

Mathis and Collins described six stages that sex offenders typically move through, though not necessarily in an orderly fashion from one stage to the next, and not without regression to earlier stages from time to time. First, the men deny their guilt. Then, after they accept their guilt, anger breaks through (against the criminal justice system, the other group members, the therapists, their families, etc.). Next, there appears disappointment at the lack of therapeutic progress, followed by improvement. Finally, separation anxiety is experienced as the therapy moves toward its conclusion.

Effectiveness of Treatment Programs

Quinsey and associates (1993) concluded that the effectiveness of treatment programs for sex offenders has not yet been demonstrated. Still, recent studies indicate that certain strategies may be valuable tools for the treatment of sex offenders.

Several meta-analyses of the effectiveness of these programs have been published in recent years. In meta-analyses, the results of a number of studies are reduced to comparable statistical conclusions, and these statistics are then averaged. Hall (1995) reviewed research using recidivism (defined as subsequent sexually aggressive behavior) as a criterion for success. He found that 19 percent of those completing treatment recidivated versus 29 percent of comparison groups. The variables that contributed to treatment success included a high base rate of recidivism, length of follow-up after the program, and outpatient status. Treatment programs using cognitive-behavioral strategies and hormonal treatments seemed to be more effective than programs using behavioral strategies.

Let us look at one of these outcome studies in greater detail. Marshall and Barbaree (1988) reported on the results of comprehensive cognitive-behavioral treatment program for child molesters. They excluded molesters who denied the offense, those who refused to participate in treatment because they felt able to control themselves in the future, and those suffering from brain damage or psychosis. Their subjects, therefore, admitted their offenses and indicated a willingness to be treated.

Of 126 child molesters, 68 completed treatment while 58 were not able to because they were incarcerated or lived too far away to attend the clinic. Marshall and Barbaree noted that the "untreated" molesters may have received some treatment in prison or in the community by participating in other programs.

The recidivism rates were:

	Untreated	Treated
Molesters of Non-family Girls	42.9%	17.9%
Molesters of Non-family Boys	42.9%	13.3%
Incest Offenders	21.7%	8.0%
Total Sample	34.5%	13.2%

These results are encouraging. However, Marshall and Barbaree do not report how many child molesters were eliminated from the study (because of denial of the offenses and brain damage/psychosis), and so we do not what proportion of child molesters might have responded to the treatment program. Also, the study provides no suggestions as to how we might deal with child molesters who do deny or who do have brain damage/psychosis.

Hall's review illustrates the problems with evaluation research. Hall identified 92 published studies of treatment outcomes with sex offenders published since an earlier review in 1989, and it is important to note that some studies are never published. This undetermined number may affect the conclusions drawn from any review. Hall eliminated 32 studies because the number of sex offenders in the study was fewer than 10. Forty-eight studies were eliminated because they failed to compare the outcome for the sex offenders with a control or comparison group or did not report recidivism data. Only 12 studies remained. The conclusion from these data is that treatment studies of sex offenders, if they are to be useful, must be methodologically sound.

Hanson and Bussiere (1998) located and reviewed 61 follow-up studies of sex offenders (which provided information on 28,972 sexual offenders), and they found being young, single, and with a criminal lifestyle, an antisocial personality disorder, and more prior offences predicted recidivism in these studies. However, those who stayed in the treatment programs were less likely to commit new sexual offences than those who failed to complete the treatment programs. Although individual treatment programs may fail to provide evidence for their effectiveness (e.g., Hanson, Bloom & Stephenson, 2004), others have proven to be successful (Seabloom et al., 2003). Overall, the conclusion is that some treatment programs are successful in rehabilitating at least some sex offenders.

Conclusion

It is not easy to help the motivated sex offender although, as we have seen, there appears to be growing success using some treatment strategies. Many sex offenders are not motivated for treatment, and the rehabilitation of these offenders remains difficult. Jenkins-Hall (1994) found that motivational factors (such as acceptance of their problems, attendance at treatment sessions, level of participation in the sessions, and arriving on time for the sessions) were powerful predictors of success in the treatment of child molesters.

Patients in general have a well-established right to refuse treatment. This right may be somewhat limited for convicted sex offenders, but it is more pertinent in cases of experimental treatments, for which the need to obtain informed consent from the offender is stronger (Bohmer, 1983).

There are categories of sex offenders for whom treatment may be especially difficult. For example, although Murphy, Coleman, and Haynes (1983) thought that the standard treatment strategies could be used for mildly or borderline retarded sex offenders, not all of the techniques are useful for the profoundly or severely retarded individual (see also Nolley, Muccigrosso & Zigman, 1996).[5]

Those treating sex offenders must comply with legal requirements. They must inform clients at the outset that not everything the offender says will be confidential. If the offender reports other offenses, these may have to be reported. If the offender is an adolescent and reports being the victim of sexual and physical abuse, this too may have to be reported.[6] These limitations of confidentiality may impede the development of good rapport with sexual offending clients, thereby impeding effective treatment (DiGiorgio-Miller, 1994).

The treatment of sex offenders can also be threatening to the therapist. Discussion of the intimate details of sexual offenses may make the therapist uncomfortable, especially if the victims of the offenses are similar in sex and age to the therapist. DiGiorgio-Miller (1994) decided not to work with a male offender who had participated in a gang rape of a female her age and who acted seductively during the first interview and seemed to have poor ego boundaries. Transference of sexual feelings to the therapist during treatment may occur and, while this is not necessarily destructive of the treatment process, it can arouse anxiety in the therapist. Ennis and Horne (2003) found some symptoms of post-traumatic stress disorder in sex offender therapists, especially if they felt that they received little peer support, and so therapists working with sex offenders should carefully monitor their own level of distress.

Notes

[1]   This type is commonly called the "lover boy" rapist by police officers.

[2]   As well as alleviating depression, the SSRIs also may increase impulse control and decrease sexual desire.

[3]   There are also standards of care for the provision of appropriate treatment under suitable conditions for sex offenders that should be adhered to—see Coleman et al. (1996) for a suggested set of standards.

[4]   Even improving personal skills can assist in the treatment of sex offenders. For example, Metz and Sawyer (2003) described their treatment of an exhibitionist, which included treatment for his erectile dysfunction (impotence).

[5]   Behavioral strategies may be appropriate for the profoundly retarded sex offenders, but obtaining informed consent for treatment from those who are profoundly retarded is a problematic because it is difficult to be sure that they understand what it is they are agreeing to.

[6]   Suicidal and homicidal ideation in all offenders, sexual and nonsexual, may also have to be reported.

Key Concepts and Terms

aversion therapy
aversive imagery
behavioral strategies
clinical interview
cognitive strategies
covert sensitization
empathy training
extinction

masturbatory conditioning
penile plethysmography
physiological strategies
relapse prevention
role-playing
Sex Offender Aftercare Program
Sex Offender Treatment and Evaluation Project
social skills training

Discussion Questions

1.   Compare and contrast organic with behavioral treatment strategies.

2.   Why is relapse prevention an important adjunct to treatment for sex offenders?

3.   What are the advantages of group therapy over individual therapy for sex offenders?

4.   Discuss the ethical problems involved in treating sex offenders.

Chapter 12

Treating Substance Abuse in Offender Populations

Patricia Van Voorhis and Gail Hurst

According to recent estimates, drug and alcohol addiction affect at least 75 percent of all incarcerated offenders (Mumala, 1999). Furthermore, substance abuse is known to place substance abusers at clear risk for future offending (Gendreau, Little & Goggin, 1996; U.S. Bureau of Justice Statistics, 1992). From this perspective, substance-abusing offenders place a heavy demand on all correctional agencies.

Fortunately, recent advances in the technology of substance abuse treatment (Wexler, 1994) offer much support to correctional efforts to provide viable treatment. These include developments in assessments, treatment models, relapse prevention strategies, drug courts, and methods for accommodating offender responsivity. In addition, research shows a clearer picture of "what works" in the treatment of this very important social problem (Anglin & Hser, 1990; Miller et al., 1995; Pearson & Lipton, 1999). None of this is to suggest that treatment of the substance abuser is a straightforward endeavor. There are many "paths" to substance abuse and many different types of substance abusers (Wanberg & Milkman, 1998). In addition, we now recognize that effective treatment should accommodate the substance-abusing offender's readiness to change. That is, interventions designed for offenders who are in denial about the existence of an addiction should differ from those delivered to offenders who are actively seeking to change or those who hope to maintain sobriety (Prochaska & DiClemente, 1986; Miller & Rollnick, 2002). Likewise, there is no consensus about what should be the underlying philosophy of treatment, particularly whether we should consider substance abuse a disease or a learned behavior (Miller & Hester, 1995). Finally, while most treatment models adhere to a requirement of abstinence from addictive substances, others advocate harm-reduction approaches, such as controlled drinking, methadone maintenance, and needle exchange programs (MacCoun, 1998; Marlatt & Witkiewitz, 2002; Marlatt, Blume & Parks, 2001).

This chapter offers an overview of the main approaches and philosophies to treating the substance-abusing offender. As in the treatment of other mental health problems, most interventions rest on the theoretically based systems of therapy discussed in earlier chapters (e.g., psychodynamic, radical-behavioral, family, social learning, and cognitive-behavioral approaches). In this chapter, we also discuss assessment, responsivity, support groups, and harm reduction models. With few exceptions, treatments for drug addictions are not viewed as distinct from those for alcohol addictions, because the addiction is the treatment target—more so than the addictive substance (Wanberg & Milkman, 1998).

Models of Substance Abuse

The wide array of interventions for substance abuse differ rather dramatically in terms of their definitions of who the substance abuser is and how he or she came to become addicted to drugs or alcohol. Treatment implications, of course, follow from each model's core philosophy. In discussing the history and patterns of treatments for alcoholism, for example, Miller and Hester (1995) set forth the 11 models shown in Figure 12.1. Many of the models discussed in Figure 12.1 also apply to drug abuse.

Figure 12.1
Models of Alcohol Intervention (Miller and Hester, 1995)

Moral Model: Probably the longest-standing conceptualization of alcoholism views it as a sin, incurred as the result of personal choice. To this day, some churches continue to hold this view. Even Alcoholics Anonymous defines alcoholism as a "spiritual deficit." This perspective suggests that alcoholism and other addictions be addressed through various means of spiritual direction and social control, including criminal sanctions.

Temperance Model: Through the late 1800s to the repeal of Prohibition in 1933, alcoholism was viewed as caused by a harmful drug—alcohol. Although the Temperance Movements of those days had support from many religious circles, they did not necessarily fault the drinker. Instead, they blamed alcohol and its destructive qualities. "Treatment" from this perspective did not require treatment of the alcoholic but rather legislation that prohibited use and distribution of alcohol, a policy not unlike current approaches to illegal drugs.

Disease Model: Conceptualizing alcoholism as a disease began with the end of Prohibition and the formation of Alcoholics Anonymous. The disease model views alcoholics as physiologically distinct from nonalcoholics in that their biological makeup renders them incapable of drinking in moderation. With this condition, drinking progresses to a point where the drinker acquires an irreversible compulsion to drink, which can only be arrested through abstinence. "Recovery" from the disease requires recognition of the condition and its effects, abstinence, and support from other recovered alcoholics. In the United States, the Disease Model receives strong support from medical arenas as a disease requiring medical treatment. The Disease Model is less widely supported outside of the United States.

Figure 12.1, *continued*

Educational Models: This approach views alcoholism as caused by ignorance of the harms and effects of alcohol. Indeed, in the United States, education has long been one of the common preventive approaches to addiction. Its applicability appears most relevant to primary prevention efforts, strategies that are administered to the general population.

Characterological Model: Most relevant to psychodynamic interventions, this model asserts that alcoholism results from fundamental personality problems. One can fault developmental difficulties such as fixation of normal psychological development, early trauma, excessive use of certain defense mechanisms, and other factors. For some clinicians and scholars, this model has initiated a search for the "alcoholic personality" or the "addictive personality." Treatment from this perspective would involve resolution or interpretation of underlying conflicts and sources of anxiety.

Conditioning Model: Alcoholism and other addictions are learned through the same behavioral mechanisms through which other behaviors are learned. Causation, then, is rooted in classical and operant conditioning models of learning. Drinking and drug use are reinforced through peer approval, tension reduction, improved social confidence, and festivity (operant conditioning). At the same time, addicts come to appreciate the various stimuli of addictive behaviors, e.g., certain friends, settings, and paraphernalia (classical conditioning). Treatment involves reconditioning, contingency management, and stimulus control.

Social Learning/Cognitive Behavioral Model: As noted in Chapters 8 and 9, behaviors can be learned vicariously in the presence of peers and others who model a behavior that is then imitated. Both the behaviors and the cognitions associated with substance abuse may be learned in this manner. Treatment models operating from this approach teach new skills, particularly coping skills, and seek to alter individuals' relationships with their environments and the individuals with whom they associate. In addition, these interventions endeavor to change thought patterns that are viewed as associated with addictive behavior. The Social Learning/Cognitive-Behavioral Model is becoming the preferred approach to treating the substance-abusing offender.

Biological Models: Not to be confused with the disease models, these approaches attempt to identify and target specific genetic or physiological causes of alcoholism. Since the 1970s, biological research has: (a) identified inherited risk factors of alcoholism; (b) identified abnormal forms of metabolizing alcohol; (c) studied brain sensitivity to alcoholism; and (d) studied the manner in which drinking escalates to alcoholism. Treatment from this approach may involve genetic counseling, counseling abstinence, or controlled drinking.

General Family Systems Model: This model views substance abuse as occurring within dysfunctional family systems. That is, addiction is just one symptom of family dysfunction. Treatment addresses the needs of all family members as members of a system. Treatment targets may include enabling behaviors, poor boundaries among family members, communication problems, and trust issues.

Sociocultural Models: These models recognize that some social environments and cultures support drug and alcohol abuse more than others. What follows from the sociocultural model are attempts to regulate drinking establishments and alcohol/drug distribution patterns in order to prevent undue encouragement of substance abuse. Thus, illegal drugs, liquor taxation, licensure requirements for bars and restaurants, advertising restrictions, regulation of hours for drinking establishments, and age restrictions are examples of sociocultural efforts to control alcohol and drug use.

Public Health Model: Seeks to integrate important aspects of the approaches listed above. The Public Health Model encourages a multifaceted approach to addictions focusing on: (a) the agent (alcohol/illegal drugs); (b) the host (the substance abuser); and (c) the micro and macro environments (family, peers, and society). The Public Health Model advocates simultaneous attention to the hazardous nature of alcohol, individual susceptibilities to alcohol, and social policies that regulate its distribution.

The preceding list presents an array of competing approaches to the treatment of substance abuse. In practice, interventions for substance-abusing offenders are more likely to be eclectic than conform to a single policy or model of service delivery. Even so, some of the models differ dramatically on such issues as: (a) who is responsible for the addiction (the addict or a disease that the addict cannot help having); (b) whether the addict is a moral individual; (c) whether abstinence is required; or (d) what should be targeted in treating the addiction (knowledge, physiological factors, spirituality, social skills, or cognitions). Importantly, the debate often manifests itself at policy levels, such as when agencies debate whether they should support the **disease model** or cognitive-behavioral approaches.

In keeping with the main approach to this text, we focus on the treatment models themselves, offering an overview of substance abuse treatment from each of the treatment systems discussed in earlier chapters.

Psychodynamic Approaches

Although **psychodynamic** approaches are not suitable for most correctional clients, the psychoanalytic/ psychodynamic tradition has much to say about substance abuse. Even with the advent and widespread implementation of more popular social learning and cognitive-behavioral approaches, some continue to maintain that psychodynamic therapy can enhance our understanding of some substance-abusing clients and improve the effectiveness of our efforts (Francis, Franklin & Borg, 1994). Psychodynamic approaches may work with some clients as a therapy in itself (or in combination with other educational, cognitive-behavioral, or support group approaches), but its use with offender clients is likely to be confined to private therapy.

In keeping with recent trends in psychodynamic therapy, treatment tends to focus on developmental and structural deficits, such as limited ego control. Affective difficulties (depression, especially) and certain ego defenses (defense mechanisms) seem especially relevant, particularly those associated with early developmental difficulties. From this perspective, substance abuse may be an attempt to "medicate" feelings of emptiness, rage, or depression (Wurmser, 1984); powerlessness (Dodes, 1990); or persistent shame (Lewis, 1987). In addition, earlier relationship difficulties that then pose problems with object relations, such as fears of intimacy or dependency (Khantzian, Halliday & McAuliffe, 1990), are also important to consider.

Psychodynamic therapy utilizes many of the same strategies discussed in Chapter 3. Early in therapy, the focus is on working with the client's denial about his or her substance abuse and "working through" the denial in order to accept responsibility for one's situation. Denial is seen from this perspective as a defense mechanism. Much emphasis is placed on the therapeutic relationship that, in itself, is considered a vehicle for change. The therapeutic relationship then serves as an opportunity to interpret transference, countertransference, and defenses directed toward the therapist. Later, it becomes possible to address additional defenses, such as interpretations of projections of blame or using the effects of drugs or alcohol in order to rationalize one's behavior while "under the influence."

Therapists are likely to assess a client's history, particularly early relationships with parents and siblings, for its impact on object relations, thus examining current conflicts or relationship problems as they relate to the past. Uncovering the sources of the client's dependence on alcohol or drugs and shifting that dependence to dependence on others, such as the therapist, family members, spiritual support, support group members, and a sponsor is an important, though temporary, step forward.

Influences on ego and superego development are also examined, because often it is necessary to strengthen ego controls and self-esteem, or a client's ability to manage feelings and deal with shame. In keeping with the basic psychodynamic model, interpretation of free associations, slips, and dreams assist in the process of uncovering unconscious links to the substance abuse as well as unconscious conflicts that may lead to relapse (Dodes & Khantzian, 1991).

If used at all, psychodynamic therapy is most appropriate for more verbal clients who are tolerant of insight-oriented approaches. Francis, Franklin, and Borg (1994) note that the most successful clients are likely to be intelligent, interested, insightful, psychologically minded, and motivated to secure a better understanding of themselves. Higher incomes, marital stability, and not having a diagnosis of psychopathy, organic brain injury, or psychosis are also precursors to success. Finally, those whose substance abuse involves defensive behaviors and anxiety also seem quite appropriate.

While nonpsychodynamic group therapies are more likely to be used with substance-abusing offenders, some clients may fear groups or be more reluctant to disclose personal issues in group settings. In these cases, individual therapy is recommended (Zimberg, 1994). Individual therapy, whether psychodynamic or some other therapy, however, cannot furnish much-needed social support or identification with recovering alcoholics. In most instances, a combination of approaches (group and individual therapy or individual therapy supplemented by AA or NA) is favored. Finally, psychodynamic approaches do not speak to the physiological craving for drugs or alcohol (Zimberg, 1994). Thus, as with other models, an eclectic approach is warranted (Miller & Hester, 1995).

Radical Behavioral Approaches

Strategies appearing under the rubric of classical or operant conditioning include aversion therapies, contingency contracting, token economies, covert sensitization, stimulus control, and community reinforcement. Some of these approaches stand alone as substance abuse interventions in themselves; others are components of such other programs as therapeutic communities or relapse prevention programs. Use of these strategies makes sense for a variety of reasons. One has only to think about how drug and alcohol use actually conforms to classical and operant conditioning to see the applicability of both learning models to the treatment of the substance abuser. Addiction can be viewed as being encouraged and maintained by the addictive substances and their effects. Drinking, for example, is often encouraged by such antecedents (stimuli) as days of the week, times of the day, activities associated with drinking, familiar drinking establishments, drinking buddies, certain meals, and emotional states. Similarly, drinking is reinforced by such effects as reduction in stressful feelings, a "buzz," increased social comfort, and peer approval. Radical behavioral therapies seek to reverse these processes by controlling the stimuli that encourage substance abuse and by reinforcing controlled drinking, abstinence, and other prosocial substitute behaviors.

Classical conditioning therapies for substance abuse treatment consist primarily of aversion therapy and stimulus control. **Aversion therapies** work directly with a client's desire for an addictive drug; they attempt to reverse these desires. These early approaches paired aversive stimuli with consumption of drugs or alcohol. The aversive stimuli included drug-induced nausea, drug-induced breathing difficulties (apnea), foul odors, and electric shock (Wilson, 1987). The goal of treatment was to cause clients to associate the addictive substance with the aversive stimulus (UCS), thereby developing an avoidance reaction to the alcohol or drugs. Given the pain and stress associated with these approaches, however, more recent applications of aversion therapy use a more benign form of classical conditioning: covert sensitization.

As described in Chapter 4, **covert sensitization** employs aversive imagery rather than aversive experiences. Clients imagine the aversive events or feelings rather than directly experiencing them (Cautela, 1977). Sometimes, however, a nauseating odor may be used to accompany the images. Rimmele, Miller, and Dougher's (1989) approach to covert sensitization with alcoholics includes the following steps: (a) preliminary assessment; (b) constructions of various scenes specific to each client; (c) administration of stimulus scenes; (d) administration of sensitization or aversive scenes; and (e) administration of escape or avoidance scenes. The preliminary assessment obtains information concerning a client's drinking preferences, patterns, and motivations. A variety of drinking scenes incorporate the situations and details that would typically accompany a client's drinking habits. The aversive scenes construct situations that find the client experiencing either nausea or strong emotional reactions (e.g., embarrassment, disgust, guilt, or horror). Rimmele, Miller, and Dougher (1989) offer the following poignant example of one such scene:

> [After leaving the bar] you have just entered your car, and are preparing to back out of the driveway, on your way to the store. With one hand on the hot steering wheel, you reach forward to insert the key in the ignition. As you feel it slide in, you swallow and notice the taste of beer in your mouth. You can smell it, as if you just swallowed a large sip. You turn the key, and the engine surges to life. As you pull the shift lever into reverse, you glance over your shoulder to make sure it is clear behind the car. The car gives a sickening lurch as if you ran over a small bump. The taste of beer is strong in your mouth as you open the door and look toward the back of the car. You are horrified to see a small foot sticking out from behind your rear tire. You jump from the car, and find a small crumpled body pinned under the rear of the car. You're down on your hands and knees, and as you peer under the car, you can clearly see the blood puddling under the small child's body. There is no movement, and you cannot tell if the child is alive. The smell of beer is strong on your breath, and the smell mixes with the warm odor of blood on the ground. You are horrified, you cannot think straight, as you stare at the broken body. You notice that the child's arms are bend unnaturally, and you see the stark white color of bone protruding through the clothing. The sour taste of beer surges into your mouth, and burning fear and horror fills you, as you see the child's limbs give a series of twitches.

It goes without saying that the aversive scene is constructed to elicit a strong response from the client. When this occurs, the client informs the therapist or demonstrates that he or she is uncomfortable. The therapist then shows an aversion relief scene (getting help for the child) or an escape scene (never going to the bar in the first place). The goal to be achieved after exposure to several stimulus and aversive scenes, however, is to have this escape scene become a conditioned response. Ultimately, the client will come to express the desire to escape before the conclusion of the aversive scene or perhaps even before the aversive scene begins. In successful therapy, the conditioned response will occur for the client in similar situations outside of therapy.

Applications of classical conditioning are also seen in recent relapse prevention programs. One of the goals of relapse prevention is to alert clients to situations (or stimuli) that place clients at a higher risk of relapse than if they were not in the presence of such stimuli. Initially, we may encourage clients to avoid such stimuli, but in the case of family holidays and other situations, this is not always possible. In the terminology of the relapse prevention approach, such times are referred to as **high-risk situations**. Treatment involves helping clients to identify their own "high risk" situations and to develop coping skills and plans for dealing with them (Marlatt & Barrett, 1994; Parks, Marlatt & Anderson, 2001).

Unfortunately, excessive alcohol/drug use is reinforced by the effects of such use. Drinking, for example, may lead to immediate reward/reinforcement (a "buzz," tension reduction, or peer approval). Although use may also be followed by negative consequences, these usually are delayed (e.g., physical discomfort, disease, social disapproval, financial loss, decreased self-esteem). **Operant conditioning** models attempt to change the ways in which substance abuse is reinforced. These approaches are seen primarily as components of other approaches. Therapeutic communities, for example, may make use of token economies or other systems of behavioral rewards and punishments (see Chapters 4, 5, and 8) as a means of increasing accountability and responsibility. In these cases, residents progress through levels of treatment and earn privileges as rewards for using prosocial substitute behaviors. Residents are rewarded with things such as restaurant coupons for positive achievements, while also being held accountable for negative behaviors (Inciardi & Lockwood, 1994).

Additional examples of operant conditioning include community reinforcement and contingency contracting. Many therapies integrate behavioral contracts (**contingency contracts**) in which access to jobs, family, friends, recreation, and other community reinforcers are contingent upon the client's ongoing sobriety (Smith & Meyers, 1995). A contingency contract is often used with adolescents or following an intervention (see page 69).

The **community reinforcement** approach (CRA) (Hunt & Azrin, 1973; Miller, Meyers & Hiller-Sturmhofel, 1999) seeks to provide alcoholics with the incentives (reinforcements) to stop drinking. This involves disrupting positive reinforcements for drinking and developing positive reinforcements for sobriety. In the early phases of CRA, therapists work to increase clients' motivation to stop drinking. An "inconvenience review" inventories all of the problems associated with the client's drinking, including work, marital, and health problems. Identification of the client's "high risk situations" and drinking-related reinforcements is also done early in therapy. A number of additional approaches are selected that are planned to increase the client's sources of positive reinforcement for not drinking. For example, these could include reducing the client's alcohol-induced isolation and increasing his or her hobbies, recreational outlets, and social interactions with friends who do not drink. Help in removing barriers to positive pursuits may also be given, such as when the client is assisted with employment efforts or with coping and social skills. Sometimes relationship counseling is offered through CRA along with teaching family members to use reinforcers (e.g., spending time with the client during times of sobriety and not while under the influence). CRA has also been used with drug offenders.

Finally, recognizing that sobriety removes a major source of enjoyment (reinforcement) from a client's life, relapse prevention programs recommend the introduction of new sources of enjoyment. Clients should have, in other words, a healthy balance between "shoulds" and "wants" (Marlatt & Gordon, 1985). This finds therapists encouraging clients to make lifestyle changes that develop new interests and sources of enjoyment. Otherwise, focusing on the deprivations of sobriety, and creating a life overburdened by "shoulds" could increase the likelihood of relapse.

Where do the radical behavioral approaches stand in terms of their effectiveness? The earlier classical conditioning and aversion models have not fared well. In addition, the idea that addicts can be punished into not drinking or using drug has been shown to be ineffective. Studies are somewhat more supportive of the incentive-based models (Miller et al., 1998). In a meta-analysis of behavioral and cognitive behavioral programs, researchers found programs to be effective in reducing recidivism and drug abuse, but the cognitive-behavioral/social learning programs were more effective than programs that relied primarily on the radical behavioral model (Pearson et al., 1999). We now turn to those approaches.

Social Learning and Cognitive-Behavioral Approaches

The most recent advances in substance abuse treatment utilize social learning and cognitive-behavioral approaches. As discussed in Chapters 8 and 9, these treatment models overlap; cognitive therapies use role models and reinforcement to model new cognitive skills, and social learning approaches often target cognitive patterns. As noted earlier, however, the fundamental vehicle for change within a social learning paradigm is the role model who can be imitated by others and offer feedback to those who are trying to change. Role models have a long history in substance abuse treatment. Members of Alcoholics Anonymous and Narcotics Anonymous, for example, are encouraged to work with **"sponsors."** These are NA or AA members who have been in "recovery" for a significant period of time. Through their own example, sponsors also offer other members the opportunity to see that sobriety can have its rewards. Sponsors model skills of relationship building, responsibility, and support, although not as formally as role models might in the social learning approaches discussed below. As will be seen, a good deal of attention must also be given to the thought processes of substance abusers, particularly how their thinking supports or does not support their recovery.

Therapeutic Communities

During the last few decades, **therapeutic communities** (see Chapter 5) have become a common form of treatment for offenders diagnosed with substance abuse problems (DeLeon, 2000; Inciardi & Lockwood, 1994). Therapeutic communities (TCs) are in-patient forms of treatment in which clients spend three months to one year in a residential setting. The philosophy of most TCs is that substance abuse is learned from environmental influences and experiences such as underemployment, poverty, job stress, and marital discord (Milhorn, 1990). In fact, residents in therapeutic communities are viewed as being in need of habilitation as a population of individuals whose skill deficits, vocational strengths, and level of psychological disturbance is more pronounced than offender clients in other treatment settings (Shore, 1994). Substance abuse is viewed as a disorder of the whole person. That is, the problem is the person, not the drug (Pan et al., 1993).

TC staff members may be former substance abusers who have themselves been resocialized in therapeutic communities (Pan et al., 1993; Schuckit, 1995). While staff are expected to act as peer role models and encourage mutual self-help, the traditional therapeutic community model also seeks to use all aspects of the environment (e.g., leadership, staff's use of authority, rules) as "models" to residents (Jones, 1968). The objectives of TCs involve changing negative patterns of behavior, thinking, and feelings that act as predispositions to drug abuse (Pan et al., 1993). There is a strong emphasis on the clients' help in maintaining the community (Milhorn, 1990). Other types of treatment found within the TC include tutorial learning sessions, remedial and formal education classes, and vocational training (Anglin & Hser, 1990).

Over time, the term therapeutic community has come to mean many different things. In fact, a recent comprehensive evaluation of drug treatment programs reported that the group of therapeutic communities contained in the large sample of studies did not offer uniform approaches to treating substance abuse (Pearson & Lipton, 1999). This sometimes creates confusion about just what intervention is represented by therapeutic communities (Taxman & Bouffard, 2002). We see in some TCs a design that focuses on cognitive-behavioral intervention, social learning, and positive peer culture. The TCs run by the Federal Bureau of Prisons, for example, are cognitive-behavioral. Moreover, it is not unusual for TCs to use the same cognitive-behavioral curricula that are used for general offender populations.

While peer role modeling and mutual self-help are components of many TCs, what constitutes good role modeling may be far from the criteria set forth in Chapter 8. Most criticized in this regard is a highly confrontational procedure known as **peer encounters**, where much of the "therapy" consisted of staff and peers challenging the behavior of an addict. Such groups also required members' adherence to the ideology of the group. For example, Synanon, a program established in the 1960s for heroin addicts, used confrontational strategies closely patterned after those used in Guided Group Interaction (See Chapter 5). Founders of Synanon claimed that the peer group was an important vehicle for breaking through the manipulation, denial, and lying common to addictive behaviors. Peer encounters were seen as a way of "heightening a resident's awareness of the images, attitudes, and conduct that need to be modified" (Pan et al., 1993). Others viewed the Synanon brand of peer encounter as dangerous, especially with substance abusers. Critics argued that substance-abusing offenders often evidence serious self-esteem problems that are aggravated by confrontations (Khantzian, 1993). Instead, abusers are believed to require consistency, empathy, and firm but nonpunitive confrontation. Most TCs have moved away from inappropriate levels of confrontation to approaches that stress mutual helping.

Notwithstanding questions about what treatment modalities are used, these programs have shown favorable results in a recent meta-analysis funded by the National Institute of Drug Abuse (Pearson & Lipton, 1999), as well as in more recent evaluations (Knight, Simpson & Hiller, 1999; Martin et al., 1999; Pelissier et al., 1998; Wexler et al., 1999). The most effective programs are those that provide community-based aftercare following release (Griffith et al., 1999).

Coping and Social Skills Training

Used in a variety of situations, including approaches to non-abusing offenders, cognitive-behavioral programs that teach coping and social skills have clear applicability to substance-abusing offenders. These programs target a number of the social and coping skill deficiencies known to affect substance-abusing offenders. These include problem solving (Beck et al., 1993), self-efficacy (Marlatt, 1985; Wanberg & Milkman, 1998), and a variety of skills pertinent to social competency and emotional control (Monti et al., 1995). Relapse prevention programs focus on skills pertinent to recognizing and dealing with high-risk situations (Annis & Davis, 1989; Marlatt & Barrett, 1994; Parks et al., 2001).

The basic steps to skills training in the substance abuse programs are similar to those mentioned in Chapter 8. For example, Monti and associates (1995) set forth the following steps to teaching the skill of refusing a drink:

1. The group leader gives **a rationale** for acquiring the skill, by explaining that being pressured for a drink is a "high risk" situation. Clients are reminded that alcohol is so readily available that they are likely to encounter situations in which drinks will be offered. Turning down the drink is not easy, but requires specific skills;

2. The group leader gives **guidelines** for using the skill, including: Saying "no" in a clear manner; suggesting an alternative; asking persisters to stop; avoiding excuses or acting indecisive; and making eye contact with the person offering the drink;

3. The group leader **models** an ineffective and then an effective response to a sample situation;

4. The group members **role-play** responses to similar situations;

5. The group members are **reinforced** for effective demonstrations of the skill or components of the skill;

6. The group members receive constructive **feedback** on how the skill might be improved;

7. The group members are encouraged to comment on their own use of the skill; and

8. The group members **rehearse the skill in increasingly difficult situations**.

Additional skills taught in these types of programs include giving positive feedback, giving criticism, receiving criticism, listening, conversational skills, developing sober supports, conflict resolution skills, nonverbal communication, expressing feelings, assertiveness, refusing requests, coping with cravings, managing negative thinking, relaxation, and managing stress.

Relapse Prevention Training

A subset of the skills training programs for substance abusers deals exclusively with **relapse prevention**. This extremely important innovation in substance abuse intervention has come to be recognized as a major stage of therapy, which does not occur until clients have initiated change toward abstinence. The goal of relapse prevention is to maintain that change (Annis & Davis, 1989). Underlying most relapse prevention programs is Albert Bandura's theory of **self-efficacy** (1978), which holds that self-efficacy greatly facilitates clients' efforts to cope. In the case of substance abuse, it is assumed that self-efficacy is crucial to coping with high-risk situations and maintaining sobriety. That is, offenders who are confident in their skills for coping with a high-risk situation are less likely to relapse than those who are not (Annis & Davis, 1989; Parks et al., 2001). The role of self-efficacy is illustrated in Figure 12.2.

A high-risk situation either elicits an effective coping response or results in a lapse into drinking or drug use. The two situations, however, have different effects on self-efficacy. Successful coping—avoiding the lapse—increases self-efficacy and the expectancy of positive outcomes in future situations. Ineffective coping decreases self-efficacy, increasing the positive expectancies for the effects of the drug/alcohol, and ultimately increasing the likelihood of full relapse. Additional goals of relapse prevention include teaching clients to recognize and cope with high-risk situations and preventing a lapse from deteriorating into a relapse.

These approaches recognize that the road to recovery often occurs in fits and starts, and that a lapse is not as important as a relapse. Lapses do, however, result in guilt, feelings of failure, and perceived loss of control, feelings that Marlatt and Gordon (1985) refer to as the **Abstinence Violation Effect (AVE).** Unless addressed, AVEs lead to demoralization, reduced self-efficacy, and the loss of one's motivation to remain abstinent. Thus, relapse prevention devotes considerable attention to helping offenders prevent lapses from reducing self-efficacy.

Figure 12.2
Cognitive-Behavioral Model of the Relapse Process (Marlatt & Barrett, 1994).

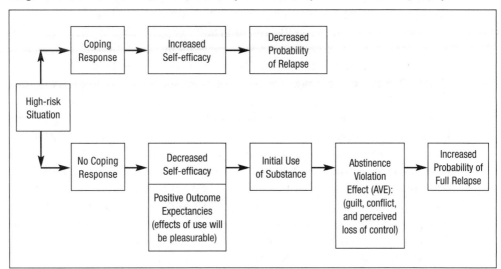

The relapse prevention therapy begins with the client's completion of the Inventory of Drinking Situations (IDS) (Marlatt & Gordon, 1985). The IDS rates each client on his or her risk potential in eight potentially high-risk situations: (a) unpleasant emotions (anxiety, depression, frustration, anger, boredom); (b) physical discomfort; (c) pleasant emotions; (d) testing personal control; (e) temptations to drink; (f) conflict with others (arguments); (g) social pressure to drink; and (h) pleasant times with others. Alternatively, Marlatt recommends keeping a log of troubling situations and the strategies used to cope with them. Either method is designed to present clients with full awareness of the types of situations in which it is especially difficult for them to cope. It is usually possible to order the situations in a hierarchy from least to highest risk, but some clients may have flat profiles, in which all situations are high risk.

Following recognition of the nature of the situations that are likely to lead to relapse, clients work to develop and rehearse plans for coping with each type of situation. In doing so, they develop an inventory of their existing strengths, such as their support network (e.g., friends, family, therapists, support groups), their knowledge of times in which they had been able to cope, or their cognitive strengths (e.g., a belief in self-discipline). Discussions, role-playing, and homework assignments are used to encourage clients to draw on these coping skills and to develop new skills. For each problem situation, clients and therapists work on a tentative plan of action for how they will deal with the event. Clients plan ahead and rehearse alternative responses, become mentally prepared, and practice in increasingly difficult situations. Over time, the client is exposed to more difficult and more varied situations, with the goal of achieving mastery of these situations and building confidence or self-efficacy. The goal is to increase self-efficacy over time. The process usually includes assessments of clients' self-efficacy at different times throughout the relapse prevention therapy (Annis & Graham, 1988).

The types of coping skills and alternative approaches to high-risk situations include: assertiveness, stress management, relaxation training, anger management, communication skills, marital therapy, and social and dating skills. Clients are encouraged to focus on their successes. With growing self-efficacy, relapse, if it occurs, may be less likely to lead to a full return to one's full substance abuse pattern. Marlatt and Barrett (1994) also teach clients to modify cognitive reactions to lapses and AVEs in order to prevent a single lapse from becoming a relapse. In particular, clients are taught to restructure or reframe self-defeating attitudes or reactions to lapses, recognizing, for example, that recovery is a learning process that takes time. In addition to the methods for dealing with specific situations, they also encourage lifestyle balancing strategies. For example, meditation, mindfulness, and exercise are viewed as strengthening a client's overall coping capabilities and reducing the intensity of urges.

Relapse prevention can be a stand-alone program as a general self-control approach, but it is typically used as a post-treatment strategy. Empirical studies indicate that the model, in most cases, reduced recidivism (Parks et al., 2001).

Drug Courts

Drug courts emerged in the late 1980s to deal with the influx of cases generated by the "War on Drugs." The courts, which proliferated dramatically during the past 15 years, differ tremendously across jurisdictions. Some divert offenders contingent upon their completion of therapy and/or refraining from future offending; others suspend a sentence based on similar contingencies. Both juvenile and adult drug courts exist. In contrast to other criminal courts, the bench has a greater role in case monitoring and supervision. That is, offenders return to court for routine status checks, relapse, failure to attend treatment, or other problematic behavior. In some cases, the judge may issue a continuance and the formulation of a modified plan of treatment. In more serious cases, a deferred sentence may be imposed or a diverted offender may proceed to conviction. In all cases, judicial authority is used as a tool for encouraging compliance with drug court conditions (U.S. General Accounting Office, 1997). Drug courts are intended to offer a more reasonable and less costly response to substance abuse than incarceration.

It is important to realize that drug courts, themselves, are administrative rather than therapeutic entities. They are part of a larger group of problem-solving courts such as mental health courts, but cannot be associated with any specific type of treatment modality (e.g., behavioral, cognitive-behavioral). Specific modalities vary considerably across courts; some offer multiple therapeutic options and others offer no therapy (Bouffard & Taxman, 2004; Goldkamp, White & Robinson, 2001).

Generally, the courts have shown some effectiveness in reducing drug-related offenses (Listwan et al., 2003). A recent meta-analysis summarizing outcomes across 22 studies, for example, reported an average reduction in recidivism of 7.5 percent (Lowenkamp, Holsinger & Latessa, 2002). Another meta-analysis of 38 studies noted that the overall reduction in recidivism was 26 percent (Wilson, Mitchell & MacKenzie, 2003). In all of these studies, there were too few programs to test the effectiveness of specific program modalities. However, Wilson and associates (2003) note that the most effective courts: (a) provide a clear incentive for completing the program, such as rewarding offenders with either dismissed charges, differed sentencing, or completion of a condition of probation; and (b) relied on a single service provider. Other reports have shown that courts using single service providers are often adhering to cognitive-behavioral interventions (Peyton & Gossweiler, 2001). Researchers also note that sufficient "dosage," or length of time in the drug court program, matters (Peters, Haas & Hunt, 2001).

Family Therapy Approaches

Few would question whether families are seriously affected by the substance abuse of a family member. In addition to coping with the stress of living with a person who is abusing drugs or alcohol, family members are viewed as having key roles in supporting the alcoholic's or the addict's efforts to recover. In many instances, family members have developed behaviors that initially helped them to cope with an addict but later proved to be dysfunctional. For example, some members may have inadvertently **enabled** a family member to drink or use drugs, e.g., by making up excuses as to why the member cannot go to work, taking over the substance abuser's family responsibilities, purchasing alcohol, or refusing to allow other family members to discuss the substance abuse. Finally, having inherited a physiological predisposition to addiction, and having lived in an addicted family system, some family members must also examine their own susceptibility to addiction.

Family therapy for alcoholism and drug addiction spans the family therapy models presented in Chapter 10; these include psychodynamic, behavioral, communications, and family systems approaches. With the exception of psychodynamic therapy, all of the approaches discussed in Chapter 10 noted at least one evaluation pertinent to substance abusers. Key to family therapy for substance abuse, however, is the assumption that the substance abusing client, technically referred to as the **"identified patient" (IP)** is not the only person in the family who is in need of therapy. Because the system is an entity that is considered to be as troubled as members within the system, it may not work to treat one member apart from the system.

Each of the family therapy models discussed below views alcoholism or drug addiction in a different manner. **Psychodynamic family therapies** assess the IP and other family members in terms of histories and "family of origin" issues. In this way, therapy attempts to help family members understand how past relationships and problems may be replayed in the present (Framo, 1981). In addition, therapists may attempt to identify and interpret members' resistance to change. Interestingly, members other than the IP will often demonstrate behaviors, habits, or communication patterns (e.g., denial, inability to deal with conflict, or reluctance to discuss angry reactions) that prevent change in the IP or the family system (Anderson & Stewart, 1983). Transference, projective identification, and countertransference must also be interpreted and incorporated into tasks that help to set new behaviors in place.

Some consider the psychodynamic model of family therapy to be inadequate for the treatment of addiction, because it is not a "here and now" approach (Kaufman, 1985). In addition, substance abuse requires more of an active emphasis on limit-setting and coping with present-day crises than is focused on in the psychoanalytic approach.

Behavioral family therapies rely mostly on a social learning theoretical framework. From this perspective, the family is alerted to behaviors that may be reinforcing excessive drinking or drug use, e.g., enabling or attention. Similarly, family members may be shielding the IP from the consequences of his or her drug use; in experiencing no costs to his or her excessive use, the addict continues to abuse. The family learns of sequences of behaviors that may be setting up stimulus-response patterns for substance abuse, e.g., poor communication and conflict resolution strategies that then precipitate excessive drinking.

Behavioral family approaches encourage members to set specific behavioral goals, such as to stop "taking care" of the alcoholic, to maintain "family detoxification," or to rehearse alternative behavioral sequences (e.g., better communication patterns). Thus, the IP and family members: (a) become alert to the behaviors that stimulate drinking or drug use; (b) rearrange contingencies (e.g., reinforce sobriety); (c) monitor sobriety rather than ignore drug/alcohol abuse; and (d) learn new skills for interacting with one another (e.g., assertiveness, problem solving, refraining from blaming) (McCrady, 1990). Behavioral family therapy approaches are widely used, especially for adolescent substance abusers (Kaufman, 1985).

Family systems models seek to identify family routines, regulatory behaviors, rituals, or problem-solving strategies that have developed to deal with substance abuse within the family (Steinglass et al., 1987). Unfortunately, when family matters become directed primarily toward coping with the alcoholism or drug addiction of a family member, other important family functions, such as child rearing, support, and the family's financial well-being, may suffer. Such processes also encourage the intergenerational transmission of substance abuse. One of the goals of family systems therapy is to change "alcoholic family systems" to "families with an alcoholic member." An "alcoholic family system," according to Steinglass (1994), organizes itself around its core issue of dealing with an alcoholic member or members. In contrast, a "family with an alcoholic member" is not organizing most of its activities and behaviors to accommodate the alcoholic.

Another goal of family systems therapy is to alter the family "structures" that sustain addiction. From this model, family therapy targets problem-solving strategies and dysfunctional family roles (e.g., a child who has assumed adult responsibilities). At the same time, it seeks to restore an appropriate family hierarchy (parents supervise children) and appropriate boundaries to family relationships (e.g., extending some separation to overly enmeshed systems and shifting alliances) (Kaufman, 1985).

Communications therapy can also apply to the task of treating family systems. Here, altering dysfunctional family communication patterns helps to create more healthy family structures. Such changes may include: (a) discontinuing the practice of triangulation (e.g., talking *about* someone rather *to* someone); (b) communicating directly to individuals rather than expecting them to read minds; (c) accurately describing problems rather than renaming them or "mystifying" them; and (d) clarifying the intentions of another person, rather than making assumptions.

Finally, **Multisystemic Family Therapy** addresses the family systems issues discussed above, but also provides intensive "wraparound" services to families in which substance abuse or other problems have diminished the family's ability to meet the basic needs of its members or work with extra-family systems in a healthy manner (Henggeler et al., 1996; Randall et al., 2001).

In addition to these five family therapy models, families coping with substance abuse may benefit from the following:

1. **Support groups for family members:** As discussed below, self-help groups exist for family members of alcoholics and addicts. These are specific to the family member's role within the family; there are groups for spouses, young children, teenagers, and adult children. These groups paralleled the development of Alcoholics Anonymous and while they are specific to the developmental needs of family members, they use many of the same principles as AA, including 12 steps and sponsorship.

2. **Interventions and Confrontations:** Alcoholics and substance abusers often resist treatment until long after their behavior has become destructive and costly to those around them. Interventions offer one method for motivating uncooperative addicts to change. Family interventions are typically facilitated by a substance abuse counselor who provides opportunities for family members, employers, and friends to confront the addict about his or her behavior. These individuals explain how the behaviors have hurt them and their rela-

tionships with the addict. Some give an ultimatum, that ongoing commitment to their relationship with the addict will require the addict to participate in treatment and maintain abstinence. Such sessions are not announced ahead of time to the addict/alcoholic, and they often conclude with the substance abuser's leaving for treatment either immediately or shortly after the intervention. Substance abuse therapists hold three or four preparatory sessions with participants prior to conducting the intervention (O'Farrell, 1995).

The Importance of Support Groups

Self-help groups and **support groups** have become important adjuncts to therapy for a vast array of personal, medical, and social problems. The prototype for self-help groups for substance abusers is Alcoholics Anonymous (AA), formed in Ohio in 1935. The approach of AA fits within the "disease model." Alcoholism is viewed as a physical, mental, and spiritual disease. AA also assumes that alcoholism has a common set of symptoms, genetic basis, and a disease progression. Total cure of the disease is not possible; one can only arrest its development through lifetime abstinence.

AA operates on a 12-step model, encouraging alcoholics to grow from an initial acknowledgement of the fact that alcohol is making their lives unmanageable to: (a) a reliance on spiritual support to assist in the recovery process; (b) acknowledgement of "defects of character" and how these have harmed others; (c) making amends to people whom they have harmed; (d) ongoing spiritual involvement; and (e) a commitment to helping other alcoholics.

AA does not view itself as engaging in a psychological model of therapy. In fact, one of the Twelve Traditions of AA states: "AA should remain forever nonprofessional . . ." Still, one sees in the 12 steps a number of the therapeutic goals of well-established clinical approaches, including: (a) dealing with denial; (b) reliance on role models; and (c) development of coping strategies and healthier relationships with others (McCrady & Irving, 1989). Some maintain that AA shares similarities with behavioral and cognitive-behavioral therapies. Both AA and behavioral skills approaches, for example, emphasize avoidance of settings in which drinking takes place (i.e., "high-risk situations"), coping skills for high-risk situations, social support, improvement of relationships through communication training, and the development of new social networks. Both AA and cognitive-behavioral programs endeavor to change self-defeating thoughts and thought processes, such as "either-or thinking" (also called "stinkin' thinkin' ") and self-centered definitions of situations.

In contrast to AA, however, the cognitive-behavioral models see substance abuse as more complex than a disease with a common set of symptoms and causes. From the cognitive-behavioral model, there are many types of substance abusers. Moreover, some of the messages given by AA and NA (such as substance abuse is a disease that one has no control over or one that a higher power will control) runs contrary to the messages of most cognitive-behavioral approaches, which offer a more direct approach to offender responsibility.

Since the beginning of AA, other groups have formed to offer support and self-help for other types of substance abuse, e.g., Narcotics Anonymous (NA), Cocaine Anonymous (CA), and for specific types of individuals, e.g., gays and lesbians, professionals, and gender-specific groups, such as Women for Sobriety. Groups for family members offer important support services, especially to those who may not be able to afford the family approaches discussed above. Such groups are usually specific to the family role and age of the family member, e.g., Alanon (for spouses), Alateen, Ala-tot, and Adult Children of Alcoholics. Self-help groups for the addict, as well as his or her family members, are also viewed as valuable supplements to therapy and family therapy. Whether viewed as treatment for the substance abusing offender or treatment for his or her family, support groups are considered helpful in focusing on issues of self-esteem; coping with loneliness and social stigma; dealing with feelings; offering role models and hope; support in working through family problems; and practice, feedback, and dealing with adjustments to a new way of living (Francis et al., 1994).

Does this mean that AA or NA can be the only "therapy" offered within a correctional agency? Unfortunately, this happens in corrections, either on an ongoing basis in some cases or during periods of fiscal constraint when agencies cut more intensive forms of therapy in order to save money. For a number of reasons, AA/NA cannot be advocated as the only form of substance abuse treatment that an agency needs to provide. First, it has not and cannot be subjected to an appropriate degree of evaluation research. In fact, its organizing principles discourage tests of its effectiveness. Second, there is no supervision of groups and how they are conducted. There are guidelines for such groups, and the national organizations hope to encourage adherence to them, but without oversight, groups, particularly offender groups, can "drift" into more antisocial directions. Just the same, the substance abuse groups are important supplements to more intensive substance abuse treatment.

Pharmacological Approaches

Pharmacological agents offer a well-known approach to the treatment of opiate addictions. Chief among these are Naltrexone, a narcotic antagonist that blocks the euphoric effects of opiates, and Methadone, which acts as a substitute for opiates (Anglin & Hser, 1990; Peters, 1993).

Methadone maintenance is a form of outpatient treatment that involves giving patients daily doses of methadone, under supervision, as a substitute for such opiates as heroin, morphine, and Percodan (Caulum, 1994). Dosages of methadone are closely monitored; ideally, doses are gradually reduced until the patient is drug-free (Marion & Coleman, 1991). The duration of methadone maintenance is generally longer than the duration of other treatment modalities; clients may stay in methadone treatment three years or more (Nurco et al., 1993). Many programs will provide additional services, such as vocational training and drug counseling. Such programs are aimed at reducing criminal behavior, reducing needle-borne diseases (e.g., AIDS and hepatitis), and enhancing vocational and social stability (Landry et al., 1994).

Of all drug treatment options, methadone maintenance appears to be the most controversial. Many argue that methadone clients have simply shifted their dependence to a legal narcotic. Other critics warn that some methadone clients may "continue to use heroin and other drugs intermittently, and continue to commit crimes, including the sale of their take-home methadone" (Institute of Medicine, 1990). From an alternative standpoint, methadone maintenance may be viewed as a long-term therapy similar to the treatment of any other chronic health disorder. That is, just as the diabetic needs insulin, the addict needs methadone for treatment (Milhorn, 1990). Still, methadone maintenance has been found to be an effective strategy in reducing withdrawal symptoms and drug cravings.

Outpatient, non-methadone treatment ranges from one-time assessment and referrals to drop-in and "rap" centers to outpatient therapeutic communities. Clients in outpatient TCs usually report three days per week for two to three hours (Milhorn, 1990). Services found in outpatient, non-methadone programs are similar to those in the TC; group and individual counseling are available. Because outpatients continue to live in the community and have more ready access to drugs, they usually receive more frequent urine tests (Milhorn, 1990).

The goals of methadone maintenance are somewhat different from the goals of the other forms of substance abuse treatment. Most substance abuse interventions seek to reduce consumption to zero, but the overriding goal of methadone maintenance is to reduce drug use by an appreciable amount (Institute of Medicine, 1990). The goal of totally reducing the use of drugs is lower on the list of priorities in most methadone maintenance programs. Secondary goals include improving productivity, social behavior, and psychological well-being (Anglin and Hser, 1990).

In this sense, methadone maintenance programs appear to be focusing on **harm reduction** rather than abstinence. As a harm reduction method, methadone maintenance has more in common with needle exchange programs, controlled drinking, and "safe use" educational programs, than with the interventions covered throughout this chapter. The harm reduction strategies are well-received outside of the United States, but in the United States they are seen as "sending the wrong message" (MacCoun, 1998). Perhaps they also run counter to public preferences for retributive and deterrent approaches.

Responsivity Considerations in the Treatment of the Substance-Abusing Offender

As noted in Chapter 7, good treatment programs usually address the responsivity principle (Andrews & Bonta, 2003). A program attends to the responsivity of its clients when it chooses programs that are suitable to offender populations. In addition, programs should recognize client characteristics that are likely to affect the client's ability to participate in a program. The program staff then consider these factors when "matching" clients to appropriate programs or program components.

What client differences should we focus on? In answering this question, we must consider the nature of the criminogenic need that we are treating. Responsivity characteristics important to substance abuse treatments, for example, may not be the same characteristics that should be considered when addressing client literacy. In addition, we cannot accommodate every client characteristic, because there would not be enough program resources to differentiate among numerous client characteristics. We have to set priorities.

Three types of client responsivity characteristics are considered important in the treatment of the substance-abusing offender. First, programs should recognize that clients differ in their readiness to change substance-abusing behaviors, and should therefore consider the client's Stage of Change (Prochaska & DiClemente, 1986; Miller & Rollnick, 2002; Wanberg & Milkman, 1998). Prochaska and DiClemente (1986), for example, set out five **Stages of Change**, and each stage suggests different treatment goals. The definition of each stage along with the treatment recommendations for each stage are shown in Figure 12.3.

It would be preferable to have an assessment tool for classifying clients into one of the five stages, but early attempts to do so have either been unsuccessful or have not yet been completed. These include the Stages of Change Readiness and Treatment Eagerness Scale (SOCRATES) (Miller & Tonigan, 1996); the Adult Self-Assessment Questionnaire (AdSAQ) (Wanberg & Milkman, 1993); and additional work in Canada by Serin and Kennedy (1997).

A second set of client considerations attempts to target the problems and individual conditions that co-occur with substance abuse. As noted, particularly by the proponents of cognitive interventions, the paths to and problems resulting from substance abuse are many. Some substance-abusing offenders drink for greater enjoyment of social situations, others seek to medicate depression and stress. Some have experienced employment and/or marital problems; others have not. Some have incurred tissue and organ damage as a result of their substance abuse, and others have not (Wanberg & Milkman, 1998). Each of these problems identifies important treatment targets and excludes others. Accommodating these differences requires correctional agencies to use offender-specific assessment strategies, such as: (a) the Adult Substance Use Survey (Wanberg, 1993); (b) the Symptom Checklist 90

(Derogatis, 1977); (c) Life Situation Questionnaire (Wanberg, 1995); (d) the Offender Profile Index (Inciardi et al., 1993); and (e) the Addiction Severity Index (McLellan et al., 1992).

Figure 12.3
Stages of Change (Prochaska and DiClemente, 1986)

Stage	Definition	Treatment Goal
Precontemplation	People do not intend to change, because: (a) they don't think they have a problem; (b) they are defensive; and (c) are discouraged about their ability to change.	Consciousness raising, e.g., interventions, observations, interpretations of substance abuse-related life events. Awareness of defenses.
Contemplation	People intend to change in the foreseeable future (within the next 6 months). They seem more confident in their ability to change. Still, they are ambivalent about the values of change, e.g., benefits do not clearly outweigh the costs.	Education and evaluation of the costs of their addiction. Self-appraisal of values toward themselves and addiction.
Preparation	People intend to change within the next month, and are more confident that they can control their addiction. They have a plan to change and are willing to take small steps toward change.	Same as precontemplation, plus some counterconditioning and stimulus control to begin to reduce the use of addictive substances.
Action	People engage in behaviors that demonstrate change, such as abstaining from alcohol or drugs.	Emphasis on self-liberation, self-efficacy, increased use of counterconditioning and stimulus control, contingency management, formation of support systems.
Maintenance	People work to consolidate gains achieved during the action phase in order to prevent relapse. They have attained self-efficacy toward dealing with high-risk situations.	Relapse prevention: Identification of high-risk situations, continued building of self-efficacy, strategies for coping with high-risk situations and relapse.

Third, substance abuse intervention services would do well to consider the needs and strengths specific to diverse populations, by accommodating factors pertinent to race, gender, and social class. Within these broad categories of diversity, substance abuse can have different meanings, contexts, associated norms, traditions, and antecedents (see Wanberg & Milkman, 1998). Tools for accommodating such differences, however, are fairly new to correctional programming. In fact, many of the needs assessments specific to special populations are only now being conducted. The questions posed by these groups, however, are numerous. For example, what considerations should be taken in building the self-efficacy of groups that have experienced racial, sexual, or class discrimination? The fact that such images are internalized by minority clients and reinforced by society poses additional challenges to programs attempting to build self-efficacy. Counselors and correctional staff, for example, should be sensitive to social stereotypes that may portray such individuals as "low achievers" (Wallace, 1991). On the other hand, how shall we capitalize on the cultural competence of groups who, by virtue of their cultural identity, may enjoy strong levels of family and community support and spiritual strength?

Furthermore, some ethnic groups may have values that discourage participation in therapy. While mental health services in Western societies appear to value work ethics, individualism, action orientations, self-disclosure, scientific method, and competition, these may not be as highly valued among certain ethnic groups. Differences in language, communication style, use of body language, and verbal skills may also contribute to misunderstandings (Sue & Sue, 1990).

It is unfortunate that treatment needs of specific groups are underresearched, but the following offers a few concerns (Wanberg & Milkman, 1998):

- While African-American males do not appear to differ from other ethnic groups in terms of the consequences and symptoms of their drug use, they experienced the largest increase in incarceration rates during the 1980s;

- Latino women are more likely than Latino men to be shamed within their own culture for substance abuse;

- Studies have not confirmed differences in alcohol metabolism between Native American groups and other ethnic groups in the United States;

- Women tend to become heavy drinkers at a later age than men.

- Women are more likely than men to: (a) drink alone; (b) use alcohol with other drugs; and (c) use alcohol and drugs for purposes of medication;

- Childhood abuse of girls is more likely to result in a progression from child abuse to depression to substance abuse to crime, than it is for boys (McClellan, Farabee & Crouch, 1997).

While more research is needed in order to move away from a "one size fits all" approach to substance abuse, and much needs to be done to design culture-specific and gender-specific treatment programs, a number of suggestions can be offered:

- Diversity awareness training with the goal of developing "**culturally competent**" staff, who appreciate diversity, adapt to differences, and seek culturally specific understanding of others;

- Adherence to a model of non-judgmental interactions;

- Ongoing sensitivity to one's own areas of ethnocentrism and bias, and appreciation for the need to self-evaluate one's attention to diversity issues;

- Openness to culturally sensitive treatment models;

- Use of culturally fair assessments, especially the avoidance of assessments that have not been normed for use with certain populations;

- Attention to diversity in hiring;

- Sensitivity in dress and office environments, e.g., avoiding expression of expensive tastes when dealing with economically disadvantaged clients;

- Attention to needs such as childcare, transportation, disabilities, homelessness;

- Sensitivity to the influences of discrimination and prejudice on clients.

A number of recent state and federal policy initiatives have focused on the treatment needs of female offenders—substance-abusing women, especially. The 1980s "War on Drugs" has been especially hard on women in poverty (Austin et al., 2000). Women's prison populations have grown at a faster pace than men's and most of this is attributable to increases in the number of female substance abusers (Beck, 2000). Incarcerated female offenders are also more likely than males to have coexisting psychiatric disorders, test HIV-positive, and have substance abuse patterns that are closely linked to their relationships with men (Peters et al., 1997; Langan & Pelissier, 2001).

For female offenders, substance abuse often co-occurs with depression and abuse (Covington, 2002; McClellan, Farabee & Crouch, 1997). That alone should put a decidedly different face on the types of substance abuse programs they receive (Bloom, Owen & Covington, 2003). Covington (2002), for example, proposed an approach that operates from three theoretical perspectives:

1. **The Theory of Addiction.** For women, addiction must be seen holistically (as a function of factors such as genetic predisposition, poor health, shame, isolation, and abuse). Addiction is a disease rather than the result of a disorder (including cognitive disorders);

2. **The Theory of Women's Psychosocial Development.** Women develop through relationships and mutuality. Relationships factor into their substance abuse and must be considered in their treatment and recovery;

3. **The Theory of Trauma.** A history of abuse predisposes women to substance abuse.

From this perspective on the causation of women's substance abuse, Covington (2002) developed the following Guiding Principles of Women's Treatment:

1. Develop and use women-only groups;

2. Recognize the multiple issues involved, and establish a comprehensive, integrated, and collaborative system of care;

3. Create an environment that fosters safety, respect, and dignity;

4. Develop and use a variety of therapeutic approaches;

5. Focus on women's competence and strength;

6. Individualize treatment plans, and match treatment to women's strengths and issues;

Programs based on this model are seen in many correctional agencies (Covington, 1999). There are not many structured, gender-responsive program models, comparable to those available for the general offender populations, but note Moving On (Van Dieten, 1999), a cognitive-behavioral approach discussed in Chapter 9. Additionally, Wanberg and Milkman's (1998) cognitive-behavioral curriculum has been rewritten for women, but was not in print at the time this book went to press.

Key to the new directions for women's programming and therapy is the **relational model of self** or recognition. This theory was developed through research conducted at the Stone Center for Developmental Studies at Wellesley College (Miller, 1976; Gilligan, 1982). The relational model recognizes that men and women form self-identity differently. Women do so through attachments and connections with others, and men are more comfortable with separation and individuation. The models listed above have yet to be evaluated. Lack of research on effectiveness continues to affect our ability to plan gender-responsive strategies for women.

With substance-abusing female offenders sharing the additional burdens of poverty, unemployment, single parenting, and child custody, it is not difficult to see the relevance of the "wraparound services" discussed in Chapter 10 (Bloom et al., 2003) or community centers that house both women and their children (van Wormer, 2002) as an important transition to independent living.

Effectiveness of Substance Abuse Interventions

Although substance abuse treatment has a long history, use of the formalized, theoretically-based approaches discussed above only began in the 1960s (Wanberg & Milkman, 1998). The earliest evaluations of programs for substance-abusing offenders showed overly high relapse rates, but research now supports a number of specific program models and programmatic conditions. Literature reviews supporting behavioral, social learning, and cognitive-behavioral approaches (Anglin & Hser, 1990; Institute of Medicine, 1990; Monti et al., 1995; Prendergast et al., 1995; Wexler & Lipton, 1993) have since been supported by meta-analyses (Pearson & Lipton, 1999; Miller et al., 1995). Specifically, Miller and his associates (1995) report that the most successful programs were behavioral and cognitive-behavioral approaches, such as social skills training, community reinforcement, behavior contracting, relapse prevention, and motivational enhancement. Marital therapy was more likely to "work" when behavioral and communication treatment models were also used. The least successful approaches consisted of **educational**, unspecified general counseling models, psychotherapy, and confrontational approaches.

Despite these favorable results, experts warn that there is no "magic bullet" or single treatment that is effective with everyone (Palmer, 1992). A growing body of literature suggests rather generically that some treatment is better than no treatment (Harris & Miller, 1990; Prendergast et al., 1995). For example, in a recent comparative evaluation of three well-known treatment models—cognitive-behavioral therapy, motivational enhancement, and Facilitated 12-Step programming—authors of Project MATCH reported that all three achieved client improvements (Project MATCH Research Group, 1997). Similar findings were noted in an earlier study when Brandsma, Maultsby, and Welsh (1980) compared AA, insight therapy, and rational behavioral therapy among court-referred subjects. All treatment groups achieved more favorable results on drinking and legal problems than members of a comparison group. With offender populations, therapeutic communities, once considered ineffective, have recently shown more favorable outcomes. The new TC models, however, are very different from their predecessors.

Conclusion

Correctional agencies appear to be assuming increasing responsibility for treating substance-abusing offenders. At the same time, it may seem that these same offenders consume very large proportions of correctional treatment budgets. In response, new organizational structures have been developed, such as drug courts, drug testing, and day reporting centers. Improved therapies and treatments show encouraging outcomes.

Even with these advances, however, few substance-abusing offenders actually receive treatment relative to the number who have substance abuse histories (Beck, 2000). It makes little sense to ignore the tremendous advances in the technology of assessing and treating the substance-abusing offender. Yet there are many ways in which this happens. First, the demand for such services is high and overwhelming to many agencies. In such settings, the treatment needs of some offenders may never be met. Second, some agencies have misinterpreted options such as drug courts, day treatment, and drug testing as treatments when they really are not. Without effective treatment programs, they simply contain substance-abusing behaviors without changing them. Third, in an effort to move all substance-abusing clients into some form of treatment, agencies often contract with outside providers (e.g. mental health agencies, hospitals, or private therapists) without knowing what is actually occurring in the contract programs. Important questions must be asked of such service providers, such as: (a) are they using an established model of treatment known to be effective with substance-abusing offenders? (b) are their assessments normed and validated to offender populations? and (c) do they operate from other principles of effective intervention? (see Chapter 13) Finally, correctional officials need to take a "helicopter" view of these services, asking whether they cover the needs of different types of substance abusers, e.g., those who deny the need for services, those who suffer from related brain injury, those who need relapse prevention services, those who need social support, and others.

Key Concepts and Terms

Abstinence Violation Effect (AVE)
aversion therapies
behavioral family therapies
classical conditioning
cognitive-behavioral approaches
communications therapy
community reinforcement
contingency contracts
covert sensitization
culturally competent
disease model
drug courts
educational model
enabled
family systems model
harm reduction
high-risk situations
identified patient
interventions

Methadone maintenance
Multisystemic Family Therapy
operant conditioning
peer encounters
psychodynamic family therapies
relapse prevention
relational model of self
self-efficacy
self-help groups
social learning approaches
sponsors
Stages of Change
support groups
temperance model
theory of addiction
theory of trauma
theory of women's psychosocial
    development
therapeutic communities

Discussion Questions

1. Compare and contrast the various models of substance abuse treatment.

2. Discuss pharmacological and cognitive-behavioral treatment approaches to the problem of substance abuse. What are the advantages and disadvantages of each?

3. What are some of the ways in which the goals of methadone maintenance differ from other substance abuse treatment programs?

4. What strategies are most effective for treating substance abuse?

5. What treatment targets should be considered in treating the family members of substance abusers?

6. What does relapse prevention do in the course of reducing an offender's chances of relapse?

7. What factors should be taken into account when counselors consider the responsivity principle for substance-abusing offenders?

8. Should substance abuse programs be modified for ethnic groups and women? How should this be done?

Chapter 13

Correctional Treatment: Accomplishments and Realities

Paula Smith, Paul Gendreau, and Claire Goggin

The purpose of this chapter is to summarize the offender treatment outcome evaluation literature with respect to our knowledge about the success of various types of treatment strategies in reducing offender recidivism. In addition, we provide some new data on the quality of offender treatment programs routinely found in the corrections field.

Accomplishments

One of the impressive accomplishments in the area of offender rehabilitation is that so much useful knowledge has been generated in a relatively short period (cf. Gendreau, 1996a). In the 1960s, corrections professionals had little idea of "what worked"; there were few treatment outcome evaluation studies at that time and little indication of effectiveness by any type of intervention (Martinson, 1974). In his review of the literature, for example, Martinson (1974) analyzed the results from 231 studies of offender treatment programs. He concluded ". . . that with few and isolated exceptions, the rehabilitative efforts that have been reported so far have had no appreciable effect on recidivism" (Martinson, 1974:48). Although his "nothing works" credo had a tremendous impact on popular and professional thinking, it should be noted that Martinson's (1974) review had a number of shortcomings. Only 138 of 286 effect sizes reported recidivism as an outcome. Of these, only 73 were based on recognizable treatment categories. Furthermore, the number of outcomes per category were limited, with considerable heterogeneity among treatment types (Cullen & Gendreau, 2000).

Presently, a huge evaluation literature exists that can only be summarized adequately by quantitative research synthesis techniques (also known as meta-analysis). There are at least three dozen of these quantitative reviews available, and they encompass approximately 1,000 studies (McGuire, 2002). Assessments of these quantitative reviews have been undertaken for the purposes of generating a set of guidelines, or **principles of effective intervention** with offenders (e.g., Andrews, 1995; Andrews & Bonta, 2003; Gendreau, 1996b; Gendreau & Andrews, 1990). A brief summary of the results of **meta-analyses** and the principles of effective intervention are outlined below.

Results of the Meta-Analyses

How successful are we at rehabilitating offenders? First, summarizing across all evaluation studies, regardless of their nature, it has been reported that about 64 percent of the programs studied reduce recidivism, with the average reduction being 10 percent (cf., Lipsey, 1992). This outcome, in itself, is noteworthy. If only cynics in criminal justice were not so parochial (Gendreau & Ross, 1979), they would be astonished to learn that results of this magnitude are often deemed quite acceptable in a wide variety of other service-delivery areas (Lipsey & Wilson, 1993; Rosenthal & DiMatteo, 2001). But it is not sufficient to simply summarize across all studies; the next step is to determine what characteristics, if any, reliably distinguish studies that reduce recidivism from those that do not. If we can do this—find some order in this universe—then we can make enormous strides in engineering better treatment services for offenders in the future. Fortunately, we can. Studies that share certain programmatic features, or what are called **"appropriate" interventions** (Andrews et al., 1990), reduce recidivism by approximately 25 to 30 percent (Andrews & Bonta, 2003; Andrews, Dowden & Gendreau, 1999), whereas studies designated as **"inappropriate"** produce slight increases in recidivism. Appropriate treatment programs also produce substantial reductions in other measures of antisocial behavior (e.g., prison misconduct) that are correlated with recidivism (French & Gendreau, in press). Finally, appropriate treatment programs set in the community generally produce two to three times greater reductions in recidivism than prison-based programs (Andrews et al., 1990).

The Principles of Effective Intervention

What are these appropriate treatments? Given the intended audience of this text, for a detailed presentation of these issues, it is recommended that the reader consult Andrews and Bonta (2003), Cullen & Gendreau (2000), Gendreau (1996b), as well as Andrews (1995). The reader is also encouraged to inspect exemplary individual studies (e.g., Alexander, Pugh & Parsons,

1998; Bourgon & Armstrong, in press; Gibbs, Potter & Goldstein, 1995; Goldstein, 1999; Gordon, Graves & Arbuthnot, 1995; Henggeler et al., 1998). Listings of these and others can be found, for the most part, in Andrews et al. (1990:403-404), Andrews et al. (1999) and Gendreau (1996b:114-120). The principles of effective intervention underlying appropriate treatments are as follows:

1. The treatment is based on behavioral strategies (e.g., radical behavioral, social learning, or cognitive-behavioral) (Andrews et al., 1990; Gendreau, 1996b; Gendreau, Little & Goggin, 1996). As such, program facilitators should engage in the following therapeutic practices: anti-criminal modeling, effective reinforcement and disapproval, problem-solving techniques, structured learning procedures for skill building, effective use of authority, cognitive self-change, relationship practices, and motivational interviewing (see Andrews & Carvell, 1997).

2. The program has a manual that describes the theory and data justifying the program, as well as a curriculum that details the discrete steps to be followed in presenting the material (for an example of a comprehensive program manual, see Gibbs et al., 1995).

3. The treatment is located, preferably, in the offender's natural environment.

4. The treatment is multimodal. In other words, the program offers a variety of interventions and is equipped to minister to a range of offender needs, particularly criminogenic needs.

5. The intensity of treatment should be approximately 100 hours of direct service over a three- to four-month period.

6. The treatment emphasizes positive reinforcement contingencies for prosocial behavior, and is individualized as much as possible. Offenders should spend at least 40 percent of their program time acquiring prosocial skills. Furthermore, the ratio of reinforcers to punishers should be at least 4:1 (see Gendreau, French & Gionet, 2004).

7. The behaviors targeted are those that are predictive of future criminal behavior and are dynamic in nature (e.g., antisocial attitudes and associates) (see Bonta, 2002; Gendreau et al., 1996; Gendreau et al., 2004; Simourd, 2004). In identifying such problems, it is crucial for programs to use valid actuarial assessments (Gendreau, Goggin & Smith, 2002). Furthermore, and this point cannot be stressed enough, it is the medium- to higher-risk offenders who will benefit the most from treatment. This is the **risk principle** (see Chapter 7).

8. The treatment should be designed to match key offender characteristics and learning styles with relevant therapist characteristics and program features in order to facilitate the learning of prosocial values. This is the **responsivity principle** (see Chapter 7).

9. Once the formal phase of treatment has ended, continuity through aftercare on an as-needed basis is required. Especially with chronic problems such as sex offenses and substance abuse, relapse prevention program models are useful (Dowden, Antonowicz & Andrews, 2003).

10. Several system factors must be in place for effective service delivery (see Andrews & Bonta, 2003; Gendreau et al., in press; Gendreau, Goggin & Smith, 2001). These center on the quality of program implementation, the training and credentials of program directors and staff, the degree to which the organization engages in inter-agency communication and advocacy brokerage, the involvement of program directors in the design and day-to-day operations of the program, the degree to which the organization engages in meaningful attempts at knowledge dissemination to line staff, the participation of staff in program decision making, the care taken to monitor changes in clients' behavior for effective case management, and the quality of the therapeutic practices of the staff.

Finally, the principles above apply to both juvenile and adult samples and, on the basis of more limited evidence, to females and minority groups. The components of the responsivity principle, however, may differ considerably across different samples of offenders.

What Does Not Work

In comparison with appropriate treatment programs, the programmatic features underlying inappropriate strategies are as follows:

1. Inappropriate programs are based on psychodynamic, nondirective, phenomenological, and medical-model treatments. As well, programs that are based on threats, inculcating fear, and/or **"punishing smarter strategies,"** such as boot camps, drug testing, electronic monitoring, restitution, and shock incarceration, have been unmitigated failures (Andrews et al., 1990; Gendreau 1996b; Gendreau, Goggin & Fulton, 2000; Gendreau et al., 1993; Smith, Goggin & Gendreau, 2002).

2. Sociological perspectives that underscore the importance of respect for an offender's culture, diversion from the correction system, or providing access to legitimate opportunities for the disadvantaged are associated with slight increases in recidivism (cf. Andrews & Bonta, 2003; Gendreau et al., 2004).

3. Programs that treat low-risk offenders or target behaviors that are weak predictors of criminal behavior (e.g., self-esteem, depression, anxiety) rarely demonstrate effectiveness (Andrews, Bonta & Hoge, 1990; Gendreau et al., 1996).

The Realities of Correctional Treatment

While it is one thing to document the fact that certain types of exemplary treatment programs (published in the research literature) can have a meaningful effect on reducing offender recidivism, another reality exists: it is highly likely that these exemplary studies are far from representative of the programming typically found in government and private agencies in the field (Gendreau & Goggin, 1991; Lab & Whitehead, 1990). In an attempt to address this crucial issue, the **Correctional Program Assessment Inventory—2000** (CPAI, 2000) was developed several years ago to measure **therapeutic integrity**, or program quality (Gendreau & Andrews, 2001). The instrument now consists of 131 items derived from the "what works" literature reviewed previously. The CPAI—2000 assesses programs on eight dimensions: organizational culture, program implementation/maintenance, management/staff characteristics, client risk-need practices, program characteristics, several aspects of core correctional practices, interagency communication, and evaluation. The CPAI—2000 documents the strengths and weaknesses of a program in each of the dimensions and provides an overall percentage score of program quality.

At this point, the CPAI has been applied to almost 400 offender treatment programs (Gendreau et al., 2001; Lowenkamp, 2004). Recently, two studies, one involving a meta-analysis (Nesovic, 2003), and the other based on an analysis of numerous treatment programs in Ohio (Lowenkamp, 2004), determined that scores on the CPAI were highly predictive of recidivism ($r < .25$ to $.50$).

Results of the CPAI Research

In 1990, the CPAI was administered to 170 adult offender substance abuse programs (Gendreau & Goggin, 1991). Program respondents were instructed to provide the authors with a complete dossier of all facets of their functioning, as well as answer a detailed questionnaire. The 101 programs that responded produced a mean CPAI score of 25 percent. Programs that were community-based (versus those in prisons) and "contracted out" (versus those run by institutions) had higher scores on the CPAI, but even in these two cases, mean CPAI scores were less than 40 percent. Two programs received a very satisfactory score, eight were judged to be satisfactory, and 12 almost received a passing grade (40-49%).

The fact that only 10 percent of programs received a satisfactory grade seemed somewhat low given that the survey was conducted within a correctional organization that was considered a leader in offender rehabilitation. Subsequently, another survey (Hoge, Leschied & Andrews, 1993) was undertaken of agencies providing services for juvenile offenders within a Canadian province that has had a very progressive history in correctional service delivery. Adequate data for the purposes of scoring the CPAI was available for 135 programs. The overall mean CPAI score for all programs was 35 percent. Furthermore, the mean percentage scores on the CPAI subcomponents were all less than 50 percent, with the evaluation component recording by far the lowest scores (20%). CPAI scores did not differ whether scoring was based on a file review or an actual site visit by the evaluators. The researchers also found that programs with a specialized focus (e.g., substance abuse, sex offenders) produced slightly higher CPAI scores (39% versus 32%). Programs in probation settings had lower CPAI scores than institution-based programs. As with the Gendreau and Goggin (1991) study, few programs (10%) scored satisfactory or better. Of some encouragement is that a new provincial innovation in service delivery—intensive community-based interventionist agencies that targeted the youth and family—was generally (7 out of 9) of satisfactory or very satisfactory quality. Most recently, the CPAI has been administered by the authors to a number of individual programs and by various colleagues (e.g., Edward Latessa and the University of Cincinnati group) to small samples of specialized programs (e.g., attendance centers, day reporting programs, and prison sex offender programs).

The pessimistic conclusion reached in the earlier surveys remains the same. What should be done about this sorry state of affairs? One school of thought is to declare a pox on the treatment enterprise and essentially "throw in the towel" (Lab & Whitehead, 1990). On the other hand, a productive strategy for dealing with the issue is to begin the arduous task of identifying the most frequently occurring programming deficits for programs "in the field" with the objective of rectifying the problems (Gendreau & Goggin, 1991).

We now turn to a brief summary of the major program deficiencies we and our colleagues have catalogued in our evaluations.

The shortcomings listed below have occurred at least 50 percent of the time; regrettably, in some cases the incidence is 70 percent or more. The reader will quickly recognize the fact that some of the chapters in this text (see Chapters 4, 7, 8, and 9) and the literature reviewed previously in this chapter speak directly to several of the concerns described. The major deficiencies, with commentary where appropriate, are as follows:

1. Implementation

   a. Program directors and staff are not adequately familiar with the literature. Moreover, they do not conduct a thorough review of the literature on the proposed treatment and its effectiveness prior to implementing the program. As a result, they may find themselves "following a hunch," repeating the mistakes of others, or chasing the latest panacea (see Van Voorhis, Cullen & Applegate, 1995).

   b. The professional credibility (i.e., training, experience with successful programs) of program designers is often suspect.

   c. Granted, the corrections literature is very sparse in the program implementation area (e.g., Gendreau, 1996b; Gendreau & Andrews, 1979; Harris & Smith, 1996); however, there is extensive literature on technology transfer that demonstrates how to establish programs effectively in other social science/service and management fields (Backer, Davis & Soucy, 1995) that invariably is ignored by program designers in corrections.

2. Client preservice assessment

   a. Somewhat surprisingly, given all that has been written about **actuarial risk assessment** (Bonta, 1996; Bonta, 2002), the traditional **clinical subjective/intuitive assessment** persists. Indeed, there is virtually no recognition of the classic literature concerning the inadequacy of this approach to assessment (e.g., Little & Schneidman, 1959; Meehl, 1954).

   b. Among the programs that employ actuarial systems (or tests) to assess offenders, it is not unusual to find a preoccupation with **static risk factors** (e.g., previous criminal history, type of offense), while the assessment of **dynamic risk factors** (e.g., attitudes, values, and behaviors) is overlooked. It is impossible to monitor treatment effectiveness unless the latter are assessed because they represent the targets for behavioral change (Gendreau et al., 1996).

   c. There is still confusion as to which dynamic factors should be appraised. Programs still place major importance on the assessment of self-esteem, anxiety, and depression, which are among the weakest predictors of recidivism, while directing negligible attention to robust predictors, such as criminal attitudes (Gendreau et al., 1996).

3. Program characteristics

   a. Programs either did not use any appropriate treatments (i.e., those known to be effective) or they diluted the overall effectiveness of the program by employing inappropriate strategies along with effective ones. In one specific instance (Gendreau

& Goggin, 1991), it was found, similar to the findings of Hester and Miller's (1995) comprehensive analysis of the alcoholism treatment literature, that the most frequently used interventions were empirically established failures.

b. The **dosage** level (i.e., intensity) of treatment is often insufficient (e.g., several hours per week). Offenders simply do not spend enough time in treatment.

c. The responsivity principle is almost totally neglected. This lack of attention to individual differences is striking; it reflects a long-standing bias in theory development in criminology (cf. Andrews & Wormith, 1989) and evolving management practices in corrections that are macro-level, input-output oriented with little concern directed toward the needs of the individual offender (Gendreau et al., 1996). In these common instances, offenders are treated as if they are all alike (see Chapter 7).

d. Very few programs incorporate a meaningful system of reinforcers (see Chapter 4).

e. **Relapse prevention** strategies are underutilized (see Chapter 12).

f. A sound index of therapeutic integrity in a program is a treatment manual that outlines, in ample detail, the theory underlying the treatment, the daily treatment task schedule (i.e., lesson plan, homework exercises, teaching aid materials), and the process evaluation assessment tools. The manual should be of sufficient quality that an "external" therapist should be able to come into the program and conduct a class session with relative ease. Such manuals are, in our experience, quite rare. Furthermore, few programs monitor, in any quantifiable way, the quality of the instruction per se. We are aware of only two measures developed in this regard (i.e., Gendreau & Andrews, 2001; Mitchell & Egan, 1995).

g. Many programs have experienced problems finding any relevant/useful community services to which clients may be referred for ongoing service.

4. Staff characteristics

The foregoing should be read more as an indictment of the lack of quality control exhibited by employers and the paucity of relevant training programs in academic settings. For the most part, we have found treatment staff to be dedicated and eager to upgrade their skills when the opportunity presents itself.

a. It is not unusual to find staff hired for a treatment program on characteristics other than clinical experience and training relevant to the task at hand. Program staff commonly have less than a university degree; postgraduate training is rare. In addition, we have not discovered one hiring protocol that employed an actuarial assessment of the characteristics (e.g., clarity, honesty, empathy, fairness; see Gendreau & Andrews, 2001) that have been found to be associated with effective counseling skills (see Chapters 1 and 2).

b. Time and again, when questioning staff, we have encountered large gaps in knowledge regarding: (i) the criminological theories of criminal behavior and the psychological theories of personality and their relevance to treatment; (ii) basic concepts of classical and operant conditioning, without which it is impossible to undertake any sort of effective counseling. These are strong comments to be sure, but with respect to this last point, how could it be otherwise when some programs have difficulty identifying a varied menu of reinforcers and punishers, let alone demonstrating awareness of the principles of how to reinforce and punish behavior? Seldom have we seen the classic texts on the modification of behavior referenced by programmers (Masters et al., 1987; Matson & DiLorenzo, 1984; Spiegler & Guevremont, 1998). Therefore, in our opinion, much of what goes on under the guise of cognitive therapy are really nondirective "chats" with no guarantee that prosocial behavior is reinforced and antisocial behavior is not reinforced or punished. Recommended reading on how counselors should function as competent role models can be found in Chapter 8 of this text and in Andrews and Bonta (2003:311-319).

5. Evaluation

a. Systematic and thorough evaluation practices are, for all intents and purposes, nonexistent. Process evaluation, or how the client is progressing in treatment, is sporadic at best; follow-up outcome evaluation is even more so.

b. Consumer satisfaction surveys are infrequent.

There is only one avenue to pursue in order to alleviate these shortcomings, and it is better education and training. This topic has been discussed in detail elsewhere (Gendreau, 1996a). Unfortunately, there are few opportunities for training in offender assessment and treatment. There are, at best, only a handful of academic psychology/criminal justice programs in the United States that have an in-depth curriculum in the offender treatment area. Nevertheless, it does not need to be a Herculean task to bring about needed changes (e.g., Ax & Morgan, 2002; Gendreau, 1996a:156; Henggeler, Schoenwald & Pickrel, 1995). A few key academic programs and a greater awareness of how to effect knowledge dissemination (Gendreau, 1995, 1996b) will, in our view, lead to a new generation of offender treatment programs that will be better able to benefit the clientele and protect the public.

Key Concepts and Terms

actuarial versus clinical subjective/
    intuitive assessment
appropriate versus inappropriate
    interventions
Correctional Program Assessment
    Inventory—2000 (CPAI)
dosage
meta-analyses

principles of effective intervention
punishing smarter strategies
relapse prevention
responsivity principle
risk principle
static versus dynamic risk factors
therapeutic integrity

Discussion Questions

1. Realistically speaking, how effective can we expect offender treatment programs to be? According to Smith, Gendreau, and Goggin, is this more or less effective than for other interventions in human services?

2. What offender problems and behaviors should programs target for purposes of intervention? What problems should not be targeted?

3. What, according to Smith, Gendreau, and Goggin, would be the characteristics of a "high-quality" correctional treatment program?

4. Why should program directors and staff be familiar with the treatment effectiveness literature prior to designing a program?

6. According to Smith, Gendreau, and Goggin, what types of knowledge should correctional treatment staff possess in order to perform their jobs effectively?

References

Abrahams, J. & L. McCorkle (1946). "Group Psychotherapy of Military Offenders." *American Journal of Sociology*, 51, 455-464.

———— (1947). "Group Psychotherapy at an Army Rehabilitation Center." *Diseases of the Nervous System*, 8, 50-62.

Ackerman, N. (1966). "Family Psychotherapy—Theory and Practice." *American Journal of Psychotherapy*, 20, 405-414

Adler, G. (1982). "Recent Psychoanalytic Contributions to the Understanding and Treatment of Criminal Behavior." *International Journal of Offender Therapy and Comparative Criminology*, 26, 281-287.

Agee, V. (1979). *Treatment of the Violent, Incorrigible Adolescent*. Lexington, MA: Lexington Books.

———— (1987). "The Treatment Program at Paint Creek Youth Center." Unpublished manuscript, Paint Creek Youth Center. Bainbridge, OH.

———— (1995). "Managing Clinical Programs for Juvenile Delinquents." In B. Glick & A. Goldstein (eds.), *Managing Delinquency Programs that Work*. Laurel, MD: American Correctional Association.

Aichorn, A. (1935). *Wayward Youth*. New York, NY: Viking Press.

Akers, R. (1973). *Deviant Behavior: A Social Learning Approach*. Belmont, CA: Wadsworth.

———— (2001). "Social Learning Theory." In R. Paternoster & R. Bachman (eds.), *Explaining Criminals and Crime*. Los Angeles: Roxbury.

Aldarondo, E. & M. Strauss (1994). "Screening for Physical Violence in Couples Therapy: Methodological, Practical, and Ethical Considerations." *Family Process*, 33, 425-439.

Alexander, J. (1973). "Defensive and Supportive Communications in Normal and Deviant Families." *Journal of Consulting and Clinical Psychology*, 40, 223-231.

Alexander, J. & B. Parsons (1973). "Short-Term Behavioral Intervention with Delinquent Families: Impact on Family Process and Recidivism." *Journal of Abnormal Psychology*, 81, 219-225.

———— (1982). *Functional Family Therapy*. Belmont, CA: Brooks/Cole.

Alexander, J., C. Pugh & B. Parsons (1998). *Functional Family Therapy: Book Three in the Blueprints and Violence Prevention Series*. Boulder, CO: University of Colorado, Center for the Study and Prevention of Violence.

Alexander, J., J. Waldron, A. Newberry & N. Liddle (1988). "Family Approaches to Treating Delinquents. Mental Illness, Delinquency, Addictions, and Neglect." In E. Nunnally & C. Chilman (eds.), *Families in Trouble Series*. Newbury Parks, CA: Sage Publications.

American Association of Correctional Psychologists Standards Committee (2000). "Standards for Psychology Services in Jails, Prisons, and Correctional Facilities and Agencies." *Criminal Justice and Behavior*, 27, 433-493.

American Bar Association (1989). *ABA Criminal Justice and Mental Health Standards*. Washington, DC: American Bar Association.

American Counseling Association (ACA) (1995). *ACA Code of Ethics and Standards of Practice*. Alexandria, VA: American Counseling Association.

American Psychiatric Association (2000). *Diagnostic and Statistical Manual of Mental Disorders*, Fourth Edition. Text Revision. Washington, DC: American Psychological Association.

Anderson, C. & S. Stewart (1983). *Mastering Resistance: A Practical Guide to Family Therapy*. New York: Guilford Publications.

Andrews, D. (1980). "Some Experimental Investigations of the Principles of Differential Association through Deliberate Manipulations of the Structures of Service Systems." *American Sociological Review*, 45, 448-462.

_____ (1982). *The Level of Supervision Inventory (LSI): The First Follow-Up*. Toronto: Ontario Ministry of Correctional Services.

_____ (1995). "The Psychology of Criminal Conduct and Effective Treatment." In J. McGuire (ed.), *What Works: Reducing Re-offending*. New York: John Wiley & Sons.

Andrews, D. & J. Bonta (2003). *The Psychology of Criminal Conduct*, Third Edition. Cincinnati, OH: Anderson Publishing Co.

_____ (1995). *The Level of Supervision Inventory-Revised (LSI-R)*. North Tonawanda, NY: Multi-Health Systems.

Andrews, D., J. Bonta & R. Hoge (1990). "Classification for Effective Rehabilitation: Rediscovering Psychology." *Criminal Justice and Behavior*, 17, 19-52.

Andrews, D. & C. Carvell (1997). *Core Correctional Treatment-Core Correctional Supervision and Counseling: Theory, Research, Assessment and Practice*. Ottawa, Ontario: Carleton University.

Andrews, D., C. Dowden & P. Gendreau (1999). "Clinically Relevant and Psychologically Informed Approaches to Reduced Re-Offending: A Meta-Analytic Study of Human Service, Risk, Need, Responsivity, and Other Concerns in Justice Contexts." Unpublished manuscript. Ottawa, Ontario: Carleton University.

Andrews, D., D. Gordon, J. Hill, K. Kurkowski & R. Hoge (1993). "Program Integrity, Methodology, and Treatment Characteristics: A Meta-Analysis of Effects of Family Intervention with Young Offenders." Unpublished manuscript, Ottawa, ON:Carleton University.

Andrews, D. & S. Wormith (1989). "Personality and Crime: Knowledge Destruction and Construction in Criminology." *Justice Quarterly*, 6, 289-309.

Andrews, D., I. Zinger, R. Hoge, J. Bonta, P. Gendreau & F. Cullen (1990). "Does Correctional Treatment Work? A Psychologically Informed Meta-Analysis." *Criminology*, 28, 369-404.

Anglin, D. & Y. Hser (1990). "Treatment of Drug Abuse." In M. Tonry & J. Wilson (eds.), *Drugs and Crime*. Chicago: University of Chicago Press.

Annis, H. & C. Davis (1989). "Relapse Prevention." In R. Hester & W. Miller (eds.), *Handbook of Alcoholism Treatment Approaches: Effective Alternatives*. New York: Pergamon Press.

Annis, H. & J. Graham (1988). *Situation Confidence Questionnaire (SCQ): User's Guide*. Toronto: Addiction Research Foundation of Ontario.

Antonowicz, D. & R. Ross (1994). "Essential Components of Successful Rehabilitation Programs for Offenders." *International Journal of Offender Therapy and Comparative Criminology*, 38, 97-104.

Arboleda-Florez, J. & H. Holley (1989). "Predicting Suicide Behaviours in Incarcerated Settings." *Canadian Journal of Psychiatry*, 34, 668-674.

Arcaya, J. (1989). "The Police and the Emotionally Disturbed: A Psychoanalytic Theory of Intervention." *International Journal of Offender Therapy and Comparative Criminology*, 33, 37-48.

Arlow, J. & C. Brenner (1988). "The Future of Psychoanalysis." *Psychoanalytic Quarterly*, 57, 1-14.

Armstrong, T. (2003). "The Effects of Moral Reconation Therapy on the Recidivism of Youthful Offenders: A Randomized Experiment." *Criminal Justice and Behavior*, 30(6), 668-687.

Auburn, T. & S. Lee (2003). "Doing Cognitive Distortions." *British Journal of Social Psychology*, 42, 281-298.

Austin, J. (1986). "Evaluating How Well Your Classification System is Operating: A Practical Approach." *Crime and Delinquency*, 32, 302-333.

Austin, J. & K. McGinnis (2004). *Classification of High-Risk and Special Management Prisoners: A National Assessment of Current Practices*. Washington, DC: National Institute of Corrections.

Austin, J., M. Bruce, L. Carroll, P. McCall & S. Richards (2000). "The Use of Incarceration in the United States: A Policy Paper Presented by the National Policy Committee to the American Society of Criminology." Columbus, OH: American Society of Criminology.

Ax, R. & R. Morgan (2002). "Internship Training Opportunities in Correctional Psychology: A Comparison of Settings." *Criminal Justice and Behavior*, 29, 332-347.

Ayllon, T. & N. Azrin (1968). *The Token Economy: A Motivational System for Therapy and Rehabilitation*. New York: Appleton-Century-Crofts.

Azrin, N., B. Donohue, V. Betsalel, E. Kogan & R. Acierno (1994). "Youth Drug Abuse Treatment: A Controlled Outcome Study." *Journal of Child and Adolescent Substance Abuse*, 3, 1-16.

Backer, T., S. Davis & G. Soucy (eds.) (1995). *Reviewing the Behavioral Science Knowledge Base on Technology Transfer*. (NIDA Research Monograph 155). Rockville, MD: U.S. Department of Health and Human Services, Public Health Service, National Institute of Health.

Baird, C., R. Heinz & B. Bemus (1979). "The Wisconsin Case Classification/Staff Deployment Project." *Project Report No. 14*. Madison, WI: Department of Health and Social Services, Division of Corrections.

Baird, C., R. Prestine & B. Klockziem (1989). *Revalidation of the Wisconsin Probation/Parole Classification System*. Madison, WI: National Council on Crime & Delinquency.

Baird, C., D. Wagner & D. Neuenfeldt (1992). "Using Risk Assessment to Structure Decisions About Services. Protecting Children: The Michigan Model." *NCCD Focus*, March.

Balduzzi, E. (2003). "A Transition Program for Post-Release Sex Offenders." *Dissertation Abstracts International*, 64B, 407.

Bandura, A. (1965). "Influence of Models' Reinforcement Contingencies on the Acquisition of Imitative Responses." *Journal of Personality and Social Psychology*, 1, 589-595.

_____ (1973). *Aggression: A Social Learning Analysis*. Englewood Cliffs, NJ: Prentice-Hall.

_____ (1977). "Self-Efficacy: Toward a Unifying Theory of Behavioral Change." *Psychological Review*, 94, 191-215.

_____ (1978). "Reflections on Self-Efficacy." *Advances in Behavioral Research and Therapy*, 1, 237-269.

Bandura, A., D. Ross & S. Ross (1963). "Vicarious Reinforcement and Imitative Learning." *Journal of Abnormal and Social Psychology*, 67, 601-607.

Bandura, A. & R. Walters (1963). *Social Learning and Personality Development*. New York: Holt, Rinehart & Winston.

Bank, L., J. Marlowe, J. Reid, G. Patterson & M. Weinrott (1991). "A Comparative Evaluation of Parent Training Interventions for Families of Chronic Delinquents." *Journal of Abnormal Child Psychology*, 19, 15-33.

Barbaree, H. (1990). "Stimulus Control of Sexual Arousal: Its Role in Sexual Assault." In W. Marshall, D. Laws & H. Barbaree (eds.), *Handbook of Sexual Assault*. New York: Plenum Press.

Barker, J. & M. Miller (1968). "Aversion Therapy for Compulsive Gambling." *Journal of Nervous and Mental Disease*, 146, 285-302.

Barnhill, L. & D. Longo (1978). "Fixation and Regression in the Family Life Cycle." *Family Process*, 17, 469-478.

Barrett, M., T. Trepper & L. Fish (1990). "Feminist-informed Family Therapy for the Treatment of Intrafamily Child Sexual Abuse." *Journal of Family Psychology*, 4, 151-166.

Barriga, A., J. Landau, B. Stinson, A. Liau & J. Gibbs (2000). "Cognitive Distortions and Problem Behaviors in Adolescents." *Criminal Justice and Behavior*, 27(1), 36-56.

Barton, C., J. Alexander, H. Waldron, D. Turner & J. Warburton (1985). "Generalizing Treatment Effects of Functional Family Therapy: Three Replications." *American Journal of Family Therapy*, 13, 16-26.

Bateson, G., D. Jackson, J. Haley & J. Weakland (1956). "Toward a Theory of Schizophrenia." *Behavioral Science*, 1, 251-264.

Baumrind, D. (1985). "Familial Antecedents of Adolescent Drug Use: A Developmental Perspective." In C. Jones & R. Battjes (eds.), *Etiology of Drug Abuse: Implications for Prevention* (NIDA Research Monograph No. 56). Washington, DC: U.S. Government Printing Office.

Baxter, D., H. Barbaree & W. Marshall (1986). "Sexual Responses to Consenting and Forced Sex in a Large Sample of Rapists and Nonrapists." *Behaviour Research and Therapy*, 24, 513-520.

Beck, A. (2000). *Prisoners in 1999*. Washington, DC: U.S. Department of Justice, Bureau of Justice Statistics.

Beck, A. & G. Emory (1985). *Anxiety Disorders and Phobias: A Cognitive Perspective*. New York: Basic Books.

Beck, A., A. Rush, B. Shaw & G. Emory (1979). *Cognitive Therapy of Depression*. New York: Guilford Publications.

Beck, A., F. Wright, C. Newman & B. Liese (1993). *Cognitive Therapy of Substance Abuse*. New York: Guilford Publications.

Becker, J., J. Alpert, D. BigFoot, B. Bonner, L. Geddie, S. Henggeler, K. Kaufman & C. Walker (1995). "Empirical Research on Child Abuse Treatment: Report by the Child Abuse and Neglect Treatment Working Group, APA." *Journal of Clinical Child Psychology*, 24, 23-46.

Bedrosian, C. (1982). "Using Cognitive Systems Interventions in the Treatment of Marital Violence." In L. Barnhill (ed.), *Clinical Approaches to Family Violence*. Rockville, MD: Aspen.

Belknap, J. & K. Holsinger (1998). "Understanding Incarcerated Girls: The Results of a Focus Group Study." *Prison Journal*, 77(4), 381-404.

Berenson, D. (1986). "The Family Treatment of Alcoholism." *Family Therapy Today*, 1, 1-2, 6-7.

Berne, E. (1961). *Transactional Analysis in Psychotherapy*. New York: Grove Press.

Bixby, F.L. & L. McCorkle (1951). "Guided Group Interaction in Correctional Work." *American Sociological Review*, 16, 455-459.

Bloom, B., B. Owen & S. Covington (2003). *Gender-Responsive Strategies: Research, Practice, and Guiding Principles for Women Offenders*. Washington, DC: U.S. Department of Justice. National Institute of Corrections.

Bohmer, C. (1983). "Legal and Ethical Issues in Mandatory Treatment: The Patient's Right versus Society's Rights." In J. Greer & I. Stuart (eds.), *The Sexual Aggressor: Current Perspectives on Treatment*. New York: Van Nostrand Reinhold Co.

Bohn, M. (1979). "Classification of Offenders in an Institution for Young Adults." *FCI Research Reports*, 1-31.

Bonta, J. (1996). "Risk-needs Assessment and Treatment." In A.T. Harland (ed.), *Choosing Correctional Options that Work: Defining the Demand and Evaluating the Supply*. Thousand Oaks, CA: Sage Publications.

———— (2002). "Offender Risk Assessment:Guidelines for Selection and Use." *Criminal Justice and Behavior*, 29, 355-379,

Bonta, J., S. Wallace-Capretta & J. Rooney (2000). "A Quasi-Experimental Evaluation of an Intensive Rehabilitation Supervision Program." *Criminal Justice and Behavior*, 27, 312-329.

Borduin, C., S. Henggeler, D. Blaske & R. Stein (1990). "Multisystemic Treatment of Adolescent Sexual Offenders." *International Journal of Offender Therapy and Comparative Criminology*, 34, 105-113.

Borduin, C., B. Mann, L. Cone, S. Henggeler, B. Fucci, D. Blaske & R. Williams (1995). "Multisystemic Treatment of Serious Juvenile Offenders: Long-term Prevention of Criminality and Violence." *Journal of Consulting and Clinical Psychology*, 63, 569-578.

Boszormenyi-Nagy, I. & D. Ulrich (1981). "Contextual Family Therapy." In A. Gurman & D. Kniskern (eds.), *Handbook of Family Therapy*. New York: Brunner/Mazel.

Bouffard, J. & F. Taxman (2004). "Looking Inside the "Black Box" of Drug Dourt Treatment Services Using Direct Observations." *Journal of Drug Issues*, 34(1), 195-218.

Bourgon, G. & B. Armstrong (in press). "Transferring the Principles of Effective Intervention to a "Real World" Setting." *Criminal Justice and Behavior*.

Bowen, M. (1978). *Family Therapy in Clinical Practice*. New York: Aronson.

Bowker, A. (1994). "Handle with Care: Dealing with Offenders who are Mentally Retarded." *FBI Law Enforcement Bulletin*, July, 12-16.

Bowlby, J. (1969). *Attachment and Loss*. New York, NY: Basic Books.

_____ (1988). *A Secure Base: Clinical Implications of Attachment Theory*. London: Routledge & Kegal Paul.

Brandsma, J., M. Maultsby & R. Welsh (1980). *Outpatient Treatment of Alcoholism: A Review and Comparative Study*. Baltimore, MD: University Park Press.

Braswell, M., T. Fletcher & L. Miller (1990). *Human Relations and Corrections*, Third Edition, Prospect Heights, IL: Waveland Press, Inc.

Braswell, M. & T. Seay (1984). *Approaches to Counseling and Psychotherapy*, Second Edition. Prospect Heights, IL: Waveland Press, Inc.

Brodsky, S. (1975). *Families and Friends of Men in Prison: The Uncertain Relationship*. Lexington, MA: D.C. Heath.

Bronfenbrenner, U. (1979). *The Ecology of Human Development: Experiments by Nature and Design*. Cambridge, MA: Harvard University Press.

Brown, S. (1990). "Dynamic Factors and Recidivism: What Have We Learned from the Case Needs Review Project?" *Forum*, 10, 46-51.

Brunk, M., S. Henggeler & J. Whelan (1987). "Comparison of Multisystemic Therapy and Parent Training in the Brief Treatment of Child Abuse and Neglect." *Journal of Consulting and Clinical Psychology*, 55, 311-318.

Buchanan, R., K. Whitlow & J. Austin (1986). "National Evaluation of Objective Prison Classification Systems: The Current State of the Art." *Crime and Delinquency*, 32, 272-290.

Buffone, G. (1980). "Exercise as Therapy." *Journal of Counseling and Psychotherapy*, 3, 101-117.

Burdon, W., D. Farabee, M. Prendergast, N. Messina & J. Cartier (2002). "Prison-Based Therapeutic Community Substance Abuse Programs: Implementation and Operational Issues." *Federal Probation*, 66(3), 3-8.

Bureau of Justice Statistics (2003). *2000 Arrestee Drug Abuse Monitoring: Annual Report* (NCRJ-193013). Washington, DC: U.S. Government Printing Office.

Burgess, A. (1987). *The Clockwork Orange*. New York: Norton.

Burns, D. (1980). *Feeling Good*. New York: Morrow.

Buschman, J. & D. van Beek (2003). "A Clinical Model for the Treatment of Personality Disordered Sexual Offenders." *Sexual Abuse*, 15, 183-199.

Bush, J. & B. Bilodeau (1993). *OPTIONS: A Cognitive Change Program*. Washington, DC: National Institute of Corrections.

Bush, J., J. Taymans & B. Glick (1998). *Thinking for a Change*. Washington, DC: U.S. Department of Justice, National Institute of Corrections.

Butcher, J., W. Dahlstrom, W. Graham, A. Tellegen & B. Kaemmer (1989). *Manual for the Restandardized Minnesota Multiphasic Personality Inventory: MMPI-2. An Interpretative and Administrative Guide*. Minneapolis, MN: University of Minnesota Press.

Caplan, P. & I. Hall-McCorquodale (1985). "Mother-Blaming in Major Clinical Journals." *American Journal of Orthopsychiatry*, 55, 345-353.

Caputo, G.A. (2004). "Treating Sticky Fingers: An Evaluation of Treatment and Education for Offenders." *Journal of Offender Rehabilitation*, 38, 49-68.

Carr, K., B. Hinkle & B. Ingram (1991). "Establishing Mental Health and Substance Abuse Services in Jails." *Journal of Prison and Jail Health*, 10, 77-89.

Cashdan, S. (1988). *Object Relations Therapy: Using the Relationship*. New York: Norton.

Castellano, T. & T. Soderstrom (1992). "Therapeutic Wilderness Programs and Juvenile Recidivism: A Program Evaluation." *Journal of Offender Rehabilitation*, 17, 19-46.

Cattell, R. & A. Cattell (1973). *Culture Fair Intelligence Tests*. San Diego, CA: EdiTS.

Caulum, S. (1994). "Drug and Alcohol Treatment Options." Paper presented to the National Association of Sentencing Advocates. Washington, DC.

Cautela, J. (1967). "Covert Sensitization." *Psychological Record*, 20, 459-468.

Center for Addiction and Mental Health (1999). *1999 Resources*. Toronto:

Chamow, L. (1990). "The Clinician's Role in Treating Spouse Abuse." *Family Therapy*, 17, 123-128.

Cheek, F., C. Franks, J. Laucious & V. Burtle (1971). "Behavior-Modification Training for Wives of Alcoholics." *Quarterly Studies of Alcoholism*, 32, 456-461.

Chesney Lind, M. (2000). "What to Do About Girls? Thinking About Programs for Young Women." In M. McMahon (ed.), *Assessment to Assistance: Programs for Women in Community Corrections*. Lanham, MD: American Correctional Association.

Clear, T. (1988). "Statistical Prediction in Corrections." *Research in Corrections*, 1, 1-39.

Clements, C., J. McKee & S. Jones (1984). *Offender Needs Assessments: Models and Approaches*. Washington, DC: National Institute of Corrections.

Cohen, B. & I. Sordo (1984). "Using Reality Therapy with Adult Offenders." *Journal of Offender Counseling, Services and Rehabilitation*, 8, 25-39.

Cohen, M., R. Garofalo, R. Boucher & T. Seghorn (1971). "The Psychology of Rapists." *Seminars in Psychiatry*, 3, 307-327.

Coleman, E., S.M. Dwyer, G. Abel, W. Berner, J. Breiling, J. Hindman, F.H. Knopp, R. Langevin & F. Pfafflin (1996). "Standards of Care for the Treatment of Adult Sex Offenders." In E. Coleman, S. M. Dwyer & N. J. Pallone (eds.), *Sex Offender Treatment*. Binghamton, NY: Haworth.

Collins, H. & D. Collins (1990). "Family Therapy in the Treatment of Child Sexual Abuse." In M. Rothery & G. Cameron (eds.), *Child Maltreatment: Expanding Our Concept of Helping*. Hillsdale, NJ: Lawrence Erlbaum Associates.

Conley, R., R. Luckasson & G. Bouthilet (1992). *The Criminal Justice System and Mental Retardation: Defendants and Victims*. Baltimore, MD: P.H. Brookes Publishing Co.

Corley, M. (1996). "Correctional Education Programs for Adults with Learning Disabilities." *Linkages*, 3, 2, 1-25. National Adult Literacy & Learning Disabilities Center. Retrieved January 24, 2003, from the National Institute for Literacy Website. http://www.nifl.gov/nifl/ld/archive/vol3no2.html.

Corsini, R. (1973). *Current Psychotherapies*. Itasca, IL: F.E. Peacock Publishers.

Covington, S. (2002). "Helping Women Recover: Creating Gender-Responsive Treatment." In S. Straussner & S. Brown (eds.), *The Handbook of Addiction Treatment for Women*. San Francisco, CA: Jossey-Bass.

Creswell, J.W. (1994). *Research Design: Qualitative & Quantitative Approaches*. Thousand Oaks, CA: Sage Publications.

Cullen, F. & P. Gendreau (2000). "Assessing Correctional Rehabilitation: Policy, Practice, and Prospects." In J. Horney (ed.), *Criminal Justice 2000: Changes in Decision Making and Discretion in the Criminal Justice System*. Washington, DC: U.S. Department of Justice, National Institute of Justice.

Cullen, F. & J. Wright (1996). "The Future of Corrections." In B. Maguire & P. Rodosh (eds.), *The Past, Present, and Future of American Criminal Justice*. New York: General Hall.

Cullen, F., J. Wright & B. Applegate (1995). "Control in the Community: The Limits of Reform?" In A. Harland (ed.), *Choosing Correctional Interventions that Work: Defining the Demand and Evaluating the Supply*. Newbury Park, CA: Sage Publications.

Deitch, D. & J. Zweben (1984). "Coercion in the Therapeutic Community." *Journal of Psychoactive Drugs*, 16(1), 35-41.

DeLeon, G. (2000). *The Therapeutic Community: Theory, Model, and Method*. New York, NY: Springer Publishing Company.

Denkowski, G. & K. Denkowski (1985). "The Mentally Retarded Offender in the State Prison System: Identification, Prevalence, Adjustment, and Rehabilitation." *Criminal Justice and Behavior*, 12, 55-76.

Dennison, G. (1969). *The Lives of Children*. New York: Random House.

Derogatis, L. (1977). *SCL-90 Administration: Scoring and Procedures Manual*. Baltimore, MD: Johns Hopkins University Press.

_____ (1994). *Brief Symptom Inventory: Administration, Scoring, and Procedures Manual*. Minneapolis, MN: National Computer Systems, Inc.

Dicks, H. (1963). "Object Relations Theory and Marital Studies." *British Journal of Medical Psychology*, 36, 125-129.

DiGiorgio-Miller, J. (1994). "Clinical Techniques in the Treatment of Juvenile Sex Offenders." *Journal of Offender Rehabilitation*, 21(1/2), 117-126.

Dignam, J.T. (2003). "Correctional Mental Health Ethics Revisited." In T.J. Fagan & R.K. Ax (eds.), *Correctional Mental Health Handbook*. Thousand Oaks, CA: Sage.

DiIulio, J. (1991). *No Escape: The Future of American Corrections*. New York, NY: Basic Books.

Dillard, J. (1987). *Multicultural Counseling*. Chicago: Nelson-Hall.

Dishion, T. & D. Andrews (1995). "Preventing Escalation in Problem Behavior with High-Risk Young Adolescents: Immediate and One-year Outcomes." *Journal of Consulting and Clinical Psychology*, 63, 538-548.

Dodes, L. (1990). "Addiction, Helplessness and Narcissistic Rage." *Psychoanalytic Quarterly*, 59, 398-419.

Dodes, L. & E. Khantzian (1991). "Individual Psychodynamic Psychotherapy." In R. Francis & S. Miller (eds.), *Textbook of Addiction Disorders*. New York: Guilford Publications.

Dowden, C. & D. Andrews (2000). "Effective Correctional Treatment and Violent Reoffending: A Meta-Analysis." *Canadian Journal of Criminology*, 42, 449-467.

Dowden, C., D. Antonowicz & D. Andrews (2000). "The Effectiveness of Relapse Prevention with Offenders: A Meta-Analysis." *International Journal of Offender Therapy and Comparative Criminology*, 47, 516-528.

Dodson, K. & M. Braswell (2003). "Correctional Counselors and Other Treatment Professionals." In J. Whitehead, J. Pollock & M. Braswell (eds.), *Exploring Corrections in America*. Cincinnati, OH: Anderson Publishing Co.

Drapeau, M., A.C. Korner & L. Brunet (2004). "When the Goals of Therapists and Patients Clash: A Study of Pedophiles in Treatment." *Journal of Offender Rehabilitation*, 38, 69-80.

Dunlap, G., L. Kern-Dunlap, S. Clarke & F. Robbins (1991). "Functional Assessment, Curricular Revision, and Severy Behavior Problems." *Journal of Applied Behavior Analysis*, 24(2), 387-397.

Edleson, J. & R. Grusznski (1988). "Treating the Men Who Batter: Four Years of Outcome Data from the Domestic Abuse Project." *Journal of Social Service Research*, 12, 3-22.

Eissler, K. (1949). "Some Problems of Delinquency." In K. Eissler (ed.), *Searchlights on Delinquency*. New York: Inter University Press.

Eliasoph, E. (1955). "Concepts and Techniques of Role Playing and Role Training Utilizing Psychodramatic Methods in Group Therapy with Adolescent Drug Addicts." *Group Psychotherapy*, 8, 308-315.

Elliott, D., D. Huizinga & S. Ageton (1985). "Reconciling Race and Class Differences in Self-Reported and Official Estimates of Delinquency." *American Sociological Review*, 45, 95-110.

Elliott, W. (2002). "Managing Offender Resistance to Counseling." *Federal Probation*, 66, 172-178.

Elliott, W. & G. Walters (1991). "Coping with Offenders' Resistance to Psychoeducational Presentations on the Criminal Lifestyle." *Journal of Correctional Education*, 42, 172-177.

Elliott, W. & G. Walters (1997). "Conducting Psychoeducational Interventions with Drug Abusing Offenders: The Lifestyle Model." *Journal of Drug Education*, 27, 307-319.

Elliot, W. & V. Verdeyen (2002). *Game Over! Strategies for Managing Inmate Deception*. Lanham, MD: American Correctional Association.

Ellis, A. (1962). *Reason and Emotion in Psychotherapy*. Secaucus, NJ: Lyle Stuart.

———— (1973). *Humanistic Psychotherapy*. New York: Julian.

_____ (1979). "The Sex Offender." In H. Toch (ed.), *Legal and Criminal Psychology*. New York, NY: Holt, Rinehart & Winston.

Emerick, R. & W. Dutton (1993). "The Effect of Polygraphy on the Self-Report of Adolescent Sex Offenders" *Annals of Sex Research*, 6, 83-103.

Empey, L. & S. Lubeck (1971). *The Silverlake Experiment: Testing Delinquency Theory and Community Intervention*. Chicago, IL: Aldine.

Endicott, J. & R. Spitzer (1978). "A Diagnostic Interview: The Schedule for Affective Disorders and Schizophrenia." *Archives of General Psychiatry*, 35, 837-844.

Ennis, L. & S. Horne (2003). "Predicting Psychological Distress in Sex Offender Therapists." *Sexual Abuse*, 15, 149-157.

Epps, K. (1996). "Sex Offenders." In C. Hollin (ed.), *Working with Offenders*. New York: John Wiley & Sons.

Erez, E. (1988). "Myth of the New Female Offender: Some Evidence from Attitudes Toward Law and Justice." *Journal of Criminal Justice*, 16(6), 499-509.

Ernst, R. & W. Keating (1964). "Psychiatric Treatment of the California Felon." *American Journal of Psychiatry*, 120, 974-979.

Erskine, R., P. Clarkson, R. Goulding & M. Groder et al. (1988). "Ego State Theory: Definitions, Descriptions, and Points of View." *Transactional Analysis Journal*, 18(1), 6-14.

Exner, J. (1993). *The Rorschach: A Comprehensive System*. Vol. 1, Third Edition. New York: John Wiley & Sons.

Eysenck, H. (1952). "The Effects of Psychotherapy: An Evaluation." *Journal of Consulting Psychology*, 16, 319-324.

_____ (1970). *Crime and Personality*. London, UK: Paladin.

Eysenck, H. & M. Eysenck (1983). *Mindwatching: Why People Behave the Way They Do*. New York: Anchor Press.

Feeley, M. & J. Simon (1992). "The New Penology: Notes on the Emerging Strategy of Corrections and its Implications." *Criminology*, 30, 449-474.

Feinstein, S. (2003). "School-Wide Positive Behavior Supports." *Journal of Correctional Education*, 54(4), 163-173.

Finn, P. (1998). *The Delaware Department of Corrections Life Skills Program*. Washington, DC: U.S. Department of Justice, Office of Justice Programs.

First, M., R. Spitzer, M. Gibbon & J. Williams (1997). *Structured Clinical Interview for the DSM-IV Axix I Disorders (SCID-I) Clinical Version*. Washington, DC: American Psychiatric Press.

Fishman, L. (1988). "Prisoners and Their Wives: Marital and Domestic Effects of Telephone Contacts and Home Visits." *International Journal of Offender Therapy and Comparative Criminology*, 32, 55-65.

Flemons, D. (1989). "An Ecosystemic View of Family Violence." *Family Therapy*, 16, 1-10.

Foa, E., B. Olasov-Rothbaum & G. Steketee (1993). "Treatment of Rape Victims." *Journal of Interpersonal Violence*, 8, 256-276.

Forehand, R. & B. Kotchick (1996). "Cultural Diversity: A Wake-Up Call for Parent Training." *Behavior Therapy*, 27(2), 187-206.

Framo, J. (1970). "Symptoms From a Family Transactional Viewpoint." In N. Ackerman (ed.), *Family Therapy in Transition*. Boston, MA: Little, Brown & Co.

_____ (1981). "Integration of Marital Therapy with Sessions with Family of Origin." In A. Gurman & D. Kniskern (eds.), *Handbook of Family Therapy*. New York, NY: Brunner Mazel.

Francis, R., J. Franklin & L. Borg (1994). "Psychodynamics." In M. Galanter & H. Kleber (eds.), *Textbook of Substance Abuse Treatment*. Washington, DC: American Psychiatric Press, Inc.

French, S. & P. Gendreau (in press). "Reducing Prison Misconducts: What Works!" *Criminal Justice and Behavior*.

Friedman, A. (1989). "Family Therapy vs. Parent Groups: Effect on Adolescent Drug Abusers." *The American Journal of Family Therapy*, 17, 335-347.

Gaes, G.G., T.J. Flanagan, L. Motiuk & L. Stewart (1999). "Adult Correctional Treatment." In M. Tonry (ed.), *Crime and Justice: A Review of Research*, vol. 26. Chicago: University of Chicago Press.

Garrett, C. (1985). "Effects of Residential Treatment on Adjudicated Delinquents: A Meta-Analysis." *Journal of Research in Crime and Delinquency*, 22, 287-308.

Gaudin, J. & D. Kurtz (1985). "Parenting Skills Training for Child Abusers." *Journal of Group Psychotherapy, Psychodrama and Sociometry*, 31, 35-54.

Gaudin, J., J. Wodarski, M. Arkinson & L. Avery (1991). "Remedying Child Neglect: Effectiveness of Social Network Interventions." *Journal of Applied Social Sciences*, 15, 97-123.

Gendreau, P. (1995). "Technology Transfer in the Criminal Justice Field." In T. Backer, S. Davis & G. Soucy (eds.), *Reviewing the Behavioral Science Knowledge Base on Technology Transfer*. (NIDA Research Monograph 155). Rockville, MD: U.S. Department of Health and Human Services, Public Health Service, National Institutes of Health.

_____ (1996a). "Offender Rehabilitation: What We Know and What Needs to be Done." *Criminal Justice and Behavior*, 23, 144-161.

_____ (1996b). "The Principles of Effective Intervention with Offenders." In A. Harland (ed.), *Choosing Correctional Options That Work: Defining the Demand and Evaluating the Supply*. Thousand Oaks, CA: Sage Publications.

Gendreau, P. & D. Andrews (1979). "Psychological Consultation in Correctional Agencies: Case Studies and General Issues." In J. Platt & R. Wicks (eds.), *The Psychological Consultant*. New York: Grune & Stratton.

_____ (1990). "Tertiary Prevention: What the Meta-analysis of the Offender Treatment Literature Tells Us About 'What Works'." *Canadian Journal of Criminology*, 32, 173-184.

_____ (2001). *Correctional Program Assessment Inventory (CPAI-2000)*. Saint John, NB: University of New Brunswick.

Gendreau, P., C. Goggin, S. French & P. Smith (in press). "Practicing Psychology in Correctional Settings." In A. Hess & I. Weiner (eds.), *The Handbook of Forensic Psychology*, Third Edition. Hoboken, NJ: Wiley.

Gendreau, P., S. French & A. Gionet (2004). "What Works (What Doesn't Work): The Principles of Effective Correctional Treatment." *Journal of Community Corrections*, 13, 4-6, 27-30.

Gendreau, P. & C. Goggin (1991). *Evaluation of Correctional Service of Canada Substance Abuse Programs*. Research Report No. 16. Ottawa, ON: Research and Statistics Branch, Correctional Service of Canada.

_____ (in press). "Principles of Effective Correctional Programming with Offenders." *Forum on Corrections Research*.

Gendreau, P., C. Goggin & B. Fulton (2000). "Intensive Supervision in Probation and Parole." In C.R. Hollin (ed.), *Handbook of Offender Assessment and Treatment*. Chichester, UK: John Wiley & Sons.

Gendreau, P. & C. Goggin & P. Smith (2001). "Implementation Guidelines for Correctional Programs in the 'Real World.'" In G.A. Bernfeld, D. Farrington & A. Leschied (eds.), *Offender Rehabilitation in Practice*. West Sussex, UK: John Wiley & Sons.

_____ (2002). "Is the PCL-R Really the "Unparalleled" Measure of Offender Risk?" *Criminal Justice and Behavior*, 29, 397-426.

Gendreau, P., T. Little & C. Goggin (1996). "A Meta-Analysis of the Predictors of Adult Offender Recidivism: What Works?" *Criminology*, 34, 575-607.

Gendreau, P., M. Paparozzi, T. Little & M. Goddard (1993). "Does 'Punishing Smarter' Work? An Assessment of the New Generation of Alternative Sanctions in Probation." *Forum on Corrections Research*, 5, 31-34.

Gendreau, P. & R. Ross (1979). "Effective Correctional Treatment: Bibliotherapy for Cynics." *Crime and Delinquency*, 25, 463-489.

_____ (1987). "Revivification of Rehabilitation: Evidence from the 1980s." *Justice Quarterly*, 4, 349-409.

Gibbs, J., G. Potter & A. Goldstein (1995). *The EQUIP Program: Teaching Youth to Think and Act Responsibly through a Peer-Helping Approach*. Champaign, IL: Research Press.

Gilligan, C. (1982). *In a Different Voice*. Boston, Ma: Harvard University Press.

Glasser, W. (1965). *Reality Therapy: A New Approach to Psychiatry*. New York: Harper and Row.

_____ (2000). *Reality Therapy in Action*. New York, NY: Harper Collins Publishers.

Glesne, C. (1999). *Becoming Qualitative Researchers*. New York, NY: Longman.

Goffman, E. (1999). "The Characteristics of Total Institution." In R. Matthews (ed.), *Imprisonment*. Brookfield, VT: Ashgate.

Golden, L. (2002). *Evaluation of the Efficacy of a Cognitive Behavioral Program for Offenders on Probation: Thinking for a Change*. Dallas, TX: University of Texas Southwestern Medical Center at Dallas.

Goldkamp, J., M. White & J. Robinson (2001). "Do Drug Courts Work? Getting Inside the Drug Court Black Box." *Journal of Drug Issues*, 31(1), 27-72.

Goldstein A. (1999). *The Prepare Curriculum: Teaching Prosocial Competencies*, Revised Edition. Champaign, IL: Research Press.

Goldstein, A. & B. Glick (1995a). *The Prosocial Gang: Implementing Aggression Replacement Training*. Thousand Oaks, CA: Sage.

_____ (1995b). "Artful Research Management: Problems, Process and Products." In A. Goldstein & B. Glick (eds.), *Managing Delinquency Programs That Work*. Laurel, MD: American Correctional Association.

Goldstein, A., B. Glick, M. Irwin, C. Pask-McCartney & I. Rubama (1989). *Reducing Delinquency: Intervention in the Community*. New York: Pergamon Press.

Goldstein, A., B. Glick & J. Gibbs (1998). *Aggression Replacement Training: A Comprehensive Intervention for Aggressive Youth,* Revised Edition. Champaign, IL: Research Press.

Gordon, D. & J. Arbuthnot (1987). "Individual, Group, and Family Interventions." In H. Quay (ed.), *Handbook of Juvenile Delinquency*. New York: Wiley.

Gordon, D., J. Arbuthnot, K. Gustafson & P. McGreen (1988). "Home-Based Behavioral-Systems Family Therapy with Disadvantaged Juvenile Delinquents." *American Journal of Family Therapy*, 16, 243-255.

Gordon, D., K. Graves & J. Arbuthnot (1995). "The Effects of Functional Family Therapy for Delinquents on Adult Criminal Behavior." *Criminal Justice and Behavior*, 22, 60-73.

Gottfredson, M. & T. Hirschi (1990). *A General Theory of Crime*. Stanford, CA: Stanford University Press.

Gottschalk, R., W. Davidson, L. Gensheimer & J. Mayer (1987). "Community-based Interventions." In H. Quay (ed.), *Handbook of Juvenile Delinquency*. New York: John Wiley & Sons, Inc.

Gottschalk, R., W. Davidson, J. Mayer & J. Gensheimer (1987). "Behavioral Approaches with Juvenile Offenders: A Meta-Analysis of Long-Term Treatment Efficacy." In E. Morris & C. Braukmann (eds.), *Behavioral Approaches to Crime and Delinquency: A Handbook of Application, Research, and Concepts*. New York: Plenum Press.

Graham, J. (2000). *MMPI-2: Assessing Personality and Psychopathology*, Third Edition. New York, NY: Oxford University Press.

Greenberg, I. (1974). *Psychodrama*. New York: Behavioral Publications.

Greenwood, P. & S. Turner (1993). "Evaluation of the Paint Creek Youth Center: A Residential Program for Serious Delinquents." *Criminology*, 31, 263-279.

Gregory, R. (1987). *Adult Intellectual Assessment*. Boston, MA: Allyn and Bacon.

Griffith, J., M. Hiller, K. Knight & D. Simpson (1999). "A Cost-Effectiveness Analysis of In-Prison Therapeutic Community Treatment and Risk Classification." *The Prison Journal*, 79(3), 352-368.

Grossman, H. (ed.) (1983). *Classification in Mental Retardation*. Washington, DC: American Association of Mental Deficiency.

Groth, N. (1983). "Treatment of the Sexual Offender in a Correctional Institution." In J. Greer & I. Stuart (eds.), *The Sexual Aggressor: Current Perspectives on Treatment*. New York: Van Nostrand Reinhold Co.

Groth-Marnat, G. (2003). *Handbook of Psychological Assessment*, Fourth Edition. New York: John Wiley & Sons.

Grove, W. & P. Meehl (1996). "Comparative Efficiency of Informal (Subjective, Impressionistic) and Formal (Mechanical, Algorithmic) Prediction Procedures: The Clinical Statistical Controversy." *Psychology, Public Policy, and Law*, 2(2), 293-323.

Guerin, P. (1976). *Family Therapy: Theory and Practice*. New York: Gardner Press.

Haapala, D. & J. Kinney (1988). "Avoiding Out-of-Home Placement of High-Risk Status Offenders Through the Use of Intensive Home-Based Family Preservation Services." *Criminal Justice and Behavior*, 15, 334-348.

Haas, S. (1999). "High School Aggression: A Social Learning Analysis." Unpublished doctoral dissertation. Cincinnati, OH: University of Cincinnati.

Hairston, C. (2002). "Prisoners and Families: Parenting Issues During Incarceration." Paper presented at the Urban Institute's From Prison to Home Conference. Washington, DC, January 30-31.

Haley, J. (1976). *Problem-Solving Therapy*. San Francisco: Jossey-Bass.

Hall, G. (1995). "Sexual Offender Recidivism Revisited: A Meta-Analysis of Recent Treatment Studies." *Journal of Consultant and Clinical Psychology*, 63, 802-809.

Hamberger, L. & J. Hastings (1988). "Skills Training for Treatment of Spouse Abusers: An Outcome Study." *Journal of Family Violence*, 3, 121-130.

Hanson, R.K., I. Bloom & M. Stephenson (2004). "Evaluating Community Sex Offender Treatment Programs." *Canadian Journal of Behavioural Science*, 36, 87-96.

Hanson, R.K. & M.T. Bussiere (1998). "Predicting Relapse: A Meta-Analysis of Sexual Offender Recidivism Studies." *Journal of Consulting and Clinical Psychology*, 66, 348-362.

Hanson, R. & A. Harris (2000). *The Sex Offender-Need Assessment Rating (SONAR): A Method for Measuring Change in Risk Levels*. User Report No. 2000-01. Ottawa, Ontario: Solicitor General Canada.

Hanson, R. & D. Thornton (1999). *Static 99: Improving Actuarial Risk assessments for Sex Offenders*. User Report No. 1999-02. Ottawa, Ontario: Solicitor General Canada.

Hardyman, P., J. Austin & J. Peyton (2004). *Prisoner Intake Systems: Assessing Needs and Classifying Prisoners*. Washington, DC: National Institute of Corrections.

Hardyman, P., J. Austin & O. Tulloch (2002). *Revalidating External Prison Classification Systems: The Experience of Ten States and Model for Classification Reform*. Washington, DC: National Institute of Corrections.

Hardyman, P., J. Austin, J. Alexander, K. Dedel Johnson & O. Tulloch (2002). *Internal Prison Classification Systems: Case Studies in Their Development and Implementation*. Washington, DC: U.S. Department of Justice, National Institute of Corrections.

Hardyman, P. & P. Van Voorhis (2004). *Developing Gender-Specific Classification Systems for Women Offenders*. Washington, DC: U.S. Department of Justice, National Institute of Corrections.

Hare, R. (2003). *Hare Psychopathy Checklist—Revisited*, Second Edition. North Tonawanda, NY: Multi-Health Systems.

———— (1993). *Without Conscience: The Disturbing World of the Psychopaths Among Us*. New York: Pocket Books.

Harris, G. (1995). *Overcoming Resistance: Success in Counseling Men*. Lanham, MD: American Correctional Association.

Harris, G., M. Rice & C. Cormier (1991). "Psychopathy and Violent Recidivism." *Law and Human Behavior*, 15, 625-637.

Harris, K. & W. Miller (1990). "Behavioral Self-Control Training for Problem Drinkers: Components of Efficacy." *Psychology of Addictive Behaviors*, 4, 82-90.

Harris, P. (1988). "The Interpersonal Maturity Level Classification System: I-Level." *Criminal Justice and Behavior*, 15, 58-77.

Harris, P. & S. Smith (1996). "Developing Community Corrections: An Implementation Perspective." In A. Harland (ed.), *Choosing Correctional Options that Work: Defining the Demand and Evaluating the Supply*. Thousand Oaks, CA: Sage Publications.

Hartmann, H. (1951). "Ego Psychology and the Problem of Adaptation." In D. Rapaport (ed.), *Organization and Pathology of Thought: Selected Sources*. New York: Columbia University Press.

Haskell, M. & H. Weeks (1960). "Role Training as Preparation for Release from a Correctional Institution." *Journal of Criminal Law, Criminology and Police Science*, 50, 441-447.

Hazelrigg, M., H. Cooper & C. Borduin (1987). "Evaluating the Effectiveness of Family Therapies: An Integrative Review and Analysis." *Psychological Bulletin*, 101, 428-442.

Heide, K. (1983). "Classification of Offenders Ordered to Make Restitution by Interpersonal Maturity Level and by Specific Personality Dimensions." In W. Laufer & J. Day (eds.), *Personality Theory, Moral Development, and Criminal Behavior*. Lexington, MA: Lexington Books.

Henggeler, S. (ed.) (1982). *Delinquency and Adolescent Psychopathology: A Family-Ecological Systems Approach*. Littleton, MA: Wright.

Henggeler, S. & C. Borduin (1990). *Family Therapy and Beyond: A Multisystemic Approach to Treating the Behavior Problems of Children and Adolescents*. Pacific Grove, CA: Brooks/Cole.

Henggeler, S., C. Borduin, G. Melton, B. Mann, L. Smith, J. Hall, L. Cone & B. Fucci (1991). "Effects of Multisystemic Therapy on Drug Use and Abuse in Serious Juvenile Offenders: A Progress Report from Two Outcome Studies." *Family Dynamics of Addiction Quarterly*, 1, 40-51.

Henggeler, S., G. Melton & L. Smith (1992). "Family Preservations Using Multisystemic Therapy: An Effective Alternative to Incarcerating Serious Juvenile Offenders." *Journal of Consulting and Clinical Psychology*, 60, 953-961.

Henggeler, S., S. Mihalic, L. Rone, C. Thomas & J. Timmons-Mitchell (1998). *Multi-Systemic Therapy: Book Six in the Blueprints in Violence Prevention Series*. Boulder, CO: University of Colorado, Center for the Study and Prevention of Violence.

Henggeler, S. & T. Lee (2003). "Multisystemic Treatment of Serious Clinical Problems." In A. Kazdin (ed.), *Evidence-Based Psychotherapies for Children and Adolescents*. New York, NY: Guilford Press.

Henggeler, S., S. Pickrel, M. Brondino & J. Crouch (1996). "Eliminating (Almost) Treatment Dropout of Substance Abusing or Dependent Delinquents Through Home-Based Multisystemic Therapy." *American Journal of Psychiatry*, 153, 427-428.

Henggeler, S., J. Rodick, C. Borduin, C. Hanson, S. Watson & J. Urey (1986). "Multisystemic Treatment of Juvenile Offenders: Effects on Adolescent Behavior and Family Interaction." *Developmental Psychology*, 22, 132-141.

Henggeler, S., S. Schoenwald, C. Borduin, M. Rowland & P. Cunningham (1998). *Multisystemic Treatment of Antisocial Behavior in Children and Adolescents*. New York, NY: Guilford Press.

Henggeler, S., S. Schoenwald & S. Pickrel (1995). "Multisystemic Therapy: Bridging the Gap between University- and Community-based Treatment." *Journal of Consulting and Clinical Psychology*, 63, 709-717.

Hepburn, J. (1989). "Prison Guards as Agents of Social Control." In L. Goodstein & D. MacKenzie (eds.), *The American Prison: Issues in Research and Policy*. New York: Plenum Press.

Herman, M. (2000). "Psychotherapy with Substance Abusers: Integration of Psychodynamic and Cognitive-Behavioral Approaches." *American Journal of Psychotherapy*, 54(4), 574-579.

Hester, R. & W. Miller (eds.) (1995). *Handbook of Alcoholism Treatment Approaches: Effective Alternatives*, Second Edition. Needham Heights, MA: Simon & Schuster Company.

Hickey, J. & P. Scharf (1980). *Toward a Just Correctional System*. San Francisco, CA: Jossey-Bass.

Higgins, S. & K. Silverman (1999). *Motivating Behavior Change Among Illicit-Drug Abusers: Research on Contingency Management Interventions*. Washington, DC: American Psychological Association.

Hill, A., P. Briken C. Kraus, K. Strohm & W. Berner (2003). "Differential Pharmacological Treatment of Paraphilias and Sex Offenders." *International Journal of Offender Therapy and Comparative Criminology*, 47, 407-421.

Hirsch, R. & J. Imhof (1975). "A Family Therapy Approach to the Treatment of Drug Abuse and Addiction." *Journal of Psychedelic Drugs*, 7, 181-185.

Hislop, J. (2001). *Female Sex Offenders: What Therapists, Law Enforcement, and Child Protection Services Need to Know*. Ravensdale, N.J: Issues Press.

Hodges, J., N. Guiliotti & F.M. Porpotage II (1994). "Improving Literacy Skills of Juvenile Detainees." *Juvenile Justice Bulletin*. Washington DC: Office of Justice Programs. Office of Juvenile Justice and Delinquency Prevention.

Ho, M.K. (1987). *Family Therapy with Ethnic Minorities*. Newbury Park, CA: Sage Publications, Inc.

Hoffman, L. (1981). *Foundations of Family Therapy*. New York: Basic Books.

Hoffman, P. (1983). "Screening for Risk: A Revised Salient Factor Score (SFS-81)." *Journal of Criminal Justice*, 11, 539-547.

————— (1994). "Twenty Years of Operational Use of a Risk Prediction Instrument: The United States Parole Commission's Salient Factor Score." *Journal of Criminal Justice*, 22, 477-494.

Hoge, R., A. Leschied & D. Andrews (1993). *An Investigation of Young Offender Services in the Province of Ontario: A Report of the Repeat Offender Project*. Toronto: Ministry of Community and Social Services.

Hollin, C. (1990). *Cognitive-Behavioral Interactions with Young Offenders*. New York, NY: Pergamon Press.

Holtfreter, K., M.D. Reisig & M. Morash (2004). "Poverty, State Capital, and Recidivism Among Women Offenders." *Criminology and Public Policy*, 3, 185-208.

Horvath, A. & B. Symonds (1991). "Relation Between Working Aliance and Outcome: A Meta-analysis." *Journal of Counseling Psychology*, 38(2), 139-149.

Houston, J. (1998). *Making Sense with Offenders' Personal Constructs, Therapy, and Change*. New York: Wiley.

Howing, P., J. Wodarski, J. Gaudin & P. Kurtz (1989). "Effective Interventions to Ameliorate the Incidence of Child Maltreatment." *Journal of Consulting and Clinical Psychology*, 51, 424-431.

Hunt, G. & N. Azrin (1973). "A Community-Reinforcement Approach to Alcoholism." *Behavior Research and Therapy*, 11, 91-104.

Inciardi, J. & D. Lockwood (1994). "When Worlds Collide: Establishing CREST Outreach Center." In B. Fletcher, J. Inciardi & A. Horton (eds.), *Drug Abuse Treatment:The Implementation of Innovative Approaches*. Westport, CT: Greenwood Press.

Inciardi, J., D. McBride & B. Weinman (1993). "The Assessment and Referral of Criminal Justice Clients: Examining the Focused Offender Disposition Program." In J. Inciardi (ed.), *Drug Treatment and Criminal Justice*. Newbury Park, CA: Sage Publications.

Institute of Medicine (1990). "Treating Drug Problems." In D. Gerstein & H. Harwood (eds.), *Treating Drug Problems*. Washington, DC: National Academy Press.

Ivey, A. & L. Simek-Downing (1980). *Counseling and Psychotherapy: Skills, Theories and Practice*. Englewood Cliffs, NJ: Prentice-Hall.

Izzo, R. & R. Ross (1990). "Meta-Analysis of Rehabilitation Programs for Juvenile Delinquents: A Brief Report." *Criminal Justice and Behavior*, 17, 134-142.

Jackson, D. (1961). "Family Therapy in the Family of the Schizophrenic." In M. Stern (ed.), *Contemporary Psychotherapies*. Glencoe, IL: The Free Press.

_____ (1967). "The Myth of Normality." *Medical Opinion and Review*, 3, 28-33.

Janeksela, G. (1979). "Mandatory Parental Involvement in the Treatment of 'Delinquent' Youth." *Juvenile and Family Court Journal*, 30, 47-54.

Janzen, C. (1977). "Families in Treatment of Alcoholism." *Journal of Studies on Alcoholism*, 38, 114-130.

Jenkins-Hall, K. (1994). "Outpatient Treatment of Child Molesters." *Journal of Offender Rehabilitation*, 21(1/2), 139-150.

Jennings, W., R. Kilkenny & L. Kohlberg (1983). "Moral Development Theory and Practice for Youthful and Adult Offenders." In W. Laufer & J. Day (eds.), *Personality Theory, Moral Development and Criminal Behavior*. Lexington, MA: Lexington Books.

Jenuwine, M.J., R. Simmons & E. Swies (2003). "Community Supervision of Sex Offenders." *Federal Probation*, 67(3), 20-27.

Jesness, C. (1975). "Comparative Effectiveness of Behavior Modification and Transactional Programs for Delinquents." *Journal of Consulting and Clinical Psychology*, 43, 759-799.

_____ (1988). "Jesness Inventory Classification System." *Criminal Justice and Behavior*, 15, 78-91.

_____ (1996). *The Jesness Inventory Manual*. North Tonawanda, NY: Multi-Health Systems.

_____ (2003). *The Jesness Inventory-Revised: Technical Manual*. North Tonawanda, NY: Multi-Health Systems.

Jesness, C. & R. Wedge (1983). *Classifying Offenders: The Jesness Inventory Classification System*. Sacramento, CA: Youth Authority.

Joanning, H., F. Thomas, W. Quinn & R. Mullen (1992). "Treating Adolescent Drug Abuse: A Comparison of Family Systems Therapy, Group Therapy, and Family Drug Education." *Journal of Marital and Family Therapy*, 18, 345-356.

Jones, G. (1972). "The Renaissance of Psychosurgery." *Journal of the Medical Society of New Jersey*, 69(1), 53-57.

Jones, I. & D. Frei (1977). "Provoked Anxiety as a Treatment of Exhibitionism." *British Journal of Psychiatry*, 131, 295-300.

Jones, M. (1968). *Beyond the Therapeutic Community*. New Haven, CT: Yale University Press.

_____ (1973). "Therapeutic Community Principles." In L. Irvine & T. Brelje (eds.), *Law, Psychiatry and the Mentally Disturbed Offender*. Vol. 2. Springfield, IL: Charles C Thomas.

Jones, P. (1996). "Risk Prediction in Criminal Justice." In A. Harland (ed.), *Choosing Correctional Options that Work: Defining the Demand and Evaluating the Supply*. Thousand Oaks, CA: Sage Publications.

Kaplan, H. & B. Sadock (2000). *Modern Synopsis of Comprehensive Textbook of Psychiatry*, Seventh Edition. Baltimore, MD: Lippincott, Williams & Wilkins.

Kaslow, F. (1987). "Couples or Family Counseling for Prisoners and Their Significant Others." *The American Journal of Family Therapy*, 15, 352-360.

Katz, L. & J. Gottman (1993). "Patterns of Marital Conflict Predict Children's Internalizing and Externalizing Behaviors." *Developmental Psychology*, 29, 940-950.

Kaufman, D. (1985). *Substance Abuse and Family Therapy*. Orlando, FL: Grune & Stratton.

Kaufman, E. & P. Kaufman (1992). *Family Therapy of Drug and Alcohol Abuse*, Second Edition. Needham Heights, MA: Allyn & Bacon.

Kauffman, K. (1988). *Prison Officers and Their World*. Cambridge, MA: Harvard University Press.

Kazdin, A. (1987). *Conduct Disorders in Childhood and Adolescence*. Homewood, IL: Dorsey.

_____ (1989). *Behavior Modification in Applied Settings*. Pacific Grove, CA: Brooks/Cole.

_____ (1997). "Parent Management Training: Evidence, Outcomes, and Issues." *Journal of the American Academy of Child and Adolescent Psychiatry*, 36 (10), 1349-1357.

_____ (2000). *Parent Management Training*. Washington, DC: American Psychological Association.

Kazdin, A., J. Mazurick & T. Siegel (1994). "Treatment Outcomes Among Children with Externalizing Disorder Who Terminate Prematruely Versus Those Who Complete Psychotherapy." *Journal of the American Academy of Child and Adolescent Psychiatry*, 33, 549-557.

Kennedy, D. (1984). "Suicide While in Police Custody." *Journal of Police Science and Administration*, 12, 191-200.

Khantzian, E. (1993). "The Ego, the Self, and the Opiate Addiction: Theoretical and Treatment Considerations." In J. Blaine & D. Julius (eds.), *Psychodynamics of Drug Dependence*. Northvale, NJ: Jason Aronson Inc.

Khantzian, E., K. Halliday & W. McAuliffe (1990). *Addiction and the Vulnerable Self*. New York: Guilford Publications.

Kinney, J., D. Haapala, C. Booth & S. Leavitt (1991). "The Homebuilders Model." In E. Tracy, D. Haapala, J. Kinney & P. Pecora (eds.), *Intensive Family Preservation Services: An Instructional Sourcebook*. Cleveland, OH: Mandel School of Applied Social Sciences.

Kirby, E., R. Milich & M. Hundley (2003). "Attributional Biases in Aggressive Children and Their Mothers." *Journal of Abnormal Psychology*, 112, 698-708.

Kirsch, I., A. Jungeblut, L. Jenkins & A. Kolstad (1993). *Adult Literacy in America: A First Look at the Results of the National Adult Literacy Survey*. Washington, DC: U.S. Government Printing Office.

Klein, N., J. Alexander & B. Parsons (1977). "Impact of Family Systems Intervention on Recidivism and Sibling Delinquency: A Model of Primary Prevention and Program Evaluation." *Journal of Consulting and Clinical Psychology*, 45, 469-474.

Knight, D., D. Simpson & M. Hiller (1999). "Three-Year Incarceration Outcomes for In-Prison Therapeutic Community Treatment in Texas." *The Prison Journal*, 79(3), 337-351.

Knight, R. & R. Prentky (1987). "The Developmental Antecedents and Adult Adaptations of Rapist Subtypes." *Criminal Justice and Behavior*, 14, 403-426.

_____ (1990). "Classifying Sexual Offenders." In W.L. Marshall, D.R. Laws & H.E. Barbaree (eds.), *Handbook of Sexual Assault*. New York: Plenum.

Kohlberg, L. (1976). "Moral Stages & Moralization." In T. Lickona (ed.), *Moral Development and Behavior*. New York: Holt, Rinehart & Winston.

Kohlberg, L., A. Colby, J. Gibbs, B. Speicher-Dubin & D. Candee (1979). *Standard Form Scoring Manual*. Cambridge, MA: Harvard University Press.

Krauft, V. (1974). "Transactional Analysis Group Interaction with Sixth Grade Behavioral Problem Boys." *Dissertation Abstracts International*, 34A, 3864-3875.

Kropp, P., S. Hart, C. Webster & M. Derek Eaves (1997). *Spousal Assault Risk Assessment Guide (SARA)*. North Tonowanda, NY: Multihealth Systems.

Kumpfer, K. (1999). *Strengthening America's Families: Exemplary Parenting and Family Strategies for Delinquency Prevention*. Washington, DC: U.S. Department of Justice, Office of Justice Programs, Office of Juvenile Justice and Delinquency Prevention.

Kumpfer, K., J. DeMarsh & W. Child (1989). "Strengthening Families Program: Children's Skills Training Curriculum Manual, Parent Training Manual, Children's Skill Training Manual, and Family Skills Training Manual." Unpublished manuscript, Social Research Institute, University of Utah.

Kurtines, W. & J. Szapocznik (1996). "Family Interations Patters: Structural Family Therapy within Contexts of Cultural Diversity." In E. Hibbs & P. Jensen (eds.), *Psychosocial Treatments for Child and Adolescent Disorders: Empirically Based Strategies for Clinical Practice*. Washington, DC: American Psychological Association.

Kushner, M. & J. Sandler (1966). "Aversion Therapy and the Concept of Punishment." *Behaviour Research and Therapy*, 4, 179-186.

Lab, S. & J. Whitehead (1990). "From 'Nothing Works' to the 'Appropriate Works': The Latest Step in the Search for the Secular Grail." *Criminology*, 28, 405-417.

Landry, M., D. Smith & M. Morrison (1994). *Understanding Drugs of Abuse: The Process of Addiction Treatment and Recovery*. Washington, DC: American Psychiatric Press.

Langan, N. & B. Pelissier (2001). "Gender Differences among Prisoners in Drug Treatment." *Journal of Substance Abuse*, 13(3), 291-301.

Lanza, M., J. Anderson, C. Boisvert, A. LeBlanc, M. Fardy & B. Steel (2002). "Assaultive Behavior Intervention in the Veterans Administration: Psychodynamic Group Psychotherapy Compared to Cognitive Behavior Therapy." *Perspectives in Psychiatric Care* 38(3), 89-97.

Larzelere, R. & G. Patterson (1990). "Parental Management: Mediator of the Effects of SES on Early Delinquency." *Criminology*, 28, 301-323.

Law, M. (2004). *A Longitudinal Follow-up of Federally Sentenced Women in the Community: Assessing the Predictive Validity of the Dynamic Characteristics of the Community Intervention Scale.* Unpublished doctoral dissertation. Ottawa, Ontario: Carleton University.

Laws, D. & C. Osborn (1983). "How to Build and Operate a Behavioral Laboratory to Evaluate and Treat Sexual Deviance." In J. Greer & I. Stuart (eds.), *The Sexual Aggressor: Current Perspectives on Treatment.* New York: Van Nostrand Reinhold Co.

Lennon, B. (2000). "From 'Reality Therapy' to 'Reality Therapy in Action.'" *International Journal of Reality Therapy* 20(1), 41-46.

Lester, D. (1977). "The Sex Offender: A Behavioral Analysis." *Police Law Quarterly*, 8(1), 19-27.

_____ (1982). "The Treatment of Exhibitionists." *Corrective and Social Psychiatry*, 28(3), 94-98.

Levinson, R. (1988). "Development in the Classification Process." *Criminal Justice and Behavior*, 15, 24-38.

Lewis, H. (1987). "Shame and the Narcissistic Personality." In D. Nathanson (ed.), *The Many Faces of Shame.* New York: Guilford Publications.

Liddle, H. & G. Dakof (1995). "Efficacy of Family Therapy for Drug Abuse: Promising but Not Definitive." *Journal of Marital and Family Therapy*, 21, 511-543.

Liebert, R. & M. Spiegler (1994). *Personality: Strategies and Issues.* Pacific Grove, CA: Brooks/Cole.

Lipsey, M. (1992). "Juvenile Delinquency Treatment: A Meta-Analytic Inquiry into the Variability of Effects." In T. Cook, H. Cooper, D. Cordray, H. Hartmann, L. Hedges, R. Light, T. Louis & F. Mosteller (eds.), *Meta-Analysis for Explanation.* New York: Russell Sage Foundation.

Lipsey, M., G. Chapman & N. Landenberger (2001). "Cognitive-Behavioral Programs for Offenders." *The Annals* (of the American Academy of Political and Social Science), 578 (November), 144-157.

Lipsey, M. & D. Wilson (1997). "Effective Intervention for Serious Juvenile Offenders: A Synthesis of Research." In R. Loeber & D. Farrington (eds.), *Serious and Violent Juvenile Offenders: Risk Factors and Successful Interventions.* Thousand Oaks, CA: Sage.

_____ (1993). "The Efficacy of Psychological Educational and Behavioral Treatment: Confirmation from Meta-analysis." *American Psychologist*, 48, 1181-1209.

_____ (2001). *Practical Meta-Analysis.* Thousand Oaks, CA: Sage Publications.

Lipton, D. (1996). "Prison-based Therapeutic Communities: Their Success with Drug-abusing Offenders." *National Institute of Justice Journal*, 230, 12-20.

LIS, Inc. (2002). *Services for Families of Prison Inmates.* Longmont, CA: National Institute of Corrections.

Listwan, S., K. Sperber, L. Spruance & P. Van Voorhis (2004). "Anxiety in Correctional Settings: It's Time for Another Look." *Federal Probation*, 68(1), 43-50

Listwan, S., J. Sundt, A. Holsinger & E. Latessa (2003). "The Effect of Drug Court Programming on Recidivism: the Cincinnati Experience." *Crime & Delinquency*, 49(3), 389-411.

Little, G. & K. Robinson (1986). *Juvenile MRT: How to Escape Your Prison*. Memphis. TN: Eagle Wing Books.

Little, K. & E. Schneidman (1959). "Congruencies among Interpretations of Psychological Test and Anamnestic Data." *Psychological Monographs: General and Applied*, 73, 1-42.

Loeber, R. & T. Dishion (1983). "Early Predictors of Male Delinquency." *Psychological Bulletin*, 94, 68-99.

Loeber, R. & D. Hay (1994). "Developmental Approaches to Aggression and Conduct Problems." In M. Rutter & D. Hay (eds.), *Development Through Life: A Handbook for Clinicians*. Oxford, UK: Blackwell Scientific Publications.

Loevinger, J. (1966). "The Meaning and Measurement of Ego Development." *American Psychologist*, 21, 195-217.

Loftus, E. & J. Palmer (1974). "Reconstruction of Automobile Destruction: An Example of the Interaction Between Language and Memory." *Journal of Verbal Learning and Verbal Behavior*, 13, 585-589.

Long, N. & W. Morse (1995). *Conflict in the Classroom*. Austin, TX: Pro-Ed.

Lösel, F. (1995). "Increasing Consensus in the Evaluation of Offender Rehabilitation? Lessons from Recent Research Synthesis." *Psychology, Crime & Law*, 2, 19-39.

Lowenkamp, C. (2004). "A Program-Level Analysis of the Relationship Between Correctional Program Integrity and Treatment Effectiveness." Unpublished doctoral dissertation. Cincinnati, OH: University of Cincinnati.

Lowenkamp, C. & E. Latessa (2002). *Evaluation of Ohio's Community-Based Correctional Facilities and Halfway House Programs*. Cincinnati, OH: University of Cincinnati.

Lowenkamp, C., A. Holsinger & E. Latessa (2002). *Are Drug Courts Effective? A Meta-Analytic Review*. Cincinnati, OH: University of Cincinnati.

Lutzker, J. (1990). "Behavioral Treatment of Child Neglect." *Behavior Modification*, 14, 301-315.

Lynch, J. & W. Sabol (2001). *Prisoner Reentry in Perspective*. Washington, DC: Urban Institute.

MacCoun, R. (1998). "Toward a Psychology of Harm Reduction." *American Psychologist*, 53, 1199-1208.

MacKenzie, D. (1989). "Prison Classification: The Management and Psychological Perspectives." In L. Goodstein & D. MacKenzie (eds.), *The American Prison: Issues in Research and Policy*. New York: Plenum Press.

Maletzky, B. (1980). "Assisted Covert Sensitization." In D. Cox & R. Daitzman (eds.), *Exhibitionism: Description, Assessment, and Treatment*. New York: Garland.

_____ (1991). *Treating the Sexual Offender*. Newbury Park, CA: Sage Publications.

Mann, B., C. Borduin, S. Henggeler & D. Blaske (1990). "An Investigation of Systemic Conceptualizations of Parent-Child Coalitions and Symptom Change." *Journal of Consulting and Clinical Psychology*, 58, 336-344.

Marion, T. & K. Coleman (1991). "Recovery Issues and Treatment Resources." In D. Daly & M. Raskin (eds.), *Treating the Chemically Dependent and Their Families*. Newbury Park, CA: Sage Publications.

Marlatt, G. (1985). "Cognitive Factors in the Relapse Process." In G. Marlatt & J. Gordon (eds.), *Relapse Prevention: Maintenance Strategies in the Treatment of Addictive Behaviors*. New York: Guilford Publications.

Marlatt, G. & K. Barrett (1994). "Relapse Prevention." In M. Galanter & H. Kleber (eds.), *Textbook of Substance Abuse Treatment*. Washington, DC: American Psychiatric Press, Inc.

Marlatt, G. & J. Gordon (eds.) (1985). *Relapse Prevention: Maintenance Strategies in the Treatment of Addictive Behaviors*. New York: Guilford Publications.

Marlatt, G. & K. Witkiewitz (2002). "Harm Reduction Approaches to Alcohol Use: Health Promotion, Prevention, and Treatment." *Addictive Behaviors*, 27(6), 867-886.

Marlatt, G., A. Blume & G. Parks (2001). "Integrating Harm Reduction Therapy and Traditional Substance Abuse Treatment." *Journal of Psychoactive Drugs*, 33(10, 13-21.

Marques, J., D. Day, C. Nelson & M. West (1994). "Effects of Cognitive-Behavioral Treatment of Sex Offender Recidivism: Preliminary Results of a Longitudinal Study." *Criminal Justice and Behavior*, 21, 28-54.

Marshall, W. (1996). "Assessment, Treatment, and Theorizing about Sex Offenders." *Criminal Justice and Behavior*, 23, 162-199.

Marshall, W. & H. Barbaree (1988). "The Long-Term Evaluation of a Cognitive-Behavioral Treatment Program for Child Molesters." *Behavior Research and Therapy*, 26, 499-511.

Martin, S., C. Butzin, C. Saum & J. Inciardi (1999). "Three-year Outcomes of Therapeutic Community Treatment for Drug-involved Offenders in Delaware." *The Prison Journal*, 79(3), 294-320.

Martinson, R. (1974). "What Works? Questions and Answers About Prison Reform." *The Public Interest*, 35, 22-54.

Masters, J., T. Burish, S. Hollon & D. Rimm (1987). *Behavior Therapy: Techniques and Empirical Findings*, Third Edition. New York: Harcourt Brace Jovanovich.

Mathis, J. & M. Collins (1970a). "Mandatory Group Therapy for Exhibitionists." *American Journal of Psychiatry*, 126, 1162-1167.

Mathis, J. & M. Collins (1970b). "Progressive Phases in the Group Therapy of Exhibitionists." *International Journal of Group Psychotherapy*, 20, 163-169.

Matson, J. & T. DiLorenzo (1984). *Punishment and its Alternatives: A New Perspective for Behavior Modification*. New York: Springer Publishing Company.

Maultsby, M. (1975). "Rational Behavior Therapy for Acting-Out Adolescents." *Social Casework*, 56, 35-43.

Maxwell, J.A. (1996). *Qualitative Research Design: An Interactive Approach*. Thousand Oaks, CA: Sage Publications.

McCawley, A. (1965). "Exhibitionism and Acting-Out." *Comprehensive Psychiatry*, 6, 396-409.

McClellan, D., D. Farabee & B. Crouch (1997). "Early Victimization, Drug Use, and Criminality." *Criminal Justice and Behavior*, 24, 455-476.

McCollum, A. (1994). "Prison College Programs." *The Prison Journal*, 74, 15-51.

McCrady, B. (1990). "The Marital Relationship and Alcoholism." In R. Collins, K. Leonard & J. Searles (eds.), *Alcohol and the Family: Research and Clinical Practice*. New York: Guilford Publications.

McCrady, S. & S. Irving (1989). "Self-Help Groups." In R. Hester & W. Miller (eds.), *Handbook of Alcoholism Treatment Approaches*. New York: Pergamon.

McGuire, J. (2002). "Evidence-based Programming Today." Draft Paper for the International Community Corrections Association (ICCA) Annual Conference 2002, Boston, MA.

McLaren, L. (1988). "Fostering Mother-Child Relationships." *Child Welfare*, 67, 343-365.

McLellan, A., H. Kushner, D. Metzger & F. Peters (1992). "Fifth Edition of the Addictions Severity Index." *Journal of Substance Abuse Treatment*, 9, 199-213.

McLellan, A., L. Luborski, J. Cacciola, J. Griffith, F. Evans, H. Barr & C. O'Brien (1985). "New Data from the Addiction Severity Index: Reliability and Validity in Three Centers." *Journal of Nervous and Mental Disease*, 173, 412-423.

McMackin, R.A., R. Tansi & J. LaFratta (2004). "Recidivism among Juvenile Offenders over Periods Ranging from One to Twenty Years Following Residential Treatment." *Journal of Offender Rehabilitation*, 38, 1-15.

Meehl, P. (1954). *Clinical versus Statistical Prediction*. Minneapolis, MN: University of Minnesota Press.

Meeks, D. & C. Kelly (1970). "Family Therapy with the Families of Recovering Alcoholics." *Quarterly Journal of Studies on Alcohol*, 31, 399-413.

Megargee, E. & M. Bohn (1979). *Classifying Criminal Offenders: A New System Based on the MMPI*. Beverly Hills, CA: Sage Publications.

Megargee, E., J. Carbonnell, M. Bohn & G. Sliger (2001). *Classifying Criminal Offenders with the MMPI-2: The Megargee System*. Minneapolis, MN: University of Minnesota Press.

Meichenbaum, D. (1977). *Cognitive-Behavioral Modification: An Integrative Approach*. New York: Plenum Press.

Meichenbaum, D. & J. Deffenbacher (1988). "Stress Inoculation Training." *The Counseling Psychologist*, 16, 69-90.

Meichenbaum, D. & M. Jaremko (1982). *Stress Prevention and Management: A Cognitive-Behavioral Approach*. New York: Plenum Press.

Melnick, M. (1984). "Skills through Drama." *Journal of Psychotherapy, Psychodrama and Sociometry*, 37, 104-116.

Metz, M.E. & S.P. Sawyer (2003). "Treating Sexual Dysfunction in Sex Offenders." *Journal of Sex and Marital Therapy*, 30, 185-197.

Milhorn, T.H. (1990). *Chemical Dependence*. New York: Springer-Verlag.

Miller, J. (1976). *Toward a New Psychology of Women*. Boston, MA: Beacon Press.

Miller, G. (1985). *The Substance Abuse Subtle Screening Inventory Manual*. Bloomington, IN: SASSI Institute.

Miller, G., N. Andrews, P. Wilbourne & M. Bennett (1998). "A Wealth of Alternatives: Effective Treatments for Alcohol Problems." In W. Miller & N. Heather (eds.), *Treating Addictive Behaviors: Processes of Change,* Second Edition, pp. 203-216. New York: Plenum Press.

Miller, M. (1960). "Psychodrama in the Treatment Program of a Juvenile Court." *Journal of Criminal Law, Criminology and Police Science*, 50, 453-459.

Miller, W., J. Brown, T. Simpson, N. Handmaker, T. Bien, L. Luckie, H. Montgomery, R. Hester & J. Tonigan (1995). "What Works? A Methodological Analysis of the Alcohol Treatment Outcome Literature." In R. Hester & W. Miller (eds.), *Handbook of Alcoholism Treatment Approaches*, Second Edition. Boston, MA: Allyn & Bacon.

Miller, W. & R. Hester (1995). "Treatment for Alcohol Problems: Toward an Informed Eclecticism." In R. Hester & W. Miller (eds.), *Handbook of Alcoholism Treatment Approaches*, Second Edition. Boston, MA: Allyn & Bacon.

Miller, W., R. Meyers & S. Hiller-Sturmhofel (1999). "The Community Reinforcement Approach." *Alcohol Research and Health*, 23(2), 116-120/

Miller, W. & S. Rollnick (2002). *Motivational Interviewing: Preparing People for Change,* Second Edition. New York, NY: Guilford Press.

Miller, W. & J. Tonigan (1996). "Assessing Drinker's Motivation for Change: The Stages of Change Readiness and Treatment Eagerness Scale (SOCRATES)." *Psychology of Addictive Behaviors*, 10, 81-89.

Millon, T. (1997). *Millon Clinical Multiaxial Inventory III Manual*. Minneapolis, MN: National Computer Systems.

———— (1998). *Millon Clinical Multiaxial Inventory III (MCMI-III) Corrections Report*. Minnetonka, MN: NCS.

Minuchin, P. (1985). "Families and Individual Development: Provocations from the Field of Family Therapy." *Child Development*, 56, 289-305.

Minuchin, P., J. Colapinto & S. Minuchin (1998). *Working With Families of the Poor*. New York, NY: Guilford Press.

Minuchin, S. (1974). *Families and Family Therapy*. Cambridge, MA: Harvard University Press.

Minuchin, S. & H. Fishman (1981). *Family Therapy Techniques*. Cambridge, MA: Harvard University Press.

Minuchin S., B. Rosman & L. Baker (1978). *Psychosomatic Families: Anorexia Nervosa in Context*. Cambridge, MA: Harvard University Press.

Mitchell, C. & J. Egan (1995). *Quality of Instruction Inventory*. Boston, MA: Department of Corrections, Program Services Division.

Monahan, J. (1980). *Who Is the Client?* Washington, DC: American Psychological Association.

Monti, P., D. Rohsenow, S. Colby & D. Abrams (1995). "Coping and Social Skills Training." In R. Hester & W. Miller (eds.), *Handbook of Alcoholism Treatment Approaches*, Second Edition. Boston, MA: Allyn & Bacon.

Morash, M., T. Bynum & B. Koons (1998). *Women Offenders: Programming Needs and Promising Approaches*. Washington, DC: National Institute of Justice.

Moreno, J. (1934). *Who Shall Survive?* Washington, DC: Nervous and Mental Disease Publishing Co.

Morgan, R. (2003). "Basic Mental Health Services: Services and Issues." In T.J. Fagan & R.K. Ax (eds.), *Correctional Mental Health Handbook.* Thousand Oaks, CA: Sage.

Mowatt, D., J. Van Deusen. & D. Wilson (1985). "Family Therapy and the Drug Using Offender." *Federal Probation*, 49, 28-34.

Mumala, C. (1999). *Substance Abuse and Treatment: State and Federal Prisoners.* Washington, DC: Bureau of Justice Statistics.

_____ (2000). *Incarcerated Parents and Their Children.* Washington, DC: Bureau of Justice Statistics.

Murphy, W. (1990). "Assessment and Modification of Cognitive Distortions in Sex Offenders." In W. Marshall, D. Laws & H. Barbaree (eds.), *Handbook of Sexual Assault Issues, Theories and Treatment of the Offender.* New York, NY: Plenum Press.

Murphy, W., E. Coleman & M. Haynes (1983). "Treatment and Evaluation Issues with the Mentally Retarded Sex Offender." In J. Greer & I. Stuart (eds.), *The Sexual Aggressor: Current Perspectives on Treatment.* New York: Van Nostrand Reinhold Co.

Myers, L. & D. Jackson (2002). *Reality Therapy and Choice Theory: Managing Behavior for Today, Developing Skills for Tomorrow.* Lanham, MD: American Correctional Association.

Nagayama Hall, G. (1995). "Sexual Offender Recidivism Revisited: A Meta-Analysis of Recent Treatment Strategies." *Journal of Consulting and Clinical Psychology*, 63, 802-809.

Napier, A. & C. Whitaker (1980). *The Family Crucible.* New York: Bantam Books.

National Institute of Correctional Education (2004). *The United Nations Economic and Social Council Resolution 20.* Retrieved January 27, 2004, from the National Institute of Correctional Education Web site. http://www.iup.edu/nice.

National Institute of Corrections (1979). *Classification Instruments for Criminal Justice Decisions, Volume 3: Institutional Custody.* Washington, DC: National Institute of Corrections.

Nelson, K. (1991). "Populations and Outcomes in Five Family Preservation Programs." In K. Wells & D. Biegel (eds.), *Family Preservation Services: Research and Evaluation.* Newbury Park, CA: Sage Publications.

Nelson, M., P. Deess & C. Allen (1999). *The First Month Out: Post-Incarceration Experiences in New York City.* New York: Vera Institute of Justice.

Nesovic, A. (2003). "Psychometric Evaluation of the Correctional Program Assessment Inventory." *Dissertation Abstracts International*, 64 (09), 4674B. (UMI No. AAT NQ 83525).

Nichols, M. & R. Schwartz (1998). *Family Therapy: Concepts and Methods*, Fourth Edition. Needham Heights, MA: Allyn & Bacon.

Nolley, D., L. Muccigrosso & E. Zigman (1996). "Treatment Success with Mentally Retarded Sex Offenders." In E. Coleman, S. Dwyer & N. Pallone (eds.), *Sex Offender Treatment.* Binghamton, NY: Haworth.

Novaco, R. (1979). "The Cognitive Regulation of Anger and Stress." In P. Kendall & S. Hillon (eds.), *Cognitive-Behavioral Interventions: Theory, Research and Procedures.* New York: Academic Press.

Nurco, D., T. Kinlock & T. Hanlon (1993). "Drug Abuse Treatment in the United States: Nature, Status, and New Directions." Paper presented at the Medical and Surgical Faculty of Maryland 4th Annual Conference on Addiction, December.

O'Connell, M., E. Leberg & C. Donaldson (1990). *Working with Sex Offenders: Guidelines for Therapist Selection*. Newbury Park, CA: Sage Publications.

O'Farrell, T. (1995). "Marital and Family Therapy." In R. Hester & W. Miller (eds.), *Handbook of Alcoholism Treatment Approaches, Second Edition*. Boston, MA: Allyn & Bacon.

O'Leary, K. & G. Wilson (1975). *Behavior Therapy*. Englewood Cliffs, NJ: Prentice-Hall.

Olson, D., C. Russell & D. Sprenkle (1980). "Marital and Family Therapy: A Decade Review." *Journal of Marriage and the Family*, 42, 973-993.

Palmer, T. (1974). "The Youth Authority's Community Treatment Project." *Federal Probation*, 38, 3-14.

———— (1978). *Correctional Intervention and Research*. Lexington, MA: D.C. Heath.

———— (1992). *The Re-emergence of Correctional Intervention*. Newbury Park, CA: Sage Publications.

———— (1994). "Issues in Growth-Centered Intervention with Serious Juvenile Offenders." *Legal Studies Forum*, 18, 263-298.

———— (2002). *Individualized Intervention with Young Multiple Offenders: The California Community Treatment Project*. Hampton, CT: Garland Press.

Pan, H., F. Scarpitti, J. Inciardi & D. Lockwood (1993). "Some Considerations on Therapeutic Communities in Corrections." In J. Inciardi (ed.), *Drug Treatment and Criminal Justice*. Newbury Park, CA: Sage Publications.

Pardeck, J. (1989). "Family Therapy as a Treatment Approach to Child Abuse." *Family Therapy*, 16, 113-120.

Parent, D. & L. Barnett (2003). *Transition from Prison to Community Initiative*. Washington, DC: U.S. Department of Justice, National Institute of Corrections.

Parkinson, A., I. Dulfano & C. Nink (2003). *Removing Barriers: Research-based Strategies for Teaching Those Who Learn Differently*. Centerville, UT: Management and Training Corporation Institute.

Parks, G., G. Marlatt & B. Anderson (2001). "Cognitive-Behavioral Alcohol Treatment." In H. Nick, T. Peters et al., (eds.), *International Handbook of Alcohol Dependence and Problems*. New York, NY: John Wiley & Sons.

Patterson, G. (1974). "Intervention for Boys with Conduct Problems: Multiple Settings, Treatments, and Criteria." *Journal of Consulting and Clinical Psychology*, 42, 471-481.

———— (1982). *A Social Learning Approach: Coercive Family Process*. Eugene, OR: Castalia.

Patterson, G., P. Chamberlain & J. Reid (1982). "A Comparative Evaluation of a Parent-Training Program." *Behavior Therapy*, 13, 638-650.

Patterson, G. & T. Dishion (1985). "Contributions of Families and Peers to Delinquency." *Criminology*, 23, 63-79.

Patterson, G., T. Dishion & P. Chamberlain (1993). "Outcomes and Methodological Issues Relating to Treatment of Antisocial Children." In T. Giles (ed.), *Handbook of Effective Psychotherapy*. New York: Plenum.

Patterson, G. & M. Fleischman (1979). "Maintenance of Treatment Effects: Some Considerations Concerning Family Systems and Follow-Up Data." *Behavior Therapy*, 10, 168-185.

Patterson, G. & M. Gullion (1976). *Living with Children: New Methods for Parents and Teachers*. Champaign, IL: Research Press.

Patterson, G., J. Reid & T. Dishion (1992). *Antisocial Boys*. Eugene, OR: Castalia.

Pavlov, I. (1927). *Conditioned Reflexes: An Investigation of the Physiological Activity of the Cerebral Cortex*. G. Anrep (trans.). London, UK: Lawrence & Wishart.

Pearson, F. & D. Lipton (1999). "A Meta-Analytic Review of the Effectiveness of Corrections-based Treatments for Drug Abuse." *Prison Journal*, 79(4), 384-410.

Pearson, F., D. Lipton, C. Cleland & D. Yee (2002). "The Effects of Behavioral/Cognitive-Behavioral Programs on Recidivism." *Crime and Delinquency*, 48(3), 476-496.

Pelissier, M., G. Gaes, W. Rhodes, S. Camp, J. O'Neil, S. Wallace & W. Saylor (1998). *TRIAD Drug Treatment Evaluation Project Six-Month Interim Report*. Washington, DC: Federal Bureau of Prisons, Office of Research and Evaluation.

Peters, R. (1993). "Substance Abuse Services in Jails and Prisons." *Law and Psychology Review*, 17, 85-116.

Peters, R., A. Haas & W. Hunt (2001). "Treatment 'Dosage' Effects in Drug Court Programs." In J. Hennessy & N. Pallone, (eds.), *Drug Courts in Operation*. New York, NY: Haworth Press.

Peters, R., W. Kearns, M. Murrin, A. Dolente & R. May (1993). "Examining the Effectiveness of In-Jail Substance Abuse Treatment." *Journal of Offender Rehabilitation*, 19, 1-39.

Peters, R. & C. Matthews (2003). "Substance Abuse Treatment Programs in Prisons and Jails." In T.J. Fagan & R.K. Ax (eds.), *Correctional Mental Health Handbook*. Thousand Oaks, CA: Sage.

Peters, R., A. Strozier, M. Murrin & W. Kearns (1997). "Treatment of Substance-Abusing Jail Inmates: Examination of Gender Differences." *Journal of Substance Abuse Treatment*, 14, 339-349.

Petersilia, J. (2003). *When Prisoners Come Home: Parole and Prisoner Reentry*. Oxford: Oxford University Press, Inc.

Peyton, E. & R. Gossweiler (2001). *Treatment Services in Adult Drug Courts: Report on the 1999 National Drug Court Treatment Survey*. Washington, DC: National Institute of Justice.

Petrik, N., L. Gildersleeve-High, J. McEllistrem & L. Subotnik (1994). "The Reduction of Male Abusiveness as a Result of Treatment: Reality or Myth?" *Journal of Family Violence*, 9, 307-316.

Phipps, P., K. Korinek, S. Aos & R. Lieb (1999). *Research Findings on Adult Corrections' Programs: A Review* (Doc# 99-01-1203). Olympia, WA: Washington States Institute for Public Policy.

Phillips, E., E. Phillips, D. Fixsen & M. Wolf (1973). "Achievement Place: Behavior Shaping Works for Delinquents." *Psychology Today*, 6, 75-79.

Piaget, J. (1948). *The Moral Judgment of the Child*. Glencoe, IL: The Free Press.

Polansky, N., M. Chalmers, D. Williams & E. Buttenwieser (1981). *Damaged Parents: An Anatomy of Child Neglect*. Chicago, IL: University of Chicago Press.

Pollock, J.M. (1998). *Counseling Women in Prison*. Thousand Oaks, CA: Sage.

Prendergast, M., D. Anglin & J. Wellisch (1995). "Treatment of Drug-Abusing Offenders Under Community Supervision." *Federal Probation*, 59, 66-75.

Prendergast, M., E. Hall, H. Wexler, G. Melnick & Y. Cao (2004). "Amity Prison-Based Therapeutic Community: 5-Year Outcomes." *The Prison Journal*, 84, 36-60.

Prochaska, J. & C. DiClemente (1986). "Toward a Comprehensive Model of Change." In W. Miller & N. Heather (eds.), *Treating Addictive Behaviors: Processes of Change*. New York: Plenum.

Project MATCH Research Group (1997). "Matching Alcoholism Treatment to Client Heterogeneity: Project MATCH Post-treatment Drinking Outcomes." *Journal of Studies on Alcohol*, 58, 7-29.

Purkiss, M., M. Kifer, C. Hemmens & V. Burton (2003). "Probation Officer Functions—A Statutory Analysis." *Federal Probation*, 67 (1), 12-24.

Quay, H. (1983). *Technical Manual for the Behavioral Classification System for Adult Offenders*. Washington, DC: U.S. Department of Justice.

————— (1984). *Managing Adult Inmates: Classification for Housing and Program Assignments*. College Park, MD: American Correctional Association.

Quay, H. & R. Parsons (1972). *The Differential Behavioral Classification of the Juvenile Offender*. Washington, DC: U.S. Department of Justice.

Quinsey, V., G. Harris, M. Rice & M. LaLumiere (1993). "Assessing Treatment Efficacy on Outcome Studies of Sex Offenders." *Journal of Interpersonal Violence*, 10, 85-105.

Quinsey, V. & W. Marshall (1983). "Procedures for Reducing Inappropriate Sexual Arousal: An Evaluation Review." In J. Greer & I. Stuart (eds.), *The Sexual Aggressor: Current Perspectives on Treatment*. New York: Van Nostrand Reinhold Co.

Randall, J., S. Henggeler, P. Cunningham, M. Rowland & C. Swenson (2001). "Adapting Multisystemic Therapy to Treat Adolescent Substance Abuse More Effectively." *Cognitive and Behavioral Practice*, 8, 359-366.

Raymond, M. (1956). "Case of Fetishism Treated by Aversion Therapy." *British Medical Journal*, 2, 854-857.

Redl, F. & H. Toch (1979). "The Psychoanalytic Perspective." In H. Toch (ed.), *Psychology of Crime and Criminal Justice*. New York: Holt, Rinehart & Winston.

Redl, F. & D. Wineman (1951). *Children Who Hate*. New York: The Free Press.

Reid, J., G. Patterson & J. Snyder (eds.) (2003). *Antisocial Behavior in Children and Adolescents: A Developmental Analysis and Model for Intervention*. Washington, DC: American Psychological Association.

Reitsma-Street, M. & A. Leschied (1988). "The Conceptual Level Matching Model in Corrections." *Criminal Justice and Behavior*, 15, 92-108.

Revised Beta Examination, Second Edition (1978). Cleveland, OH: Psychological Corporation.

Rimmele, D., W. Miller & M. Dougher (1989). "Aversion Therapies." In R. Hester & W. Miller (eds.), *Handbook of Alcoholism Treatment Alternatives: Effective Alternatives*. Elmsford, NY: Pergamon Press.

Ritchie, G. (1968). "The Use of Hypnosis in a Case of Exhibitionism." *Psychotherapy*, 5, 40-43.

Rogers, C. (1951). *Client-centered Therapy*. Boston, MA: Houghton-Mifflin.

Rosenthal, R. & M. DiMatteo (2001). "Meta-analysis Recent Developments in Quantitative Methods for Literature Reviews." *Annual Review of Psychology*, 52, 59-82.

Ross, R. & E. Fabiano (1985). *Time to Think: A Cognitive Model of Delinquency Prevention and Offender Rehabilitation*. Johnson City, TN: Institute of Social Science and Arts.

Ross, R., E. Fabiano & R. Ross (1989). *Reasoning and Rehabilitation: A Handbook for Teaching Cognitive Skills*. Ottawa, Ontario: Flix Desktop Services.

Rubins, J. (1968). "The Neurotic Personality and Certain Sexual Perversions." *Contemporary Psychoanalysis*, 4, 53-72.

Russell, C., D. Olson, D. Sprenkle & R. Atilano (1983). "From Family Symptom to Family System: Review of Family Therapy Research." *The American Journal of Family Therapy*, 11, 3-14.

Rutan, J. & W. Stone (1984). *Psychodramatic Group Psychotherapy*. Lexington, MA: Collamore.

Ryan, T. (1995). "Correctional Education: Past is Prologue to the Future." *Journal of Correctional Education*, 46 (2), 60-65.

Samenow, S. (1984). *Inside the Criminal Mind*. New York, NY: Times Books.

_____ (1989). *Before It's Too Late*. New York, NY: Times Books.

_____ (2001). "Understanding the Criminal Mind: A Phenomenological Approach." *Journal of Psychiatry & Law*, 29(3), 275-293.

Sameroff, A. (1989). "Commentary: General Systems and the Regulation of Development." In M. Gunnar & E. Thelen (eds.), *Systems and Development: The Minnesota Symposia on Child Psychology*. Hillsdale, NJ: Lawrence Erlbaum.

Sampson, R. & J. Laub (1993). *Crime in the Making: Pathways and Turning Points through Life*. Cambridge, MA: Harvard University Press.

Santsaver, H. (1975). "Behavior Modification Paired with TA." *Transactional Analysis Journal*, 5, 137-138.

Satir, V. (1967). *Conjoint Family Therapy*. Palo Alto, CA: Science and Behavior Books.

_____ (1972). *Peoplemaking*. Palo Alto, CA: Science and Behavior Books.

Saunders, D. (1996). "Feminist-Cognitive-Behavioral and Process-Psychodynamic Treatments for Men Who Batter: Interaction of Abuser Traits and Treatment Models." *Violence and Victims*, 11, 393-414.

Saunders, D. & S. Azar (1989). "Treatment Programs for Family Violence." In L. Ohlin & M. Tonry (eds.), *Family Violence*. Chicago, IL: University of Chicago Press.

Schoenfeld, C. (1971). "A Psychoanalytic Theory of Juvenile Delinquency." *Crime & Delinquency*, 17, 469-480.

Schoenwald, S. & S. Henggeler (1997). "Combining Effective Treatment Strategies with Family-Preservation Models of Service Delivery." In R. Illback & C. Cobb (eds.), *Integrated Services for Children and Families: Opportunities for Psychological Practice*. Washington, DC: American Psychological Association.

Schorsch, E., G. Galedary, A. Haag, M. Hauch & H. Lohse (1990). *Sex Offenders: Dynamics and Psychotherapeutic Strategies*. New York: Springer-Verlag.

Schrink, J. (1976). "Strategy for Preparing Correctional Reports." *Federal Probation*, 40, 33-40.

Schrumski, T., C. Feldman, D. Harvey & M. Holiman (1984). "A Comparative Evaluation of Group Treatments in an Adult Correctional Facility." *Journal of Group Psychotherapy, Psychodrama and Sociometry*, 36, 133-147.

Schuckit, M. (1995). *Drug and Alcohol Abuse*. New York: Plenum Medical Book Co.

Schwartz, R.K. (2003). "Services for Special Populations." In R.K. Schwartz (ed.), *Correctional Psychology: Practice, Programming, and Administration*. Kingston, NJ: Civic Research Institute.

Scott, T., C. Nelson, C. Liaupsin, K. Jolivette, C. Christle & M. Riney (2002). "Addressing the Needs of At-Risk and Adjudicated Youth through Positive Behavior Support: Effective Prevention Practices." *Education and Treatment of Children*, 25(4), 532-551.

Seabloom, W., M. Seabloom, E. Seabloom, R. Barron & S. Hendrickson (2003). "A 14- to 24-year Longitudinal Study of a Comprehensive Sexual Health Model Treatment Program for Adolescent Sex Offenders." *International Journal of Offender Therapy and Comparative Criminology*, 47, 468-481.

Selzer, M. (1971). "The Michigan Alcoholism Screening Test: The Quest for a New Diagnostic Instrument." *American Journal of Psychiatry*, 127(12), 1653-1658.

Serin, R. & S. Kennedy (1997). *Treatment Readiness and Responsivity: Contributing to Effective Correctional Programming*. Ottawa, ON: Correctional Services of Canada.

Serketich, W. & J. Dumas (1996). "The Effectiveness of Behavioral Parent Training to Modify Antisocial Behavior in Children: A Meta-Analysis." *Behavioral Therapy*, 27, 171-186.

Shadish, W., L. Montgomery, P. Wilson, M. Wilson, I. Bright & T. Okwumabua (1993). "Effects of Family and Marital Psychotherapies: A Meta-Analysis." *Journal of Consulting and Clinical Psychology*, 61, 992-1002.

Sherman, L., D. Gottfredson, D. MacKenzie, J. Eck, P. Reuter & S. Bushway (1997). *Preventing Crime: What Works, What Doesn't, What's Promising*. Washington, DC: National Institute of Justice, U.S. Department of Justice.

Shipley, W. (1983). *Shipley Institute of Living Scale*. Los Angeles, CA: Western Psychological Press.

Shore, J. (1994). "Community-Based Treatment." In M. Galanter & H. Kleber (eds.), *Textbook of Substance Abuse Treatment*. Washington, DC: American Psychiatric Press, Inc.

Silverman, K., C. Wong, A. Umbricht-Schneiter, I. Montoya, C. Schuster & K. Preston (1998). "Broad Beneficial Effects of Cocaine Abstinence Reinforcement Among Methadone Patients." *Journal of Consulting and Clinical Psychology*, 66(5), 811-824.

Simourd, D. (1997). "Criminal Sentiments Scale-Modified and Pride in Delinquency: Psychometric Properties and Construct Validity of Two Measures of Criminal Attitudes." *Criminal Justice and Behavior, 24,* 52-70.

_____ (2004). "Use of Dynamic Risk/Need Assessment Instruments Among Long-Term Incarcerated Offenders." *Criminal Justice and Behavior*, 31(3), 306-323.

Skinner, B. (1953). *Science and Human Behavior*. New York: Macmillan.

_____ (1971). *Beyond Freedom & Dignity*. New York: Knopf.

Smith, C., B. Algozzine, R. Schmid & T. Hennly (1990). "Prison Adjustment of Youthful Inmates with Mental Retardation." *Mental Retardation*, 28, 177-181.

Smith, P., C. Goggin & P. Gendreau (2002). "The Effects of Prison Sentences and Intermediate Sanctions on Recidivism: General Effects and Individual Differences." *A Report to the Corrections Research Branch*. Ottawa, Ontario: Solicitor General of Canada.

Smith, R.R. & V.S. Lombardo (2001). "Cognitive Interventions for Dealing with Domestic Violence." In B.K. Welo (ed.), *Tough Customers: Counseling Unwilling Clients*. Lanham, MD: American Correctional Association.

Smith, J. & R. Meyers (1995). "The Community Reinforcement Approach." In R. Hester & W. Miller (eds.), *Handbook of Alcoholism Treatment Approaches*, Second Edition. Boston, MA: Allyn & Bacon.

Sperber, K. (2004). *Potential Applications of an Existing Offender Typology to Child Molesting Behaviors*. Unpublished doctoral dissertation. Cincinnati, OH: University of Cincinnati.

Spiegler, M. & D. Guevremont (1993). *Contemporary Behavior Therapy*, Second Edition. Pacific Grove, CA: Brooks/Cole.

Spiegler, M. & D. Guevremont (1998). *Contemporary Behavior Therapy*, Third Edition. Pacific Grove, CA: Brooks/Cole.

Spiropoulis, G., L. Spruance, P. Van Voorhis & M. Schmitt (forthcoming). "Pathfinders vs. Problem Solving: Comparative Effects of Cognitive-Behavioral Programs for Men and Women Offenders. *Journal of Offender Rehabilitation*.

Stanchfield, P. (2001). "Clarifying the Therapist's Role in the Treatment of the Resistant Sex Offender." In B.K. Welo (ed.), *Tough Customers: Counseling Unwilling Clients*. Lanham, MD: American Correctional Association.

Stanton, M. (1994). "Family Therapy for Drug Abuse." Paper Presented at the National Conference on Marital and Family Therapy Outcome and Process Research: State of the Science, Philadelphia, PA.

Stanton, M., T. Todd & Associates. (1982). *The Family Therapy of Drug Abuse and Addiction*. New York: Guilford Publications.

Stein, D. & E. Smith (1990). "The 'Rest' Program: A New Treatment System for the Oppositional Defiant Adolescent." *Adolescence*, 25, 891-904.

Steinem, G. (1994). *Moving Beyond Words*. New York, NY: Simon & Schuster.

Steinglass, P. (1994). "Family Therapy." In M. Galanter & H. Kleber (eds.), *Textbook of Substance Abuse Treatment*. Washington, DC: American Psychiatric Press, Inc.

Steinglass, P., L. Bennett, S. Wolin & D. Reiss (1987). *The Alcoholic Family*. New York: Basic Books.

Steurer, S.J. & L.G. Smith (2003). *Education Reduces Crime: Three State Recidivism Study, Executive Summary*. Lanham, MD: Correctional Education Association.

Stierlin, H. (1977). *Psychoanalysis and Family Therapy*. New York: Jason Aronson.

Stith, S. & K. Rosen (1990). "Family Therapy for Spouse Abuse." In S. Stith, M. Williams & K. Rosen (eds.), *Violence Hits Home: Comprehensive Treatment Approaches to Domestic Violence*. New York: Springer Publishing Co.

Strordeur, R. & R. Stille (1989). *Ending Men's Violence Against Their Partners: One Road to Peace*. Thousand Oaks, CA: Sage Publications.

Stuart, R. (1971). "Behavioral Contracting Within Families of Delinquents." *Journal of Behavior Therapy and Experimental Psychiatry*, 2, 1-11.

Sue, D. & D. Sue (1990). *Counseling the Culturally Different*, Second Edition. New York: Wiley.

Sullivan, C., M. Grant & D. Grant (1957). "The Development of Interpersonal Maturity: An Application to Delinquency." *Psychiatry*, 20, 373-385.

Sullivan, H. (1953). *The Interpersonal Theory of Psychiatry*. New York, NY: Norton.

Sykes, G. (1958). *The Society of Captives*. Princeton, NJ: Princeton University Press.

Sykes, G. & D. Matza (1957). "Techniques of Neutralization: A Theory of Delinquency." *American Sociological Review*, 22, 664-670.

Szapocznik, J., J.W. Kurtines, F. Foote, A. Perez-Vidal & O. Hervis (1983). "Conjoint Versus One-person Family Therapy: Some Evidence for the Effectiveness of Conducting Family Therapy through One Person." *Journal of Consulting and Clinical Psychology*, 51, 889-899.

Szapocznik, J., A. Rio, E. Murray, R. Cohen, M. Scopetta, A. Rivas-Vazquez, O. Hervis, V. Posada & W. Kurtines (1989). "Structural Family Therapy Versus Psychodynamic Child Therapy for Problematic Hispanic Boys." *Journal of Consulting and Clinical Psychology*, 57, 571-578.

Taxman, F. & J. Bouffard (2002). "Assessing Therapeutic Integrity in Modified Therapeutic Communities for Drug-Involved Offenders." *Prison Journal*, 82(2), 189-212.

Taymans, J. & S. Parese (1998). *Problem Solving Skills for Offenders: A Social Cognitive Intervention*. Washington, DC: George Washington University.

Thornberry, T., A. Lizotte, M. Krohn, M. Farnsworth & S. Jang (1994). "Delinquent Peers, Beliefs, and Delinquent Behavior: A Longitudinal Test of Interactional Theory." *Criminology*, 94, 47-83.

Thorndike, E. (1913). *The Psychology of Learning (Educational Psychology, II)*. New York: Teachers College.

Truax, C., D. Wargo. & L. Silber (1966). "Effects of Group Psychotherapy with High Accurate Empathy and Nonpossessive Warmth upon Female Institutionalized Delinquents." *Journal of Abnormal Psychology*, 71, 267-274.

U.S. Bureau of Justice Statistics (1992). *Compendium of Federal Justice Statistics, 1989*. Washington, DC: U.S. Department of Justice.

U.S. General Accounting Office (1997). *Drug Courts: Overview of Growth, Characteristics and Results*. Washington, DC: U.S. General Accounting Office.

Van Dieten, M. (1998). "Applying the Principles of Effective Correctional Interventions." Presentation to NIC Workshop on Effective Interventions with High Risk Offenders, July, 1998.

_____ (1999). "Moving On: A Program for Criminal Justice Involved Women." Unpublished Manuscript.

Van Voorhis, P. (1987). "Correctional Effectiveness: The High Cost of Ignoring Success." *Federal Probation*, 51, 56-62.

_____ (1994). *Psychological Classification of the Adult Male Prison Inmate.* Albany, NY: SUNY Press.

Van Voorhis, P. & K. Brown (1996). *Risk Classification in the 1990s.* Washington, DC: U.S. Department of Justice, National Institute of Corrections.

Van Voorhis, P., F. Cullen & B. Applegate (1995). "Evaluating Interventions with Violent Offenders: A Guide for Practitioners and Policymakers." *Federal Probation*, 59, 17-28.

Van Voorhis, P., J. Pealer & G. Spiropoulis (2001). *Validation of the Offender Custody Classification and Needs Assessment Systems for Incarcerated Women Offenders in the Colorado Department of Corrections.* Cincinnati, OH: University of Cincinnati.

Van Voorhis, P. & L. Presser (2001). *Classification of Women Offenders: A National Assessment of Current Practices.* Washington, DC: U.S. Department of Justice, National Institute of Corrections.

Van Voorhis, P. & G. Spiropoulis (2003). *Evaluation of Adult Work-Release Services.* Cincinnati, OH: University of Cincinnati, Center for Criminal Justice Research.

Van Voorhis, P., L. Spruance, N. Ritchie, S. Listwan, R. Seabrook & J. Pealer (2002). *The Georgia Cognitive Skills Experiment: Outcome Evaluation, Phase II.* Cincinnati, OH: University of Cincinnati, Center for Criminal Justice Research.

van Wormer, K. (1988). "All-or-Nothing Thinking and Alcoholism: A Cognitive Approach." *Federal Probation*, 52, 28-33.

_____ (1999). "The Strengths Perspective: A Paradigm for Correctional Counseling." *Federal Probation*, 63 (1), 51-59.

_____ (2002). "Addictions and Women in the Criminal Justice System." In S. Straussner & S. Brown (eds.), *The Handbook of Addiction Treatment for Women.* San Francisco, CA: Jossey-Bass.

Vogel, E. & N. Bell (1960). "The Emotionally Disturbed Child as the Family Scapegoat." In N. Bell and E. Vogel (eds.), *The Family.* Glencoe, IL: The Free Press.

Vorrath, H. & L. Brentro (1985). *Positive Peer Culture*, Second Edition. Chicago, IL: Aldine.

Wallace, B. (1991). *Crack Cocaine: A Practical Treatment Approach for the Chemically Dependent.* New York: Brunner/Mazel.

Walsh, E. (2003). "Legal and Ethical Issues Related to the Mental Health Treatment of Incarcerated Persons." In R.K. Schwartz (ed.), *Correctional Psychology: Practice, Programming, and Administration.* New York, NY: John Wiley.

Walters, G. (1990). *The Criminal Lifestyle: Patterns of Serious Criminal Conduct.* Newbury Park, CA: Sage.

Walters, G.D. (1998). *Changing Lives of Crimes and Drugs: Intervening with the Substance Abusing Offender*. New York: John Wiley.

Walters, G.D. (2001). "Overcoming Offender Resistance to Abandoning a Criminal Lifestyle." In B.K. Welo (ed.), *Tough Customers: Counseling Unwilling Clients*. Lanham, MD: American Correctional Association.

Wanberg, K. (1993). *The Adult Substance Use Survey (ASUS)*. Arvada, CO: Center for Addictions Research and Evaluation.

_____ (1995). *The Life Situation Questionnaire*. Arvada, CO: Center for Addictions Research and Evaluation.

Wanberg, K. & H. Milkman (1993). *The Adult Self Assessment Questionnaire (AdSAQ)*. Arvada, CO: Center for Addictions Research and Evaluation.

Wanberg, K. & H. Milkman (1998). *Criminal Conduct and Substance Abuse Treatment: Strategies for Self-Improvement and Change*. Thousand Oaks, CA: Sage Publications.

Warren, M. (1971). "Classification of Offenders as an Aid to Efficient Management and Effective Treatment." *Journal of Criminal Law, Criminology and Police Science*, 62, 239-268.

_____ (1983). "Application of Interpersonal Maturity Theory to Offender Populations." In W. Laufer & J. Day (eds.), *Personality Theory, Moral Development, and Criminal Behavior*. Lexington, MA: Lexington Books.

Warren, M. & the Staff of the Community Treatment Project (1966). *Interpersonal Maturity Level Classification: Diagnosis and Treatment of Low, Middle, and High Maturity Delinquents*. Sacramento, CA: California Youth Authority.

Watson, J. (1916). "The Place of the Conditioned Reflex in Psychology." *Psychological Review*, 23, 89-116.

Wechsler, D. (1997). *WAIS-III Administration and Scoring Manual*. San Antonio, TX: Psychological Corp.

Welo, B.K. (2001). "Taking Care of Yourself in the Process: Counselor Self-Care in Brutal Environments." In B.K. Welo (ed.), *Tough Customers: Counseling Unwilling Clients*. Lanham, MD: American Correctional Association.

Westen, D. (1991). "Social Cognition and Object Relations." *Psychological Bulletin*, 109, 429-455.

Wexler, H. (1994). "Progress in Substance Abuse Treatment: A Five Year Report." *Journal of Drug Issues* 24(1-2), 349-360.

Wexler, H., G. DeLeon, D. Kressel & J. Peters (1999). "The Amity Prison TC Evaluation: Reincarceration Outcomes." *Criminal Justice and Behavior*, 26, 147-167.

Wexler, H. & D. Lipton (1993). "From Reform to Recovery Advances in Prison Drug Treatment." In J. Inciardi (ed.), *Drug Treatment and Criminal Justice*. Newbury Park, CA: Sage Publications.

Wexler, H., G. Melnick, L. Lowe & J. Peters (1999). "Three-Year Reincarceration Outcomes for Amity in-Prison Therapeutic Community and Aftercare in California." *Prison Journal*, 79, 321-336.

Whitaker, C. (1976). "The Family is a Four-Dimensional Relationship." In P. Guerin (ed.), *Family Therapy: Theory and Practice*. New York: Gardner Press.

White, T.W. (1999). *How to Identify Suicidal People: A Systematic Approach to Risk Assessment.* Philadelphia PA: Charles Press.

Whitehead, J. & S. Lab (1989). "A Response to 'Does Correctional Treatment Work?'" Unpublished paper.

Wickramasekera, I. (1968). "The Application of Learning Theory to the Treatment of a Case of Sexual Exhibitionism." *Psychotherapy*, 5, 108-112.

Wilson, D., L. Allen & D. MacKenzie (2000). "A Qualitative Review of Structures, Group-Oriented, Cognitive-Behavioral Programs for Offenders." Unpublished Manuscript, University of Maryland, College Park.

Wilson, D., C. Gallagher & D. MacKenzie (2000). "A Meta-Analysis of Corrections-Based Education, Vocation, and Work Programs for Adult Offenders." *Journal of Research in Crime and Delinquency* 37(4), 347-368.

Wilson, D., O. Mitchell & D. MacKenzie (2003). *A Systematic Review of Drug Court Effects on Recidivism.* Unpublished manuscript.

Wilson, J. (1987). "Strategic Opportunities for Delinquency Prevention." In J. Wilson & G. Loury (eds.), *From Children to Citizens.* New York: Springer-Verlag.

Winkler, G. (1992). "Assessing and Responding to Suicidal Jail Inmates." *Community Mental Health Journal*, 28, 317-326.

Wolf, M., C. Braukmann & K. Ramp (1987). "Serious Delinquent Behavior as Part of a Significantly Handicapping Condition: Cures and Supportive Environments." *Journal of Applied Behavior Analysis* 20(4), 347-359.

Wolpe, J. (1958). *Psychotherapy by Reciprocal Inhibition.* Palo Alto, CA: Stanford University Press.

Wright, K., T. Clear & P. Dickson (1984). "Universal Application of Probation Risk-Assessment Instruments: A Critique." *Criminology*, 33, 113-134.

Wrightsman, L. (1991). *Psychology and the Legal System.* Pacific Grove, CA: Brooks/Cole.

Wulach, J. (1983). "August Aichorn's Legacy: The Treatment of Narcissism in Criminals." *International Journal of Offender Therapy and Comparative Criminology*, 27, 226-234.

Wurmser, L. (1984). "The Role of Superego Conflicts in Substance Abuse and Their Treatment." *International Journal of Psychoanalytic Psychotherapy*, 10, 227-258.

Yablonsky, L. (1955). "Preparing Parolees for Essential Social Roles." *Group Psychotherapy*, 8, 38-40.

————— (1976). *Psychodrama.* New York: Basic Books.

Yalom, I. (1995). *The Theory and Practice of Group Psychotherapy,* Fourth Edition. New York: Basic Books.

Yochelson, S. & S. Samenow (1976). *The Criminal Personality, Vol. 1: A Profile for Change.* New York: Jason Aronson.

————— (1977). *The Criminal Personality: Vol. II. The Change Process.* New York: Jason Aronson.

Yonas, D. & T. Garland (1994). "Recognizing and Utilizing Ethnic and Cultural Diversity in Counseling Approaches." In P. Kratcoski (ed.), *Correctional Counseling and Treatment*, Third Edition. Prospect Heights, IL: Waveland Press, Inc.

Zager, I. (1988). "MMPI-Based Criminal Classification System: A Review, Current Status, and Future Directions." *Criminal Justice and Behavior*, 15, 39-57.

Zechnich, R. (1976). "Exhibitionism." *Transactional Analysis Journal*, 6, 307-310.

Zigler, E., C. Taussig & K. Black (1992). "Early Childhood Intervention: A Promising Preventative for Juvenile Delinquency." *American Psychologist*, 47, 997-1006.

Zimberg, S. (1994). "Individual Psychotherapy." In M. Galanter & H. Kleber (eds.), *Textbook of Substance Abuse Treatment*, Washington, DC: American Psychiatric Press, Inc.

Zuk, G. (1975). *Process and Practice in Family Therapy*. Haverford, CT: Psychology and Behavioral Science Books.

Zussman, R. (1989). "Forensic Evaluation of the Adolescent Sex Offender." *Forensic Reports*, 2, 25-45.

Name Index

Subject Index

Drugs, operant conditioning for treatment
   of abuse of, 73. *See also* Substance
   abuse; Substance dependent
DSM-IV-TR, 128
   defined, 117
   mental retardation, 120-122
   mood disorders, 118-119
   personality disorders, 122-123
   psychotic disorder, 119-120
   substance abuse and dependence, 123-
      125
Dual or multiple relationships, 30
Dual relationships, 31
Dyad, 224
Dynamic assessment, 114
Dysfunctional homeostasis, 233
Dysthymic disorder, 118

Early interventions, radical behavioral
   approaches to, 72-73
Educational model, 259
Educational programs, recidivism rates in,
   13
Educational specialists, 12-13
Educators, as institutional counselors, 11
Effective risking, 9
Ego, 42, 95
Ego control, 56-57
Ego deficits, 49-52
   delinquent superego, 52
   ego strengths, 51-52
Ego developmental theory, 198
Ego failures, 50-51
Ego ideal, 42
Ego psychology, 45
Ego state, 95
Ego strengths, 51-52
Electric shock, 251
Empathic understanding, 89
Empathy training, 249
Empty chair technique, 99
Enabled, 271
Enmeshed system, 216, 223
Entitlement, 26
Environment, brutality of prison, 36-37
EQUIP program, 104, 176, 203
Ethical dilemma, 22, 29-33
   boundaries of competence, 30
   confidentiality, 30-31
   definition of client, 29-30
   dual or multiple relationships, 30
   maintaining expertise, 30
   treatment versus security dichotomy,
      29

Ethical Standards, of American Counsel-
   ing Association, 29, 31-32
Ethnically diverse offender population, 7
Ethnic groups, 279
Ethnic skewing, 34
Ethnocentrism, 34
Exercise, as therapy, 14
Exhibitionist, 65-66, 248
   case of angry, 48-49
   treatment of, 251
Expertise, maintaining, 30
Exposure therapy, 66
External reinforcement, 173
Extinction, 248
Extortion, as power and control tactic, 27

Fade, 70
Family boundaries, 222
Family member, as inmate, 235-236
Family preservation, 230
Family structure, 222-223
Family systems, 210-211, 271
   models of, 272-273
   qualities of systems, 214-215
Family therapy, 209-238
   behavioral and social learning models,
      225-227, 271
   communications, 219-221, 271, 273
   and criminal justice applications, 230-
      231
   domestic violence, 231-233
   earliest approaches to, 213
   for families with adolescent abusers,
      234
   history and overview of, 212-217
   models of, 214, 217-230
   multisystemic treatment, 227-230, 273
   psychodynamic, 217-219, 271
   structured, 221-225
   substance abuse, 233-234
   for substance abuse, 271-274
   when family member is incarcerated,
      235-236
Fears, 66. *See also* Anxiety
Federal Bureau of Prisons, 25, 152, 266
Federal Coming Home Initiative, 236
Flooding, 66
Free association, 46
Freud, Sigmund, 41-43, 45, 95
"Freudian slips," 46
Functional behavioral assessments, 74
Functional Family Therapy, 225-226
Functional value, 172